Ireland: The Autobiography

Ireland:
The Autobiography

*One hundred years in the life of the nation,
told by its people*

Edited by

JOHN BOWMAN

PENGUIN
IRELAND

For Eimer

PENGUIN IRELAND

UK | USA | Canada | Ireland | Australia
India | New Zealand |South Africa

Penguin Ireland is part of the Penguin Random House group of companies
whose addresses can be found at global.penguinrandomhouse.com.

First published 2016
001

Selection and editorial copyright © John Bowman, 2016

The 'Sources' on pp. 469–78 constitute an extension of this copyright page

The moral right of the author has been asserted

Typeset in Bembo Book MT Std 12/14.75 pt by
Palimpsest Book Production Limited, Falkirk, Stirlingshire
Printed in Great Britain by Clays Ltd, St Ives plc

A CIP catalogue record for this book is available from the British Library

ISBN: 978–1–844–88158–1

www.greenpenguin.co.uk

Contents

Introduction

The role of the anthologist differs from that of the historian. The anthologist offers glimpses of history: telling glimpses, one hopes. I hope that the whole of this book is greater than the sum of its parts, and that an illuminating picture of Irish life will emerge from the testimony of men and women in the century since 1916.

In assembling this anthology, I have ranged widely over many kinds of sources: books, journals, newspapers, parliamentary debates, private letters and diaries. Some of the ground I covered was new to me, and some was familiar: I have been researching and writing on the past hundred years of Irish history all my adult life. Since my student days, I have had the opportunity of interviewing survivors of the revolutionary period and of the early governments of the Irish Free State. And since the 1960s, as a current affairs broadcaster, I have been covering many of the stories and themes reflected in this book as they have unfolded. There are documents included here which I first came across many years ago and have never forgotten. In some cases I filed them in anticipation of working on some such volume as this. Unusually for an anthology, the selection includes a high proportion of archival material – much of it never before published.

The seven years from the Easter Rising in April 1916 to the end of the Civil War in May 1923 went by as quickly as the period from 2009 to 2016. But those first years of the century covered by this anthology were formative – of the independent Irish state, of Northern Ireland, and of the political and social dynamics that have defined them – and so they are represented with a disproportionately generous selection here. Much of the material I have chosen from these years may not be known even to readers who are knowledgeable about the period. I have deliberately selected texts representing many strands of Irish opinion – some of them neglected. Inevitably, most of the documents from this period are concerned with high politics, diplomacy and war. But the reader will also find texts on a variety of other subjects: a polemic protesting the adoption by Ireland of Greenwich Mean Time; an advertisement by a Waterford Convent School promising a curriculum especially suited to farmers' daughters; a journal article warning of the perils of the cinema in 1918; an essay on the Dublin accent; and an account of how fifteen-year-olds fared when recruited for farm work at Ulster's hiring fairs.

In choosing pieces I have, of course, tried to represent key events and themes. But I have also been on the lookout for arresting voices, and this is one reason why I have included a number of personal letters. Bishop Michael Fogarty's excoriation of the Irish Parliamentary Party, just before its humiliation at the hands of Sinn Féin in the 1918 election, may not be the most balanced or insightful treatment of the subject, but his verdict that he was 'sick of the House of Commons with its plutocratic record of oppression, corruption and chicanery' conveys the raw anger of which Irish nationalists were capable at this juncture. Frank Gallagher served as government press secretary under Eamon de Valera, and was well versed in the arts of equivocation; but his unguarded 1940 letter to a party supporter rails against those who talk 'every kind of flapdoodle' about utopian economic schemes where 'no one does a day's work and everyone is to have a Rolls-Royce'.

A number of recurring themes emerge from the chosen documents. One such is the widespread naivety or self-deception that often led Irish nationalists to play the Catholic card while simultaneously preaching the virtues of a united Ireland. In the case of two of the seminal events covered in this book, the Easter Rising and de Valera's 1937 Constitution, senior figures were dispatched in advance to the Vatican to seek a papal endorsement. And in 1945, when de Valera brought all Irish diplomats home for a briefing on how to seek support in the post-war world, he described the Catholic Church as 'the best propaganda organisation in the world' and advised his diplomats to impress the clergy 'with the role filled by Ireland as a Catholic nation'. The Irish living outside Ireland could see more clearly the limitations of the Catholic card. Bernard Shaw warned in 1928 of the danger that, 'having broken England's grip of her', the country might slip 'back into the Atlantic as a little grass patch in which a few million moral cowards are not allowed to call their souls their own by a handful of morbid Catholics'. In that case the world would let the Irish 'go their own way into insignificance without the smallest concern' and would no longer 'even tell funny stories about them'. This verdict of Shaw's has been much quoted, but what has often been overlooked is the subject of the essay in which he offered it. Shaw was writing about the Censorship Bill, which proposed to limit information on birth control.

Contraception remained a battleground for several decades, and the references to it in this anthology provide, in microcosm, a remarkable insight into how Ireland has evolved over the past century. Along with Shaw's essay, there is the intemperate and insulting commentary in the *Irish Press* about how its British rival, the *Sunday Times*, had covered birth control in 1931; and also the verdict on this spat from Rosamond Jacob's contemporary diary. Women remained in the vanguard on this issue, and when the law was finally changed, some decades later, it was largely due to the work of feminists. In May 1971 the Irish Women's Liberation Movement made the mischievous but wholly constructive decision to publicize a day-trip to Belfast to purchase all manner of contraceptives and defy Dublin Customs officials to enforce the law. The rapidity of the change, when it came, was remarkable. In the space of a single decade, the question asked about contraception on television programmes moved from 'Is it a sin?' to 'Is it a crime?' to 'Why is it not a civil right?' As June Levine's account of the 'Contraceptive Train' shows, the feminists were using embarrassment to tackle the bishops, politicians, judges and doctors who were so far behind them on this issue.

Researching this book involved some surprises for me. I thought I was aware of how oppressive Irish society was in the aftermath of the Second World War, but until I explored that period more closely I was unaware of just how very sheltered Irish society was. The examples quoted from the column of the agony Jesuit in 1948 volumes of the *Irish Messenger* are, at one level, amusing. But they are also revealing of the state of Irish Catholicism during this period. Many of the readers' letters begin with the question, 'Is it a sin ...?' One writer wonders if he can say his morning prayers with his hat on while cycling to work!

The book reflects the remarkable shift in Irish values over the century which it covers. Read, for instance, how boy met girl in Ennistymon as recorded by Arensberg and Kimball in their Harvard anthropological study of life in Clare in the 1930s. Other documents reveal how preoccupied the clergy were with dancing as an occasion of sin: one bishop advised fathers to 'lay the lash' upon their daughters' backs if they were late home from a dance. The selection also reveals how the censors – official and unofficial – busied themselves with curbing ideas, books, films and the 'wrong' music. Jazz was a special target.

By the 1950s, the marriage rate was so low that an American-published book was devoted to the question of whether there was any future at all for the Irish race in Ireland. John V. Kelleher argued in 1957 that Irish ills were 'largely psychosomatic', the truth being that compared with so many other countries Ireland had had 'an almost fatally easy time of it', at least in the twentieth century. Kelleher feared 'that Ireland may do what no other nation has ever tried, and perish by sudden implosion upon a central vacuity'.

This mood of pessimism was one of the important contexts for T. K. Whitaker's attempt to reorient the Irish economy. The extract from *Economic Development* chosen here is a reminder that Whitaker was not merely a great economic thinker, but also someone who grasped the importance of psychology in economics. And, bearing in mind how much ground the Hierarchy has been obliged to cede over the timeframe covered here, I gladly join in his salute to Dr William Philbin, the Bishop of Clonfert, from whose writings Whitaker found inspiration. He quotes especially Philbin's complaint that the Irish version of history had 'tended to make us think of freedom as an end in itself and of independent government – like marriage in a fairy story – as the solution of all ills'. But freedom was surely 'useful in proportion to the use we make of it'. In 1958 that was an important message, and it remained at the heart of Whitaker's transforming initiative.

For ninety-five of the past hundred years, Ireland has been partitioned politically – and often culturally too. This book does not distinguish between material originating from the two political entities, but it cannot but reflect the divergent histories and experiences. The Northern experience of the world wars, for example, was different in important ways from that of the South; and the thirty-years war that began in the late 1960s was overwhelmingly fought in the North. The island remains partitioned, of course, but the endorsement of the Good Friday Agreement by 85 per cent of voters on the island was surely the single greatest expression of self-determination in all of Irish history.

As the years pass, the anthology's range becomes, if anything, wider. Attitudes to the Irish language, sport, drink, tourism, theatre, short skirts and censors of all kinds are all represented. There are examinations of emigration, the experience of flying Ryanair, the property bubble of the 2000s, the politics of water, the limbo that's reserved for asylum-seekers, the experience of inmates of custodial institutions run by religious orders, and the same-sex marriage referendum of 2015. The Irish expertise in begrudgery is noted. There are cameos: the young Brendan Behan sympathetically observed at Borstal; Patrick Kavanagh taking his libel case. Visitors are recalled: Kennedy in 1963, the Pope in 1979, the 'returned Yank' in 1917 – and not much changed since. Also Robinson's presidency, O'Malley's 'conduct unbecoming', Haughey's farewell. I would like to say of this anthology that all human life is here – but of course no such gathering could ever claim to be comprehensive. Another anthologist could, under the same title, produce a book with entirely different contents.

The simplest way to arrange documents in an anthology is to run them chronologically, by date of publication. But I have taken the view that where a document describes a particular moment or period, then it belongs with other documents from that period. So, for example, Elizabeth Bowen's account of Easter Week 1916 at the Shelbourne Hotel, though published in 1951, appears here alongside other accounts of the Rising. Some of those documents are contemporaneous, and others are taken from testimony to the Bureau of Military History some thirty years after the events described. But they all give graphic eyewitness accounts of what happened that week, and presenting them together gives a more coherent picture of the events of that period.

All editorial elisions from documents are marked with a square-bracketed ellipsis [. . .]. I have silently corrected small errors of punctuation and spelling, but I have not attempted to impose uniform stylings on the original documents. These texts come from a wide range of sources over the span of a hundred years, and their idiosyncrasies of voice and usage are part of what makes them interesting.

The book is intended for the general reader. I have tried, in the headnotes, to supply essential context; but of course some of the interpretative work must be done by the reader. I hope that the chosen documents will encourage some to pursue further reading on this period in Irish history.

The Rising: Seen from Archbishop's House

MICHAEL J. CURRAN (1916)

In 1916 Monsignor Michael J. Curran was secretary to the Archbishop of Dublin. On the morning of Easter Monday, Curran was in the garage at Archbishop's House. The following is from his witness statement to the Bureau of Military History.

Towards noon on Easter Monday I have noted in my diary the page-boy came down again to the garage [. . .] to say that Count Plunkett had called and was waiting to see me. I told the boy I would be there in a minute. I guessed, of course, that there was some new development. At five minutes past twelve I interviewed Count Plunkett. He said he had come to see the Archbishop. I informed him that the Archbishop was ill in bed and that nobody was allowed to see him except the doctor. I gathered, of course, that it was something urgent, obviously on account of the circumstances. 'Well,' he said, 'it is not necessary that I would see him personally but, if you would tell him, it would be alright.'

Count Plunkett then told me that there was going to be a Rising, that he had been to see the Pope and that he had informed Benedict XV of the whole Irish situation and the intended Insurrection. He briefly went over the incidents of his audience. Count Plunkett informed His Holiness that a rising for national independence was arranged, that the Volunteers would strike in the course of Easter Sunday and that His Holiness should not be shocked or alarmed. Count Plunkett explained that the movement was purely a national one for independence, the same as every nation had a right to. At the end of his discussion, he asked the Pope's Blessing for the Volunteers. According to him, the Pope showed great perturbation and asked was there no peaceful way out of the difficulty; that the news was extremely grave, and asked had he seen the Archbishop of Dublin. Count Plunkett answered every question, making it plain that it was the wish of the leaders of the movement to act entirely with the goodwill or approval, I forget which now, of the Pope and to give an assurance that they wished to act as Catholics. It was for that reason they came to inform His Holiness. All the Pope could do was to express his profound anxiety and how much the news disturbed him, and asked could their object not be achieved in any other way, and counselled him to see the Archbishop. Count Plunkett informed the Pope that he intended to see the Archbishop as soon as he arrived home. At this time, he was only just back in Ireland.

I have noted in my diary that, while I was still talking with Count Plunkett on Easter Monday, the telephone bell in the Secretaries' study rang and I was called to answer it. I said to the Count, 'Wait a moment!', and I went to the 'phone. The call came from a Mr Stokes, a jeweller, who rang me up to say that the GPO was seized by the Volunteers and the Castle was attacked, and he asked could the Archbishop stop it. I told him that was impossible but that I would go down town. I returned to Count Plunkett and told him the Rising had already begun. Count Plunkett, although he implied it was to take place immediately, had not told me when. It was then a quarter past twelve. [. . .]

I had to hasten up and tell the Archbishop all about Count Plunkett's report and the telephone news of the seizure of the GPO. He thought less of the poor Count than of Eoin MacNeill. He looked on the Count as a simple soul and could not conceive a man like him being at the head of a revolution as it really was. Never in my life did I tell so much or so grave a report in such a brief time.

Curran then cycled 'to the GPO to see the situation'.

The first person I saw in the portico outside the GPO was James Connolly in uniform with a huge Colt revolver, shouting out orders. Volunteers were battering out window-panes. When James Connolly saw me, he called out, 'All priests may pass!', as the Volunteers were keeping the inquisitive on-lookers at some distance. The crowd then showed comparatively little excitement. I passed in to the building. The newly arranged central hall was a scene of immense activity but nobody was unduly excited. It must have been then shortly after half past twelve.

Speaking to one of the first Volunteers I met in the GPO, I gave my name and said I wanted to see Mr Pearse. 'Commandant Pearse?' he corrected. 'Yes,' I said. He went off and got Pearse, whom, of course, I knew well. He was flushed but calm and authoritative. I at once said that we had just got word by telephone of this attack, that I had informed the Archbishop of the position and told him I was coming down to ascertain the facts and that, if there was anything that could be done, I would do it. 'But,' I said, 'I see now that nothing can be done.' 'No,' he said, 'we are going to see it out.' 'You know my feelings; if there is any possible thing I can do, I will be very glad to do it,' I said. I thought there might possibly be some message or other. 'No,' he said, 'but some of the boys would like to go to Confession and I would be delighted if you would send over word to the Cathedral.' I promised I would do that, left the GPO and went over to the Pro-Cathedral . . . I telephoned Archbishop's House, reported all the information I had, saying I would remain on. I took lunch at the Gresham Hotel.

Before 2 p.m. the crowds had greatly increased in numbers. Already the first looting had begun; the first victim was Noblett's sweetshop. It soon spread to the neighbouring shops. I was much disgusted and I did my best to try to stop the looting. Except for two or three minutes, it had no effect. I went over and informed the Volunteers about the GPO. Five or six Volunteers did their best and cleared the looters for some five or ten minutes, but it began again. At first all the ringleaders were women; then the boys came along. Later, about 3.30 p.m., when the military were withdrawn from the Rotunda, young men arrived and the looting became systematic and general, so that Fr John Flanagan of the Pro-Cathedral, who had joined me, gave up the attempt to repress it and I left too.

The Rising: Seen by a postal worker

MICHAEL DEMPSEY (1916)

On Easter Monday, 1916, Michael Dempsey, a postal worker, was
'due for duty in the Central Telegraph Office at the GPO, which was
on the top floor'. He worked there until noon, when he went to the
dining room, also on the top floor.

Being a Bank Holiday, there were not many people in the Dining
Room at that hour. When I was a short time there I could not help
noticing some commotion or excitement and it seemed to be increasing rather than diminishing. People were gathering at the windows,
which were at the Prince's Street side of the room and from which it
was possible to see a portion of Lower O'Connell Street in the direction of Clery's and Lower Abbey Street. It was obvious that something
unusual was occurring in the street, though naturally at the time, I
did not realise what it was. Without hurrying, I finished my lunch
and could see that there were far fewer people in the room than when
I had entered it over half an hour earlier. From a window I saw a
body of Citizen Army men crossing at the double, from Lower
Abbey Street towards the front of the GPO. They carried rifles.
Leaving the Dining Room with one or two others, I went back along
the corridors towards the Central Telegraph Office and looked in
there. It was almost deserted and work seemed to have ceased. I could
see people at the opposite end of the room, which was a very big one,
carrying office furniture chairs, tables, etc., through the doors leading from the Prince's Street stairway. Most likely they were Volunteers
collecting material for barricades. They could scarcely have been
British sentries as by that time such had probably become prisoners. I
turned back along the corridors, noticed a few people going in various directions and I also recollect passing some armed men, Volunteers
no doubt, but certainly not in full uniform. On reaching the yard I
noticed that the big doors leading to Prince's Street were closed.
There were three or four others with me and we were approached by

a fully uniformed officer, the late Gearóid O'Sullivan, whom I had seen from time to time in the Keating Branch of the Gaelic League during the previous winter. I recollect that he was surprised to see any of the GPO staff still on the premises. It could not have been far off one o'clock at the time. He asked us to wait a while to see if any more would turn up and advised me against going to the cloak-room at the Henry Street side for my hat and coat. Eventually, being apparently satisfied that no more of the staff were on the premises, he opened one of the big doors and let us into Prince's Street.

I stood for some time at Mansfield's corner Middle Abbey Street and then at Purcell's corner junction of Westmoreland and D'Olier streets. While there, I saw Lancers coming in single file, at little more than walking pace, by the Gresham Hotel towards Nelson Pillar. When the leading two or three had passed the Pillar and were turning towards the GPO, a volley rang out, one or two horses fell and the remainder doubled back towards Parnell Square at a much livelier pace.

The Rising: Seen from the Shelbourne Hotel

ELIZABETH BOWEN (1916)

Elizabeth Bowen's 1951 book on the history of Dublin's Shelbourne
Hotel includes this account of the role played by the Shelbourne as
the Easter Rising unfolded.

All through Easter Week while the fighting lasted the sun shone. The
burning blue April weather, which hung over Dublin like a spell,
gave even more unreality to the horror – what was happening was
not easy to grasp. That Monday morning, early, everything was still
as it should be. Bank Holiday quietness filled the streets; the squares,
whose trees were bursting out into leaf, were full of the song and
twittering of birds. An ideal race-day, thought many, looking out of
their windows – happily, it was for Fairyhouse races that the majority of the Shelbourne people, together with hundreds of Dubliners,
were bound. The hotel, as always for Fairyhouse, was packed: this
year the race-going people up from the country were fitted in somehow on top of the wartime complement of officers' wives and
families, officers in transit, officers on leave. Fred Barnes, the popular
light comedian, booked this week to perform at the Gaiety, had
arrived, and was also under the Shelbourne roof.

In order to live through a Great War, it is sometimes necessary to
forget it. For today, the War was eagerly banished from all minds.
Those most bent on forgetting – young men on leave from the Front
– were assisted by others naturally prone to do so: the Irish gift for
good-timing came in well. Yes, over the Shelbourne hung the azure
sky of an Easter holiday: not a cloud, not a presentiment marred that
sky. The bustle always involved in getting all the people off to the
races having at last subsided, the hotel drew breath; and Miss Mabel
Young went out to spend the rest of the morning in Phoenix Park.

Miss Mabel Young, the painter, had come to the Shelbourne in 1914
to help her elder sister, who was manageress, with the extra pressure
of work war had entailed. Sometimes she was at the reception desk;

her other duties, which varied from day to day, were not less interesting – she entered deeply into the human drama of the hotel. This Easter another sister was over from England on a few days' holiday; and Miss Mabel Young, with an hour or two to spare, decided to show her the beauties of Phoenix Park – which, at the edge of Dublin, extending superbly into the countryside, has its most accessible gate at the far end of the quays, across the river from Kingsbridge station. For the two ladies the agreeable morning went by only too fast: they emerged at lunch-time, ready to board a tram. Amazingly, everywhere was depopulated, empty and still as death. The sinister silence of the quays had no sooner struck them than it was rent by gunfire – distant but unmistakable.

Round here all trams had stopped. The Miss Youngs therefore began to foot it along the river towards O'Connell's Bridge, their usual link with home. From the doorways of quayside houses, white-faced people called out, warning the sisters back. It was dangerous to go farther into the city: fighting had broken out. [. . .]

Miss Mabel Young felt that, in any event, she should get back to duty as soon as possible. She saw and succeeded in stopping a jaunting-car, which she and her sister mounted without ado. The man at first did not want to drive them: on learning their destination he agreed to try. Whipping his horse to a gallop, he crossed a nearby bridge, to pursue a course through that network of narrow streets on the south bank, between Dame Street and the river. In this quarter, depressed and primitive, illusion had at no time set her well-shod foot: one believed all that one heard, and imagined more. Lamentation sounded and panic reigned. Wild-haired women rushed out, snatched at the bridle, and attempted to turn the horse, wailing of death ahead. The carman, nettled, laid around with his whip. 'Get out, get back!' he yelled. 'Are you crazy mad? These ladies are going to the *Shelbourne*!' [. . .]

The green-white-and-orange tricolour [. . .] rose over Dublin. Bank Holiday family parties, trickling back into town from Howth and the North Strand as the day went on, raised their eyes and saw it. The two Miss Youngs, headed southward on their careering car, did not. They were full of other concerns. From the clamour set up by their wailing informants, their ears had detached one phrase: 'The rebels are in the Green!' Was this so? If so, what of the Shelbourne? As the car turned out of Kildare Street, both questions answered themselves. The rebels were in the Green. The Shelbourne was just the same as ever.

Barricades – carts and vans pulled crosswise – had, it is true, been set up across the roadway which runs between the hotel and the Green's railings. At what point these were, or how the car got round them, I unhappily fail to be quite clear. I only know that the carman, pulling up with the flourish always accorded to that august porch, set down the ladies, who found themselves slightly late for lunch. In the Coffee-room service proceeded smoothly. In the hall three or four guests had gathered, and, in company with the head porter, were gazing across at the Green through the glass doors. Disappointingly little was to be seen. The thicket inside the railings screened the insurgent troops – green uniforms merged into the bosky shadows: here the glint of a rifle-barrel, there the turn of a head in a bandolier hat were to be spotted from time to time. Whatever they might be doing inside in there, they were dead quiet – so far, that is to say.

Countess Markievicz supplied the first touch of drama. In the uniform of a colonel of Volunteers she emerged from the Green and marched up and down, gun on shoulder, in full and rewarding view of the Shelbourne windows. This practice [. . .] was to continue for several days of what became the siege of the Shelbourne. The fact that British troops were moving up into position all round the Green, ready to shoot from houses or along confluent streets, did not apparently for some time deter her. It is the stern opinion of some of the hotel staff that 'the Countess took unfair advantage of her sex.' [. . .]

It was the custom of gaiety-seeking Dubliners who for any reason did not attend the races to go for tea to the Shelbourne on Easter Monday. The function (for such it had come to be) occasioned, in the sunny and splendid Drawing-room, a second showing of Easter hats. This afternoon, while the waiters were spreading cloths on the tables, while pastries were being set out and bread-and-butter cut, the Green's silence was broken by one or two shots. Mr Olden ordered people away from the glass doors and commanded the closing of the strong wooden outer ones – generally left open till late at night. It was now, however, that bobbing millinery and smiling faces appeared on the farther side of the barricades; and, scrambling nimbly round the obstruction, the tea-time parties began to come surging in. The idea of transferring tea to the Writing-room, at the safer back of the Shelbourne, met with disfavour: so many faces fell that the waiters carried on where it was. While the Drawing-room filled up with talk and laughter, sporadic rifle-fire resumed: now and then a shot spattered against the hotel front. Not till a bullet entered obliquely through the bay window, shearing the tip of a rose-petal from the hat of a lady seated against the wall, did the guests reconsider their choice of scene. One by one, cups in hand, followed by trays and waiters, the parties moved slowly through the door. Not long after they had been settled into the Writing-room, a further claim on the staff's attention arose – the Fairyhouse people started arriving back. They had had a great day's racing and were in the best of spirits – so much taken up with themselves, indeed, were they that anything odd about Dublin, as they tore home through it, had not struck them. Only now were they asking to know what the matter was.

The murder of Francis Sheehy Skeffington

HANNA SHEEHY SKEFFINGTON (1916)

Francis Sheehy Skeffington, journalist, feminist and pacifist, was among the earliest victims of Easter Week. On the Tuesday, he called a meeting with the aim of organizing a militia to oppose looting. While walking home to Rathmines, he was followed by a crowd of hecklers, and arrested by soldiers under orders to keep Portobello Bridge clear. At Portobello Barracks, he was in the charge of Captain J. C. Bowen-Colthurst, who brought him along as a human shield when raiding a tobacconist's shop. During the raid, Bowen-Colthurst took four hostages: a Labour Party councillor, a boy called James Coade, and two journalists. In the days that followed, Francis Sheehy Skeffington's widow, the nationalist and feminist Hanna Sheehy Skeffington, reconstructed what happened next.

Shortly before 10 o'clock the next morning Colthurst again demanded my husband from the guard, together with the two other editors. Besides Wilson and Dobbin, Lieutenant Tooley was in charge of the guard of eighteen men. To them he stated he was 'going to shoot Skeffington and the other two'. According to their own testimony these subordinate officers delivered the three prisoners to Colthurst without protest. They also told off seven men with rifles to accompany Colthurst to the barracks' yard. This yard was about 12 feet long and 6 feet wide. As the three prisoners walked away from the firing squad, and when they had reached the end of the yard, Colthurst gave the order to fire, and all three dropped in their tracks, dead. The British authorities prevented my ever seeing my husband's body, and when I attempted to have an inquest held, refused permission.

Colthurst presently made a report of the triple murder after Major Rosborough ordered him to do so, and it was duly sent to headquarters at Dublin Castle. The report was altogether a fabrication and, subsequently, he was ordered to make a second report. Meantime, however, he kept his command without even a reprimand. [...]

Meanwhile, I was vainly seeking my husband. All sorts of rumours reached me: that he had been wounded and was in a hospital; that he had been shot by a looter; arrested by the police. I also heard that he had been executed, but this I refused to believe, it seemed incredible. I clung to the belief that even if he had been condemned to die, he would be tried before a jury, for martial law did not apply to non-combatants, and that I would be notified. Of course, the reason of the silence is now clear. It was hoped my husband's case would be like that of so many others who 'disappeared' and whose whereabouts could never be traced. Thirteen days after the murder of my husband and the other two editors, Mr Tennant stated in the House of Commons in answer to a question that 'no prisoner has been shot in Dublin without a trial.'

All day Wednesday and Thursday I enquired in vain, and Friday came without my having any positive information of my husband's fate. On Friday I tried to see a physician connected with the Portobello Barracks, but the police stopped me. [. . .] To allay my terrible anxiety my two sisters, Mrs Kettle and Mrs Culhane, agreed to try to get into Portobello Barracks. On their arrival they were immediately put under arrest and a drumhead court martial held upon them. Colthurst presided. Their crime was that they had been seen talking to Sinn Féiners. Colthurst refused to give them any information, declaring he knew nothing whatever of Sheehy Skeffington. Finally, they were marched off under armed guard and admonished not to mention what had taken place.

That afternoon I managed to find the father of the murdered boy Coade. He told me he had seen my husband's body in the barracks' mortuary when he had gone for his son's body. This a priest later confirmed, but he could give me no other information. I went home shortly after 6 o'clock, and was putting my little boy to bed when the maid noticed soldiers lining up around the house. She became terrified and dashed out the back door, carrying my son with her. I ran after them, for I knew the house would be surrounded and feared they might be shot down if seen running. As I ran down the hall a volley was fired through the front door and windows. The shots were fired without warning, and without any demand having been made on us to open the door. They broke in the windows with their rifle butts and swarmed all over the house, some going to the roof. Colthurst was in command. He rushed upon us and ordered us to throw up our hands. Behind him was a squad of men with fixed bayonets . . . Colthurst ordered us to be removed to the front room to be shot if we stirred. For three hours they searched the house while we stood motionless, closely guarded by men with drawn bayonets, with others outside the house with levelled rifles pointed at us. The house was sacked, everything of value being removed, books, pictures, toys, linen and household goods. I could hear officers and men jeering as they turned over my private possessions. One of the soldiers (a Belfast man) seemed ashamed, and said, 'I didn't enlist for this. They are taking the whole bloomin' house with them.'

Bread panic in Rathmines

T. K. MOYLAN (1916)

T. K. Moylan was a clerk in the mental hospital at Grangegorman.
On the Wednesday of Easter Week, with public transport suspended,
he attempted to walk to work from his home in Rathmines, but got
no further than Thomas Street, where soldiers advised him that a few
people had been shot in the vicinity a short time before, and that 'the
Insurgents were in the houses at the back of me.' Thus warned, he
turned back towards home, as he recorded in his unpublished diary.

In Rathmines I met J. shopping, which was also the principal occupation of half Rathmines, the other half were gossiping about the road
and occasionally combining shopping and gossip. Here might be seen
the extraordinary spectacle of all the toffs and lady toffs, nuts of the
highest type wending their way homewards with a plain cottage loaf
or two under their arms, without even a scrap of newspaper to hide
its nakedness. Furthermore the possessors of the loaves seemed quite
'cocky' over their possessions. His Honour, Judge Brereton Barry,
was seen pedalling along Belgrave Square with two loaves under his
arm, and even motor cars carried round ladies who sat with a naked
loaf on their lap. 'Bread' was the cry, the main topic of conversation
was 'bread', not that there was any great shortage, but the non-arrival
of the breadcars before breakfast had brought high and low into the
breadshops for the staff of life, and everyone was in high good
humour at the novelty. The day was beautifully fine and a holiday
spirit was about. Never have I seen together so many people in Rathmines whose faces are familiar to me. Those whom one only saw
passing to and from business were all here lining that portion of the
road from Castlewood Avenue to Leinster Road. When we woke in
the morning, about eight, we had heard a few shots from a big gun,
which seemed to come from the direction of the Liffey. Also from
time to time, through the clear, sunny air came the indescribable rat-
a-tat of a machine gun. J. was told by a girl in Findlater's, who lives

at the Pigeon House Road and who had to come in to business via Ballsbridge, that a gun boat had come up the river and opened fire from a small gun. We laid in a supply of various necessaries such as flour, bacon, preserved meat and potatoes, and also five dozen sods of turf, as we could not get coal.

The long way across O'Connell Street

LESLIE PRICE (1916)

Leslie Price, a member of Cumann na mBan since 1914, was mobilized
on Good Friday 1916. Although anxious to participate in the Easter
Rising, she was initially told to go home to avoid danger. But she and
her friend Bríd Dixon walked to O'Connell Street, seeking a role.
Once in the GPO, she was initially assigned to duties in the kitchen;
later in the week, she and Dixon were promoted to work as couriers.

I remember Bríd and myself on the following day, Thursday, being
sent from the Post Office to the King Street area. This time it was a
written despatch. It was daytime. We came to a barricade and the
man in charge of the barricade was Diarmuid Hegarty. I remember
we had to climb over it, and in and out of a cab. I cannot recollect if
we gave the despatch to Diarmuid Hegarty. We all knew him very
well. The members of the Keating Branch and the Árd Craobh of the
Gaelic League were very united. I have an idea we passed the despatch to Diarmuid there and came back to the Post Office. This was
about four o'clock.

We had done our midnight job so well and got back so easily that
Seán MacDermott said up in the dining-room that we were to be
treated as officers. We were promoted on the field. When we went up
to Louise Gavan Duffy officers were given separate tables, and we
were given a table to ourselves. We thought it was marvellous.

I don't think we slept at all in the Post Office. At night we sat on
the steps going into Prince's Street. We were talking to Gearóid
O'Sullivan. We talked all the time. There was no activity for us,
except for the cooks and first-aid people. We were despatch carriers.
We were told not to go into the kitchens or do washing or anything,
nor first-aid. We had our own special function.

I remember about four o'clock on the Thursday evening when
Tom Clarke called for me. Being a despatch carrier was a most miserable job. It turned out to be very sad, for my courage. At four o'clock

he called for me and said, 'You are to cross O'Connell Street to the Presbytery and get a priest.' Probably a priest had come in and gone away. He had the intention of now bringing a priest in and keeping him on the premises. I suppose, from the military point of view, he knew the GPO was practically surrounded then. I remember I had seen Connolly brought in when he had gone out under the arches in the front of the Post Office and had been wounded. I remember saying to myself, 'Here's good-bye to you.' Tom Clarke looked at me. He had sort of steely eyes. He said, 'You are to cross O'Connell Street.' I could have cried but, when I looked at his courageous old face, I said, 'Alright.' I did not cry. I am sure I said to Bríd Dixon and Gearóid, 'This is frightful!'

I went to the small door on Henry Street side that opens opposite Moore Street. Whoever was on that door must have seen I was terrified at my job. They said on no account to go across O'Connell Street but to cross Moore Street, go across Parnell Street by the Rotunda and back again. I came out of the Post Office and I darted across to Moore Street I crawled along by the walls on the right-hand side until I came to the top of Moore Street and Parnell Street. There was no barricade on Moore Street. [. . .] I turned into Parnell Street and came up to a public house in front of the Rotunda, Conway's I think, at the corner of a laneway. People were drinking. They had looted the public house. Now I came to my corner of O'Connell Street, and people were saying, 'Go in! Go into a house and stay there!' They were calling from windows. I said to myself I had to take this message and I would go. Somebody told us that the British had a barricade at the top of Parnell Square, just at Findlater's Church. They were gradually coming down into O'Connell Street. I had anticipated a bullet from there. I made a dart across to the Parnell statue and then another dart to the other side of O'Connell Street. I kept in by the walls again and turned into Marlborough Street. At that time the Education Office was occupied by the British. I crawled along. In Marlborough Street there were railings and I could not keep very close to the houses. All the ladies in the halls said, 'Go home, child!'

I got safely to the door of the Presbytery. I kicked the door. All these women told me the soldiers were in the Education Office, and the hall door could be seen from there. I kicked and kicked, and pressed all the bells. There was no answer. I kicked and kicked again, and finally a voice asked me, 'Who is there?' I said, 'I have come from the Post Office.' That is all I said. The door was opened a little bit and I was let in by a priest, Fr Michael O'Flanagan. [. . .] I said to him, 'I have been sent over by Tom Clarke for the priest.' He said, 'You are not going to the Post Office. You are staying here. No one here will go into the Post Office. Let these people be burned to death. They are murderers.' Mrs Wyse Power was the only one to whom I ever told this.

I knew then, by some other remark Fr O'Flanagan made, that it was the linking up with the Citizen Army he did not like. It took a certain amount of courage to fight a priest. I said, 'If no priest is going to the Post Office, I am going back alone. I feel sure that every man in the Post Office is prepared to die, to meet his God, but it is a great consolation to a dying man to have a priest near him.' Whatever effect I had on him, he said, 'Very well! I will go.'

I stayed near him in the hall, and he said, 'We won't go that way. We will go out the back way.' We came out the laneway at the back of the Gresham. We went up that laneway, and it brought us out to Gloucester Street. We went from Gloucester Street back to Parnell Monument again. I told him I had come across by the Rotunda. We turned into Moore Street. We came to a laneway on the left in Moore Street. I was very impressionable at that time. We passed a man in Moore Street who had been shot and was dying on the road, but he had drink taken. The priest did not stop for him. I was horrified. Further down Moore Street on the left we came to Henry Place, I think. At that place, a white-haired man was shot but not dead. He was lying, bleeding, on the kerb. This was the second wounded man, a civilian. Someone had picked out of this old man's pocket a note, or card, or envelope; it was Eimer O'Duffy's father or grandfather. He was an old man. I remember the priest knelt down to give him Absolution. You see the difference! Here he knew a man who was respectable. I stood aside while he heard his Confession. Then we left him and went on. I said to Fr O'Flanagan, 'Isn't it extraordinary you did not kneel beside the other man?'

We got to the Post Office and I brought Fr O'Flanagan to Tom Clarke. I remember Tom Clarke took Mick Staines aside, and he said on no account was he (the priest) to be let out of the Post Office. That was Thursday, and it must have been about six o'clock when I finished that job.

Pearse writes to his mother

PATRICK PEARSE (1916)

Patrick H. Pearse – educationalist, poet and co-founder of the Irish Volunteers – was appointed the President of the Provisional Government of the Irish Republic and Commandant General of the republican forces in the 1916 Rising. After surrendering on the Saturday of Easter Week, Pearse wrote a letter to his mother and entrusted it to one of his guards at Arbour Hill Prison, Sergeant G. Goodman, for delivery. Instead, Goodman gave the letter to General Sir John Maxwell – who had come to Ireland as 'military governor' – as evidence for Pearse's court martial. The postscript, with its reference to Pearse's approval of the prospect of German help, proved especially incriminating. Whether Pearse deliberately added this reference to hasten his execution and martyrdom remains open to question.

Arbour Hill Barracks, Dublin, 1 May 1916

Dearest Mother,

You will, I know, have been longing to hear from me. I don't know how much you have heard since the last note I sent you from the GPO. On Friday evening the Post Office was set on fire, and we had to abandon it. We dashed into Moore Street, and remained in the houses in Moore Street until Saturday afternoon. We then found that we were surrounded by troops, and that we had practically no food. We decided in order to avoid further slaughter of the civil population and in the hope of saving the lives of our followers, to ask the General commanding the British forces to discuss terms. He replied that he would receive me only if I surrendered unconditionally, and this I did. I was taken to the Headquarters of the British

Command in Ireland, and there I wrote and signed an order to our men to lay down their arms. All this I did in accordance with the decision of the members of our Provisional Government who were with us in Moore Street. My own opinion was in favour of one more desperate sally before opening negotiations but I yielded to the majority, and I think now the majority were right, as the sally would have resulted only in losing the lives of perhaps fifty or one hundred of our men, and we should have had to surrender in the long run, as we were without food.

I was brought here on Saturday evening and later on all the men with us in Moore Street were brought here. Those in the other parts of the city have, I understand, been taken to other barracks and prisons. All here are safe and well. Willie [Pearse, his brother] and all the St Enda's boys are here. I have not seen them since Saturday, but I believe that they are all well, and that they are not now in any danger. Our hope and belief is that the Government will spare the lives of all our followers but we do not expect that they will spare the lives of the leaders. We are ready to die and we shall die cheerfully and proudly. Personally I do not hope or even desire to live. But I do hope and desire and believe that the lives of all our followers will be saved, including the lives dear to you and me (my own excepted), and this will be a great consolation to me when dying. You must not grieve for all this. We have preserved Ireland's honour and our own. Our deeds of last week are the most splendid in Ireland's history. People will say hard things of us now, but we shall be remembered by posterity and blessed by unborn generations. You too will be blessed because you were my mother.

If you [indecipherable] would like to see me, I think you will be allowed to visit me, by applying to the Headquarters Irish Command, near the Park. I shall, I hope, have another opportunity of writing to you. Love to W. W., M. B., Miss Byrne, and to your own dear self. P.

P.S. I understand that the German expedition on which I was counting actually set sail – but was defeated by the British.

At his court martial Pearse called no witnesses in his defence but made the following statement:

My sole object in surrendering unconditionally was to save the slaughter of the civil population and to save the lives of our followers who had been led into this thing by us. It is my hope that the British Government who has shown its strength will also be magnanimous and spare the lives and give an amnesty to my followers, as I am one of the persons chiefly responsible, have acted as C-in-C and President of the Provisional Government. I am prepared to take the consequences of my act, but I should like my followers to receive an amnesty. I went down on my knees as a child and told God that I would work all my life to gain the freedom of Ireland. I have deemed it my duty as an Irishman to fight for the freedom of my country. I admit I have organised men to fight against Britain. I admit having opened negotiations with Germany. We have kept our word with her and as far as I can see she did her best to help us. She sent a ship with arms. Germany has not sent us gold.

Pearse was executed between 3.30 and 4.00 a.m. on 3 May 1916.

James Connolly's farewell

NORA CONNOLLY (1916)

Because of the serious injuries he suffered in the GPO during Easter
week, James Connolly was imprisoned in a small ward in the officers'
quarter of the hospital wing in Dublin Castle. It was there that he was
court-martialled and condemned to death on 9 May. Later that day,
his wife, Lillie, and eldest daughter, Nora, visited him. They were still
hopeful that, because of his injuries, he might be reprieved. On the
following day, Connolly was told that he would be executed at dawn
on 11 May, but this was later changed: 'Execution suspended by prime
minister's orders' is handwritten on his file. This order, in turn, was
superseded by General Sir John Maxwell. Late at night on 11 May,
there was a knock at the door of the Connolly home, where James
Connolly's wife and eldest daughter were informed that he wished to
see them again.

There was an ambulance outside the door; and there was a military
Captain with it. He said the message he brought to us was: James
Connolly was very weak, and wanted to see his wife and eldest
daughter. Mama had seen him the day before, and he was very weak;
and she half believed him; but I guessed what it was. We were brought
in the ambulance up to the Castle. I remember it so well. You know
the part of the Castle, where there are a porch and pillars outside;
there is a staircase landing above, which branches into corridors; they
had soldiers on every step of the staircase; and on the landing they
had little mattresses; there were soldiers lying on them; and there
were soldiers at every door.

We were brought into the room where Daddy was. He lifted his
head, and said: 'I suppose you know what this means?' Mama was
terribly upset. I remember he said to me — we were talking about
various things — he said: 'Put your hand under the bedclothes.' He
slipped some paper into my hand. He said: 'Get that out, if you can.
It is my last statement.' Mama could hardly talk. I remember he said:

'Don't cry, Lillie. You will unman me.' Mama said: 'But your beautiful life, James,' she wept. 'Hasn't it been a full life? Isn't this a good end?' he said.

Then they took us away; and we got home. We just stood at the window, pulled up the blind, and watched for the dawn; and, after we knew he was gone, the family all came in; and I opened the last statement, and read it: – 'To the Field General Court Martial, held at Dublin Castle, on 9th May, 1916. I do not wish to make any defence, except against the charge of wanton cruelty to prisoners. These trifling allegations that have been made, if they record facts that really happened, deal only with the almost unavoidable incidents of a hurried uprising against long established authority, and nowhere show evidence of set purpose to wantonly injure unarmed persons. We went out to break the connection between this country and the British Empire, and to establish an Irish Republic. We believed that the call we then issued to the people of Ireland, was a nobler call, in a holier cause, than any call issued to them during this war, having any connection with the war. We succeeded in proving that Irishmen are ready to die endeavouring to win for Ireland those national rights which the British Government has been asking them to die to win for Belgium. As long as that remains the case, the cause of Irish Freedom is safe. Believing that the British Government has no right in Ireland, never had any right in Ireland, and never can have any right in Ireland, the presence, in any one generation of Irishmen, of even a respectable minority, ready to die to affirm that truth, makes that Government forever a usurpation and a crime against human progress. I personally thank God that I have lived to see the day when thousands of Irish men and boys, and hundreds of Irish women and girls, were ready to affirm that truth, and to attest it with their lives, if need be.' JAMES CONNOLLY, COMMANDANT GENERAL, DUBLIN DIVISION, ARMY OF THE IRISH REPUBLIC. [...]

Afterwards, we went to the Castle to demand his body. We knew they would refuse it, but we had to make the request. They refused our request. While we were standing there, a nurse came along, and said: 'Mrs Connolly, I clipped this off your husband's head.' She gave her a lock of his hair. I have that still. Then we met Father Aloysius, who was with him before he was executed. I asked Father Aloysius: 'How did they shoot him?' He told me he had not known Daddy. Of all those men, Daddy was the only one he had not known personally. He felt it was a great favour to have met him before he died. I said: 'How did they shoot him?' He said: 'They came in an ambulance. They carried him on a stretcher to the ambulance. I accompanied him in the ambulance, and drove to Kilmainham. They carried the stretcher to the yard, and put him in a chair. Before he was executed, I said to your father: "Will you say a prayer for the men who are about to shoot you?"' My father's answer was: 'I will say a prayer for all brave men who do their duty.' Then he was shot.

Dublin after the executions

John Dillon was the leading nationalist politician after Parnell's death
and, with John Redmond, at the centre of all Home Rule negotiations from 1910 to 1916. In a letter dated 11 June 1916 to David Lloyd
George, the Minister of Munitions, he is critical of the regime of
martial law imposed by General Sir John Maxwell.

The temper of the country is extremely bad, and the temper of the
city *ferocious*. Major [Ivor] Price – the head spy, who gave such blackguard evidence before the Commission, is I am told much worse than
Maxwell, and is Maxwell's right-hand man. The never failing inge-
nuity of the Celt has discovered a method of evading martial law,
and a series of great demonstrations are now going on at high masses
for the souls of the executed men. The relations are received on their
leaving the church by enormous cheering crowds, and gradually
these crowds are developing into processions and demonstrations
singing patriotic songs. Kitchener's picture at the Rotunda Cinema-
tograph on Thursday had to be instantly withdrawn, and disloyal
demonstrations are now known at the theatres.

It is inevitable that accounts of these proceedings should reach
England, and I fully appreciate the truth of all you say as to the
possible consequences. Do you wonder now at the bitterness with
which I spoke when I came over fresh from observing the effect of
the executions? When the fighting was over and the insurrection
crushed – if there had been no executions – the country would
have been *solid* behind us, and we could have done what we liked
with it. The tragedy of the situation is – and it is one of the greatest
tragedies of all history – that but for the blunders and perversities
of your Government – Ireland would be today as loyal to your
cause as Canada, and you could have had easily double the number
of Irish soldiers fighting at the front, including many hundreds of

those who took part in the rebellion, and many thousands who are now cursing England and eager for her defeat . . .

The wholesale, and wholly unnecessary arrests and house-searchings in districts where there was no disturbance, and very little sympathy with the Sinn Féiners, have done incalculable mischief. I have no doubt there is an effort on the part of Price and Co. to make any Home Rule settlement impossible by irritating the people to such a state of madness that our influence over them will be wiped out. That is the almost avowed policy of the Kildare Street Club and the *Irish Times*, and the horrible irony of the situation is that by giving the soldiers and Price a free hand you are making yourselves the instruments of your worst enemies to defeat your own policy. [. . .] You have let Hell loose in Ireland, and I do not see how the country is to be governed.

Ulstermen at the Somme

TWO VETERANS (1916)

The Battle of the Somme started on 1 July 1916 and lasted until November. It was the battle that, more than any other, came to symbolize the horror of the new industrialized combat. It also demonstrated the incompetence of the generals and the futility of trench warfare. By the end of the battle, the casualties on both sides numbered over one million. Some of those had died within minutes of their first going over the top, many of them members of the 36th Ulster Division. R. H. Stewart collected the testimony of numerous veterans, including the first, unnamed veteran whose recollections appear below. Major H. Singleton's account comes from a letter to General C. H. Powell. The words underlined were marked 'omit' – perhaps by the censor or, later, by the Ulster Unionist Council, which published the letter.

Unnamed veteran: We had a young officer not as old as some of us, and as hard-faced, crooked a sergeant as ever walked on two feet. As we moved across no-man's-land a shell landed on our left. It could have been one of our own landing a bit short. Anyway it killed the officer and wounded the sergeant and a bit of it hit me on the upper part of my left arm and cut me, but not too badly. The old sergeant kept going till we reached the German lines. With the first bomb he threw the door off a deep dugout, and the next two he flung inside. He must have killed every German in it. We left him sitting just below the parapet with a grenade in each hand ready for the next live German that came along. We did not stay that long in that line but moved on to the next. Then to the 3rd line . . . It was here that the real fighting started. I had never killed a man with a bayonet before and it sent cold shivers up and down my spine many's a night afterwards just thinking about it. It must have taken our lot about a quarter of an hour to clear a hundred yards or so of the trench. I was one of them left to hold the line because I had to get my arm bandaged. We found some food the Germans had and it was worse than our own rations but we were so hungry we ate them.

Major H. Singleton: To go into deeds of gallantry would be impossible: every man that went over the Parapet was a Hero, and as I heard one Brigadier remark: he looked upon them as Gods. The carnage was terrible, and some Companies that went over the Parapet 180 strong returned about 20. I have served with Regulars, Volunteers, Colonials, but never in my life have I ever seen such deeds of heroism and gallantry as those displayed by Ulstermen. They may be equalled, but cannot be surpassed. <u>And now, the Ulster Division has practically ceased to exist; at any rate for the time being. We are withdrawn into reserve to re-organise and recoup.</u> Doubtless we shall fill up from Englishmen and others, but we still have a smattering to go on with, and, although most of the Ulstermen are now no more, still, the spirit of the Ulster Division must continue, and doubtless we have glorious times for us in the future – *La Division est mort, vive la Division.* One mustn't imagine that, because we got badly knocked here that the whole offensive is being badly treated elsewhere. On the contrary we hear good reports from the South. It was our luck and we must make the best of it.

Time! Gentlemen

D. P. MORAN (1916)

In August 1916 a bill was put before the Parliament at Westminster to introduce Greenwich Mean Time to Ireland, whose time zone was thirty minutes later than that of GMT. It was believed in Ireland that the rebuilding of O'Connell Street after the Rising was made dependent on Ireland's acceptance of GMT. The Irish Parliamentary Party was opposed, as was D. P. Moran's *Leader* newspaper.

England has got a distinct place in the sun, but hasn't got shares in him. And 'tis a good job she hasn't. I expect he will continue to go on in his old accustomed way notwithstanding her Daylight Saving Acts and other expedients for getting to windward of him. The union of Irish with English clocks is the latest piece of one-and-indivisible amelioration to which we are asked to submit. I wonder will Wm. M. Murphy organise Ireland against it? Or will Mr Jones support it on the ground that under Martial Law, which he voted for, it would clear all mere Irishmen off the streets 25 minutes earlier every night?

Why let England play Sequaw with us altogether, and, under cover of the noise of her guns and drums and oratory, operate as she likes on us? The fingering of a clock seems a small matter, but the principle is much the same whether a stranger puts his finger on your clock or in your pocket. What right has he to do it? Why should an Englishman lay down for me the time I am to get up in the morning or go to bed at night? Is it because England is determined never to let us have anything, not even daylight, except as it suits her own convenience, that she is taking over the business of winding our clocks for us?

'Convenience?' it will be said. 'But, my dear boy, the change will be wholly to *our* convenience. There's not a businessman in Ireland but will be thankful for it.' Just so. That's exactly it. The businessmen in Ireland are so thoroughly reconciled to looking to England for everything that it is a convenience to them to even get out of bed half an hour earlier in order to attend to orders. They would rather do that than take the trouble to order things themselves. Their commercial news, the arrivals and sailings of their ships, their stock quotations, even their betting wires, are ruled by Greenwich time, and they never want, or hope, it to be otherwise. What they want is to be more completely, and therefore more comfortably, huxters, and to let England do their business for them with the outside world. For, of such is the kingdom of slavery.

To leave principles and right, and come to details and expediency, will the imperialising of our clocks convenience even our huxters? The effect of it in brief will be that in summer our clocks will be an hour and a half, and in winter half an hour, ahead of the sun. That is all right for such an early-rising nation as we are, but will we rise any the earlier if our clocks are ordered to register Greenwich time? Not necessarily. The most loyal time-servers amongst us are our railway companies and they frame their time-tables to fall in with the time-tables of the English companies. Although therefore our clocks will be put forward, our trains, we may be sure, will be run correspondingly later, and, as everyone knows, business is mostly done as per the trains, not as per the clocks. The main result to us will be that in summer we will lose half an hour of daylight as compared with England, while in winter, when there is no daylight to gain, we will gain half an hour of it as compared with England! In fact, it is the Act of Union over again. Our shares of sunshine now, like our Exchequers then, are being assimilated for England's convenience and our befoolment.

'An anachronism and a nuisance', is what one of the Dublin newspapers lately enthusiastic for Ireland one and indivisible calls the arrangement by which Ireland keeps her own time. Of course it is a nuisance, just as Home Rule would be a nuisance and for the same reason. The ideal arrangement would be Ireland one and indivisible, swallowed, clocks and all, by England.

Let me not be too serious, however, this hot weather. When we get Home Rule, we can rule our own clocks, I suppose. Meanwhile, and pending Home Rule, a good many of our own and our MPs' sons will be studying for jobs in the Imperial Civil Service and I would submit to them a sample of one of the arithmetical questions they will very likely be set: 'Irish was assimilated with English railway time on October 1st, 1916. The Summer Time Act having been in force in both countries, at what hour (local time) should the member for Mayo [John Dillon] have started from Ballaghaderreen in order to arrive in Westminster in time to be up to the Coalition Ministry?'

Yours, Convict 12

CONSTANCE MARKIEVICZ (1916)

As a member of the Irish Citizen Army, Constance Markievicz participated in the Rising in the St Stephen's Green area and in the College of Surgeons. She was sentenced to death for her role but was reprieved because of her sex. Initially jailed in Mountjoy, she was transferred to Aylesbury Prison in July 1916. The following is a letter to her sister, Eva Gore-Booth.

Aylesbury Prison, 8 August 1916

Dearest old darling, the one thing I have gained from my exile is the privilege of writing a letter, but there is very little to say, as I do not suppose 'an essay on prison life' would pass the Censor, however interesting and amusing it might be! What you have called my 'misplaced sense of humour' still remains to me, and I am quite well and cheerful.

I saw myself, for the first time for over three months, the other day, and it is quite amusing to meet yourself as a stranger. We bowed and grinned, and I thought my teeth very dirty and very much wanting a dentist, and I'd got very thin and very sunburnt. In six months I shall not recognise myself at all, my memory for faces being so bad! I remember a fairy tale of a princess, who banished mirrors when she began to grow old. I think it showed a great lack of interest in life. The less I see my face, the more curious I grow about it, and I don't resent it getting old.

It's queer and lonely here, there was so much life in Mountjoy. There were sea-gulls and pigeons, which I had quite tame, there were 'Stop Press' cries, and little boys splashing in the canal and singing Irish songs, shrill and discordant, but with such vigour. There was a black spaniel, too, with long, silky ears, and a most attractive convict-baby with a squint, and soft Irish voices everywhere. There were the trains, 'Broadstone and Northwall' trams, and even an old melodeon, and a man trying to play an Irish tune on a bugle over the wall! Here it is so still and I find it so hard to understand what anyone says to me, and they seem to find the same trouble with me. 'English as she is spoke' can be very puzzling. One thing nice here is the hollyhocks in the garden. They seem to understand gardening here. There is a great crop of carrots, too, which we pass every day, going to 'exercise' round and round in a ring – like so many old hunters in a summer.

I had the loveliest journey over here. My escort had never been on the sea before and kept thinking she was going to be ill. I lay down and enjoyed a sunny porthole and a fresh breeze. There was a big airship (like the picture of a Zeppelin) cruising about when we arrived. I was awfully pleased, as I had never seen one. I do so long to fly! Also I'd love to dive in a submarine.

My darling, I repeat – *don't* worry about me. I am quite cheerful and content, and I would have felt very small and useless if I had been ignored. I am quite patient and I believe that everything will happen for the best. One thing I should enjoy getting out for, and that would be to see the faces of respectable people when I met them! I don't like to send anyone my love, for fear that that most valuable offering would be spurned. I expect, though, that Molly has a soft spot for me somewhere. Very best love to Esther and to Susan and to all the 'rebelly crew' if ever you come across them. [. . .] Send me a budget of news and gossip, when you can write, about all my pals and my family, and anything amusing at all.

Yours, Convict 12

A Southern unionist on nationalism in Cork

M. H. FRANKS (1917)

James Mackay Wilson – southern unionist and friend of Edward
Carson – was an active collector of intelligence on militant nationalists (referred to under the umbrella term 'Sinn Feiners'). One of his
informants, M. H. ('Harry') Franks of Garrettstown, Co. Cork,
wrote to him on 5 March 1917.

I have chatted with chaps who at one time were Redmondites, but
they have now become ardent supporters of Sinn Feiner policy. [. . .]
They complain Ireland has been sold by Redmond & Co., and all
denounce his action which they say favoured recruiting, and his
silence in the House of Commons when the Rebels were being shot.
[. . .] Indeed the enmity to the Irish party is nearly as great as the
hatred of England. The change has been created in this way: among
all parties – the Redmondite and O'Brienite – there is and has been a
terrible fear of being conscripted. For a time they lived in daily dread
of it; and to prevent the Act applying to Ireland they would I believe
sell body and soul. They believe the best means of preventing it is to
give help to the rebels, as they think if conscription is moved to be
applied the Sinn Feiners will give trouble, and that that trouble will
not be worth the big force of soldiers who will be employed in
rounding up the conscripts, whose dream it is to flee to the mountains. Such trouble they say will prevent conscription. If conscription
was out of the way, it is doubtful if so many would extend sympathy
to Sinn Fein, but hatred of John Redmond for Imperial feelings re
the war sent many of his followers to the extreme side. The danger at
present is this – the active Sinn Feiners are all young and intelligent
men, generally teetotallers. Unlike the ordinary political fellow, they
do not patronise public-houses and talk there over matters. They are
silent and know how to keep their mouths closed, but they think and
plot the more. Perhaps if they had a little latitude to let off steam at
say a public meeting, it would act as a safety-valve. But the fact is

they are – a great many of them – 'brainy' in well-to-do positions; they speak little in public, and, as in all secret political gatherings – suffering as they think under great wrongs – there is a danger of an outburst. Of course you know in Cork, we always talk and do not act – that may be the case, but this silence on a matter which is deep in the hearts of thousands of young fellows in the city is to say the least very ugly and portends something more than usual happening unless they [are] pulled up in time.

The School for Farmers' Daughters

ADVERTISEMENT (1917)

The following advertisement appeared in the *Catholic Bulletin* in April 1917.

The Practical School, Convent of St Louis, Ramsgrange, Waterford. (Under Department of Agriculture and Technical Instruction.)

THE SCHOOL FOR FARMERS' DAUGHTERS

Trained and specially qualified teachers, appointed and paid by Department. Practical instruction in milking, dairying, poultry-keeping, cookery, dressmaking, household economy, laundry work, horticulture. Thirty free places available every year, granted by Department. Full particulars from The Sister in Charge.

'The strong thing is the just thing'

KATHLEEN LYNN AND RICHARD HAYES (1918)

Sinn Féin's 'Public Health Circular No. 1' called for dramatic action to prevent syphilis being spread by Irish soldiers returning from the Great War. It also argued that the costs of such a programme should not be borne by Irish county councils but rather fall upon the 'proper shoulders'. As a public-health proposal, it was a non-starter; as an expression of nationalist attitudes to Great War soldiers and the ostensible sexual purity of Ireland, it was eloquent propaganda.

Endeavouring in this Circular to impress on our fellow-countrymen and women the evil that threatens us, we should at the same time like to emphasise the fact that the problem is more of a social than a purely medical one. Public representatives and National Organizations must grapple with it at once if the solution is to be really successful – public opinion must be roused. The British military authorities, or whatever governing body there is at present in this country, must be made aware that the Irish people are interested in this vital question and realise thoroughly the grave consequences of dumping down and letting loose among us those under their immediate control affected with this contagion. Mere half-measures to combat it are worse than none, and must not be tolerated.

It must be demanded and insisted on that the blood of every one of these soldiers returning to our country shall be tested, and those of them found to be in an infectious condition from this disease shall be detained in institutions till pronounced free from contagion as determined by the blood test.

The enormous advances made by Medical Science for the past few years in the treatment and especially in the diagnosis of the disease, will do much to help us in carrying this out.

We shall be told that this measure is too drastic – we reply that none other will cope with the evil, and that in dealing with it the methods hitherto in vogue of combating such evils by treating effects rather than causes must be abandoned. 'The strong thing is the just thing' – now and always. It shall be said that it interferes too much with the liberty of the subject – one might with equal reason speak of interfering with his liberty when a homicidal maniac is placed under restraint. Some will say that the expenditure on such a scheme of treatment would be very heavy – we reply that on the contrary it will mean a big economic saving by reason of its effect on the child life of the nation, on adult productive power, on the cost of upkeep and administration of Homes, Asylums, Schools, Hospitals, etc. Above all, that it is the only measure that will keep from our doors one of the most hideous of modern Social Evils.

Kathleen Lynn, F.R.C.S.I., Richard Hayes, L.R.C.P. and S.I., Sinn Féin Public Health Department, Dublin, February 1918

Court in a cowshed

JOSEPH KINSELLA (1918)

Sinn Féin's strategy was to 'hollow out' the British government's administration in Ireland, and among their targets were local government and policing. Joseph Kinsella was an intelligence officer with the 4th Battalion of the Dublin Brigade of the IRA. In early 1918 he was instructed 'to concentrate on police work', and a sergeant and fifty-four Volunteers were placed at his disposal. Kinsella later told the Bureau of Military History that 'These men were exempt from all other duties . . . the idea being that each section would deal with crime in its own Company area.' He went on to recount the following example of their police work.

There was an old lady living alone in Crumlin. She had a little property of her own and her savings amounted to about £80. It was reported to me that thieves had broken into her house and stolen her savings. I instructed members of my police unit to watch out for any individuals who appeared to be lavish in spending money. Shortly afterwards I was told that two men, Reilly and Coleman, who were not normally well off, were spending money much beyond their means. This threw suspicion on them. We arrested both men and extracted a confession from each of them. By a little rough handling they openly admitted that they had broken into this lady's house and had stolen the money. Reilly had most of the money, amounting to between £50 and £60, in his possession. He explained that the balance had been spent on the purchase of a gramophone, a watch and wearing apparel. He surrendered all the cash he had and most of the articles purchased with the remainder of the money. These articles were later taken back to where they had been purchased, and when the position was explained to the proprietor the money was refunded.

These two men were brought before a Battalion Court at which Peadar Ó Briain presided. The court was held in a cowshed at the rear of Wellington House, Templeogue. The prisoners were defended by a young solicitor named Burke, a relation of Liam T. Cosgrave. The prosecuting officer was by the name of Andy Walsh who was a Company Captain. The case was presented as legally as we could manage. The sentence of the court was that the cash available would be paid over in full to the woman from whom it had been stolen, and that the outstanding balance was to be paid by weekly instalments by both culprits. Any damage that had been done to the house was to be made good. Glass had to be replaced in a window which had been broken, and paint had to be procured for painting round the glass. The case ended very satisfactorily. The lady was paid in full and expressed her appreciation of the way in which we had dealt with the matter.

'Better remain in our ignorance'

JOHN RYAN (1918)

In an article in the Jesuit quarterly *Studies*, John Ryan described cinema as 'the most revolutionary development' that had taken place 'since the Flood'. He feared that this 'new piper of Hamelin' had 'all the children at his heels' and was 'luring them to a sure doom'.

It has brought into our midst vivid representations of the manners and lives of other nations; it demonstrates their social customs and their mechanical devices; it shows us their mountains, their rivers and their waterfalls; it teaches us how they make money and how they spend it. Twenty years ago it was necessary to go abroad in order to enlarge one's mind by travel; to-day any urchin who can lay hands on twopence is able to explore the world from 'Greenland's icy mountains to Afric's coral strand'. What shall we have to pay for all this? There is one price that we cannot afford to pay. We cannot afford to barter the Irish ideals of humour and virtue for those that obtain in the busy marts of England, of America, or upon the Continent of Europe. Better remain in our ignorance; better not to know the machinery of other lands; better to be content with our own innocent mirth than to participate in the cosmopolitan gaiety of sin. [. . .]

It may be asked naturally, whether some Dublin [picture] houses are good and some bad? The question would be a difficult one to answer; undoubtedly some managers are less particular than others, and I have had to walk out of certain picture houses and shake the dust off my feet. In one case I left a large gathering of ladies and gentlemen wrapped up in a disgusting plot, so bad a one that I have no intention of visiting that house again. But the problem is a very peculiar one: the Dublin proprietors and managers are at the mercy of others, at the mercy of the film-makers, at the mercy of the viewers and the reporters, and at the mercy of the Censors. A Dublin manager invests money in a film which he has not himself seen. It has been passed by the British Censors, approved in various towns by local Censors, and is well reported on. Perhaps he does not see it till the second day of its appearance; he then finds to his surprise that it has bad features, and he has to decide whether he will lose his money or let it run through. A few men may make the sacrifice and put up with the loss, but I expect that most of them would throw the onus on the Censor's judgment. [. . .]

At present the Cinema industry is a wild, untrained colt, needing to be harnessed for the common good, much too powerful an influence to be left unguarded. State Censorship is certainly needed, for though the present system has done good, it is clearly wanting in authority. Local and voluntary Censorships are palliatives merely, not efficacious remedies. Next to an Official Authority with power to enforce its decrees, the best safeguard is a strong public opinion ready to resent there and then every infringement of morality or good taste. To this end it is desirable that the clergy and prominent citizens should frequent the picture houses as a matter of duty, and give a lead in denouncing whatever may be wrong. Failing this, the young men's confraternities should act promptly and fearlessly.

We want the Irish picture houses to be clean and crowded with patrons, above all with the clergy and strong-minded laymen who will insist on healthy pictures. It is no good boycotting the greatest educational and social influence that has arisen in any age. We must master the 'movies' or they will master us! Much more important than Censorship is a strong and articulate public opinion, but as yet Dublin audiences are essentially timid.

Just now one can only suggest a remedy that is far from perfect: Let every parish priest take cognisance of the houses in his own district, and recommend to his parishioners those which are known to be careful in the selection of their subjects. A recommendation of this kind would be so valuable that every effort would be made to secure it.

But after all the most radical cure is the manufacture of our own Irish films, in order that they may be healthy and racy of the soil. In his day, [Andrew] Fletcher of Saltoun said, 'Let who will make the laws of a country, if I may write its ballads.' If he were living at the present time, he could add the further reflection: 'And I care not who makes the ballads of a country, if I may produce its films.'

'On the straight road to massacre'

ALICE STOPFORD GREEN (1918)

Alice Stopford Green, historian and Irish nationalist, was a well-respected advocate of Sinn Féin policies. She wrote to the South African statesman J. C. Smuts in the immediate aftermath of Lloyd George's proposal to extend conscription to Ireland and in the wake of the report of the Irish Convention. On 18 April the Mansion House Conference of representatives of Sinn Féin, the Irish Parliamentary Party, the All-for-Ireland League and the Irish Labour Party agreed to campaign against conscription.

There is no hope from voluntary enlistment now, and we are on the straight road to massacre. The new young stuff of Irish boys is as fine a material as any country ever produced, and as things stand I see only one use reserved for them. They are not pro-Germans, if they are anti the Castle, and they will be mad to prove that it is not as cowards and shirkers that they are staying at home. That sting is driven in by those who do not want voluntary enlistment, and who now think they can settle the Irish Question once for all. Well, you know how brave men should be led. Fables for the foolish are no use at this time. You would need tremendous guarantees *now* to get enlistment at all. You can't wait for an atmosphere unless it is to bring a massacre. [. . .] A year ago I would have hailed a Colonial Conference. But now I see the power of the London propaganda and the London 'atmosphere'. I don't wonder at it in the fury of the war. It is as natural and as dangerous as a tornado. To sail a ship through it! I wish there was an administration fit for the time of danger.

The returned Yank

FRANCIS HACKETT (1918)

Francis Hackett, journalist and novelist, emigrated to the United States, and later lived in France and Denmark. In his 1918 book *Ireland: A Study in Nationalism*, Hackett examined one of 'the regular tragicomedies of Irish life': the 'Returned American'.

Fresh from Chicago or Boston, the prosperous visiting emigrant finds himself in a strange relation to the old familiar life. Still a child when he left home, humble, timid and inexperienced, he knew nothing beyond his native parish, and his life was hemmed and subdued. Without a penny of his own, he lived in obedience to his father, his schoolmaster and his priest; and his radius was the radius of the ass's cart. Flung into the medley of American life he was compelled to struggle with giants he had never even conceived, to fit his senses to the mad traffic of a metropolis, to become way-wise in the factory, to learn the methods of a harsh, crass, bristling civilization. He who had thought Leitrim or Limerick illimitable found himself engulfed in a whirlpool of sensations which no one could sort or describe. His own people laughed at him as a 'greenhorn', and pushed him out for himself to sink or swim. For the first time he earned and spent real money. He ate and drank what he liked. He tasted a novel independence. If he had an aptitude for the new life, he lost some of his fears, took courage in his search for work, found his value in the market, earned higher wages, broadened out. A little swaggering before any new 'greenhorn' was inevitable; and when his chance to visit the 'old country' arrived, he resolved to show the heights he had attained, the vast distance he had travelled, the colossal difference between the 'greenhorn' and the Yank.

The greatest surprise for the Returned American is the stationary life to which he comes home. He does not understand that he has himself been merely sucked into a whirlpool. He feels that it is he, not America, that has accomplished his experience; and he wonders that while he was so active, the people at home could stand still. The contrast between his own brilliant achievements and the unvarying routine he had forgotten fills him with an unbidden superiority. He sees in a new perspective the gods to whom he formerly bowed. The terrifying schoolmaster is a meek, slipshod, shabby old man. The priest is slow-moving, amiable, asthmatic, fat, and obviously inexperienced. And his mother is a respectful, blushing woman, who cannot help fingering his clothes. The subservience of his father to the tradespeople and the land agent strikes a nerve that competition has made keen. He sees no reason for all this self-effacement. He longs to assert himself against all the powers to which his childhood had been enslaved. He grows loud, aggressive, crude. He jingles his sovereigns and cocks a belligerent hat. He swears more than is good for him, and doesn't give a damn who knows it. Something tells him he is out of joint with the world he knew. He criticizes, to set himself right. People sneeringly whisper he thinks he's a great fellow. All he has seen, and been, and suffered, is locked from their eyes. The story of his life beyond is ignored, while yesterday's weather is discussed, and the bad year for hay. Three thousand miles of sea lie between himself and the men who say 'hello'. They feel he is proud of the contrast that his thick gold chain announces. He's 'too good for them'. The words that should be spoken are left unspoken, and both take refuge in idle, rasping talk. When he goes back to the Chicago car-barns, he feels a strange relief. He is, in a sad sense, going home.

But if the people in Ireland have utterly failed to appreciate the romance of the Returned American, the romance of his lonely and heroic struggle in a hard and unfriendly life, they, in turn, are acutely sensitive to the contrast he has taken pains to draw. He is no longer the modest, submissive boy they knew. He is purse-proud and vulgar. He has overlooked the improvements that meant labour and invention and pride. He has conveyed all too scornfully his desire to introduce changes, renovate, reform. They shudder at his impious hands. Things reverent from age and association have lost their value in his sharpened eyes. His religion is no longer the influence it was at home. New values, values in money and worldliness and will, have supplanted the previous truths of old. He has looked down on them as old-fashioned and behind the times. He has tried to force on them crazy ideas of class and power. The clash between generations has been accentuated by the clash between the New World and the Old. In the parish he is remembered as a Yank; and conservatism is ironic about this latest disciple of Mammon, who has splashed his money about with such immoral recklessness, and so boldly invited the anger of the gods.

For my own part, I feel sympathy with the Old World in Ireland. I dread nothing for Ireland so much as machine-slavery, the homogeneity of vulgar living that is now the rule in the world and the economic rule in small Irish towns. But, bitter as it is to risk Ireland's ascent, I do not think that passionate provincialism, either in regard to England or America, can save her without confirming a worse decay. Ireland must season its character in the world as it is, not shrink away from foreignness, or it is destined to succumb to the world.

A bishop backs Sinn Féin

MICHAEL FOGARTY (1918)

Dr Michael Fogarty was the Bishop of Killaloe from 1904 until his death in 1955. Following the death of his friend Bishop O'Dwyer of Limerick in August 1917, Fogarty's was the loudest and most articulate nationalist voice among the Irish bishops. As is clear from this letter to James O'Mara, Sinn Féin's director of elections, he was by November 1918 an outspoken opponent of the party he had once supported: the Irish Parliamentary Party. He enclosed a subscription and his 'best wishes for the success of the Sinn Féin cause in the coming elections, handicapped though that cause is by the unjust imprisonment of its leaders'.

The country is sick of the House of Commons with its plutocratic record of oppression, corruption and chicanery. Ireland, since it came under its influence a hundred years ago, has wasted and withered as badly as Armenia under the Turks. The policy of 'massaging' English ministers by our 'expert statesmen' has had an ample trial. We know where it has landed us – in the national degradation of Partition. The authors of that criminal and cowardly surrender will never be forgiven by Ireland.

I am not afraid of Abstention. It is not only a logical and long-called for protest against the pillage of our national rights in the infamous Union but, in view of the insulting policy expounded by the Prime Minister as to the share reserved for Ireland in his world-reconstruction, no other course is open to us if we have a particle of self-respect. [material heavily scored through by Fogarty and indecipherable]. Irish representatives in a House of Commons dominated by Mr L. George and his anti-Irish Coalition is a horrible imposition which it is time to terminate. That Unionist combine will work its shameless will on Ireland whether Irish members are present there or not. Why then send them there to be spat upon as paupers to come back to us with empty hands or with a few crumbs from the English kitchen garnished with rhetoric, but, as always, with the leprosy of Anglicisation visibly developed on their person for the ruin of our national spirit.

Partition is to be defeated and liberty ultimately won, not by talking to the dead sons of the House of Commons but under God, where and as emancipation was won, and landlordism broken, and conscription defeated, at home in Ireland by the determined will of the people.

John Mitchel was right when he called for the withdrawal of the Irish members and time has fully verified the words he then used in speaking of this subject. 'That parliament,' he said, 'is a lie, an imposture, an outrage – a game in which our part and lot is a disgrace and defeat for ever; to Ireland it is nothing besides a conduit of corruption, a workshop of coercion, a storehouse of starvation, a machinery of cheating, and a perpetual memento of slavery.'

Smuggling Michael Collins into police HQ

EAMON BROY (1919)

By 1918, Eamon 'Ned' Broy, a colonel of the Dublin Metropolitan Police, had switched allegiance and started passing intelligence to Michael Collins. It soon became clear to Broy that Collins 'did not understand the complete background of the detective organization', and it was decided that Broy would help smuggle Collins into the barracks so that he could read the record books himself.

So, meeting Mick one night in April 1919, I was able to tell him that I would be on duty the following night from 10 p.m. to 6 a.m. We arranged that, at twelve o'clock, he would ring up to make certain that it was I who was on duty, as there were frequently last-minute changes. He was to use the name 'Field', and my name was to be 'Long'.

In due course, I went on duty at 10 p.m. Most of the detectives, who were unmarried, usually went to bed at about 11 p.m. From about 11 p.m. that night, reports began to come in about shootings in Store St and other areas, and I wondered was fate going to take a hand. I also learned that, in the uniformed B. Division, which did duty around that office, the Inspector on night duty was Inspector Daniel Barrett. While the average uniformed officer would give the G. Division a wide berth, Barrett was an ignorant, presumptuous man, who would be quite capable of reporting that there was a light on in the office at night, the secret office being on the first floor. It was a semi-circular office, with many windows and with blinds only over the bottom windows. It became obvious to me that I could not switch on the electric light in that room. The secret small room, which held the books, had no electric light. Therefore, candles would be necessary. While thinking this out and, at the same time, receiving the messages about the shooting, Sergeant Kerr of the Carriage Office, who was a single man and sleeping in the building, was in the office talking to me, which was quite a usual practice. When it was nearly 11.30 p.m., I tried to break off the conversation with Kerr as much as I could. At about 11.45 p.m., he said he would stay up and give me a hand, in view of all the messages. Finally, we had almost a row, and he left for bed at about 11.50 p.m. At twelve o'clock, Mick rang up, saying, 'Field here. Is that Long?' I said: 'Yes. Bring a candle.'

The new building had, of course, a brand-new set of keys, and there was a master-key, in case any of the other keys got lost. I had made myself another master-key, by filing one of the ordinary keys. That key would be necessary to open the secret room. In due course, at about 12.15 a.m., Mick Collins arrived, accompanied by Seán Nunan. I had told him, and whoever came with him, to be armed and also to have sticks, because one would never know what might go wrong. I duly let them in, showed them the back way and the yard door to Townsend St in case anything happened, and gave them the general lie of the land. No sooner had I done so than a stone came through the window. I was just wondering again if the British fate was going to take a hand. I looked at them, and they looked at me. I told them to go into a dark passage and to wait near the back door, in the shadow. On looking out on Great Brunswick St, I saw a British soldier in custody of a policeman. I opened the door and inquired of the constable what was wrong. He said: 'This fellow is drunk and he is after throwing a stone in through the window.' He took the soldier to the police station next door. I went back and told Mick what had happened. On inquiring if he had brought the candle, he said: 'No.' He thought I was having a joke at his expense. [. . .] I thought of my precious master-key, opened the store and found plenty of candles, boxes of matches, soap, etc. Having taken a couple of candles and a couple of boxes of matches, I brought Michael upstairs. With the master-key I locked the main doors of the dormitories, which were on the top floor. The same key opened the political office and opened the secret small room, built into the wall, which contained the records. I gave Collins and Nunan the candles and, getting them to close the door fairly tightly, I left them to carry on their investigation. I then went downstairs. No sooner was I down than there was a heavy knock at the door. I opened it and found the same constable back again, inquiring as to the value of the broken glass. I gave him a rough estimate and he left. I went upstairs, told the boys what the noise was about, and came down to look after telephones, etc.

Michael stayed from about 12.15 till about 5 a.m. There were many reasons for his visit. He wanted to know the background of what he called the correspondence which they had received from me, the exact degree of British knowledge as regards the Volunteers, Sinn Féin and other national organisations. Michael wanted to ascertain who, of their people, were known and, still more important, who were not known. He wanted to try to gauge the mentality behind the records, and then to use the police secret organisation as a model, with suitable improvements and modifications, for Volunteer requirements. It was obvious that, sooner or later, these records would be taken to the Castle because at nearly every hour of the day a ring would come to the office asking for particulars, in writing, of Suspect So-and-So. As a matter of fact, not very long afterwards, the books were taken to the Castle.

The 'foul methods' of the First Dáil

J. J. WALSH (1919)

J. J. Walsh, an irascible, strong-willed Sinn Féin member, was elected
to the First Dáil to represent Cork in December 1918. He shared with
Michael Collins the experience of having worked as a post office clerk
in London and of having played a relatively junior role in the GPO
during the Easter Rising. In the letter to Hanna Sheehy Skeffington
extracted below, his sneer at what he describes as the careerism of the
'ambitious lad' is obviously aimed at Collins, and he explains his disdain for how Sinn Féin was using the power it had won in the 1918
election.

I was not surprised to see your apt description of our new Westminster Parliament; or, as you may fitly term it, the mongrel tail. Imagine
Irish culture after centuries of practical observation copying the foul
methods of English legislation. Unfortunately I had to clear off
before this Hon. Members' and Cabinet business came on for discussion – I had made arrangements to clear out at a given moment
– otherwise I should have spoken my mind. This Cabinet and its
attendant Foreignisms is the product of an ambitious lad who is forcing his way forward on the strength of the fact that he has made a
corner in several movements and from which, combined with the
latest elevation, he now enjoys a trifle of five or six hundred a year.

When Europe is shedding its blood for Government by the people,
the new-born Ireland produces nothing better than the disappearing
Dictatorship. See how it works – the Dáil members are called together
once every two or three months to hear reports from these Dictators.
They are then dispersed to mouch around amongst their constituents
as if they were the most insignificant of ciphers. People are asking
them have they nothing to do for their country? Do they know anything about projects industrial, social or political development –
anything about foreign affairs? But they know nothing and can do
less. In the eyes of the framers of our constitution any single 'Cabinet

Minister' knows more than half a dozen of such men: evidently their functions end with election and the endorsing of pious resolutions.

What support I will get I cannot say but I will move at the next Dáil [. . .] that our Government be run on the Committee system as we see in Corporate and County Council bodies dispensing with the Hon. Members and the Cabinet and also the self-imposed salaries of the latter which tax the organization to the tune of £4,000 per annum. You should communicate strongly and at once your views on these objectionable 'things' to one of the Irish-Ireland papers. If it isn't done now it will become an established institution and difficult to shake later on.

A poteen raid

FRANCIS TUMMON (1920)

Francis Tummon, who served as a lieutentant in the Irish Volunteers during the War of Independence, recalled in his testimony to the Bureau of Military History a raid on a farm where poteen was being distilled illegally. It was led by General Eoin O'Duffy, who would go on to be appointed Garda commissioner – and to become an alcoholic himself.

The first of these raids in the area was brought about rather accidentally. On Sunday night members of my Company joined in a dance at Clones. I was one of a small group who took part in one of these. Towards the end of the dance one of the Clones Volunteers reported that some poteen was offered for sale by a certain gentleman. On investigation, it was further learned that a small quantity had been actually made by this man. Gen. O'Duffy, to whom the matter was reported, decided to hold him prisoner and use him as a guide to find the remainder of the stock. About twelve Volunteers were selected from those remaining at the dance and some small arms were supplied by the Clones Company. O'Duffy took charge personally and off we started on bicycles, taking our prisoner along. En route it was learned that the poteen was under control of a Protestant gentleman who would possibly resist us by force. Plans were accordingly made to use surprise as the chief weapon. A large pole was secured from a hedgerow, and on arrival at the 'still house' it was used as a battering ram on the front door. I don't know if the door was locked but it did not stand up to this heavy assault and was driven in to the centre of the room. The occupant had no time to offer resistance. He was interrogated but for some time gave no information. A search of the place was ordered, and in a ditch close by a four-gallon crockery jar was located, containing about half a gallon of poteen. With due ceremony Gen. O'Duffy smashed this jar on the laneway leading to the house. It was now daylight in the morning but O'Duffy was not satisfied until the still apparatus was located. Further enquiries led to our movement about half a mile to the house of the 'salesman' of the dance. In the garden buried in potato drills the worm of the still was found. It was sawn into short lengths to prevent its further use. A shot-gun seized in the house where the poteen was found was ordered to be returned to the owner by Gen. O'Duffy, who stated it was a poteen raid he was conducting, not an arms one. My first poteen raid carried out, we were ordered to dismiss. It was well into the morning when I arrived home, had my breakfast, and commenced my usual day's work.

Big Houses under threat

LORD ORANMORE AND BROWN (1920)

The threat posed by the IRA to country estates was captured in this letter from an Irish peer, Lord Oranmore and Brown, to Walter Long, the First Lord of the Admiralty and Chairman of the Cabinet's Irish Situation Committee.

It is commonly reported in many parts of Ireland that it is the intention of Sinn Feiners shortly to inaugurate a campaign of burning country houses in order that they may be relieved from the necessity of adding their value to the compensation which they propose to offer to landlords when, under an Irish Republic, they compulsorily acquire their demesnes, and I think it is more than likely that this plan will shortly be put into operation. It was my intention, as usual, to go over to Ireland, at the end of next month, for the autumn; but I am very doubtful whether, in the present condition of the country, I shall be justified in exposing my wife and family to the risks of certain anxiety and probable danger.

Only the other day, a parlourmaid of a neighbour of mine, General Lewin [presumably General Arthur Lewin of nearby Cloghan Castle], was ordered by the Sinn Feiners to leave his employment. She did not obey, and when bicycling home from Tuam, the neighbouring town, she was ambushed by six men, who divested her of every stitch of clothing, and forced her to bicycle back to her employer's house stark naked.

An Irish unionist advises the British establishment

CABINET PAPER (1920)

W. E. Wylie, a unionist barrister in Dublin, was the prosecuting counsel at the court martial of the 1916 leaders and worked as a legal adviser in Dublin Castle between 1918 and 1920. Recognized as an astute observer of the worsening conditions in Ireland, he was given an opportunity in July 1920 to offer his analysis to all the key players on the British side: the prime minister, his Cabinet, civil servants, military leaders and Sir James Craig. That analysis is summarized in the Cabinet paper that follows. It would be twelve months before the Lloyd George-led government came to accept the logic of Wylie's analysis, agree a truce and open negotiations with Sinn Féin.

Mr Wylie said that in his view the present position in Ireland meant the parting of the ways, and only harm could come of patchwork legislation. With regard to the state of the police, he had during the last three weeks seen a large number of police officers, and had formed the strong opinion that within two months the Irish Police Force as a police force would cease to exist. He was referring now to the whole of Ireland, with the exception of the North-East Counties. In two months' time, fifty per cent of the police force would have resigned through terrorism, and the remainder would have to go about in considerable force committing counter outrages. An Irish policeman either saw white or he saw red; if he saw white he resigned from the force through terrorism; and if he saw red he committed a counter outrage. Both conditions of mind were disastrous.

With regard to the Civil Courts, the entire administration of the Imperial Government had ceased. In one town, out of forty-five appeals down for hearing only two came on. As for the revenue, everyone was determined to pay no taxes, and it was not fair to ask the revenue officers to collect them, for, if they attempted to do so, they did it at the peril of their lives. With regard to the Local Authorities, these were prepared to function so far as their own local affairs were concerned, but they would give no assistance in carrying out the instructions of the Irish Government.

There were in his opinion two remedies for the present state of affairs. The first was to proclaim at once martial law of the most stringent kind. As an Irishman, this to him was abhorrent, and afforded no solution of the problem. By proclaiming martial law it would be possible to beat the people into insensibility; but when martial law was taken off – and it must end sometime – the feelings of hatred and bitterness would be intensified, and there would be a return to the present state of affairs. The second remedy was a settlement with Sinn Fein. He was aware that the English might regard this as a condonation of the murderers, but he wished to emphasise that these murderers were not real criminals. Of that he felt convinced. Fanatics they might be, and probably were, but they were themselves convinced that through murder was the only path to freedom. These men were not committing outrages through blood-lust, but because they believed they had been tricked by the British Government, and the only way to focus the eyes of Europe on their cause was by the adoption of the methods they had pursued. The Sinn Feiners were of the opinion that the application of martial law would assist their cause.

A difficulty with regard to settling with Sinn Fein was to find anyone with whom to negotiate. He felt convinced that if England took her courage in both hands and stated that she was prepared to settle with Sinn Fein on any terms short of an Irish Republic, and that if Sinn Fein did not accept the offer, martial law would be introduced, Sinn Fein would come forward and negotiate. The Sinn Feiners were convinced that they were capable of governing Ireland, and he agreed with them. He himself had started life as a Unionist, but now, after seeing the marvellous organization which Sinn Fein had built up, he was of the opinion that the Irish were capable of governing themselves. If the Government attempted to bludgeon the Irish people, no good could possibly result, and Ireland would still remain a thorn in the side of the Empire. But if the Government played straight, within two years Ireland would be one of the strongest partners within the Empire.

The last days of Terence MacSwiney

ART O'BRIEN (1920)

The hunger-strike undertaken at Brixton Prison by Terence Mac-Swiney, the Lord Mayor of Cork, attracted worldwide attention. Art O'Brien was Sinn Féin representative in Britain from October 1919 and a regular visitor to MacSwiney in jail. He assumed the task of ensuring that the progress of the hunger-strike would be relayed to the outside world. These passages are from O'Brien's chronicle of MacSwiney's last days, which survived in his papers.

22 October 1920, 71st day of hunger-strike

The Lord Mayor continues in a delirious condition with very short intervals of semi-consciousness. He is still unable to recognise his relatives or his surroundings. For a short period during the night the delirium became violent again. The spasms and twitchings of the limbs and face continue. He went off into a sleep for about an hour. At about 4.45 a.m. he seemed to be rallying to his senses but relapsed again almost immediately. This occurred again between 7 and 8 a.m. when his sister Annie was with him. He suddenly asked, 'What was the month? What was the year? Where he was? What they were all doing here? Was the Irish Republic established and recognised? It seemed as if he might recognise his sister, but almost immediately he went off into a delirium again muttering: 'We did grand marching during the night. They were marching as well, but we beat them. It is glorious! Glorious!' The prison authorities still continue to force food into his mouth. At about 8.30 this morning the nurse held a spoon of meat-juice to his mouth. He muttered: 'No! No! Take it away,' and closed his lips firmly. This performance was repeated twice, when his head fell back from the exhaustion of the effort and the spoon was then inserted in his mouth.

On the following day, the Home Office refused to allow MacSwiney's sisters, Mary and Anne, to enter the prison and refused his other visitors the use of the prison telephone to report on his condition.

11 a.m., 24 October 1920, 73rd day of hunger-strike

The Lord Mayor remained very quiet all night. He did not open his eyes, and gave no sign that he knew anyone was present. This morning he is still unconscious. He has opened his eyes occasionally, sometimes looking straight at his Chaplain, Fr Dominic, but without any sign of recognition even when Fr Dominic spoke to him [Fr Dominic O'Connor, a Capuchin and republican sympathiser]. He lies very quietly, moaning now and again as though he were in pain. His condition seems very critical indeed. The restrictions suddenly imposed on his relatives, limiting or prohibiting their access to the Lord Mayor, and removing their facilities of communicating with their friends outside, still continue in force. Misses Mary and Annie MacSwiney remained in the waiting room of the prison all day yesterday, refusing to leave until they were allowed to see their brother. At 10 p.m. an Inspector and several police constables entered the waiting room, and sometime after the Misses MacSwiney were put out by force. The Lady Mayoress was only allowed to be with her husband for a little over an hour yesterday. This extra strain, fatigue and anxiety placed upon her by the unnecessary and inhuman restrictions of the Home Office have brought upon her an attack of indisposition. She has, consequently, been unable to go out this morning but hopes to be sufficiently recovered to visit her husband for a little while, if permitted to do so, this afternoon. The additional strain is also telling on the Misses MacSwiney. They tasted no food during their long vigil in the cold prison waiting room from an early hour yesterday morning until nearly 11 p.m. last night. Their friends are extremely anxious on their behalf. The pain caused to them by total exclusion from their brother during his dying hours is terrible to contemplate.

7 p.m., 24 October 1920, 73rd day of hunger-strike

The Lord Mayor is still unconscious. The Lady Mayoress visited the prison this afternoon, but after waiting twenty minutes she was not allowed to see him. His brother, who has been in the prison all day, has only been allowed to see him for a few minutes. His two sisters have been at the prison gate all day long, but have not been allowed to enter.

25 October 1920, 74th day of hunger-strike

The Lord Mayor of Cork died at twenty minutes to six this morning. His brother John and Father Dominic were with him. Notice was given to them at twenty-five minutes to five that they should go to him. His brother John wanted to communicate with the other relatives, but he was not allowed to use the prison telephone, nor was he allowed to leave the prison until 6.15. The Lord Mayor did not recover consciousness.

Sectarianism in the Belfast shipyards

MICHAEL CUNNINGHAM, JOE DEVLIN,
DAVID LLOYD GEORGE AND EDWARD CARSON (1920)

A letter from a Belfast native, Michael Cunningham, to Joe Devlin, MP, brought the question of anti-Catholic discrimination to the attention of the Prime Minister.

My dear Mr Devlin,

I wish to be excused for addressing you personally but as I have been exiled through no fault of my own and compelled to seek a living outside Belfast, I was inspired by your recent speech in the House of Commons, and I wish to inform you that I am an Irish Nationalist. I was three years and three months through the Great War. My son, Joseph, was through the war from the 10th of August 1914 till he was released from Germany when the Armistice was signed. My second eldest son was two years and three months through the war, joining up at the age of eighteen and six days. We have all suffered or are suffering from wounds or gas yet we are refused the right to earn a living in Belfast because we are Catholics. I am a man three months younger than yourself and as a boy I was acquainted with you in and around Derby Street, therefore as a disabled ex-serviceman who has been driven from wife and family to look for a living amongst strangers, I appeal to you to expose the infernal lie that none but Sinn Féiners was expelled from work in Belfast.

I with hundreds of other ex-servicemen was expelled for no other reason than that I was a member of the Roman Catholic Faith, and, although I was under medical treatment for injuries received in Dunkirk during the latter part of the war (and my workmates knew this fact), still I was a Fenian and deserved to be murdered, although I was fighting in France while my assailants were earning big wages in peace in Belfast.

I now claim from the government at least the right to live in

England, the country I fought and was wounded for. I have been trying to get a house in either Jarrow or Hebburn-on-Tyne, Co. Durham, so that I can bring my wife and family here to live in peace, but I have been unsuccessful up to the present, although several men with no claim to war service have obtained houses. My wages are not sufficient to keep two houses, one here, and one in Belfast, therefore I trust you will do all in your power to help me to get a house here in either Jarrow or Hebburn-on-Tyne. [. . .] I appeal to you knowing that you won't desert an old schoolmate even from Hannahstown.

Devlin forwarded Cunningham's letter to Lloyd George, with this covering letter:

Dear Prime Minister,

I did not care to trouble you to-day at your lunch when I met you but I do again desire to point out that the appointment of these 'special' constables in Belfast will be an outrage so indefensible that I fear to think of what the consequences of it will be. Only the other day a man who had served four years in the war, had been wounded, and had returned to Belfast, was kicked and badly beaten by the men who now will be the special constables in Belfast. A Judge, who was a follower of Sir Edward Carson, stated from the bench in trying the case that nothing more disgraceful he had ever heard of, that this man who had been out fighting for his assailants had been so treated by them, and that it was enough to excite the sympathy of the most callous of men. Indeed his speech was stronger than this. I have not the paper beside me now in which I read it.

I intended to send you a copy of enclosed letter but I want you to see the original, and I do beg of you to read it. This man is only typical of hundreds of others whom I know. I feel that my responsibility is a terrible one because through me these men went out to the war, and every one of these cases wrings my heart and makes me feel utterly ashamed that I asked them to make such sacrifices. I hope you will not fail to read the letter and return it to me.

Lloyd George in turn sent a copy of Cunningham's letter and of Devlin's to Sir Edward Carson, the leader of the Ulster Unionists, with this covering letter:

I enclose copy of a letter I have received from Devlin which explains itself. I have not, of course, investigated the case and do not know whether the facts can be substantiated, but if they are true, the case points to a situation which ought to be seriously dealt with by the Ulster Unionist Council. This man states that he and his sons, as Nationalist Roman Catholics, fought for the British Empire throughout the war, in which they were wounded. Yet they are now expelled from Belfast, not because they are Sinn Feiners, but apparently simply because they are Roman Catholics. If this is really true it is an act of the utmost folly which cannot fail to bring discredit both on Belfast and Ulster, and the British Empire.

I write to you as the trusted leader of the Ulster Protestants. I know that you will agree with me that men who fought for the Empire in the war ought not to be persecuted like this, and that those who have influence and authority should do everything possible to prevent these things happening and to secure justice to those who have been unfairly victimized. I shall be infinitely obliged to you if you look into this case.

Carson replied to Lloyd George:

I have received your letter and copies enclosed from Devlin. Of course such a case as he mentions is a most deplorable one and I need hardly say is most discreditable, if true, to Belfast. I have no doubt in the early outbreak in the Shipyards and elsewhere after the murders [by the IRA] of [RIC officers] Smythe and Swanzey, there were cases which were dealt with without any discrimination but you are aware that since, matters have cooled down, the various bodies of workmen have passed resolutions stating that any man who was willing to disconnect himself with Sinn Fein, should be allowed to return to work and I am in hopes that things are settling down. I believe myself that the Special Constables, if properly selected, will go far to prevent similar cases occurring and I need hardly say, that I will have this particular case investigated.

It should be remembered, I think, that many Protestants were driven out of their employment at the same time by the Sinn Fein element and that an open boycott of Ulster is being proclaimed everywhere; also that throughout the South and West it is practically impossible for any man, who served in the War, to obtain employment. I do not mention these facts as any palliation of the case referred to by Devlin but it of course very much complicates the situation.

A Black and Tan writes to his mother

'CHARLIE' (1920)

This letter from a Royal Irish Constabulary 'auxiliary', or 'Black and Tan', gives an inside account of the beginning of an extraordinary sequence of ambushes and pillaging in Cork in December 1920. The letter survives among the papers of Florence O'Donoghue, who was the IRA's head of intelligence in Cork during the War of Independence. It might have been intercepted by O'Donoghue's fiancée Josephine Marchment, later his wife, who was working undercover for the IRA while employed as a secretary in the British Army barracks in Cork.

Auxiliary Division, Dunmanway, Co. Cork

We came on here from Cork and are billeted in a workhouse, filthily dirty; half guns [soldiers] are down with Bronchitis. I am at present in bed, my camp bed which I fortunately brought with me recovering from a severe chill contracted on Saturday night last during the burning and looting of Cork in all of which I took perforce a reluctant part. We did it all right never mind how much the well-intentioned Hamar Greenwood would excuse us. In all my life and in all the tales of fiction I have read I have never experienced such orgies of murder, arson and looting as I have witnessed during the past sixteen days with the RIC Auxiliaries. It baffles description. And we are supposed to be ex-officers and gentlemen. There are quite a number of decent fellows and likewise a lot of ruffians.

On our arrival here from Cork one of our heroes held up a car with a priest and a civilian in it and shot them both through the head without cause or provocation. We were very kindly received by the people but the consequences of this cold-blooded murder is that no-one will come within a mile of us now and all shops are closed. The brute who did it has been sodden with drink for some time and has been sent to Cork under arrest for examination by experts in lunacy. If certified sane he will be court-martialled and shot. The poor old priest was 65 and everybody's friend.

The burning and sacking of Cork followed immediately upon the ambush of our men. I, as orderly sergeant, had to collect 20 men for a raid and then left the barracks in two motor cars. I did not go as I was feeling seedy. The party had not gone 100 yards from barracks when bombs were thrown at them from over a wall. One dropped in a car and wounded 8 men, one of whom has since died. Very naturally the rest of the Co[mpan]y were enraged. The houses in the vicinity of the ambush were set alight and from there the various parties set out on their mission of destruction. Many who had witnessed similar scenes in France and Flanders say that nothing they had experienced was comparable to the punishment meted out to Cork. I got back to barracks at 4 a.m.

Reprisals are necessary and loyal Irishmen agree but there is a lot done which should not be done. Of course it is frequently unavoidable that the innocent suffer with the guilty. The sooner the Irish extremists recognise that they will never gain their point by the methods they employ the better it will be for this unfortunate and misguided country.

You ask what our uniform is: the RIC Auxiliary uniform is khaki tunic and breeches and puttees: dark military great coats, dark green tam o'shanters and harp badge – harp badge on collar of tunic. Revolver, rifle and bayonet, bombs, complete our equipment. I am up today feeling a lot better but the accumulated chills have made their appearance on my face, which is plastered from forehead to Adam's apple with 'cold spots'. I am not beautiful to behold with a week's growth of hair on my face and no immediate prospect of getting it off.

We have a lot of guard duty to do, about four nights in each week: 24 hours on duty at a time, and no sleep at all for the sergeant of the guard, who has just to post his sentries every two hours – that's me. I maintain that we could not be overpaid at £5 per diem. It's the hardest life I have ever shouldered but one gets used to everything in time.

A general inspector arrived this morning to have a 'straight talk' to us about discipline, etc., as he put it. I am afraid we struck terror into him for the straight talk never materialized. He was most amicable. I could tell you much more but sufficient for the day, etc.

The weather has been bitterly cold but the frost gave this morning. I wish this play was set in the Cameroons or somewhere near the Equator, then I wouldn't mind it much. The country round here is quite pretty and very hilly. Our friends the gunmen are in their holes and we are here to round them up; they may or may not remain to face the ordeal. It is as well that you should know everything. I have named Maurice [?] as my next of kin. Ireland has to pay very substantially for every RIC casualty. A mere flesh wound is paid £250 and so on up to £5,000 to a man's widow. The widow of the young fellow who was shot in the raid in which I took part in Dublin received the latter amount.

'Seditious literature' and a burning piano

TOM CASEMENT (1921)

Tom Casement, a brother of Sir Roger Casement, was a veteran of the Second Boer War, where he had come to know Jan Smuts, by now South Africa's prime minister. In a letter dated 1 February 1921, Casement lobbied Smuts to play a constructive role in initiating dialogue between the Sinn Féin leadership and the British government at the forthcoming Imperial Conference. In the event, Smuts did play a significant role in encouraging the Anglo-Irish truce in July.

You in SA have got what every Irishman worth his salt would accept and honestly work. But no hope is ever held out to us of any decent measure of gov[ernment]. The result is that we demand a Republic but we leave room for a modification of our demands. What we have got today is Force in its most brutal form. You think it's a nightmare. I often wonder if I am awake. The condition of the people is terrible but the spirit grand; and I am proud to be an Irishman. I have seen things done since I have been home that have made my blood boil but your last words came to me and I kept a tight rein on my temper. There are today hundreds of men in gaol untried; hundreds serving sentences of from two to five years penal servitude for having been found in possession of 'seditious literature'. These men at their trials have always stated that they had no knowledge of the stuff found upon them and I have always believed them. I will now state a case that has lately happened to me.

When I left Dublin for a visit to Galway I left my writing case with a lady friend that I think you have met, Mrs Stopford Green, the historian. My case contained nothing seditious: letters and articles of my brother [Roger] that are now history. During my absence from Dublin, Mrs Green's house was raided and my writing case taken by the military to Dublin Castle. Later on it was returned. I opened it in the presence of several responsible and well-known people. All my brother's letters, photographs and many other private papers that I prized were gone. In one flap of the case I found a bundle of papers; I opened it. The contents would have got me five years if found in my possession. I at once sent them to an MP [in] London and asked him to bring the case before Hamar Greenwood when the House meets next week. It was a deliberate case of trying to trap me but it has failed. [. . .]

The women of Ireland are grand. They are suffering more than the men, but, like the women of SA in 1899, they keep the men up to the mark. In SA, when Lord Roberts [Field Marshal Frederick Roberts, commander of British forces in the Second Boer War] burned houses as a reprisal, he permitted the furniture to be removed. In Ireland everything is destroyed and the poor souls are just left stranded. The other day at an 'official reprisal' a poor fellow managed to get a £50 piano out of the house. He pleaded with the officer in charge of the operation that it might be spared as it was his daughter's. The officer refused and the piano was thrown back into the flames. Hostages are now taken on the military lorries as was done in SA. These poor fellows are kept out in the cold night and if there was an attempt to ambush the lorry there is no doubt that their number would be up. The men in the lorry would see that they did not return alive.

'Stamp out this vermin'

SIR HENRY WILSON (1921)

Sir Henry Wilson, who came from Co. Longford and who would be assassinated by the IRA in 1922, was in 1921 the Chief of the Imperial General Staff. In May of that year, when Wilson wrote to Sir Henry Rawlinson, the Commander-in-Chief for India, Lloyd George was avoiding him and not taking much heed of his advice on Ireland. Wilson held politicians in contempt, and called them 'Frocks' – a reference to the frock-coats worn on formal occasions.

In Ireland we have had one of the worst week-ends since the beginning of the rebellion, and it is perfectly clear to me that unless the 'Frocks' shout out at the top of their voices and get England on their side, and then really set to work to stamp out this vermin we shall lose Ireland, and with the loss of Ireland we have lost the Empire. I want permission from the 'Frocks', the moment England gets temporarily quiet again, to send over between 20 and 30 battalions, from here, some more cavalry, guns, aeroplanes, wireless, tanks, armoured cars, etc., to place the whole of Ireland under Martial Law, and hand it all over to [General Sir Nevil] Macready. But even with this reinforcement no promise can be made that we can really knock out the murder gang in Ireland, all that I can say is that he is more likely to be able to do so after being reinforced than he is today before he is reinforced. But to go on as we are now, which is neither trying to knock out the murderers nor handing the country over to them as a present, is sheer madness and when the weather breaks in September-October I am afraid we shall find that the troops, whoever they are, who have been separated from their wives and families for a couple of years, will be getting tired of the job and will say so, and then we shall be properly in the soup.

Since I began this letter, and when I got down to the bottom of the first page, the telephone rang and Curzon [the Foreign Secretary], who was at the other end, said that he and the PM agreed that I was to send 5 battalions back to Silesia. I told him that of course if he and the PM had settled the matter there was nothing more to be said about it except to send the battalions, but I would be failing in my duty if I did not tell him plainly that it was madness; that 5 battalions solved no problem; that they might get into a horrid mess; that we did not know how long they would be there; that they would be under the French Command, and quite possibly have a quarrel with the French troops; and so on and so forth; and then I finished up by saying that how anybody in their senses could dream of sending troops to Silesia when Ireland was in the condition she was in passed my understanding, and I told him categorically that in my opinion if we don't reinforce Ireland by every available man, horse, gun, aeroplane that we have got in the world we would lose Ireland at the end of this summer, and with Ireland the Empire. I asked him of what avail would 4 or 5 battalions be in Silesia then! He has gone to speak to the PM, who apparently won't see me for some reason, and I suppose I shall hear in the course of half an hour or so what those wonderful people have settled to do. It really is terrifying to have to deal with men who have so little idea of what is going on right under their noses.

In defence of the Dublin accent

ARTHUR CLERY (1921)

Arthur Clery was a sometime Sinn Féin TD, writer and university
professor. The following is from an article he published in *Studies*.

There is no difficulty at all in determining what is one's natural
accent. It is the accent in which a man speaks when you stick a pin in
him, or as he is running to catch a train, or when he is tired and ill.
The differences between the natural accents of the several classes in a
particular place, so apparent to the citizens themselves, scarcely count
for the stranger. The all-pervading local accent has a distinctiveness
from the accent of other places that surpasses any mere differences
between the accent of class and class in the same locality. To Cork
people, for instance, the accent of the South Mall or the City Club
seems a thing different not merely in degree but in kind from that of
the Coal Quay. We in Dublin are, I am afraid, inclined to lump them
both together as simply the Cork accent. As for our own accent, we
are in a very unhappy plight. To put it in its extreme form, one might
say that we Dubliners cannot speak any language at all. At least we
speak with an accent which neither English nor Irish will recognise.
Oxford and Ballyvourney hold our soft inoffensive tones in equal
contempt, demanding something more violent and exasperating as
the norm of their respective speeches. We, poor Dubliners, say:
'Sure, it doesn't matter.' They reply with violence that it does, or
rather: 'It dos' and 'is mor an difir i' respectively. English speakers
won't have us, whilst Irish speakers are most bitter against us, poor
Dubliners, who really don't want to injure the Irish language at all.

I heard a very learned professor say the other day that the future
of the Irish language lay with Cork Irish spoken with a Dublin
accent. And this we are told is not an Irish accent at all. Dublin Irish
is a bye-word! The truth is we, men of Dublin, are in the position of
a rightful owner who has lost his title deeds. Irish having died out in
this city and county, where it was spoken almost within living

memory, as late as 1835 at any rate, the validity of our accent as a vehicle of Irish speech is no longer admitted. Yet nothing is more certain than that Irish must have been spoken at least with a Co. Dublin accent. The accent along the south-east coast does not differ very greatly. A Drogheda accent is very like a Dublin one. When the people of Glenasmole, for instance, spoke Irish in the last century, it must have been with a Co. Dublin accent. What was the Irish accent of the Irish speakers in Howth, I wonder. 'Murryan' Square itself, to give it the correct local pronunciation, enshrines a distinct peculiarity of Leinster Irish, the pronunciation of 'bh' with 'y' sound instead of a 'v' sound. Glasnevin – with 'd aspirate' pronounced as 'v' Leinster-wise – is another example. Even Dublin city accents must preserve a good deal of Leinster Irish in them. We know that certain Irish words, the schoolboy's 'pus' and 'gob' and the milkman's 'tilly', are still universal in Dublin. 'Caise puca' for a fairy mushroom – the English call it a toadstool – is, according to Seosamh Laoide (from whom I have been quoting), in common use near Blanchardstown. I never heard it in South Dublin.

The Protestant inheritance and the new Ireland

E. J. GWYNN (1921)

The scholar E. J. Gwynn, in a personal letter to the Provost of Trinity College, J. H. Bernard, gives some indication of how discomfited some Southern Protestants felt about the imminent negotiations between Sinn Féin and the British government.

One reads de Valera's speeches and letters, thinking of the essays one has heard declaimed by the Auditor of the Historical, products of a good heart, plenty of conceit, and a blank ignorance of what has been and of what is. Well enough from boys at College, but to see this sort of thing solemnly put forth by grown men, in such a position! [. . .] this last yr has made one feel, for the first time, that I am myself essentially English and not Irish, in spite of certain sympathies and antipathies. A man is what he inherits and what he draws in from his surroundings, and for me and most of us Protestants these things are ninety per cent English or Scotch traditions, beliefs, customs, mental furniture, all that: and why I mainly fear and draw back from the new order – which I suppose will flood in upon us, sooner or later, is not so much the material loss and annoyance as the tendency to cut us away from our roots, or civilisation, which is bone of our bone, flesh of our flesh. Perhaps we ought not to blame the other side for wishing to attest their separate nationality at all points; but it is hard for a man who has children to come after him. I do not want myself and I do not want them to feel aliens in their own country.

And the college. It has got to remain here and must somehow accommodate itself to the change. We ought to be thinking about that. Some of the other side are, I believe, friendly enough disposed and we may find a *modus vivendi*, if only they are ready to recognise that we as well as they have our own ideas and traditions.

Postscript: Gwynn would succeed Bernard as the Provost of Trinity on Bernard's death in 1927.

In defence of the Treaty

MICHAEL COLLINS (1921)

The Anglo-Irish Treaty of December 1921 was agreed after some weeks of talks between the British government and an Irish delegation that included Michael Collins. The Dáil debate over the Treaty's terms took place in the Council Chamber, University College Dublin, between 14 December 1921 and 10 January 1922. On the second day of the debate, Collins reminded deputies of the 'momentous Saturday' of 3 December, when the delegation returned to Dublin for a Cabinet meeting to discuss the compromise terms which were then being offered by the British.

We came back with a document from the British Delegation which we presented to the Cabinet. Certain things happened at that Cabinet Meeting, and the Delegation, on returning, put before the British Delegation as well as they could their impressions of the decisions – I will not say conclusions – arrived at that Cabinet Meeting. I do not want unduly to press the word decisions. I want to be fair to everybody. I can only say they were decisions in this way, that we went away with certain impressions in our minds and that we did our best faithfully to transmit these impressions to paper in the memorandum we handed in to the British Delegation. It was well understood at that Cabinet Meeting that Sir James Craig was receiving a reply from the British Premier on Tuesday morning. Some conclusion as between the British Delegation and ourselves had, therefore, to be come to and handed in to the British Delegation on the Monday night. Now, we went away with a document which none of us would sign. It must have been obvious, that being so, that in the meantime a document arose which we thought we could sign. There was no opportunity of referring it to our people at home. Actually on the Monday night we did arrive at conclusions which we thought we could agree to and we had to say 'Yes' across the table, and I may say that we said 'Yes'. It was later on that same day that the document was signed. But I do not now, and I did not then, regard my word as being anything more important, or a bit less important, than my signature on a document. Now, I also want to make this clear. The answer which I gave and that signature which I put on that document would be the same in Dublin or in Berlin, or in New York or in Paris. If we had been in Dublin the difference in distance would have made this difference, that we would have been able to consult not only the members of the Cabinet but many members of the Dáil and many good friends. There has been talk about 'the atmosphere of London' and there has been talk about 'slippery slopes'. Such talk is beside the point. I knew the atmosphere of London of old and I knew many other things about it of old. If the members knew so much about 'slippery slopes' before we went there why did they not speak then? The slopes were surely slippery, but it is easy to be wise afterwards. I submit that such observations are entirely beside the point. And if my signature has been given in error, I stand by it whether it has or not, and I am not going to take refuge behind any kind of subterfuge. I stand up over that signature and I give the same decision at this moment in this assembly [applause]. It has also been suggested that the Delegation broke down before the first bit of English bluff. I would remind the Deputy who used that expression that England put up quite a good bluff for the last five years here and I did not break down before that bluff [applause, and a voice, 'That is the stuff']. And does anybody think that the respect I compelled from them in a few years was in any way lowered during two months of negotiations? That also is beside the point. The results of our labour are before the Dáil. Reject or accept. The President has suggested that a greater result could have been obtained by more skilful handling. Perhaps so. But there again the fault is not the Delegation's; it rests with the Dáil. It is not afterwards the Dáil should have found out our limitations. Surely the Dáil knew it when they selected us, and our abilities could not have been expected to increase because we were chosen as plenipotentiaries by the Dáil. The Delegates have been blamed for various things. It is scarcely too much to say that they have been blamed for not returning with recognition of the Irish Republic. They are blamed, at any rate, for not having done much better. A Deputy when speaking the other day with reference to Canada suggested that what may apply with safety to Canada would not at all apply to Ireland because of the difference in distance from Great Britain. It seemed to me that he did not regard the Delegation as being wholly without responsibility for the geographical propinquity of Ireland to Great Britain. It is further suggested that by the result of their labours the Delegation made a resumption of hostilities certain. That again rests with the Dáil; they should have chosen a better Delegation, and it was before we went to London that should have been done, not when we returned.

Collins then referred to 'another vexed question': whether the terms of reference of the talks implied 'any departure from the absolutely rigid line of the isolated Irish Republic'. He read out the exchange of letters between Lloyd George and de Valera that had immediately preceded the talks. He insisted that it was the acceptance of the invitation to the conference 'that formed the compromise'.

I was sent there to form that adaptation, to bear the brunt of it. Now as one of the signatories of the document I naturally recommend its acceptance. I do not recommend it for more than it is. Equally I do not recommend it for less than it is. In my opinion it gives us freedom, not the ultimate freedom that all nations desire and develop to, but the freedom to achieve it [applause].

A Deputy has stated that the Delegation should introduce this Treaty not, he describes, as bagmen for England, but with an apology for its introduction. I cannot imagine anything more mean, anything more despicable, anything more unmanly than this dishonouring of one's signature. Rightly or wrongly when you make a bargain you cannot alter it, you cannot go back and get sorry for it and say 'I ought to have made a better bargain'. Business cannot be done on those bases. I must make reference to the signing of the Treaty. This Treaty was not signed under personal intimidation. If personal intimidation had been attempted no member of the Delegation would have signed it. [. . .]

Now I have gone into more or less a general survey of the Treaty, apart from one section of it, the section dealing with North-East Ulster. Again I am as anxious to face facts in that case as I am in any other case. We have stated we would not coerce the North-East. We have stated it officially in our correspondence. I stated it publicly in Armagh and nobody has found fault with it. What did we mean? Did we mean we were going to coerce them or we were not going to coerce them? What was the use of talking big phrases about not agreeing to the partition of our country? Surely we recognise that the North-East corner does exist, and surely our intention was that we should take such steps as would sooner or later lead to mutual understanding. The Treaty has made an effort to deal with it, and has made an effort, in my opinion, to deal with it on lines that will lead very rapidly to goodwill, and the entry of the North-East under the Irish Parliament [applause]. I don't say it is an ideal arrangement, but if our policy is, as has been stated, a policy of non-coercion, then let somebody else get a better way out of it. Now, summing up – and nobody can say that I haven't talked plainly – I say that this Treaty gives us, not recognition of the Irish Republic, but it gives us more recognition on the part of Great Britain and the associated States than we have got from any other nation. [. . .]

In coming to the decision I did I tried to weigh what my own responsibility was. Deputies have spoken about whether dead men would approve of it, and they have spoken of whether children yet unborn will approve of it, but few of them have spoken as to whether the living approve of it. In my own small way I tried to have before my mind what the whole lot of them would think of it. And the proper way for us to look at it is in that way. There is no man here who has more regard for the dead men than I have [hear, hear]. I don't think it is fair to be quoting them against us. I think the decision ought to be a clear decision on the documents as they are before us – on the Treaty as it is before us. On that we shall be judged, as to whether we have done the right thing in our own conscience or not. Don't let us put the responsibility, the individual responsibility, upon anybody else. Let us take that responsibility ourselves and let us in God's name abide by the decision [applause].

The Treaty and 'shoneenism rampant'

MARY MACSWINEY (1921)

Mary MacSwiney, the older sister of the late Terence MacSwiney, was the Sinn Féin member of the first Dáil for Cork Borough. She had been considered by de Valera for membership of the Treaty negotiating team, but in the end her beliefs were judged too extreme. The following is from her three-hour contribution to the Dáil's Treaty debate. She reserved a particular disdain for those she considered 'shoneens', Irish people aping English ways.

Leaving official documents out of the question, let us come to the social side, the social structure we were told we would have power to build up. Some of you will realize what a hard and terrible fight it has been for our people to destroy the evils of shoneenism in this country. Here under this instrument you will have shoneenism rampant. All the worst elements of our country will gather around that Governor-General's residence. [. . .] We are not a race of archangels, and you allow that Governor-General's residence, with drawing-rooms, levees, and honours and invitations to be scattered broadcast to your wives and your sisters and your daughters, and mothers even, with all the baits that will be held out to them to come in for the first time by consent of the Irish people in the social atmosphere of the Governor-General's residence. Remember that there will be functions there which will be partly social and partly political, which will be Governmental functions. The Ministers of the Government of the Irish Free State – I will omit for the sake of argument the offensive words 'his Majesty's Ministers' – will be obliged to attend the Governor-General's functions and he will attend theirs. Wherever the Governor-General is, or the representative of the Crown in Ireland is, there you will have the Union Jack and 'God Save the King', and you will have the Union Jack and 'God Save the King' for the first time with the consent of the people of Ireland. You may say to me, some of you, that there will be, perhaps, a self-denying ordinance clause which will prevent the Ministers of the Irish Government, or any person belonging to the Irish Government, entering the portals of the Governor-General's house. You cannot. You will have to have him there as representative of the King with certain functions to perform. You cannot exclude him. [. . .] And remember what you are doing to the young girls growing up into this so-called Irish Free State. Many young girls of my own personal acquaintance, not very many, because very many of that type, I am sorry to say, have not been on our side; but some few, at all events, who had what we know as an *entrée* into vice-regal circles have been cut off from many social functions that their age entitled them to, that their position entitled them to, because they could not consistently with Republican principles go to a dance at the vice-regal lodge, or go to a dance in any place where the English military influence was uppermost. But in the Irish Free State these brave young girls who stood up against temptation can walk in unchecked. Under the Constitution of the Irish Free State you have no right to call any girl a shoneen because she walks into a dance at the vice-regal lodge. You men may sneer, some of you, at these points. Believe me they are no matters to sneer about. Those of you who are thinking men, and who are out to do the best for Ireland, know perfectly well what a hard fight we have had against that sort of thing. This you say will be sentiment, but for the first time in the history of this country you have Irish sentiment and Irish demoralisation and Irish Government all on the one side. Do you realise what that means? The papers have told us that a royal residence in the Irish Free State will be an admirable thing in Ireland; it will conduce to loyalty among the people of Ireland. It may and it may not, but if it does not it will not be the fault of the Irish Free State 'by law established', if it gets established, but it will be because we Republicans will keep up the very same plan of black flags and boycotts that we kept up until they place us where we are to-day, or rather not where we are to-day, but where we were on the 4th of December last. And, mind, when we put up black flags in the streets of Dublin, either for the Governor-General or the representative of the Crown or Viceroy, or whatever you like to call him, or the King himself, his Majesty's representative will send word to the Prime

Minister of the Irish Free State and make a complaint and get us arrested. And who is going to arrest us? I have already told Michael Collins that I will be the first rebel he will have to arrest. And mind, we Republicans are going to carry on this fight with the gloves off, if this thing is passed.

Hiring fairs

MAY BLAIR (1922)

In the following passage from her 2007 book *Hiring Fairs and Market Places*, May Blair draws upon oral reminiscences to paint a picture of the world of hiring fairs in rural Donegal and Tyrone in the early 1920s. Boys and girls paraded before the local farmers assembled to evaluate them; the lucky ones were hired on six-month contracts to engage in seasonal farm work.

Ellen was fifteen when she first left home in 1922. She had intended hiring in Letterkenny, but had mistaken the date and found herself travelling a further twenty miles to the Strabane fair, which was being held the following Monday. She knew that an Evelyn Logue who had a lodging house somewhere in the main street always welcomed boys and girls from her native Gweedore and it was to her that she made her way on arrival. Here in Ellen's own words is her story: 'I was with some other girls. We had left home anonst and we were anxious that we would hire for we didn't want to have to go back home. I hid my clothes in the hen house the night before, all ready for leavin' in the mornin'. My father was dead from we were weans [children] and I wanted to earn some money for my mother. We would all have liked to hire in the one place, but no, it was one here and one there. I had this notion that I would like to hire with a woman, and here didn't this widow-woman come up to me and says, "Are you for hirin'? I'm lookin' for a good girl to help me on the farm. I need somebody that can milk." She was a Mrs Kelly – Margaret Kelly. She had a farm near Clady and a pub in the town. Her daughters looked after the pub and her son managed the farm. She was very good to me – even better than my own mother.' [. . .]

Ellen McFadden, May Blair writes, had the good fortune to remain happily working at the Kellys' farm 'to the end of her days'; and when Margaret Kelly's son died, he stated in his will that he 'was leavin' the farm to his

*housekeeper that had been so good to him and his mother'. Blair acknowledges
that 'other servant girls weren't so lucky'.*

Sheila Gallagher travelled the same road at the same tender age. Her
parents had prepared her by sending her out to work locally at the
age of eight. She attended school in winter but come the month of
May off she went to earn a few shillings herding cattle. Oddly enough
she remembers those days with affection, especially the time spent
with the O'Donnells, who had no family and treated her like she was
their own.

However, all this was merely a preparation for the big hiring in
Strabane. Like Ellen, Sheila arrived the day before the fair and took
lodgings for the night. She was out early the next morning at the eye
of the market house along with hundreds of others – just like a herd
of cows. Those for hire always stood under the market house clock.
It was the biggest clock Sheila had ever seen. Before long a man
tapped her on the shoulder. 'Are you for hirin'?' he asked, staring
hard at her. 'I need a girl to milk the cows, wash spuds, clean the
house, help wi' the washin'.' Could Sheila do these things, he wanted
to know. Sheila replied that she had learnt to do all these things. He
offered her three pounds and she was hired. For a while she kept up
the pattern of working away from home in summer and going home
in winter but eventually hired full-time, returning to Strabane to re-
hire each May and November.

Farmer William Mehaffy hired his servant girls in Strabane.
William farmed around 90 acres in the townland of Carricklee, about
a mile and a half outside the town. He hired both men and girls, as
did his father before him and probably his grandfather before that.
Mostly hired men and women worked hard, were happy in their
work and lived as one of the family. William remembers those years:
'[. . .] Mostly I knew who I was getting but I did have to hire girls in
the hiring fair – had to make a bargain with them. I hired one girl one
time and nearly got two but she got away just in time. She used to let
the servant man in through her bedroom window when he came
home late at night and you can guess the rest. She married a neighbour man after that and had thirteen children. Sometimes you had to

clean the fleas off them but mostly they were clean and honest. The girls used to work with farmers for a year or two, then get married and get a job in Herdman's mill. That entitled them to get a mill house. They came from all over Donegal, mainly the Rosses, Bloody Foreland and the off-shore inlands. This part of the country is full of their descendants – thousands of them! Girls worked both inside and outside the house. You see long ago the water had to be carried from a well across the road. Then there were pigs and calves to feed, cows to milk by hand, hens to feed. The girls would have helped with those things. [. . .]

'The servant girl lived in. She maybe slept in a room with my sisters. When I was wee I slept with the hired help too. My brother and I slept in one bed and the hired man slept in another. The people we got were treated like ourselves – ate the same food at the same table. If they lived near, they got home on a Sunday and took their washing with them. There was no contracts; just word of mouth. We kept a wee book, a wages book, and they gradually lifted so much to keep them smoking. Sometimes at the end of six months a man would have nothing to get. One fellow we had was overdrawn and cleared off. He had done the same with the previous farmer only we didn't know that at the time. But most of them were honest.'

A country in limbo

C. H. ROBINSON (1922)

C. H. Robinson, the Resident Magistrate for Collon, near Drogheda
in Co. Louth, wrote to the Under Secretary in Dublin Castle on 1
March 1922. His letter is testimony to the political and legal vacuum
that followed the Treaty settlement, at a time when the British were
preparing to evacuate the Irish Free State and before the new administration had had an opportunity to embed itself.

The circumstances are as follows. Collon courthouse has been purchased by Messrs Rea, Timber Merchants of Antrim, who will be
engaged for another two and a half years in cutting down the timber
of the Oriel Temple Estate. Messrs Rea obtained possession of the
courthouse from the County Council, who held it as yearly tenants,
a few months ago. The firm are now erecting shafting in it for driving lathes for the manufacture of brush heads. I ordered these facts to
be reported by the Petty Sessions Clerk to the Registrar. The Registrar asked the clerk whether the Magistrates would consider the
acquirement of new premises and I directed the clerk to reply in the
terms quoted in your letter herewith attached.

The reasons for this reply are as follows. Collon Petty Sessions, in
common with all other petty sessions in my district, no longer exist
in practice. Republican Courts function everywhere and do all the
work, civil and criminal. There are no RIC to bring cases to my
courts and if any civil cases were brought, there is no body to exe-
cute our warrants or enforce our decrees. I did not therefore consider
that any useful purpose would be served by attempting to acquire a
courthouse for a court which cannot function and to arrange for the
rent thereof to be paid by a local authority which won't pay it. I
accordingly arranged with Mr Rea, senior partner of Messrs Rea, to
allow us to keep the books in a lock-up part of the courthouse and
to allow us to use the courthouse in the event of the impossible happening, namely a court being required there. I considered this

arrangement quite adequate in view of the existing condition of affairs.

There is no use in transferring the Collon business to Dunleer. There is neither a courthouse nor a court in Dunleer. The whole state of petty sessions administration is at present quite abnormal and artificial, and in this temporary chaos I think it is quite useless to attempt to deal with the situation as if it were normal. My petty sessions exist only on paper and will so continue until a stable government is set up competent to deal with the matter. Meanwhile, as matters cannot be changed, except on paper, I consider that matters should be left alone.

A farewell to the Civil War

FLORENCE O'DONOGHUE (1922)

Florence O'Donoghue was opposed to the Treaty, but, as his diary
from the earliest days of the Civil War records, he could see no purpose in taking armed action against the Irish Free State. He wrote this
letter of resignation to Liam Lynch, the Chief of Staff of the IRA.

Liam a chara, I feel it is due to you that I should send you a personal
note in explanation of my position, since I did not see you at Mallow
on the last occasion I was there. I do not know quite where I stand
now with regard to the post I held in the 1st Southern Division
because of the fact that I had worked as Adjutant General for some
time previous to my resignation from the Executive; but lest there
should be any misunderstanding about the matter I wish to clear it up
by tendering my resignation from the post of Adjutant. In the
present circumstances this of necessity involves also my resignation
from the Army.

My reasons are already known to you. I have the same fundamental objections to Civil War now that I had when I resigned from the
Executive rather than assent to an action, the logical result of which
would have been civil war. I have thought over the matter carefully
and at length, and to my mind there is nothing in the circumstances
of the origin of the present conflict which could justify me in taking
part in it. It is true that my sympathies are entirely with you but my
judgment convinces me that out of civil war will come not the
Republic, or unity, or freedom, or peace but a prolonged struggle in
which the best elements in the country will be annihilated or over-
borne with the result that the old shoneen–Unionist groups, who
care nothing for Ireland, will be returned to power again and that in
all probability the enemy will re-occupy the country.

In no circumstances could I be a party to a conflict which would
bring about such deplorable results, and it is only in the event of the
return of the English that I could take up arms again. Should that

happen, as I think it will, I'll be somewhere in the ranks. Meantime I have to find the means of living.

This decision of mine is the hardest that I have been forced to take since I joined the Army, not because it will leave me misunderstood and derided (though it will do that), but because I have to part with you all, and lay aside the work I had hoped to do for Ireland.

May I assure you and all the other Divisional officers, that I have no feelings other than of esteem and regard for each and all of you; and if at any time I could be of any use I hope you will call on me. As I cannot wish you success I will hope that your work will in its results help to bring us nearer to the ideal we have at heart.

P.S. Use your own discretion in showing this to other officers.

'A plague of minorities'

EDWARD MARTYN (1922)

Edward Martyn — dramatist and co-founder of the Irish Literary
Theatre and of the Irish Theatre — lived at Tulira Castle in south
Galway; his estate bordered Lady Gregory's Coole Park. The letter
extracted below was a reply to one from his friend John Sweetman,
which Martyn felt was 'like a breeze from the outer world to a
captive'.

I am practically imprisoned here, for although the railways are open
off and on, it is practically impossible to go to Dublin by road, so
many are the obstacles and uncertainties. I want very much to
return, but dare not risk the journey and being deprived of my
motor, as I very nearly was when coming down last Friday. Barring
all this they leave me here altogether in peace. They all say that they
do not wish to disturb me at all, although they are always prowling
about the place. I hope they may continue in this mind. I'm afraid
it's going to be a long business. We suffer [. . .] from a plague of
minorities. There is the Unionist minority, the Protestant minority,
the Ascendancy minority, the Carson minority and what not — all
wanting to impose their will on the *majority* of the Irish who are
fairly decent and reasonable: and now that they have made a treaty
with England and confirmed it by Parliament, lo and behold true to
the country's native instincts another minority leaps into national
life and seeks to impose its murderous tyranny on the majority. I
think this is probably the reason we have the reputation of not being
fit to govern ourselves. We have now certainly made as great a mess
of government as ever before. It's all along [because] of our mania
for minorities!

When I stopped to say farewell to you last Friday, I worried at the
effect I seemed to produce in your household. I seemed to throw all
into confusion. It never occurred to me until some time afterward —

that when I arrived at your house with motor and baggage unexpectedly, you must certainly have thought that I came to throw myself on your hospitality in my pitiable condition. You must have felt relieved when I departed.

'From the pulpit the Treaty is being rammed down our throats'

ELLIE RICE (1922)

Ellie Rice was the mother of J. J. Rice, Commandant of the IRA's 5th (Kenmare) Battalion, No. 2 Kerry Brigade. In this letter she complained to Bishop Charles O'Sullivan concerning 'the three priests whom you have placed over our spiritual welfare' at the Catholic Church in Kenmare.

Sunday after Sunday, Republicans have to sit there and listen to insulting remarks, cast at our men and boys whose only crime is being true to their oath of allegiance to the Republic. From the pulpit Sunday after Sunday the Treaty is being rammed down our throats. I say our because we seem to be the only family they are up against. I may add here I am mother of Commandant J. J. Rice and because he is leader of our men here, the clergy of Kenmare think it fit to snub and insult us into having to give up our religious duties. And a Fr Lynch [. . .] treated us from the altar steps to the political situation on Sunday, August 2nd, at the workhouse mass. I had to leave the chapel while his political oration was on because the IRA, when leaving the town to the Free Staters the night before, set fire to the barracks, [he] called them 'misguided youths, uneducated boys, led by leaders who were infinitely worse' and all the rest. I could not sit there and listen to insults flung at my son who is the 'Leader' and who can stand a better test of character than Fr Lynch in the town of Kenmare. My son has arrived at the age of 28 years and up to this day he has never put a glass to his mouth nor, as Fr Brennan remarked to me, has he put a cigarette between his teeth. Not so for the Revd Fr Lynch; he can go into the ordinary public house in Kenmare and take his glass of whiskey standing at the counter. Yes – and be able to tell the bar-maid the difference between the 'brands' better than she could; and to think that I should be expected to sit and listen to a man like that abuse my son or any of the IRA. If it were any of our

own priests spoke as he did, it would not have hurt me so much for I
have got quite accustomed to hear them call our boys down.

My Lord, I'm sorry to have to write thus but I'm so worked up by
the clergy of Kenmare. It was bad enough last year when the Archdeacon Marshall sided with the English enemy against us; but now
we have himself and his two curates side with one part of his congregation against the other, it showed the side he is up against
(Republicans) do not belong to his flock at all. Well we are taking
him at that and until you take up the matter we will stay outside the
Church; and if the welfare of our souls are in your keeping I trust
you will instruct the Archdeacon to pay the same respect to his
Republican flock as he is to his 'Free State' flock.

The Civil War in Connemara

REVEREND WILLIAM KELLY (1922)

This letter from a priest in Clifden, Co. Galway, to a senior cleric in Maynooth captures a dramatic sequence of fighting, and conveys the danger faced by priests attending to the wounded on both sides.

As there is a possibility that letters may go out tomorrow – a fortnight's mail to the tune of 85 bags having come in last night, I took the notion of writing to you – how Clifden was captured by the IRA with the Mallaranny Hotel boiler for an armoured car, how the victors and vanquished fraternised, shook hands and developed into a mutual admiration society after the shock of the battle was over, how Mrs Moran with her good man and eight hopefuls spent ten hours in the coal shed, and like the Miller when the mill stopped, cannot sleep now for want of the sweet rifle music; how the 5 prisoners escaped – as everyone knew they would – in real comic-opera style; how the officers of the Marconi Station garrison signed the surrender and with characteristic fidelity scooted off before the IRA came to disarm them; how there was scarcely a nerve or a pane of glass left in the town after the terrific bombardment, how Fr McHugh [Aughagower] produced his best malt and most excellent mutton for the IRA (when on their way here) thinking them to be some of the People's Army, and so on ad infinitum.

Well seriously it was a fierce fight and no opera bouffe work either. The mine explosion rattled the delf and startled the cocks over at Slyne Head. The morning was beautifully calm and I slept till ten minutes past eight without any forebodings of trouble. The car man was the first to acquaint me of the news and as we neared Ballinaboy and faced for the school on the hill-top, the fact that operations were afoot was pretty obvious. Small Congregation. A mine explosion rocks the chalice on the altar. The IRA are in position around the place, firing ceases till Mass is finished, the people dispersed, and the priest safely crouched behind a stone wall on the roadside. The troops from the Marconi Station under cover of the returning Mass-goers have made their way down near their opponents and now the duel begins. I smoke a cigarette to soothe the nerves but don't get time to finish it. A yell of pain from the Free State position, then a cry of agony. I hoist a dirty handkerchief and repair to the spot. He is lying in the swamp, weltering in blood, his rifle beside him, death in his face. His four companions, rather stupefied-looking, are obviously relieved by my advent. He is in shocking agony, fully conscious, can take Holy Communion, and talks Irish. I have finished – and now what to do with him? He cannot be left alone to die in the marsh; he is too heavy for me even to turn. 'We cannot do anything, Father. If the Irregulars see our uniforms they will snipe us all. There's a house 40 yards away.' I look for assistance. Yes, they will go with the priest – the old man too.

We bring a sort of bed with us, lift in the wounded man, plaster ourselves all over with blood, and stagger and plough our way through the bog, knee deep in water. 'Won't you come back and hear our confessions, Father' is shouted after me. We put him before the fire: the woman of the house does all that can be done but his heart's blood is pumping out. The pity of it. Back I go to the others, and lying flat on our bellies, I shrive them one by one. My heart goes out to them and I bid them goodbye, and hie to Ballyconneely. I begin 11 o'clock Mass at 12.15, thinking strange and sad thoughts.

I hasten to the scene of battle after Mass. 'For God's sake hurry, Father: there are two dead Republicans on the hill up near the school. They [the Free Staters] shot them with their hands up, Father. I saw the whole thing.' I ran till the froth was thick on my lips, and the pounding of my heart vieing with the rifle cracks. Ah, here is one of them, warm but just dead, his mouth open, the eyeballs staring wildly, a pierced bicycle-pump in his breast pocket, brain-matter bedaubing the wild heather, his head half-buried in a clump of furze – his companion [both from the same village near Ballina] is alive. A dozen people are around him. After six hours of heavy firing they appear to have got quite accustomed to the sensation, and heed not the splutter, bang, ping and crack that goes merrily on a quarter of a mile away, not to speak of the terrific bombardment in the town.

They have beads, holy water, Sacred Heart pictures, etc., some of them chanting the prayers for the dying, all of them ardent Free Staters. One of them wonders has her son been blown to bits in the Clifden barracks.

Such a handsome boy, so young, and boyish, so clean of limb, so proudly resigned – just 20, his long black unruly hair tossing about on his pale brow. He knows there's no hope for him. He is lead all over, two fingers blown away, a bullet in the forearm, one in the shoulder, one in the thigh, one through the small of the back. Yes, he thanks God for having got the rites of the Church.

How is Tom [the dead companion]? Did I get [to] him in time? Yes, they missed the main body and lost their way on the hill. Seven Free Staters came on them – the people crowd around him. 'They shot me lying down, yes, they did. I am going before my God soon but I want you all to know that they did that, and one of them used horse-language to me. But I forgive them, I forgive them.' They bear him to a house nearby. Everybody is kind to him: somehow they can't help it. He is in agonies, but offers all his sufferings for the souls in Purgatory, thanks God for the Sacraments, repeatedly calls the Holy Name, never murmurs or complains, but is so sorry that poor Tom hadn't the priest in time. So he lingered for 24 hours.

And now a man appears on the road – two civilians wounded out near the town – calling for a priest. Death to attempt going into Clifden – won't I come. Yes, through very shame at what he risked to acquaint me. We get in without mishap, although the rifles are busy all around. There's a fierce explosion, a cloud of thick, murky smoke, a shout, a cheer, one last wild crescendo of rifle and machine-gun fire, and all is over . . . The hill barrack is still standing, but though consumed with curiosity I must repair to Ballyconneely for the Novena. Devotions at 5.30 and it's now 5 o'clock. Late at night a messenger reaches me to say that no one was killed in the town. The news is incredible, though the best I've heard for a long time. I expected anything up to 50 casualties, and yet the only deaths – 3 – were all in Ballinaboy.

I went there the next day. A boat was ready. The Free State troops, all a bit shaken, got on board, with their 4 wounded and 1 dead. A feeble cheer from their dazed townspeople and they are off – 110 strong, 7 having run away from the Marconi Station. I don't know if you'll wade through this long-winded, egotistical narrative, but you will understand that as life is very uneventful down here, it looms large as an experience.

Last letter of a condemned man

ERSKINE CHILDERS (1922)

Erskine Childers was a veteran of the Boer War, author of the best-selling *Riddle of the Sands*, and a convinced separatist. By October 1922, finding his role as an anti-Treaty propagandist ineffective, he set out from Cork by bicycle and on foot to reach his boyhood home at Glendalough House in Co. Wicklow. He had determined to work on his political papers and publish his account of the Treaty negotiations. He was arrested by Free State troops in a raid on the house on 10 November and accused of bearing arms against the state, by then a capital offence. His only weapon was a personal revolver – a gift from Michael Collins in earlier days. He was court-martialled and sentenced to be shot. The following is from the last of his many letters to his wife, Molly.

Beloved wife, I have been told that I am to be shot tomorrow at 7. I am fully prepared. I think it is best so – viewing it from the biggest standpoint, and perhaps you will agree. To have followed those other brave lads is a quiet thing for a great cause. I have a belief in the beneficent shaping of our destiny, yours and mine, and I believe God means this for the best; for us, Ireland and humanity. So in the midst of anguish at leaving you, and in mortal solicitude for you, beloved of my heart, I triumph and I know you triumph with me. It is such a simple thing too, a soldier's death, what millions risk and incur, what so many in our cause face and suffer daily. There is this too; that living I was weighted with a load of prejudice, unjust, but so heavy that it may be that I have been harming our cause. Dead, I shall have a better chance of being understood and of helping the cause. I am, as I sit here, the happiest of men. I have had 19 years of happiness with you. No man ever could claim so great and precious a blessing as that. But for you I should have foundered; and died younger possibly, possibly older, but an unhappy man, a dwarfed soul, not understanding love, the secret of all, and not grasping life like a man.

You redeemed me. I understand dimly the cult of the Blessed Mother, through you with your divine intercession leading me to God, for through you I reach him. [. . .] You have never failed me. In these last years you followed me nobly and loyally into the hard rugged path which has brought me to this cell and death. [. . .]

Oh will this nation soon understand and pay reverence to what actuates our comrades in the cause and ourselves? I feel it will. If only I can die knowing that my death would somehow – I know not how – save the lives of others and arrest this policy of executions. And the blessed, darling, boys. I thank God I saw them again. (Bobby, enforced self-command until quite the end – never pathetic and wonderful to see.) They will be strong loving comrades and helpful to you, drawing from your own indomitable nerve, spirit and giving it back in their own measure. Erskine, I think, under the circumstances, should in these years concentrate on his studies and on you. You will understand what I mean. But in this and in all else, I mean to give no direction – you know that – my trust in you is absolute, oh so absolute – are not you, besides your divine self, my own best self? [. . .]

I hope one day my good name will be cleared in England. I felt what Churchill said about my 'hatred' and 'malice' against England. How well we know it is not true. What line I ever spoke or wrote justifies the charge? I die loving England and passionately praying that she may change completely and finally towards Ireland.

November 22. In case I should forget, I wish to say that my treatment while under sentence here has been very considerate and courteous – Commandant, Officers and men of the guard, and all. Nothing to complain of: on the contrary. Within the range of things allowed, food, writing material, papers and so forth, I have been given whatever I asked for. It has made a vast difference. Everything that bridges this ghastly gulf between the armies is to the good, and I hope to God nothing has been conceded to me which is not to others.

November 23, 7 p.m. Yet another day, and the last. [. . .] I have just been told it is to be tomorrow at 7. Asked to see you. Told 'not at present' – a hard answer [. . .] In case proceedings at my trial are never known, I want to say that I asked all the witnesses questions to show that a shooting fight – in the passage outside my door, when taken, would have endangered two women there, and that is why I did not use my pistol and only tried to force my way through. They admitted it was a fact. Normally of course I should have put up a fight. The pistol was in my hand. [. . .]

My beloved country, God send you courage, victory and rest and to all our people harmony and love. Whatever we may think of the course taken toward men in my position by their captors let us unswervingly follow our own righteous ideal and keep the Republic stainless.

The final words scribbled on the morning of his execution read:

You must be pleased to see how imperturbably normal and tranquil I have been this night and a.m. It all seems perfectly simple and inevitable like lying down after a long day's work. Thus our precious *equanimitas* and I draw it all from you. For me it is easy *now*, for you the hard road. But you will tread it like the gallant soul you are with the dear boys beside you. And now I am going. Coming to you, heart's beloved, sweetheart, comrade, wife. I shall fall asleep in your arms, God above blessing us – all four of us. Erskine.

The burning of Graiguenoe Park

ANNE GOOD (1923)

Anne Good, a member of the domestic staff at Graiguenoe Park, Holycross, Co. Tipperary, sent her employer, Mrs Charles Clarke, an account of the burning of the house by anti-Treaty forces in March 1923. Mrs Clarke's nephew, Hubert Butler, later quoted this letter in his essay 'Divided Loyalties'. Butler suggests that some twenty big houses were burned out in Tipperary alone. Such arson was not always unpopular locally, as the abandonment of the big estates was seen as creating opportunities for 'landless men'.

Madam, you know the bad news how Graiguenoe is burned down. Oh it was terrible to see it blazing away! Just at 5 past 12 on Wednesday night the bell was rung. I was only just in bed, so I jumped up and called the girls and went to Nolan; but he was up. They never stopped ringing till Nolan and I went to the hall-door; and there were two men with revolvers and demanded to know why we did not open before and come out; so I said, 'Surely you will give us time to get our things.' He said: Yes, if we were not too long. He wanted to know how many there were in the house. I said, 'Three girls more.' He wanted to know who were all those inside there.

I said, 'That is yourself in the mirror.' He thought (when he saw our reflections in the glass) that a lot of people were there. So we all got our things put together as quick as we could, but all of us had to leave a lot of things as they kept asking, 'Are ye ready, as we are in a hurry,' so we got out. Nolan saved three pictures out of the dining room and your dressing case and a small case under the bed and Mr Clarke's dressing bag, but they did not want him to take anything, only his own things.

He also saved the harness; he worked like a nigger but he could do nothing more. He also tried to save the harness room by throwing buckets of water on the inside and the roof; but no use. The fire got too firm a hold on everything before those demons left. They had petrol, straw and hay so they made a good job of it. The only place not burned out is the scullery and Mrs Curtin's room. We were in the coach house watching it blazing. The flames were very high but the wind was in our favour, or the outhouses would also be in flames. The laundry basket (Dublin) was in the passage and the man asked us was it ours and I said, 'Yes,' so he let us take it; also there is a basket at Thurles laundry, which I expect will come back on Monday. Will the things be sent to you? They could be packed in a box. Also we managed to grab some coats off the rack in the dark. They turned out to be your grey coat and the brown. Will I send them on also? There were about seven or eight men through the house but they told us not to stir from where we were for at least half an hour as the house was surrounded and we may be shot. They left before 1 o'clock so you see we got no time. We stayed all night. It was heartbreaking to see the house burning where we were living so long. But we were thankful Mr Clarke was not there for the story was bad enough and he may be shot. They asked several times where was the Boss. We all came up to Mrs Hilton's at 7 o'clock in the morning. Bridget has gone home, also Maggie and Josie. I am staying here with Mrs Hilton for the present. I will never forget the sight and experiences of Wednesday night. I feel sorry for you and Mr Clarke, but I'm thinking there will be no gentlemen's places soon. Hoping you and Mr Clarke are well, I am, Madam, yours respectfully, A. Good. I can't find a pen so please excuse pencil.

Lady Gregory meets Sean O'Casey

AUGUSTA GREGORY (1923)

Lady Gregory's account of the first night of Sean O'Casey's first play, *The Shadow of a Gunman*, reveals much about O'Casey's relationship to the Abbey and about his own early life; and it depicts Dublin at the conclusion of the Civil War.

12 April 1923. At the Abbey I found an armed guard; there has been one ever since the theatres were threatened if they kept open. And in the green room I found one of them giving finishing touches to the costume of Tony Quinn, who is a Black and Tan in the play, and showing him how to hold his revolver. *The Shadow of a Gunman* was an immense success, beautifully acted, all the political points taken up with delight by a big audience. Sean O'Casey the author only saw it from the side wings the first night but had to appear to make his bow. I brought him into the stalls the other two nights and have had some talk with him. Last night there was an immense audience, the largest I think since the first night of [Shaw's] *Blanco Posnet*. Many, to my grief, had to be turned away from the door. Two seats had been kept for Yeats and me, but I put Casey [i.e. O'Casey] in one of them and sat in the orchestra for the first act, and put Yeats in the orchestra for the second. I had brought Casey round to the door before the play to share my joy in seeing the crowd surging in (Dermod O'Brien caught in the queue) and he introduced me to two officers, one a Colonel. (Yeats has wanted me to go with them to a *ball* given by the army, 'good names being wanted'!)

Casey told me he is a labourer, and as we talked of masons said he had 'carried the hod'. He said, 'I was among books as a child, but I was sixteen before I learned to read or write. My father loved books, he had a big library, I remember the look of the books high up on shelves.' I asked why his father had not taught him and he said, 'He died when I was three years old, through those same books. There was a little ladder in the room to get to the shelves, and one day when he was standing on it, it broke and he fell and was killed. I said, 'I often go up the ladder in our library at home' and he begged me to be careful. He is learning what he can about Art, has bought books on Whistler and Raphael, and takes *The Studio*. All this was as we watched the crowd. I forget how I came to mention the Bible, and he asked, 'Do you like it?' I said, 'Yes, I read it constantly, even for the beauty of the language.' He said he admires that beauty, he was brought up as a Protestant but has lost belief in religious forms. Then, in talking of our war here, we came to Plato's *Republic*, his dream-city, whether on earth or in heaven not far away from the city of God. And then we went in to the play. He says he sent us a play four years ago, *Frost and Flowers*, and it was returned, but marked 'Not far from being a good play'. He has sent others, and says how grateful he was to me because when we had to refuse the Labour one, *The Crimson in the Tri-Colour*, I had said, 'I believe there is something in you' and 'your strong point is characterisation'. And I had wanted to pull that play together and put it on to give him experience, but Yeats was down on it. Perrin [the theatre's secretary, J. H. Perrin] says he has offered him a pass sometimes when he happened to come in, but he refused and said, 'No one ought to come into the Abbey Theatre without paying for it.' He said, 'All the thought in Ireland for years past has come through the Abbey. You have no idea what an education it has been to the country.' That, and the fine audience on this our last week, put me in great spirits.

A father and son differ over the Civil War

JOHN SWEETMAN (1923)

A wealthy Catholic farmer in Meath who also had a townhouse in Merrion Square, John Sweetman was a public intellectual and indefatigable letter-writer to Irish newspapers. The range of his political sympathies stretched from the Irish Parliamentary Party, to Arthur Griffith's early Sinn Féin, to the Gaelic League. He supported the Treaty and appealed to his eldest son, John, not to take up arms against the Irish Free State. When the Pope's envoy, Monsignor Salvatore Luzio, came to Ireland to attempt to mediate in the Civil War, Sweetman wrote him a letter.

Having good reason to suspect that a son of mine was joining the irregulars (or, as I call them, bandits), I wrote to him on August 20th 1922 as follows: – 'I do not know what you are doing, but I fear you are trying to destroy your country, your parents, and the rest of your family. If your father's wish has any effect on you, as your father, I forbid you to take any part against our present Irish Government, but I know my orders can have no effect on you, when you will not obey the Church, which Our Lord established to teach us. As far as I am personally concerned, I can only say "God's will be done." Why God has left me on earth for more than seventy-eight years, I know not.'

Many mad priests have satisfied these foolish youths that they are sacrificing themselves for the good of Ireland, and that they are taking part in a legitimate war, and that de Valera and his council may be considered the Government of Ireland; and further that it is a falsehood to say that these youths are simply trying to destroy all civilized government.

It is very unfortunate that these foolish youths will now be saying (although, no doubt, they should not) that the Irish bishops were evidently wrong when they condemned our robberies, assassinations and the destruction of bridges, railways and houses, as the Pope has sent over an envoy to plead for us, now that the Irish nation is proving too strong for us.

As to my son, his mother persuaded him to give up his doings, and to go to America last November. On December 8th he wrote to me from New York: 'I can get lots of work here in America but I take no interest in it. If I stay here I will end up jumping off a sky-scraper or going to the devil. I have no interest in America or indeed in myself now that I am here. You do not know me or you would not expect me to stay in this materialistic country. Why I'd go mad. I would give much worldly goods to please you but I can't give up my principles. I hope you will understand me and not worry any more about me.'

He came back to Ireland but I do not know whether he be alive or dead.

On the language fanatics

JOHN DILLON AND MYLES DILLON (1924)

The Bishop of Clonfert, John Dignan, stated in June 1924 that Ireland should be protected from 'the wave of paganism and materialism and sin that now swept the world by erecting around their coasts the barrier of the language'. From Heidelberg, where he was a student, Myles Dillon wrote to his father, John Dillon.

The bishop is rather a thrill. Not the least remarkable of his precepts was that we should use the Irish language as a barrier against the wicked knowledge of the world which might reach our island from outside. What sort of an opinion have such reverend men got of the intelligence of the Irish?

John Dillon to Myles Dillon, 16 June 1924:

I am pleased you took notice of the obscurantist declamation of the Bishop of Clonfert. It is the expression of a spirit which has been, and still is, very rampant in Ireland, and threatens to do enormous mischief. [. . .] All this bullying and compulsion will end badly for the Irish language.

On 24 July, Myles Dillon wrote to his father about the standard of lectures in Heidelberg. He found himself 'delighted and despairing' at the end of term, listening to a philosopher who spoke so widely of a number of writers, philosophers and others, but 'if he had asked me more than the names of any one of them I should have been silent.'

I cannot help blaming the organisation of the Church in Ireland for part of our ignorance, and it is a horrible fact if it is true. The divines are pleased if the people obey the commandments, whether they know why they are obeying them or not, and yet anyone would admit that it is better to do good because it is good than because you will be read from the altar or go to hell if you don't. It is the same fanaticism for the letter instead of the spirit which makes people insist on Irish words without regard to Irish mentality as if it really much mattered whether we spoke Irish or Tungusish so long as we possessed our own tradition. I hope this does not seem irreverent, which would be the reverse of what I mean, but I think it is fair.

On 2 December 1924 John Dillon replied to another letter from Myles, writing with approval of his son's return to Germany.

I can quite understand your sensation on leaving Dublin and getting back amongst the learned. Poor Dublin! I greatly fear it will be a considerable time before we can set her feet on the path to a really intellectual and artistic life. Things here, political, educational, etc., etc., are very bad and going from bad to worse. [. . .] There can be no doubt that a very formidable reaction is being stirred up by this system of trying to force Irish down the throats of all the people. I suppose you have seen Sean O'Casey in last Saturday's *Irish Statesman*. It is poor stuff for him. Nevertheless I have no doubt that it speaks the mind of a large section of the Dublin working people. What I fear is that, just as the SF campaign has killed all enthusiasm in public life and politics, so the rabid Irish language enthusiasts will kill enthusiasm for the language, and provoke a bitter and cynical reaction.

Drunkenness: The curse of Ireland

'AN IRISH CORRESPONDENT' (1925)

This article, from the *Spectator*, discusses a problem that was common north and south of the border.

In setting about the reform of the liquor laws, the Governments of Northern and Southern Ireland have laid the axe to the root of Irish ills. Drunkenness is an evil of long standing in Ireland. In the reckless eighteenth century the gentry drank claret – far too much of it – and the peasants and artisans formed the taste for spirits which is still our country's curse. In England there has grown up a public horror of intoxication which preserves the average man from excess; but in Ireland public opinion so far lags behind that of other lands that men are not shamed by being seen abroad 'under the influence'. The chief evil effect of Irish intemperance is seen in the general lack of character in the classes which should be the backbone of the nation.

Idleness, boastfulness and futility are bred in young men. The moral fibre of the race is enfeebled. The land is full of ineffective men who owe the failure of their young promise to alcohol. During the last few years, with the lowering of moral standards and the increase of temptation, orgies of drunkenness have disgraced the race, and have issued in epidemics of crime. The horrors of the conflict during 1922 and 1923 were made possible, if not caused, by drink, and they do not bear contemplation.

In the North courageous legislation has been passed at the cost of popularity. Drinking facilities have been greatly curtailed. The petty publican by the docks or the shipyards complains that he is no longer allowed to sell drink in the early morning; but the workers no longer begin their work with whiskey. In the small towns and villages the owner of licensed premises complains that he has been compelled to spend money on building a partition between the 'bar' and that part of his shop devoted to the sale of groceries and to other business. He says that men who call in for a drink go away again without his being able to introduce clasp-knives or what not to their attention. His real grievance, however, is that women calling to buy household goods are no longer tempted to drink whiskey.

Every Sunday is a 'dry' day in the North. During the past two summers this fact has led to unedifying spectacles on the border. Every Sunday excursion trains from Belfast to the pretty seaside resort, Warrenpoint, on Carlingford Lough, have been loaded with thirsty folk who alight only to swarm across the Lough in motor-boats and to crowd into the public houses of 'the wet State' as bona fide travellers. This humiliating spectacle – a sort of mass indulgence – will not be repeated for long, for the liquor laws of North and South are on the way to uniformity.

The champion of reform in the South is Mr Kevin O'Higgins, Minister of Justice. He has carried through the Oireachtas measures, less drastic indeed than those of the North, yet substantial. He has made public holidays 'dry' days. No more will St Patrick's Day be celebrated with drunkenness, nor Good Friday disgraced by tipsy rowdies in the streets. Mr O'Higgins was defeated by the free vote of the Dáil in one of his most desirable proposals: he was unable to carry a provision for the 'structural division' of shops in which other commodities are sold beside drink. Publicans in the miserable villages persuaded deputies to stand up and plead piteously the case of drink purveyors who would be compelled to spend ten pounds on a wooden partition. Only by yielding on this point was Mr O'Higgins able to carry the rest of his Bill. [. . .]

The drink traffic has, indeed, been assisted by the dullness of Irish rural life. During the past century, the 'kill-joy' has wrought havoc on the people's morale. In the old days, the young folk met at the cross-roads for hearty, innocent, traditional dances, and they were safe enough there in the public eye. The discouragement of these dances drove lads to dangerous haunts. The present writer saw these things done in a typical country parish in a single winter: (1) Evening classes suppressed to check the walking home of boys and girls arm-in-arm. (2) Dances in country houses forbidden on pain of refusal of the Sacraments. (3) The parish hall, formerly let to societies, travelling players and cinematographic shows, shut against all and sundry.

During the recent period of lost restraint and of flowing drink there has been a wave of loose conduct quite astonishing to idealists. The Bishops have been obliged to issue pastorals against bucolic imitations, in remote mountainy parishes, of the most hectic modern dancing and dressing. The making of poteen has been declared a 'reserved sin' – but in vain, for the stuff is sold by publicans of the highest respectability. Old sanctions have proved unable to maintain old standards. [. . .] It will be a happy day for Ireland when the old, political moulds are broken, and free, frank intercourse takes the place of suspicion. Decent social relations must be the basis of temperate life and self-respect. To these things, however, Ireland under the new order is groping her way. Irishmen should record their gratitude to Sir Dawson Bates in the North, and to Mr Kevin O'Higgins in the South. It needs rare fortitude in an elected representative to attack a people's beloved sin.

The reception of The Plough and the Stars

JOSEPH HOLLOWAY (1926)

Joseph Holloway, an architect who was reputed to have attended every play staged in Dublin for fifty years, left 200 volumes of diaries and cuttings to the National Library of Ireland. These are as much concerned with registering the verdicts of other theatre-goers as they are with his own opinions, which tend to be prudish and conservative. Despite his distaste for the grittier elements of Sean O'Casey's *The Plough and the Stars*, he attended not only the dress rehearsal and the opening night, but every performance in the first week of the play's run, leaving a valuable real-time record of the public's response.

Monday, February 8. There was electricity in the air before and behind the curtain at the Abbey to-night when Sean O'Casey's play *The Plough and the Stars* was first produced. The theatre was thronged with distinguished people, and before the doors opened the queue to the pit entrance extended past old Abbey Street – not a quarter of them got in. The play was followed with feverish interest, and the players being called and recalled at the end of the piece. Loud calls for 'Author!' brought O'Casey on the stage, and he received an ovation. Monty [James Montgomery, the film censor] said after Act II, 'I am glad I am off duty.' Some of the incidents in Acts I and II had proved too much for the Censor in him. Mr Reddin after Act III said, 'The play leaves a bad taste in the mouth.' [. . .]

The first-night audience stamped the play with their approval in no uncertain way. [. . .] The street outside the theatre was packed on either side with motor cars. In Abbey Street a policeman was stalking after four 'Rosie Redmonds' [prostitutes] who flew before him, and I am sure the dispersing audience found no interest in their flight, although they had applauded 'Rosie' plying her trade in *The Plough and the Stars*. The fight between the two women in the pub scene was longly applauded, yet who is not disgusted with such an exhibition when one chances on it in real life?

Tuesday, February 9. The Abbey was again thronged. [. . .] Some four or five in the pit objected to the Volunteers bringing the flag into a pub. Kevin Barry's sister was one of the objectors. The pit door had to be shut to avoid a rush being made on it, and two policemen were on the scene. The audience relished the fight of the women [. . .] and didn't object to the nasty incidents and phrases scattered here and there throughout the play. [. . .] Lord Chief Justice Kennedy frankly declared he thought it abominable. Kevin O'Higgins was silent until Monty thanked God he was off duty, and added, 'This is a lovely Irish export.' Then O'Higgins owned up he didn't like it. Meeting Dr Oliver Gogarty, Monty said, 'I hope you are not going to say you liked it?' 'I do,' owned up Gogarty (whose reputation for filthy limericks is very widespread). 'It will give the smug-minded something to think about.'

Wednesday, February 10. A sort of moaning sound was to be heard to-night from the pit during the 'Rosie Redmond' episode and when the Volunteers brought in the flags to the pub.

Thursday, February 11. The protest of Tuesday night having no effect on the management, a great protest was made to-night, and ended in almost the second act being played in dumb show, and pantomiming afterwards. People spoke from all parts of the house, and W. B. Yeats moved out from the stalls during the noise, and Kathleen O'Brennan, who came in afterwards, told me Yeats went round to *The Irish Times* office to try to have the report of the row doctored. On his return to the theatre, he tried to get a hearing on the stage, but not a word he spoke could be heard. [. . .] I am sorry to say that I was incorrect in my judgment as to what Abbey audiences could stand when I told George O'Brien on Monday that they would stand even the devils in Hell exhibiting their worst pranks in silence sooner than make another objectionable play like *The Playboy* burst into notoriety by their disapproval. But, alas, to-night's protest has made a second *Playboy* of *The Plough and the Stars*, and Yeats was in his element at last. [. . .] After Act I was the first I heard that a storm was brewing from Dan Breen, who was speaking to Kavanagh and said, 'Mrs Pearse, Mrs Tom Clarke, Mrs Sheehy Skeffington, and others were in the theatre to vindicate the manhood of 1916.' [. . .]

Few really like the play as it stands, and most who saw it are in sympathy with those who protested. Some of the players behaved with uncommon roughness to some ladies who got on the stage, and threw two of them into the stalls. One young man thrown from the stage got his side hurt by the piano. The chairs of the orchestra were thrown on the stage, and the music on the piano fluttered, and some four or five tried to pull down half of the drop curtain, and another caught hold of one side of the railing in the scene in Act III.

The players headed by McCormick as spokesman lined up onstage, and Mac tried to make himself heard without avail. Then a man came on and begged the audience to give the actor a hearing, and they did, and Mac said he wished the actors should be treated distinct from the play, etc., and his speech met with applause. Then the play proceeded in fits and starts to the end, and the whole house in a state of excitement. Mrs Fay protested to me that the play didn't get a hearing. Mrs Sheehy Skeffington from the back of the balcony during the din kept holding forth, and at the same time others were speaking in the pit; all were connected with Easter Week. A great big voice called, 'O'Casey out!' on 'Rosie Redmond' appearing. [. . .]

Friday, February 12. A detective-lined theatre presented itself at the beginning of the play to-night at the Abbey, and there was no disturbance up to the end of Act II when I left for home. [. . .] I saw O'Casey, Brinsley MacNamara, Liam O'Flaherty [. . .] and others of the dirt cult in a group in the vestibule. Mr and Mrs Yeats and Lady Gregory sat at the end of the first row of the stalls. [. . .] None was allowed to stand in the passages to make way for the 'G' men [Special Branch policemen], a body of men of evil fame in Ireland. AE was in the audience.

Sunday, February 14. On my way to the Abbey I called over to parley, had a chat with them re Thursday night. [. . .] The Darleys were pleased at the protest. They saw Sean Barlow handle roughly and throw a woman off the stage into the stalls. Fitzgerald had a stand-up fight with a man on the stage and succeeded in knocking him over into the stalls. O'Casey was surrounded by a crowd of questioning women, and his answer to one of them was, 'I want to make money!' – sums up his attitude toward art.

Holloway also quoted in his diary Hanna Sheehy Skeffington's 'dignified letter' on the protest, which appeared on 15 February in the Irish Independent:

The incident will, no doubt, help to fill houses in London with audiences that come to mock at those 'foolish dead', 'whose names will be remembered forever'. The only censorship that is justified is the free censorship of public opinion. The Ireland that remembers with tear-dimmed eyes all that Easter Week stands for, will not, and cannot, be silent in face of such a challenge.

And Holloway quoted O'Casey's reply in the Irish Times *of 19 February:*

The heavy-hearted expression by Mrs Sheehy Skeffington about 'the Ireland that remembers with tear-dimmed eyes all that Easter Week stands for' makes me sick. Some of the men cannot get even a job. Mrs Skeffington is certainly not dumb, but she appears to be both blind and deaf to all the things that are happening around her. Is the Ireland that is pouring to the picture-houses, to the dance halls, to the football matches, remembering with tear-dimmed eyes all that Easter Week stands for? Tears may be in the eyes of the navvies working on the Shannon scheme, but they are not for Ireland. When Mrs Skeffington roars herself into the position of a dramatic critic, we cannot take her seriously: she is singing here on a high note wildly beyond the range of her political voice, and can be given only the charity of our silence.

Our neglected heritage

C. P. CURRAN (1926)

C. P. Curran was an expert on the plasterwork of Georgian Dublin. In an article for *Studies* about the fledgling Irish tourism industry, he began by making large claims for the uniqueness of Ireland's 'complex of natural beauty, art and history' before discussing the neglect of that inheritance.

Consider Dublin. Its streets were nobly planned and its architecture distinguished, preserving even in decay something of dignity and reserve. But with the social disintegration of the nineteenth century, big business and shop-keepers got their untrammelled way, and a pretentious, tatterdemalion disorder set in. They thought bad manners meant good business, and entered upon ostentatious rivalry which forbade neighbourly building and broke up the harmony of the street. There followed the blatant publicity of outrageous façade advertisement, street hoardings, sky signs and posters – an orgy of waste which defeats its object; for the exhausted citizen, every sense insulted, shuts his eyes and endeavours to ignore all. When everybody yells nothing is heard. Business gains nothing, but the city loses charm and magnetic power when buildings like the Rotunda are defaced by the peculiar horrors of cinema advertising and College Green degraded by the unsightliness above Cook's agency.

Going out from the centre of the city to the suburbs, we again encounter unnecessary ugliness and waste. The canals, the Dodder and the Tolka are all potential river banks. Berlin makes a thing of beauty out of a river which is naturally little more than a drain. We present a spectacle of river and canal banks neglected or fallen in, seats broken up and trees cut down where agreeable malls might exist for the recreation of citizens. Further out, where wealth might be realized we find impoverishment. Dublin is eminently fortunate in its proximity to the mountains and the sea. In any well-ordered community Glen Dhu and Howth would be natural reservations, their beauty jealously guarded. Instead the woods are ruthlessly cut down from Killakee to Kilmashogue, and Howth is disfigured with houses that would intimidate a Viking.

I dwell upon Dublin not merely because it is the chief tourist resort in Ireland, but because the evils which afflict it are shared by every tourist resort in Ireland. Is there a town or village which, to take one instance, makes the most of its river? I know none if it is not Inistioge, where overhanging woods fall down upon the old Priory and the little lime-planted village square fronting the Nore bridged with its bridge of ten arches. Not Drogheda, most depressing of Irish towns for all its wealth of historical building; nor Navan, which turns its back upon one of the pleasantest river-stretches in Ireland; nor Galway, which hides its river; nor Limerick, though the expanse of waters which mirror the old houses of Arthur's Quay and the great walls of John's Castle and the old Cathedral is memorable; nor even Cork, with the Mardyke. Why, there is not even a service of motor boats on the Blackwater, Barrow or Boyne, or on the Killarney lakes.

So much for our neglected heritage of natural and civic beauty. The bait of antiquity and historical association is even less temptingly displayed before the tourist. I have heard our most distinguished archaeologist say that the over-growth of brambles which hide from view so many sculptured tombs and sedilia protect them at least from a worse fate. Driving through Limerick, Clare and Tipperary I found only three out of twenty old churches kept in tolerable decency. Through the rest one stumbled over and between graves hidden in long grass and through a jungle of nettles and thorns. Even in Adare the contrast between the condition of the Franciscan Friary and the golf links about it was informing. In Adare Castle as in Trim the staircase and ladders are broken, and the ascent is perilous or impossible. Superstition has hitherto protected our ring forts, but this defence is yielding to modern education and economic pressure. Nor is the public authority blameless. New Grange is in the charge of the Board of Works, and yet its souterrain is so ravaged by rat holes as to be a danger to the unwary visitor. No signposts point out his way, and when he reaches the tumulus he must turn back more than a mile towards Drogheda because no sufficient indication warns him of the whereabouts of the keys. Similarly at Dunbrody Abbey and else-where. At Monasterboice lichen is allowed to obscure the high cross.

Let us pass now to the provision made for feeding and housing the tourist; and since this matter of hotels – their food, service and charges – raises fierce passions and conflicting testimony in any com-pany in which it is discussed, it will be well to proceed with some care; in the first place hotels cannot be isolated from our social fabric. They are part of it, and to animadvert on them is to criticise our-selves, the standards we passively accept, the abuses we tolerate. They are the public evidence of the national indifference to good food and decent surroundings and of our subservience to the profiteer. Hotel food is very often bad and dear. Our own food is bad and without variety. *Il n'est de bonne cuisine que simple.* Our food is simple without being good, never ingenious, and not always agreeable. Hotels and restaurants but reflect this general or national defect.

So also with rooms and their decoration. Lagging behind in domestic architecture, the modern feeling for air, light, colour and simplicity, which profoundly affects decoration abroad, has hardly touched Ireland; and in reproaching our hotels with obtuse disregard of these things, we recognise that they are only a little behind the general Irish insensitiveness to these elements of beauty. But, having made all these allowances, the case against the average Irish hotel is deplorably strong. [. . .]

Hotel reform is antecedent to all reform. When two-thirds of the Irish hotels have been raised to a high minimum standard of effi-ciency the publicity campaign should be seriously undertaken. There is no *Baedeker* for Ireland or any Irish guide book in an inter-national series. *Murray's Hand-book*, admirable in many ways, is tinged with an obsolescent colonialism. In Stephen Gwynn we have a writer of exceptional charm, with a quite unusual faculty for historico-topographical writing and an infectious enthusiasm for fishing. His talent should be enlisted and exercised to the utmost. We want provincial guides; we want a *Wanderer in Dublin* on the lines of Lucas's well-known series; we want more D. L. Kelleher. The material in George Coffey's and Margaret Stokes's books should be widely diffused. Apart from catalogues we want handbooks to all the National Collections, and we want other manuals on sectional subjects: architecture, painting, health-resorts, spas, hunting – we have one on fishing. Posters should be commissioned from Irish painters of repute, and illustrated folders should pullulate.

One may expose and criticise these deficiencies all the more frankly because they are already fully recognised by the new Irish Tourist Association, and effective steps have been taken to remedy them. [. . .] If the example of Continental methods proves anything, it proves that such expenditure is a sound investment and that the collaboration of the State and local authorities with such a voluntary organisation as the ITA is the effective instrument of progress.

A loyal British subject faces eviction in the Free State

EMILY HARRIS (1926)

Emily Harris worked as an unpaid voluntary nurse at the British Red Cross Hospital in Kingstown, Co. Dublin, from 1915 to 1919. By the time she wrote this letter to King George V, seven years later, she had fallen on hard times. According to its headed notepaper – on which she wrote the letter – the hospital catered for wounded and sick sailors and soldiers home from the Great War. It had a fully equipped theatre and X-Ray room, and 42 beds, with accommodation for a further 14; and the letterhead boasted: 'Officers treated, Naval and Military, 56; sailors, 356; soldiers, 1128; Deaths, 0.'

His Most Excellent Majesty the King,

May it please Your Gracious Majesty, it was Your Majesty's loyal subject's delight and privilege as a daughter of the British Empire during the late Great War, to serve as an officer in Your Majesty's Army in my woman's sphere, being specially trained for that purpose in that my profession of Nursing, to make good the ravages of warfare, by building anew the wornout, maimed tissues and bodies of the sons of Your Majesty's vast Empire, fighting for the glory of their King. For the honour of the Regiment, as a soldier's daughter, I did my duty, without pay, serving my King for Love. Thus one of they who needs must, serve best.

Sunrise and sunset saw Your Majesty's devoted subject at her post holding Florence Nightingale's lamp, without weariness, continuing without a falter during the subsequent civil strife and all the bitter antagonism which fall upon the faithful's head. And for the reason Your Majesty's loyal subject was not a hired servant, I do dutifully, respectfully and humbly beg Your Gracious Majesty's protection from the stigma now vouchsafed those loyal woman who served also.

That they may not be demoralised by [being] thrown by the Sheriff's men on the roadside, or they that were injured physically during their ministrations on duty, may not be dragged from their beds and be conveyed to the Union Infirmary, such which has taken place in Kingstown recently to Miss de Cadiz. And furthermore an eviction order having been obtained against this, Your Majesty's loyal subject, now awaits her turn for the same indignity. Your Majesty's loyal subjects do not make appeals to Your Majesty's Bounty of the Private Purse. It is to Your Majesty's gracious influence on our behalf.

In grief and sorrow, my lovely Home, the trophies of my profession, has been sold by public Auction. The presents from grateful patients, each household god fraught with fragrant memories of triumph and success. And Your Majesty's loyal subject's heart is broken, having returned the Royal Red Cross, bestowed by Your Gracious Majesty, in order to obtain justice by [being] relieved of the onus of my service to my beloved King in Ireland. The Courts are for my justice. Your Majesty, this loyal subject craves only for her sovereign's protection against [being] thrown by the sheriff's men on the roadside. While Your Majesty's humble petitioner will ever pray to continue Your Majesty's most devoted loyal subject.

Emily K. Harris, A.R.R.C., [former] Commandant and Matron, British Red Cross Hospital, Corrig Castle, Kingstown

On 'company keeping', dancing and other evils

AN *IRISH INDEPENDENT* REPORT (1926)

The *Irish Independent* published a detailed account of remarks made by
Archbishop T. P. Gilmartin of Tuam at the dedication of a new
church in Co. Mayo in December 1926.

Most Reverend Dr Gilmartin, in dedicating a new church at Cloon-
goonagh, Aughamore, yesterday, referred to the growth of evils
against which the young people especially would have to be on their
guard. In recent years the dangerous occasions of sin had been multi-
plied. The old Irish dances had been discarded for foreign
importations, which, according to all accounts, lent themselves not
so much to rhythm as to low sensuality. The actual hours of sleep had
been turned into hours of debasing pleasure. Company keeping
under the stars of night had succeeded in too many places to the good
old Irish custom of visiting, chatting, story-telling from one house
to another, with the Rosary to bring all home in due time.

Parental control had been relaxed, and fashions bordering on
indecency had become a commonplace; while bad books, papers,
and pictures were finding their way into remote country places. He
felt sure that that locality was free from some of those dangers, but
yet he rejoiced that they had now a church in their midst called by
the name of Mary Immaculate, which would remind their sons and
daughters of Mary's characteristic virtues.

'A girl,' adds His Grace, 'may have money or she may have not, she
may have to go to America or she may stay at home, she may be
beautiful or she may be what is called plain, but if she is a true daughter of Mary Immaculate, if she has guarded her chastity as a pearl of
great price, if she is more distinguished by maidenly dignity than by
frivolity, then she has a rich dowry, and happy is the man who will
win her love and prove himself worthy to have this mutual love
cemented in the holy sacrament of Matrimony.

'For both girls and boys there is no surer road to temporal and eternal happiness than respect for themselves and respect for one another, the boys respecting the girls as children of Mary Immaculate and the girls taking care to respect themselves and to lead the boys not to sin, but to virtue. If boys and girls live up to this ideal there will be more, happy marriages, for the best preparation for marriage is not sinful company-keeping or outlandish dances or late hours, but the practice of those quiet, secret, domestic virtues which makes home the reflex of the home life of Jesus, Mary and Joseph in the little house of Nazareth.'

A Jesuit preaches on marriage

AN *IRISH TIMES* REPORT (1928)

A series of Lenten talks by Fr Charles Doyle, SJ, on the subject of marriage attracted such a crowd to Gardiner Street church in Dublin that loudspeakers had to be installed to carry his message to those unable to enter. One of his lectures, entitled 'Queen of the Home', was reported in the *Irish Times*.

It too frequently happened, said the lecturer, that married couples did not always find themselves well matched. The husband before long found that the romance of courtship had fled, that the feverish desire of possession was gone; and the woman discovered the man was an ordinary, prosaic, imperfect individual. As the wife could not afford to be unhappy, she should begin seriously the business of adaptation. Life was too precious to be thrown away in secret regrets or open differences. The wife should love her husband, but the love need not be the soft, sweet love of pre-marriage days. Let the woman be subject to her husband.

It was common experience that in almost every phase of life woman clung to man, and needed his help and protection. There was nothing menial in that dependency, nothing that detracted from woman's dignity in the slightest. The true relation between man and woman was the quality of dependence. In married life man was as subject to woman as woman to man. It was the woman's mission to regulate the house; to make the husband happy, and, above all, to make a man of him. The moment a woman tried to throw off dominion and sought to rival a man she quarrelled with God's design and unsexed herself. That, however, did not mean that the wife should not have a voice and hand in the affairs of the family business. Two heads were better than one, and woman's head would often think quicker and see farther than man's brain and eyes.

In the presence of their wives most husbands were like clay in the hands of the potter, ready to take any shape that the least skilful

potter wished. After all, in the family firm the husband was the senior partner, and should have the last word and say. The love and
obedience that a wife gave to her husband gave her a claim on his time
and society. She was under an obligation to make the home pleasant;
but, were the home ever so sweet and pleasant, every man has a desire
for an hour of social freedom to mix with his fellows, and to mingle
in their talk.

Here precisely was danger for the wife – for the young wife especially. She had been alone all day and she thought that her husband
should spend the evening with her. She became cross and exacting. It
irritated the man to think that his wife desired to monopolize him. 'I
have sympathy,' said the lecturer, 'with the wife who has married a
golf fiend, unless she happens to be a golf fiend herself, which a
woman with a family to look after has no business to be. Of course,
golf in moderation is a harmless and innocent occupation, except for
the bad language to which it gives rise when a man misses his stroke,
but if a man starts thinking and talking and dreaming golf, when he
makes golf an idol, oh! then he becomes an unmitigated bore and a
nuisance, and such a husband becomes a perfect brute, for every
moment is given to his new-found love, and he leaves his wife lonely
and neglected.'

On the other hand, if the wife wanted to keep her husband from
golf, from girls and from Guinness, she must seek more effective
means than reproaches and tears – she must make the home clean and
neat and comfortable. [. . .] If girls knew as much about cooking as
they did of the different ways of doing up their hair and powdering
their noses there would not be so many marriage failures. The wife
should dress neatly and tastefully, not in 'the hide your eyes skirt' or
the 'low and behold blouse'.

On the censorship bill

GEORGE BERNARD SHAW (1928)

Though he moved to London as a young man in 1876, George Bernard Shaw maintained a lifelong interest in his native country. The final paragraph of his essay 'The Censorship', published in the *Irish Statesman* in 1928, has been much quoted. But this has obscured the fact that the main theme of Shaw's essay was the then vexed question of birth control. Shaw feared that the proposed censorship bill – which was eventually passed – would make matters even worse for Irish people seeking to practise contraception.

What we have to consider in judging the special aim of the Bill is that life, especially married life, is unnecessarily troubled and occasionally wrecked because we have no technique of marriage; and this ignorance is produced by the deliberate suppression of all responsible information on the subject. England has an expert instructress in the person of Dr Marie Stopes; and the result is that – quite apart from the special technique of Birth Control, which she has at all events rescued from the uncontradicted, and in Ireland presently to become the legally uncontradictable, advertisements of the underground trade in 'specialities' – numbers of unhappy marriages have been set right by her instruction. The Irish people will not be allowed to consult either Dr Stopes or their spiritual directors. Of clandestine instruction there will be plenty; but as nobody will be allowed to criticise it, or even to mention it, everything that is evil in it will be protected and nourished, and everything that is honest and enlightening in it will be discredited and suppressed.

But we must not let our vision be narrowed by the specific and avowed objects of the Act, which are, to prevent our learning the truth about the various methods of Birth Control (some of them in urgent need of criticism) now in irresistible use, and to hide from us the natural penalties of prostitution until we have irrevocably incurred them, often quite innocently at second hand. The matter of

Censorship as opposed to constitutional law is bigger than these, its meanest instances. Ireland is now in a position of special and extreme peril. Until the other day we enjoyed a factitious prestige as a thorn in the side of England, or shall I say, from the military point of view, the Achilles heel of England. We were idealized by Pity, which always idealises the victim and the underdog. The island was hymned as one of saints, heroes, bards, and the like more or less imaginary persons. Every Don Quixote in Europe and America, and even actually in China, made a Dulcinea of Kathleen ni Houlihan and the Dark Rosaleen. We thought ourselves far too clever to take ourselves at the Quixotic valuation; but in truth even the most cynically derisive Dubliners (detestable animals!) overrated us very dangerously; and when we were given a free hand to make good we found ourselves out with a shock that has taken all the moral pluck out of us as completely as physical shell shock. We can recover our nerve only by forcing ourselves to face new ideas, proving all things, and standing by that which is good. We are in a world in which mechanical control over nature and its organization has advanced more in a single century than it had done before in a whole epoch. But the devil of it is that we have made no corresponding advance in morals, and religion. We are abject cowards when confronted with new moral ideas, and insanely brave when we go out to kill one another with a physical equipment of artificial volcanoes and atmospheres of poison, and a mental equipment appropriate to stone axes and flint arrow heads. We incite our young men to take physical risks which would have appalled the most foolhardy adventurers of the past; but when it is proposed to allow a young woman to read a book which treats sexual abnormalities as misfortunes to be pitied instead of horrors to be screamed at and stoned, an Irishman arises in the face of England and madly declares that he is prepared in the interests of family life to slay his children rather than see them free to read such a work. What sort of family life his daughter has led him since he made this amazing exhibition of Irish moral panic is a matter for shuddering conjecture; but however dearly he has paid at his own fireside for his terrors, he can hardly have got worse than he deserves.

The moral is obvious. In the nineteenth century all the world was concerned about Ireland. In the twentieth, nobody outside Ireland cares twopence what happens to her. If she holds her own in the front of European culture, so much the better for her and for Europe. But if, having broken England's grip of her, she slips back into the Atlantic as a little grass patch in which a few million moral cowards are not allowed to call their souls their own by a handful of morbid Catholics, mad with heresyphobia, unnaturally combining with a handful of Calvinists mad with sexphobia (both being in a small disliked minority of their own co-religionists), then the world will let 'these Irish' go their own way into insignificance without the smallest concern. It will no longer even tell funny stories about them.

The battle over the short skirt

SIGNE TOKSVIG (*c.* 1929)

The Danish writer Signe Toksvig lived in Ireland from 1926 to 1937 with her husband, the writer Francis Hackett. The following text survived as a manuscript among her papers from her Irish sojourn, published by Lis Pihl as *Signe Toksvig's Irish Diaries 1926–1937*.

Another war is raging in Ireland. It is being fought around, so to speak, the knee – the female knee. The Antis are as usual the most active and the most noisy; while the 'pros', following the example of Mahatma Gandhi, offer only passive resistance. The trouble is of course with the short skirt. It spread from wicked Paris to wicked Dublin and thence into the hitherto innocent country-side, reaching the smallest place beginning with Kil- or Bally-. And people who had viewed the short hair with misgiving began to view the knees, or rather to avert their eyes from them, with active alarm. Limerick led the way; after the Pope and the Irish hierarchy had expressed a wish for more modesty in women's clothes. Limerick may be a dank corpse among cities, artificially breathing a little through the Shannon scheme, but it was able to start the Modest Dress and Deportment Crusade, the main plan of which is that the skirt must measure four inches below the knee when the wearer is kneeling. And the crusaders wrote to the leading Irish newspaper.

They are still writing. The organ notes of their indignation quite drown the few timid little pip-pips in contradiction. And dreadful things are being disclosed. It is difficult to put it delicately, but it appears that only four inches of flimsy stuff stand – well, hang – between the proverbial virtue of Irishwomen and being a spiritual amoral, etc. What is even more terrible really is that, in the opinion of those who ought to know, those fatal four inches are all that protect the virtue of Irish young men. Judge from the following extracts of a letter about the 'female population' bearing in mind that the short skirt is the writer's inspiration.

'Satanic behaviour of the modern woman is incredible and intolerable — a cantankerous epidemic is claiming Europe for its victim. Ireland is catching the contagion. A horde of infidels are endeavouring to place Lucifer on the seat of Christ. Our magnificent Irish women so recently the idols of the Catholic world have become the slavish imitators of Parisian fashionmongers. Modern women, many unknowingly no doubt, are creating havoc among our virtuous young men. Are we Catholics going to stand by and see our land once hallowed by the blood of martyrs now made a place where Satan may carry on his traffic?'

You cannot deny that 'Tomas' is stirred up. So is the writer signed 'Disgusted' who wants us all to 'stand firm and wipe out the plague now' and the one signed 'Morality' who wants to invoke the law. 'Veronica', who ventured to think that Christianity had nothing to do with the short skirt, is crushed by being told that Irish girls who listened to her would risk the salvation of their souls, such big guns being wheeled against her as: 'I stated the doctrinal fact', etc.

An appeal to the Pope

SINN FÉIN STANDING COMMITTEE (1929)

The founding of Fianna Fáil and its comparative electoral success left a rump of republican irreconcilables in Sinn Féin. Their leaders still maintained that they were the 'Executive Council of the Republic of Ireland'. In this document of December 1929, the party's Standing Committee urged the Pope to consider postponing the forthcoming Eucharistic Congress in Dublin until such time as Ireland was united.

It is now announced that the Eucharistic Congress is to be held in Ireland in 1932. Our deep reverence, our Faith, and an ardent desire that a united Ireland should send up a paean of joy, unclouded by division or bitterness, make us regret that so great an event has not been postponed a little longer, till such union is possible. For how can we rejoice as we would wish, while Irishmen are in gaol because they will not bow to an alien monarch; while the traitors who have deceived the people, and the authors of the slaughter of our bravest citizens, are accorded the place of honour on an occasion so sacred; while the representative of an alien and heretic monarch is received with royal honours, and given the place and dignity allotted to a King in a Catholic land? Many thousands of those who took part in the recent celebrations of the Centenary of Catholic Emancipation tried to shut their eyes to this outrage on their national feeling, and to think only of its religious significance. One would not object to the presence of those, whom loyal citizens of Ireland stigmatise as traitors, among the rank and file of Catholics. But it is, we repeat, an outrage on national feeling that honour should be given officially to those who have betrayed the best traditions of their race and murdered loyal citizens who refused to dishonour their country or accept for her a subordinate position.

We rely on a sympathetic and paternal understanding, on the part of Your Holiness, of our view that, having waited so long for the signal favour of the Eucharistic Congress in Ireland, we should wait yet a little longer, till a united Ireland could fittingly join in that great Celebration, without the risk of a further outrage against these who had courage and patriotism enough to refuse to sell their National Birthright under a threat of immediate and terrible war.

Imploring the Apostolic Blessing, we have the honour to remain the most loyal and devoted children of Your Holiness. Executive Council, Republic of Ireland.

Red peril at the cinema

H. O'FRIEL, DEPARTMENT OF JUSTICE (1930)

Despite a prudish censorship regime, the cinema had become in the 1920s one of Ireland's most popular sources of entertainment. But the American and British films which were dominant in the commercial cinema did not exhaust the interest of some film enthusiasts. The Dublin Film Society – with a programme including works by the Soviet masters Eisenstein and Pudovkin – invited the Governor-General, James McNeill, to be their patron. It fell to the Department of Justice – which was responsible for film censorship – to try to warn him off. The departmental letter was addressed to Mr McNeill's secretary.

Strictly confidential
Dear Miss Coulson,

With further reference to your letter of 11th instant regarding the Dublin Film Society, the enquiries which I promised to make indicate in their result that the Society has as its promoters a group of persons who regard themselves as 'intellectuals'. Some of these His Excellency has no doubt heard of. Paul Farrell is a re-instated Civil Servant with artistic leanings. Miss Manning [presumably the actor and playwright Mary Manning], whose address is, as far as I know, 66, Waterloo Road, is a journalist in the film and fashion domain. The others mentioned in the circular are interested in Art and Drama. With the possible exception of Mr Farrell none of the promoters has been prominent in contemporary troubles.

Nevertheless, their programme is disturbing. The film [*Battleship*] *Potemkin* is largely Bolshevist propaganda; so also is *Mother*. *Storm over Asia* is described in a recent issue of the *Daily Express* as an anti-British film and a gross libel on the British Army; and while I have not particulars of the other films they seem to be, in the words of the circular, 'of unusual interest'. We have some reason to fear, and this fear is not dictated by reference to the personnel of the Society, that Bolshevist propaganda look to this society as a medium for the dissemination of films which would otherwise fail to secure publicity here. Apart from this I am somewhat nervous of the 'Cinema as an Art Medium' in the hands of a Society such as the present. On the whole His Excellency would, perhaps, be of opinion that it was not a project in which he would care to be prominently associated.

Yours sincerely, H. O'Friel

The censor's lament

JAMES MONTGOMERY (1930)

James Montgomery was Ireland's first film censor. In 1930, with the introduction of the 'talkies', Montgomery was rejecting so many films that the Irish Advisory Committee of the Kinematograph Renters' Society of Great Britain and Ireland complained to the Department of Justice of a 'film famine'. His letter to the Department of Justice quoted approvingly the following comment from Paul Rotha's recently published book *The Film Till Now*: 'The Cinema lost a public who loved it for itself and what it meant to them, they had no liking for vaudeville, for star turns on a big scale. In place of the old film-goer there arose a new type of audience, a vacant-minded empty-headed public, who flocked to sensations, who thrilled to sensual vulgarity, and who would go anywhere, and pay anything to see indecent situations riskily handled on the screen.'

I received so many complaints about the screening of bathing beauty parades, 'close ups' of women in single-piece bathing costumes, and of mannequins in scant underwear, that I have dealt with all the topical films [newsreels] for some time past, but not so drastically as many desire. I don't cut bathing or diving, but I do cut exhibitions of beauty parades where men are seen pawing girls in bathing suits, or vetting them as it is elegantly described, and 'close ups' which are obviously pandering to exhibitionism. [. . .]

I cannot offer any remarks on my alleged unsuitability for the position: the question of age might deprive the State of many useful public servants, but I wonder why they fixed 45 years as the limit. Do they think that the Hollywood formula might not influence a Censor over that age? They probably know that when the emotions are aroused, the critical faculty is weakened. [. . .] Knowing that the Appeal Board can reply to the contradictory statements made about my influence, I'll conclude by stating that I will continue to call the stock characters and incidents of Movie Land by their proper Police

Court names. As Appeals are pending in the cases of *Lord Richard in the Pantry* and *What Price Melody*, I'll make no comment. In *Trailing Trouble* it is interesting to note that the Australian Censor uses the words 'brothel' and 'prostitute' – in his report on that film – and in *The Czar of Broadway* the woman in the case is undoubtedly the discarded mistress of the underworld 'hero', so a rape will not be called an 'erotic impulse', a paramour will not hide behind the euphemism of 'lover' or 'sugar daddy', and I certainly will not wrap a piece of tawdry tinsel around a prostitute or mistress and call her a 'Gold Digger'.

So far as Hollywood is concerned the Free State does not exist, it is not even mentioned in their Year Book. So far as British Production is concerned we are only a territory smaller than Manchester, consequently our influence on production is negligible, but I feel that a strong stand should be made in the interests of common decency, whatever the consequences may be.

Christmas in Letterfrack

PETER TYRRELL (1930)

As a boy of eight, Peter Tyrrell was sent with his three siblings to St Joseph's Industrial School in Letterfrack, Co. Galway, which was run by the Christian Brothers. His mother was a beggar. He remained in Letterfrack until he was sixteen, then worked as a tailor. He joined the British Army, and reckoned his conditions in a German prisoner of war camp better than what he had experienced in Letterfrack. Later in life he was befriended by the Trinity senator Owen Sheehy Skeffington, and in June 1964 *Hibernia* published his account of life in Letterfrack. In 1967 Tyrrell's charred remains were found on Hampstead Heath, London. He was identified by a fragment of a postcard addressed to Skeffington. An inquest returned a verdict of death by suicide. His account of his life in Letterfrack, *Founded on Fear*, was posthumously published in 2006. It was edited by Diarmuid Whelan, who discovered it when working on Skeffington's papers for the National Library of Ireland. The text that follows is based on Tyrell's original manuscript.

It is Christmas Day and I try to pull myself together. My brother Jack has left school and I am alone, really alone. Never have I felt so lonely and miserable before. There is someone speaking to me, it is Con Murphy, he is wishing me a Happy Christmas. I am dazed and he repeats what he has been saying. As I look at his face, he is smiling, and I can see his gums. They are in a sickly condition, his teeth are discoloured and decayed, his gums are just full of mucus and I advise him to go and see the nurse, but I know he won't go, because I told him before. Many of the children have this complaint or disease, others have running ears. Many suffer from sores on the head and face and in the ears, the legs and the hands. Many walk with their heads down, and some are very round shouldered.

Dr Lavelle, a man of about forty, comes to see us about once a month, but he just walks around the yard with a dog at his heels. The dog is the biggest I have ever seen. Lavelle always wears a plus-four suit of tweed; and I have never seen him without a cigarette in his mouth. My younger brother Laurence has been in the school about a year, but I do not recognise him. He was too young to come to Letterfrack so was sent to the nuns at Kilkenny. He is a year younger than me, but is now much bigger than I am and is good at school. He was in the infirmary six months ago with poisoned hands and had to have both lanced in several places in order to let out the pus. This was due to chilblains which became septic.

The Christmas dinner is really good. Roast chicken and roast pork, green peas, followed by plum pudding and custard. There is less excitement than last year as Father Christmas did not come. I am now feeling a little better than for the last few days. It's most remarkable how the Brothers change at this time of year. Vale has been up half the night preparing the dinner, and it is really good. Brothers Fahy and Byrne, Murphy and Conway are waiting on the children. Vale, his clothes dirty and full of grease, is busy bringing out the trays of chicken from the kitchen. His face is sweating and he looks tired. Brother Kelly is going about giving everyone sweets from a very big tin.

I have not received a letter this year because I have not answered the last two. Now I know why many of the other lads stopped writing. I now feel bitter towards my parents. I want to write home and tell them everything, but always change my mind the last moment. I now feel glad that I never wrote. I think it's much better that my parents forget about me. I shall soon be fifteen and will then have only a year to do. However bad the last year is it can't be any worse than the last five and a half years, so I make up my mind to try and have fun for the next few days like the other lads. I tell myself that I am not going to worry about the awful and terrifying things the missioner has been telling us, besides they may not even be true. I find it hard to believe that the priest has seen a boy who is in Hell, and I remember the last year how the missioner explained the exact position of the chains on the condemned boys' legs.

After dinner, we go into the village. Martin Mullins and Tommy Gordon have some money and we want to buy sweets. We come to the post office and it is shut. We go across the road to the pub, and Mr Griffin is there, so the lads give Mr Griffin a shilling for a drink. He is now looking old and shabby, since his wages were cut down to sixteen shilling he has not been able to get any new clothes. We asked for sweets in the pub but they didn't sell any, but they had bottles of lemonade and ginger beer, so we had three bottles of ginger beer. Mr Griffin now teaches infants because he is unable to read the third standard book owing to his failing sight.

We stood at the door drinking the ginger beer straight from the bottle. When John Kusack [*sic*] and Tommy Mannion arrived with another farmhand, I do not know. They bought a pint for Mr Griffin and asked us to have something, but we thanked them very much and said no.

We walked along the road towards Kylemore. We were making for Rankins, because they were always open. Martin Mullins asked Gordon if ginger beer would make us drunk, and Gordon admitted he never drank any before. I didn't know because I had never been in a pub before. Just before we came to the sweet shop we met a lady who smiled and spoke to us. Tommy Gordon said she was the Protestant woman Brother Byrne used to talk about, and I then remembered a sermon a few weeks before in the chapel. It was the priest from the convent at Kylemore Abbey who said: a Protestant had as much chance of going to Heaven as would a rowing boat crossing to America in a storm.

This made me think a lot because this lady, although I never met her before, was very good and kind. I could not remember what Brother Byrne said but I should like to find out, and feel certain that he would say nothing wrong about her. After buying a lot of canned sweets we made our way back and found the boys having supper, after which there was a picture show. It was the same picture we seen about two years before, when it broke down several times: it was Charlie Chaplin.

'Always give Irish angle'

FRANK GALLAGHER (1931)

Eamon de Valera founded the *Irish Press* with the aim of redressing the imbalance in the political allegiance of national newspapers in the 1920s, all of which showed a marked antipathy to Fianna Fáil. The following is from Gallagher's memorandum to his journalistic staff in 1931 as the paper was preparing to launch.

Staff generally: Every good journalist while he is writing is one of his own readers. Ireland matters most to the *Irish Press*. [. . .] 'Women and children first': If there is a side to a story or illustration of interest to women don't ignore it. Do not make the *Irish Press* a Dublin paper: there are O'Connell Streets in other cities also. Remember the Free State is not Ireland and 'Northern Ireland' is not either Northern Ireland or Ulster – it is the Six Counties. Do not quote Judges' jokes unless they are real jokes. Give the Garda or RUC man's name, not his Number. It is not necessary to report every word of praise spoken to policemen.

Subs: Always give Irish angle in the headlines. Do not use agency headlines: the other papers will have those. Be on your guard against the habits of British and foreign news agencies who look on the world mainly through imperialist eyes. For instance: Do not pass the word 'bandits' as a description of South American revolutionaries. Pirates and robbers in China are not necessarily Communists and therefore should not be described as such. Tammany is an American institution disliked by British agencies. Be careful of one-sided accounts of its activities. These agency stories show ignorance of Catholic practice and things: check all doubtful references in such copy. Propagandist attacks on Russia and other countries should not be served up as news.

Birth control and the press

IRISH PRESS ARTICLE AND ROSAMOND JACOB (1931)

Rosamond Jacob and Dorothy Macardle – feminists and nationalists both – welcomed the *Irish Press* as redressing the political imbalance in the Irish newspapers of the time. But they were quickly disillusioned with some of the attitudes of the paper. They took particular exception to a brief article entitled 'Censorship' on the front page on Monday, 7 December 1931.

In yesterday's issue of the *Sunday Times* the principal article was one headed 'Birth Control'. It was written by Lord Buckmaster and, as its title implies, it dealt with the unnatural prevention of conception and blatantly advocated a course of action and a manner of married life repulsive to every Christian. The article was an extraordinary exhibition of how far paganism and animalism had gone in England when one of the most conservative organs stars an affront to the Christian basis of life which must disgust every decent heart in Britain. In the same issue *Lives of our Lord* are reviewed under the title 'Three more studies of the Galilean'. Here in Ireland there are so many political censors that a line cannot escape into an Irish newspaper which may even distantly offend against a series of prohibitions as long as the Wall of China. But the *Sunday Times* sold without official molestation everywhere in Irish cities yesterday.

Rosamond Jacob's diary entry for that date records Macardle's reaction to the Irish Press *articles, and her own.*

Monday, 7 December 1931. This was the day the *Irish Press* came out with a thick-type par[agraph] on the front page denouncing the Buckmaster article on birth control – the court case on abortion showing the need for b[irth] c[ontrol] in the *Sunday Times* as depth of paganism and animalism disgusting to every decent heart in England. I visited Dorothy [Macardle] that evening, and she was raging over it; the arrogant rudeness to all non-Cath[olics], the ignorance of it, let alone the devilishness of the Church attitude. She was very down-hearted over the paper altogether, with the sectarian blight over it, and FF and the country. Never heard anyone speak better. Like me, she had got the *Sunday Times* and thought the article excellent.

The joys of the Eucharistic Congress

ALICE CURTAYNE AND 'JOHN ROWE' (1932)

The Eucharistic Congress was vastly popular, with over a million people attending an open-air mass in the Phoenix Park. It was covered significantly in the 1933 *Capuchin Annual*; pieces by Alice Curtayne and a self-described 'exile' writing under the name John Rowe give a flavour of the excitement generated.

Alice Curtayne: [. . .] the Congress in Dublin was like a drama in which everyone was an actor, down to the smallest child in the darkest back alley of the City.

It was this same unanimity prompted the dwellers in the poorest quarters of Dublin to compete with the City Corporation in the matter of display. It inspired them to draw over the squalor of their surroundings a delicate veil of greenery, streamers, nosegays, flags and coloured illuminations, beneath which the drab and the commonplace disappeared. Dublin's very poorest proved they possessed an inventive fertility, a talent for artistic creation, that drew thousands around them all Congress Week. Their unity of mind with the Congress idea inspired them, too, how to spend their evenings: saying the Rosary around their central altar, duly blessed, and with lighted candles; and afterwards sitting outdoors until darkness fell, talking and admiring their transformed streets. There was one such place that attracted me repeatedly. I do not know the name of the street, but the altar had been raised on some elevated waste ground near a crossing, and over it this legend in black letters nearly a foot high on a white background: No power on earth can destroy the Priest, the Altar, or the Victim [. . .]

'John Rowe': Sunday was of course the greatest day of all. It is generally agreed that never since the beginning had such a congregation been present at the offering of the Holy Sacrifice of the Mass. We followed the ceremonies perfectly. The voices of the Celebrant and the Ministers

came through distinctly, and we got a perfect reception of the Choir's masterly rendering of the Mass. Count John McCormack's 'Panis Angelicus' soared above the things of earth; his singing was a triumph of voice and art but above all it was a prayer. There was a piercing moment when the word of command rang out to the Guard of Honour to unsheathe their swords. The same tense hush of terrible expectancy fell on us who were far away as on those who were there. The soul of Christendom joined in one grand act of adoration.

And then St Patrick's Bell. [. . .] A voice from the world of all realities. Was that bell rung for the first Mass in Ireland? Who can say now? Of a surety it was the bell of our Great Shepherd which of old called our fathers to hear the word of Christ. Now it told us that 'the Master is here.' Is it fanciful to think that not only we, the scattered ones, were there with those who filled the great spaces of the Phoenix Park, but that, in addition, all the holy ones of our race from the beginning joined with us who are still in exile in this valley of tears, in one great act of homage, which passing the confines of time and space drew together in itself all the angels and saints of Heaven and the faithful on earth.

'Nationalism is a cocaine'

SEAN O'FAOLAIN (1934)

Sean O'Faolain, who joined the Irish Volunteers in 1918 and took the anti-Treaty side in the Civil War, was a keen interpreter of Irish nationalism in post-independence Ireland. In a letter to Hanna Sheehy Skeffington, he admits that he 'cannot help' writing to her on the subject, though wisdom tells him that it was unlikely that she would be influenced by him.

I dislike this common idea that rabid Nationalism was and is necessary. At the bottom of that idea is a contempt, unconscious, for the people, and an innate disbelief in humanity. It means that a boy cannot adapt himself, and protect his individuality, other than by running away from home and then running back again. It means that nothing but violent emotionalism can direct a people. It springs from the same source as Fascism and Communism, both of which treat the people as children. It is the denial of reason.

Ireland with Pearse ran from modern Europe back to the Utopia of the Gaelic State – that accursed bugbear, jackothelantern, and whatnot of our day. Dev follows it up with his race back to the simple life. (Or, rather, proposed to do so before he got into power.) But Gaelic *simplicitas* won't wash. I look at my Lemasses and Childerses and even my Michael Collinses and my Cosgraves and even, if I may so without any malice, my Skeffingtons – AND my O'Faolains – and I see it just isn't honest with any of us. Here is Dev, today, at long last brought up bang against Europe, running back to home like the prodigal, back to factories in the cities, industrialism, diplomacy, capitalism, cheap politics, trousers and tallhats, banks, everything European and English that was once so scorned by the Pearseites that they would not even talk of such things in connection with the risen Ireland. [. . .] Irish is being 'saved' at two pounds per head per child. Irish industries are being developed by charging the worker thirty to fifty per cent more for his goods, and by developing a new class of bourgeois capitalists of the getrichquick type who don't give a damn for anything but the money to be made out of the game. I need not go on. I do not question – NOTE – the propriety of all this. That is another story. All I point out is that the old machine goes its way. It is a good way – let us suppose. But did that good oldfashioned economic policy of tariff-reform and industrial expansion need so much hysteria of emotionalism to produce? And is it decent, to say no more, to beat the drum of the *Irish Press* kind of Nationalism in pride and glory at the Risen Ireland when this is all nothing more than a resurrection of the ghost of Joe Chamberlain?

Come! Nationalism 'necessary'? Yes, if we are children. [Peadar] O'Donnell is right. De Valera is not a Republican and he is not a socialist. He is merely a tariff-reformer. His Republic is allmyeye. As I said over and over again in my biography – a bit of tinsel where the reality is quietly hidden away. Nationalism is a cocaine. It is a religion without any values and without an ethic. To supply values Dev drags in Christianity and talks of the Christian state. He takes his values from Socialism, and the Catholic Church. Nationalism is merely the gilding of the pill. OK! If our people haven't the guts to swallow Socialism and Christianity without the gilded covering then give the babbas the sugar-coating.

But agree with me, then, that it is 'necessary' only because you feel the Irish people are half-child and half-fool.

Yours cordially, Sean O'Faolain

Gaels v. jazz

'LIA FÁIL' (1934)

Fr Peter Conefrey – parish priest of Cloone, champion of flax culti-vation and weaving, and founder of the Cloone céilí band – gained some renown for a campaign against jazz music. He described jazz as 'something that should not as much be mentioned among us', as its object was 'to destroy virtue in the human soul'. Some of the worst offenders, he alleged, were the gardaí, who were regularly holding all-night jazz dances, and had persisted 'even since the Anti-Jazz cam-paign started'. The following article, published in the *Leitrim Observer*, was signed '"Lia Fáil" and Fellow-Gaels'; the paper's readers would have assumed that Conefrey was the author. Conefrey is remembered by a stained-glass window in the parish church at Cloone, and, although sometimes mocked for his opposition to jazz in Ireland, he is also credited with helping to preserve Leitrim's unique tradition of fiddle-playing.

Gaels of Breffni we are with you in the fight against the imported slush. Keep out, we say, the so-called music and songs of the Gall; his silly dances and filthy papers, too. We can never be free until this is done. The Gael has his own customs, games and amusements, and they are second to none. Why imitate the foreigner? Why follow the ancient foe? The Saxon has tried for ages to destroy our faith and our nationality. Henry, Elizabeth, Cromwell, the Yeos, Fencibles, Hes-sians, Auxiliaries and Black-and-Tans tried and failed. Now 'the mind and the heart are the centres assailed by an art that is crafty and cold'. Having failed to ruin our faith by force, Satan and Saxonland are now endeavouring to sap its foundations by sullying the virtue of the children of the Gael – the war is still waged. We must fight; and we must win again.

Let your voice be heard, Gaels of Breffni. Let it ring through Erin and beyond her shores. Let the pagan Saxon be told that we Irish Catholics do not want and will not have the dances and the music that he has borrowed from the savages of the islands of the Pacific. Let him keep these for the thirty million pagans he has at home.

Forty years ago earnest patriots founded the Gaelic League in this land to stem the tide of pagan foreign materialism. We may thank them for the freedom we to-day enjoy. Are we now to forget their labours and their suffering? Should we not follow in their wake and make our land a real Irish-Ireland – a Gaelic nation free from the ties of Anglicization and uncorrupted by its baleful influences? We must continue the good work of the Gaelic pioneers until our land is finally free from foreign sway. This is the land of the Gael; this it must remain. 'Tis righteous men and women, and these alone, that can keep our land a real Catholic Gaelic nation worthy of those who in the past toiled and suffered fought and died to snap the rusty chain.

God gave the Gael a special mission to spread real Christian civilisation and thus save the world from barbarism. That mission has been nobly fulfilled by Irish men and Irish women in the past. Are we of to-day to turn aside from the path they trod in the days of stress and peril? Are we going to disgrace the bones of the heroic saints and martyrs of our race? God forbid!

When Ireland was beaten at Wexford she called for revenge to the West. The West, we are sure, will not now slumber but rush forth again to expel the last and worst invader – the jazz of Johnny Bull and the niggers and cannibals. The brave and noble O'Rourkes of West Breffni, whose fame shall live for ever, call on you to-day, and cry out in clarion tones: 'Away with it, away with it.' And you must obey and vow like true Gaels: 'We are going to oppose and crush the Satanic stuff from Saxonland. Away with it, away with it.' The blood of your ancestors reddened the walls of Hamilton's Castle and flowed on the battle-field of Ballinamuck, when they fought for the faith and the land of Patrick. Surely, that blood still flows in your veins, and you don't forget it – surely you are not ashamed of that blood, for you are descendants of those fearless men of Breffni who vowed on many a battleplain that their clan would never bow to slavery. To be slaves of Saxonland is bad enough, but to belong to Satan! Perish the thought!

Cast aside the wiles of Satan, and Shauneen Bwee.
Be yourselves – be Gaelic, Catholic and free.
Keep out the foreigner, hold your own.
Self-abasement paves the way to villain
bonds and despots' sway.
You are getting the lead now from your
Gaelic sagarts, thank God!
Hand in hand the priests and people,
Faith it is a glorious sign.
'Tis the sign the fires are burning
brightly all along the line.
When the Gaelic sagart leads the way
your hearts can never quail.
For he'll spread the light and chase the
mists from green-robed Innisfail.

Hibernia Irredenta

J. J. MCELLIGOTT (1937)

The 1937 constitution was a central pillar in de Valera's programme to unravel the 1921 Treaty and justify his opposition to it. When the constitution was in draft form, it was circulated to senior civil servants. Article 2, which described the island of Ireland as the 'national territory', and Article 3, which allowed that the laws of the state would apply only south of the border with Northern Ireland, were a classic de Valera formula: one article declared a united Ireland; the next allowed 'not yet'. These articles did not cause public controversy at the time, but one formidable critic was J. J. McElligott, the Secretary of the Department of Finance. His concerns were ignored, but would be vindicated some sixty years later when – in the aftermath of the Good Friday Agreement – Articles 2 and 3 were amended broadly in line with his critique.

Articles 1–3. These Articles, dealing with the Nation as distinct from the State (a distinction which many political scientists would not admit), seem rather to vitiate the Constitution, by stating at the outset what will be described, and with some justice, as a fiction, and one which will give offence to neighbouring countries with whom we are constantly protesting our desire to live on terms of friendship.

Having been at such pains to expel fictions from the existing Constitution and to bring theory into line with practice, it seems inconsistent now to import an even greater fiction. Further, from the point of view of international law, it is not clear whether we are on safe ground in claiming sovereignty and jurisdiction over land recognised internationally, *de jure* and *de facto,* as belonging to another country. [. . .]

From the practical point of view, apart from the fear of consequences, these Articles will not contribute anything to effecting the unity of Ireland, but rather the reverse. Besides they will impose an additional and more severe strain on our relations with the members of the British Commonwealth of Nations, relations which are already difficult enough, and which coming events, apart from the Constitution, will make even more difficult.

It is not usual in a Constitution to define the national boundaries. Query: does the expression 'The Irish Nation' not include all Irishmen whether living in or outside Ireland?

Later in this document McElligott commented on Article 4, complaining that changing the name of the state to Éire *could prove expensive in terms of printing stamps and bank notes. He also expressed deeper misgivings:*

The adoption of the name 'Éire' may be quite justifiable from the traditional and scholarly points of view, but from a realistic point of view it seems a mistake. This land is generally known internationally as Ireland or one of the derivatives of that name, and so there will probably be a long period of confusion and misunderstanding before the unaccustomed name conveys a definite meaning to educated people throughout the world.

Some weeks later, when a revised draft was circulated, McElligott welcomed some changes to the early articles, but his central concern remained.

Articles 1–4. The Nation. These Articles take the place of Articles 1 to 3 and Article 9.1 of the previous version. The revised Articles are less emphatic and aggressive in tone and to that extent they are perhaps less likely to arouse antagonism in the two neighbouring countries. But the claim to territory which does not belong to Saorstat Éireann still subsists in Articles 3 and 4 and therefore the general criticism contained in our previous observations on this part of the Draft Constitution still stands. It gives a permanent place in the Constitution to a claim to *Hibernia Irredenta*. The parallel with Italy's historical attitude to the Adriatic Seaboard beyond its recognised territory is striking, and as in that case it is likely to have lasting ill effects on our political relations with our neighbours.

Dev woos the Vatican

JOSEPH P. WALSHE (1937)

De Valera was covetous of the Pope's approval for his new constitution. The task of winning papal approval was assigned to Joseph Walshe, the Secretary of the Department of External Affairs. In a memorandum to de Valera, Walshe reported his conversation with Cardinal Pacelli, the future Pope Pius XII. Walshe noted that Pacelli considered Ireland so important in the Catholic world that he thought 'we should have made a very special effort to give to the world a completely Catholic Constitution.'

I told him I quite realised how important the form of the Constitution was in the mind of the Vatican, but from what I had already said he would appreciate that we had abstained from using the forms in order to be able to keep the realities. In our case the full Catholic framework would destroy absolutely the building we desired to construct. We had to take the long view in order to reconcile the most hostile religious opinions, and to get all our people to work for our common country. [. . .]

But it became clear at a very early stage of our conversations that we should not succeed in getting any expression of approval of the text from the Vatican. From the nature of things they have to stake their full claim, and formal or indeed informal approval was not to be given to a text which did not come down completely on the side of strict Catholic doctrine. The Cardinal told me with a smile, but quite truthfully, that according to the strict teaching of the Church we were heretics to recognise any church but the one true church of Christ. Again I reminded him of the danger of seeing only the form, and he assured me at once that the Church would not take our heresy too seriously.

It did not shake him when I contrasted the expressly Christian character of our new Constitution with the liberalism (continental sense) of the old, though he recognised the great change for the better. He promised to have a long talk with the Holy Father and to obtain his blessing for [the Government] for having done so well in such difficult circumstances. It was clear when saying this that the Cardinal did not realise that the Holy Father was going to adopt the negative attitude which he made known to me the following day. Indeed he gave me the very clear impression that having said all *he* could say, he was going to get the Pope to bless the Government for the effort they had made to meet the Catholic viewpoint – without making any reference to the Constitution.

I need hardly say therefore that I was very disappointed when I received from the Cardinal yesterday the exact text of the words used by the Holy Father: '*Ni approvo ni non disapprovo – taceremo.*' And the Cardinal did not leave me any doubt as to the meaning. I had asked him to ensure at least that the Holy Father would not disapprove. The answer was: 'I do not approve, neither do I not disapprove – we shall maintain silence.' I tried to translate the evil out of this double negative but the Cardinal held me to the sense. He went on to show that the Holy Father was doing quite a lot in saying that he would maintain silence. It was an attitude of complete neutrality. He might have taken the text without bearing in mind all the implications of the explanations I had given, because the text after all was what counted, but he refrained from disapproving. He would not say 'I approve' and while he would not say 'I do not disapprove' he took the middle position of keeping silence. So argued the Cardinal and while he clearly wanted to give us a crumb of consolation, he had to maintain that the Pope went to the extreme limit to which his position allowed him to go. [. . .]

I insisted again and again that we regarded the fundamentally sound position of the Church in the hearts of the people as an infinitely greater safeguard for Catholic doctrine than form in any documents whether constitutions or concordats – and that that conviction was never absent from your mind when drawing up the Constitution. The Holy Father and the Cardinal would realise as our State evolved that we had acted in the best interests of the Church as well as of the people.

At the Cardinal's request we went back again to see him today,

Thursday. He told me how very ill the Pope had been and that there were several ministers accredited to the Vatican whom he had never seen and who would be annoyed if they heard – and they would hear – that he had given a private audience to me. However, there were some people whom in the normal course he had to see on a Saturday, and he would like Mr Macaulay and myself to come with them. He would be able to give us his blessing and perhaps say a word to us. [. . .]

To conclude this scanty and hastily written report, I want to express my great regret at not having been able to do what I was sent out to do. But I have learned a great deal about the attitude of the Holy See to such matters – and I can assure you, most confidently, that at the back of their adherence to rigid forms and dogmas there is very sincere respect, and even gratitude for the extent to which you have been able to go in making our Constitution Catholic, notwith-standing the very great difficulties which they understand better than they pretend to understand them.

Don't mind the ladies

LOUIS J. WALSH (1937)

Feminists and the Women's Graduate Association campaigned — unsuccessfully — against the article of the draft constitution that outlined the state's idea of the role of women: 'by her life within the home, woman gives to the State a support without which the common good cannot be achieved . . . The State shall, therefore, endeavour to ensure that mothers shall not be obliged by economic necessity to engage in labour to the neglect of their duties in the home.' Louis J. Walsh, a district justice and an Abbey playwright, seems to have thought de Valera needed support on this point.

Letterkenny, Co. Donegal, 5 June 1937

My dear President,

I regard the Bunreacht as a wonderfully well conceived instrument of Constitutional Law. The checks and balances which you have embodied in it are brilliant solutions of the special difficulties of our position. [. . .] Don't mind all the nonsense that is being talked about women. The ladies, who are so vocal, would not be elected to any office by their fellow women if the franchise was a purely feminine one. Surely, the mass of women are entitled to say what they want, and they don't want these ladies to ask for them — the duty of serving on juries in what are often our filthy courts.

Censors meet the editors

T. J. COYNE (1939)

One of the government's earliest decisions, after the outbreak of the Second World War and Ireland's declaration of neutrality, was the imposition of a strict censorship code. On 19 September, a meeting was held at the Department of Justice. Present were the editors of the *Irish Times*, *Irish Press*, *Irish Independent*, *Sunday Independent*, *Evening Herald* and *Evening Mail*, and the Dublin editor of the *Cork Examiner*. The following is from the note made on the meeting by the department's deputy controller for censorship, T. J. Coyne. At the outset of the meeting, the controller of censorship, Joseph Connolly, stressed the importance of keeping in step with the policy of the state as expressed in the decision of neutrality adopted by the Oireachtas. There were two main difficulties which he foresaw.

There was danger from what he might describe as the Right and Left sections of the people. By the Right he perhaps should explain he meant those who are by training and inheritance inclined to lean towards a strong pro-British bias, and by the Left he should describe in short those who advocated that 'England's difficulty is Ireland's opportunity.' That in short represented the two extreme points of view in this country, and it represented also the particular sections from which any difficulty would be likely to arise in opposition to the Government's declared policy of neutrality. He wished to place the Editors in possession of all the facts, and he desired to facilitate them in every possible way. The situation was a delicate one, but he again emphasised the determination of the Government to maintain strict neutrality in the existing European conflict. [. . .]

Mr Smyllie (*Irish Times*) said that at times even a journalist must act at the risk of spending a period in Mountjoy [Jail]. He would have no hesitation in condemning, for instance, a bombing attack on Belfast. He pointed out that Holland, Belgium, etc., are neutral countries. Are they so circumscribed as we? The Controller replied that we are in a very exceptional position. We are exceptionally situated, and because of recent history we have to avoid anything in the nature of a civil disturbance and all that that involves. Mr Smyllie – 'Am I then to say there is nothing to choose between both sides?' The Controller – 'As regards the War, yes.'

The Irish Times *versus the censor*

A Department of Justice file titled 'Wartime censorship: correspondence with editor, *Irish Times*, 1939–40' includes an *Irish Times* cutting
from 12 December 1939. A marginal note on the cutting is annotated:
'This paragraph indicates recruiting for the British Army.' Given the
reference to war recruitment, the censor's office would have expected
such a piece to have been submitted prior to publication; but evidently the *Irish Times* did not submit the piece. Elsewhere in this file
there are indications of the censor's dissatisfaction with the paper,
which had a tendency 'to sail very close to the line and occasionally
cross it'; and he was concerned that the paper's editor, R. M. Smyllie,
might interpret 'our leniency' as weakness or timidity.

Belfast's Nudist Colony: A correspondent writes: – Belfast has a
nudist colony, and even on these chill December days men eager to
enter are turned away in scores. Mere striplings and men well matured
come from all parts of Ulster, and from many points in Éire, to seek
it out.

I would never have known of its existence save that a man prominent in European politics turned my thoughts towards finding it. I
inquired from the police. '72 Clifton Street,' they said. I was there
bright and early next morning, and stated my name and my desire to
enter. I was ushered in. Many questions were asked, and many forms
were completed before I received the secret pass-word, 'Straight
through and up the stairs.'

I went as directed and joined a group undressing in a too-small
ante-room. Then we, nudists, filed out and along the cocoanut mat-
ting to the stairs. At the top five doctors set to work to test our fitness
for His Majesty's forces!

We were recruits.

Match-making

A COUNTRYMAN (1940)

A social-anthropological survey known as the 'Harvard Irish Survey' conducted field research in Co. Clare in the 1930s, and its findings were published by Conrad M. Arensberg and Solon T. Kimball in their 1940 book *Family and Community in Ireland*. They write of a publican in Ennistymon, then a market town of 1,200, that 'The back room of his public house reserved for special customers became one of the centres of local match-making. It was there that the fathers of both boy and girl would meet and "sit on the match". Their deliberation, to the accompaniment of many bottles of stout, threshes out the whole matter of the disposal of the properties involved, the relative status of the families, and any possible barriers to the union, such as consanguinity, insanity, or notorious crime in past ancestry.' There followed protracted bargaining 'between the "fortune" and the farm'. The following is the oral testimony of a countryman who participated in the survey.

When a young man is once on the lookout for a lady, it is put through his friends for to get a suitable woman for his wife. It all goes by friendship and friends and meeting at public houses. The young man sends a speaker to the young lady and the speaker will sound a note to know what fortune she has, will she suit, and will she marry this Shrove? She and her friends will inquire what kind of a man is he, is he nice and steady? If he suits, they tell the speaker to go ahead and draw it down. So then he goes back to the young man's house and arranges for them to meet in such a place on such a night and we will see about it. The speaker goes with the young man and his father that night, and they meet the father of the girl and his friends or maybe his son and son-in-law. The first drink is called by the young man, the second by the young lady's father. The young lady's father asks the speaker what fortune do he want. He asks him the place of how many cows, sheep, and horses it is. He asks what makings of a garden are in it; is there plenty of water or spring wells? Is it far from the road or on it? What kind of house is in it, slate or thatch? Are cabins good, are they slate or thatch? If it is too far in from the road, he won't take it. Backward places don't grow big fortunes. And he asks too is it near a chapel and the school or near town? If it is a nice place, near the road, and the place of eight cows, they are sure to ask three hundred and fifty pounds fortune. Then the young lady's father offers two hundred and fifty pounds. Then maybe the boy's father throws off fifty pounds. If the young lady's father still has two hundred and fifty pounds on it, the speaker divides the fifty pounds between them, so now it's two hundred and seventy-five. Then the young male says he is not willing to marry without three hundred pounds – but if she's a nice girl and a good housekeeper, he'll think of it. So there's another drink by the young man, and then another by the young lady's father, and so on with every second drink till they're near drunk. The speaker gets plenty and has a good day. After this, they appoint a place for the young people to see one another and be introduced. The young lady takes along her friends, and maybe another girl, and her brother and father and mother. The young man takes along his friends and the speaker. If they suit one another, they will then appoint a day to come and see the land. If they don't, no one will reflect on anybody, but they will say he or she doesn't suit. They do not say plainly what is wrong. The day before the girl's people come to see the land, geese are killed, the house is whitewashed, whiskey and porter bought. The cows get a feed early so as to look good; and maybe they get an extra cow in, if they want one. Then next day comes the walking of the land. The young man stays outside in the street, but he sends his best friend in to show the girl's father round, but sure the friend won't show him the bad points. If the girl's father likes the land, he returns, and there will be eating and drinking until night comes on them. Then they go to an attorney until the next day and get the writings between the two parties and get the father [boy's] to sign over the land. Then there comes another day to fit her for a ring. The girl and boy meet in town some day. He buys her some present. They walk the town that day and all admire the pair and gander after them.

'The only people alive in this country is the government'

FRANK GALLAGHER (1940)

Stephen O'Mara, who ran a bacon factory in Limerick, was a long-time supporter of de Valera and Fianna Fáil. His method of lobbying de Valera – whose eyesight was severely compromised – was through Frank Gallagher, the former editor of the *Irish Press*, who, as government press secretary, had daily access. This letter from Gallagher is evidently a response to some proposal from O'Mara for an innovative approach to the economy. Gallagher's unguarded reply may reveal a strand of thinking that was more widespread in the government than it ever admitted.

Isn't it time we all faced up a bit to the truth instead of going round with every kind of flapdoodle on our lips about Christian Social systems? Didn't you get to where you are by sheer hard work? Didn't I? Why shouldn't others? Because they're all waiting for the government to live their lives for them, always provided they have as little as possible to do themselves. Look back on the position of the poor in Ireland even twenty years ago and you'll see what has been done: read the annual report of the department of agriculture and you will be amazed at the literally hundreds of ways the farmers are being helped to make money out of their land; but they will not even take the help given free to them, at the cost of fellows like you and me. Around the coasts of Kerry and Cork there is the finest fertiliser in the world – seaweed. It is there by the thousands of tons. Do the young farmers collect it? Not at all; they badger the government for a subsidy on imported guano and cart it home after a good drink in Dingle. And the government is promptly blamed when it gives a ten shilling subsidy on fertilisers for not giving twenty shillings; just as the farmers having got a guaranteed price for wheat (which the Northern farmers did not get) promptly demand as well a subsidy of £2 an acre which the Northern farmer gets instead of that guaranteed price; and when they don't get it both ways they won't extend the wheat acreage though famine may be only a year away.

No, Stephen, it isn't the government but this damned curse that is on us that we won't work ourselves and when the government works for us we sit on the ditch sneering at civil servants and talking twaddle about Christian Society. Dead? The only people alive in this country is the government.

If you write anything with thought in it I'll read it to Dev but please do stand back and give me something grown up. What is it here for instance that we have not tried that has been tried elsewhere and showed any glimmer of success? Social credit? The basis of social credit is surely the production of goods. You ask what will we use for money – what else but the exchange of goods? But if I am a farmer with butter to sell and you are a bootmaker with boots for sale, and if you take so damned long over making your boots that I must give you forty pounds of butter for them, mustn't I soon go barefoot? Say the farmer can send his forty pounds of butter to Britain and get back in value the price of two pairs of boots, would you blame him for wanting a medium of exchange other than what Social Credit can give him? Or is the new world to be one in which no one does a day's work and everyone is to have a Rolls-Royce?

No: the social revolutionaries in Ireland are all of a piece with the IRA. They won't take off their coats and devise a programme and go out and tell it to the people – that requires a mind and sincerity and hard work. It is much easier to steal some high-explosive, make it into a bomb, and blow up women and children with it. The new patriotism! God spare us all, for as sure as God made little apples it's coming to that, not only in Dublin Castle, but wherever men, unwilling to work, think to justify idleness by speechmaking and ballyhooing. I know, as you said, it is hard to be restrained. But it shouldn't be so hard to be mentally honest.

'Blindness, egotism, escapism or sheer funk'

ELIZABETH BOWEN (1940)

Resident in London during the Second World War, Elizabeth Bowen was a regular visitor to her native Ireland. During these visits she wrote dispatches to the British Ministry of Information in London. This work has sometimes misleadingly been described as 'spying'; in reality, she hoped to serve the interests of both countries by ensuring that an intelligent reading of Irish opinion was available to London. In the dispatch extracted below, she instances the 'flare-up of resentment and suspicion' in Ireland following a controversial reference by Winston Churchill to the so-called 'Treaty ports'. Under the 1921 Treaty, the British had retained control of the deep-water ports of Lough Swilly, Berehaven and Spike Island, but in 1938, as part of the settlement of the Economic War, control of the ports had returned to Ireland. Churchill, who had opposed the 1938 settlement, complained of the 'heavy and grievous burden' of the unavailability of the Irish ports to Britain at a time when German submarines were operating in Atlantic waters.

The reaction in this country to Mr Churchill's remark on the Irish ports has been very unfavourable. Even were Mr de Valera likely to be amenable, he now clearly feels himself placed, with regard to public opinion in his own country, in a position of appalling difficulty.

There seems – I have gathered from talk and the Irish papers – only one basis on which Éire would consider treating for the ports. That is, on some suggestion from the British side that the Partition question was at least likely to be reconsidered. It is felt here (I do not know how correctly) that the Six Counties' intransigence comes from British support. [. . .] The childishness and obtuseness of this country cannot fail to be irritating to the English mind. In a war of this size and this desperate gravity Britain may well feel that Irish susceptibilities should go to the wall. But it must be seen (no doubt is seen) that any hint of a violation of Éire may well be used to implement enemy propaganda and weaken the British case. Also, that aggravation of feeling in this country makes one more problem to settle after the war – or, rather, is likely to make the settlement of an outstanding problem more difficult. [. . .]

It may be felt in England that Éire is making a fetish of her neutrality. But this assertion of her neutrality is Éire's first free self-assertion: as such alone it would mean a great deal to her. Éire (and I think rightly) sees her neutrality as positive, not merely negative. She has invested her self-respect in it. It is typical of her intense and narrow view of herself that she cannot see that her attitude must appear to England an affair of blindness, egotism, escapism or sheer funk. In fact, there is truth in Mr de Valera's contention. It would be more than hardship. It would be sheer disaster for this country, in its present growing stages and with its uncertain morale, to be involved in war. That Éire might lease her ports without being involved in war is a notion the popular mind here cannot grasp. I have spoken of the horrific view held here of the Nazi bombing of England. To the popular mind here, 'being involved in war' now conjures up only one picture – a bombing of Éire. The panic caused by this is intense: it is like England before Munich, twenty times more. People say: 'We could never stand it,' and they are right. One air raid on an Irish city would produce a chaos with which, in the long run, England would have to cope. [. . .] I could wish some factions in England showed less anti-Irish feeling. I have noticed an, I suppose, inevitable increase of this in England during the last year. The charge of 'disloyalty' against the Irish has always, given the plain facts of history, irritated me. I could wish that the English kept history in mind more, that the Irish kept it in mind less.

'Ireland needed a schoolmaster'

GEORGE BERNARD SHAW (1940)

Shaw maintained a close interest in Irish affairs and was invariably pragmatic in his analysis. He appreciated the wartime challenges facing de Valera. In this letter to Alfred Douglas he chides him for failing to appreciate these challenges.

14 November 1940. Childe, childe, the Irish question is going to be a very vital one. If the submarine campaign on the west coast of Ireland continues to be successful, and we come as we did before within five weeks of being starved out, we *must* seize the Irish ports or surrender. Obviously we will not surrender for the sake of the IRA's beautiful eyes. We will exterminate the whole four millions of Irish in Ireland first. Your motion of dealing with this situation is to rake up old dirt to set the Irish by the ears again, and to call de Valera a skunk and declare that you do not care two damns about his difficulties. How much farther will that get you or anyone else, do you think?

De V. is not, as a matter of passionate fact, a skunk. He is an ex-schoolmaster of unblemished character who, when, like you, he had more courage than common sense, risked his life in the Easter Rising, and escaped hanging by the skin of his teeth. He is where he is because Ireland needed a schoolmaster very badly and had enough of hanged heroes. His difficulties, about which you do not care two damns, happen to be England's difficulties as well. If I were in his place I should probably write a very private letter to the PM as follows: 'Dear Churchill: I cannot give you the ports because I should provoke an IRA rising and lose such power for good as I have. I cannot prevent you from taking the ports, as I have only four millions to your forty, and you have America at your back this time. So for God's sake *take* the ports as nicely as you can as a temporary forced loan, promising to give them back when our common enemy the atheist Hun is disposed of. Faithfully, Eamon de Valera.'

What have you to say to that, courageous but idiotic Douglas? Which cat, by the way, are you going to bell?

A month in Irish college

DERVLA MURPHY (1941)

In her memoir *Wheels within Wheels*, Dervla Murphy writes about her father's anxiety that she become fluent in the Irish language. This prompted her parents to send her, shortly after her ninth birthday, as a boarder to Ring College in the Waterford Gaeltacht.

A few days after Christmas my mother broke it to me that in January I was to go as a boarder to an Irish-speaking coeducational school. Naturally I was devastated. It had always been understood that I would go away to school at the age of ten and I could scarcely credit my parents' treachery. But in an odd way this sense of having been betrayed kept me calm. Parents who loved me so little must not be allowed to see how much I cared – a melodramatic reaction which carried me through my initial grief and disillusionment. Then suddenly going away to school began to seem an interesting idea; to my own surprise part of me was one morning quite looking forward to it, though I had never yet been separated from both my parents for more than a few days. But soon I was again shattered by the discovery that books in English were forbidden at the College. Despair overcame me; this was equivalent to depriving an alcoholic of his bottle or a chain-smoker of his packet. Yet I never made any attempt to alter my parents' decision. On details I argued interminably with them; on major issues I meekly deferred to their adult wisdom. [. . .]

This was one of the few occasions when my father made a decision, for personal reasons of his own, to which my mother only grudgingly assented. Where the use of English was totally forbidden it seemed possible that within a year even I would have acquired a working knowledge of my native tongue. For nationalistic reasons my father wished me to be as fluent an Irish speaker as himself. Besides, if I were ever to pass an examination some action had to be taken to remove whatever blockage prevented me from learning languages. Or so my parents thought; for years they would not accept the simple fact that I had not inherited their linguistic gifts. They mistook stupidity for laziness and my mother – who held no strong views about the Gaelic Revival – probably agreed to this experiment as a general disciplinary measure.

At the beginning of 1941 the 'Emergency' had not yet banished all motor-cars from Irish roads and we drove to the College on a cold, dark, wet January afternoon. The hedges were hardly visible through swirling curtains of rain and we were all, for our various reasons, apprehensively silent. Real, live boarding-school authorities were an unknown quantity to me, but I felt that they might prove much more dangerous in life than in literature so I had been afraid to pack even one illicit book. And now I was sick with anguish at the thought of parting from my parents. When the grey school buildings loomed sombrely out of the rain and fog, on their bleak and windswept cliff above the sea, I remarked that there would be no need for any lingering once my luggage had been unloaded. And my mother agreed that this was so.

When we had said our brisk good-byes my father decisively banged the car door and I turned into a long, empty corridor. Most pupils travelled by train and had not yet arrived. A young master appeared, said something curt in Irish and disappeared, carrying my suitcases. I hurried after him, down the ill-lit corridor and up a steep staircase. The whole place reeked of Jeyes Fluid and boiled onions. Then I was put in the care (not quite the mot juste) of a freckled twelve-year-old with sandy plaits and a shrill, bossy voice. I can still see her frayed pale green hair-ribbons and her look of contempt when she realised that I understood not a word she was saying.

In the icy, barn-like, whitewashed dormitory there were no cubicles but only rows of beds with vociferously broken springs and lumpy, unclean mattresses. My bed stood almost in the centre of this desolation and as I paused forlornly beside it, wondering where to hang my clothes, I realised that such a complete lack of privacy would add an unforeseen dimension to my hell. I shivered and needed to go quickly to the lavatory. Half-a-dozen older girls were gathered in a far corner, wearing overcoats and stuffing themselves with sticky buns. When I asked for the lavatory in English one of them threw a boot at me and shouted angrily in Irish. My bladder was about to fail me and I broke into a cold sweat – literally, for I remember pushing the hair out of my eyes and noting the chilly moisture on my forehead and thinking that this must be what authors meant by 'cold sweat'. I had assumed that in extremis we could talk English; now it was plain that to do so, under any circumstances, would bring some instant punishment from my uncouth and intimidating seniors. Mercifully a lavatory chain was pulled nearby at that moment and I rushed gratefully towards the sound.

Back in the dormitory I found my suitcases open and their contents scattered on the bed. The girls were examining everything critically and the discovery of my school-books provoked much mirth; I was so tall for my age that from these they deduced extraordinary stupidity. They expressed the opinion that I must be mentally retarded by using graphic traditional gestures, while shrieking with laughter. Then they came on a packet of sanitary towels – proud emblem of my recently acquired womanhood – and used other gestures, not then understood by me; no doubt their comments were to match for they lowered their voices and muffled their sniggers. As I could see no friendly – or even neutral – face anywhere I suppressed my rage and stood by helplessly until the enemy lost interest. They left the dormitory linking arms, scuffling, giggling and shouting each other down. I thought of Mrs Mansfield, who would almost have fainted to witness such behaviour, and the image of her trim little figure, with San Toy trotting regally to heel, sent me hurrying back to the lavatory to weep. Already I had resolved that my enemies would never see me weeping.

At six o'clock a jangling bell summoned us to the refectory for high tea. Most of the other pupils had now arrived, but I seemed to be the only new girl though there were several new boys – all of whom, discouragingly, spoke effortless Irish. As I took my place at one of the long, scrubbed wooden tables, each with mounds of thick bread and scrape placed at intervals down the centre, I vowed that this educational experiment must be made to fail as expeditiously as possible. Since English was forbidden, I would not speak. And when the futility of having a dumb child about the place impinged on the authorities, they would expel me. Nothing could be simpler. As I am naturally taciturn the prospect of maintaining silence for an indefinite period did not dismay me. And to compensate for the lack of books I would secretly write one myself.

Of course things did not work out quite like this. I was far too demoralised by homesickness to concentrate on writing anything more than letters and my misery, instead of diminishing as the days passed, became more acute. There was not even one remotely congenial character among either staff or pupils and I had immediately become a favourite bullying target for the more sadistic seniors. These also regularly robbed me of my weekly food parcel – an Emergency innovation – and they did use English to threaten to retaliate if I reported them. It is easy to see how I brought out the worst in these schoolmates.

To them I must have seemed intolerably priggish, precocious, precious, pedantic and pusillanimous. There was no point of contact; in every sense we spoke different languages. Inevitably my memories of this ordeal are biased and the reality may have been a trifle less barbarous than what I recollect. Yet the essence of the atmosphere remained unparalleled in my experience until I worked as a waitress, almost twenty years later, in the canteen of a home for down-and-outs in East London.

Therefore this episode, despite its brevity, was one of the most valuable in my limited educational career. At Lismore school I was subtly accorded privileges by many of the teachers because I seemed different. At Ring I was given hell for the same reason and thus I learned that standards other than my own were not only acceptable to, but preferred by, large sections of the population.

My parents wrote long letters three times a week but refrained from squandering their petrol ration on me. In my Sunday letters home I never asked for a visit but regularly reported that I was learning no Irish and cunningly emphasised the physical hardships of school life. In fact I took these in my stride – apart from the atrocious food they seemed no worse than the rigours of home life – but I felt that my mother would be more disturbed by health hazards than by complaints about bullying. So I graphically described how – after an inadequate lunch – we were driven out every afternoon, whatever the weather, to play camogie (the feminine of hurling) on pitches hock-deep in mud – and how we then had to sit in an unheated prep. hall for two hours wearing damp socks.

These letters were not greatly exaggerated and as a result of over-exposure and underfeeding I developed severe bronchitis in the middle of February. After forty-eight hours I was almost too ill to walk, yet the matron merely dosed me with some ineffectual syrup. Everyone had sniffles and coughs and she did not pause to distinguish between penny plain and tuppence coloured. So I wrote an extra letter to my parents, one Wednesday morning.

On the following afternoon they arrived unannounced, and despite a keen east wind discerned in the distance their wheezing ewe-lamb, feebly wielding a camogie stick. Moments later I was in the car, drenching my mother's shoulder with all the tears not shed since our parting. And in the headmaster's office my father was being told that I had made little progress with my Irish and seemed 'unable to fit in with the rest'. 'I should think not!' muttered my mother, as we drove off. While I was changing and packing she had had an opportunity to observe a cross-section of 'the rest'.

The Belfast Blitz

ALFRED AMBROSE (1941)

With the exception of the London Blitz, the systematic attack by 200 bombers of the Luftwaffe on Belfast on the night of 15/16 April 1941 resulted in the greatest number of casualties in any city in the United Kingdom during the war. Nine hundred people were killed and 1,500 injured. Alfred Ambrose was an air-raid warden during the attack. In his account of the raid, he records that the sirens sounded at 22.43 p.m. on Tuesday, 15 April.

Sometime later the unsynchronised drone of enemy aircraft could be heard approaching from the direction of Knockagh Hill. It was a dark night and evidently the leaders were uncertain of their bearings, for they dropped flares. These slowly drifted in a north-easterly direction eventually falling in Belfast Lough seemingly about Jordanstown or Whiteabbey. Still the engines droned overhead and Wardens gazing upward felt defenceless and impotent. An uneasy feeling in the stomach hinted to us that we were scared though no one admitted the fact openly at the time. Further flares were dropped and this time they landed in and around the Post Area. While they were descending the whole area seemed brighter than at noon in summer-time. I looked along the street and could recognise clearly two Wardens who were 100 yards away. I felt as if I were standing in the street stark naked. As the flares touched the ground they were very promptly dealt with by Wardens who quickly had them extinguished. Ack Ack fire opened up and I began to feel better as I knew that 'Jerry' was not going to have it all his own way. The Senior Warden hastened around contacting patrols and advising that all residents should immediately take cover. He came along Veryan Gardens on his way to the Post. A minute or two later he was outside the Post at 01.55 hours with the Post Warden, who suddenly called: 'Look out!' They had just time to fling themselves to the ground when a parachute mine fell in the centre of Veryan Gardens (opposite No. 44) with a vibrating crash which seemed to shatter the entire neighbourhood. This was followed almost immediately by another gigantic crash as a second parachute mine fell on open ground at the rear of 128 Whitewell Road. The [. . .] ceiling crashed down, and the windows, door and telephone were hurled across the floor. It took a matter of seconds to turn off the gas at the meter, and scarcely had the Wardens collected their faculties after the severe blast, when they witnessed an appalling sight as some hundreds of people, verging on panic and many of them injured, came running down Whitewell Road towards the Post. This must be dealt with. [. . .]

Now we had time to make a reconnaissance of the area. Numerous houses were demolished and hundreds damaged. It was still dark but the task on hand was obviously greater than we could handle unaided. A Dispatch Rider left with a message to 'B' Group Posts asking for the help of all available Wardens. School-rooms were opened as Rest Centres, where ladies carried out invaluable work in supplying tea for the homeless and keeping hundreds of people off the streets. The 'B' Group Wardens received our SOS message as the 'Raiders Passed' siren sounded at 04.54 hours, and we shall be ever grateful to them for their splendid response. When these reinforcements arrived, daylight was breaking, and the scene was one of orderly activity. [. . .]

Not long after the mines fell a small boy was picked up in Whitewell Road by a Bombardier of the Royal Artillery, who had the lad dispatched to hospital. When this was reported to the Senior Warden he asked the Rector of the Parish to make inquiries, and inside one hour he had full information, giving name, age and hospital. This was only one of innumerable services performed by Rev. Finlay Maguire during and after the raids. He at no time spared himself. The lad referred to had lived at 128 Whitewell Road with his Grandmother, Father, Mother and a little sister fifteen months old. The three adults were killed, and, as their house was only six yards from the crater, it was merely a heap of bricks and splintered timber. A party of Welch Fusiliers under a Captain came on the scene and removed every brick and piece of debris on to what had been the garden. The Senior Warden was sent for about 14.00 hours on 16th April (about twelve hours after the mine had fallen) and the Captain asked him was he satisfied that there was no one left in the site. The Senior Warden replied: 'No. I have a fifteen-months-old child missing.' The Captain gave a gesture of despair and said: 'Where can it be?' Noticing that the ground just below foundation level had a rather churned up appearance the Senior Warden asked the Captain had he disturbed it. The Captain answered: 'No.' The Senior Warden, remembering that there are no rules for blast, thought that perhaps there had been a subsidence and that the child was trapped beneath the soil. Work was restarted and after ten minutes the little hand of the child was uncovered, feverishly the work progressed and in a few moments the hood of a Tansad [pram] was uncovered, the child called 'Mamma' and the little kiddie was lifted out unhurt. The hearts of those of us who stood around, which had been frozen in our breasts throughout the long hours preceding, seemed to melt in a glow of joy, and for the first time that day we felt like cheering. We had, however, to restrain our feelings on account of the desolation and grievous loss surrounding us.

Borstal boy observed

DEPUTY GOVERNOR G. MACFARLANE (1941)

Brendan Behan was sentenced to three years' Borstal detention at Liverpool Assizes on 29 January 1940, having been found guilty of possessing explosive substances under suspicious circumstances. He served his sentence in Hollesley Bay Colony in Suffolk. This is the prison where Behan began to write. The following is from a report by Deputy Governor Macfarlane, who was in charge of St George's House, to the Governor of the prison.

He has completed sixteen months of his sentence and is the senior colonist here. This puts him in a unique position in the eyes of the other colonists, a position strengthened by the fact that he is above the average in intelligence and facility of tongue. He is very popular with the other colonists, and although he does not fit in with our idea of a 'good prisoner' he is generally liked by the staff. His mind is lively and he enjoys juggling with words and ideas, quite undeterred by being snubbed. Challenge him to stop foolish talking and get down to serious thinking and speaking and he can do it to good account. He loves the limelight and whilst playing to the gallery he is not unmindful of the stalls. It would seem that he is making an effort to compensate for a feeling of insecurity and it is, perhaps, a saving fact that he has insight into this condition. He maintains his loyalty to the Roman Catholic Church and performs small offices at the services in spite of excommunication. He proclaims his faith in the Church in matters of religion. In political matters he maintains his belief in the justice of the idea of Irish independence. A passionate nationalist, he states that his sympathies are all on the side of Britain at the moment, because she is fighting to defend principles in which he wholeheartedly believes. He considers he was in error in joining in the 'Bomb Plan' of the IRA and says that he does not intend to engage in such activities again. The leniency shown him has made a good impression on him.

Behan has intelligence enough to keep out of trouble if he so wills it. Had this case been an ordinary one I have no doubt Behan would have been recommended for discharge after twelve months.

The Governor, Cyril Joyce, minuted the following:

I concur with all the opinions expressed therein. In my opinion Behan is deteriorating as a result of continued detention, and I consider that the best interests of the lad himself would be served by as early a discharge as is possible. He is quite clearly worried about the future, and, in spite of his constant quips and jests about religion, he is more perturbed than he would have us know about his excommunication. Whatever leniency may be possible would be appreciated by him.

This recommendation was submitted to the Home Office. In June 1941 the commissioners recommended, subject to the approval of the Secretary of State, that Behan be released 'as soon as the Borstal Association can arrange'. Indecision followed, with both the Dominions Secretary, Viscount Cranborne, and the Home Secretary, Herbert Morrison, involved. Eventually the British authorities decided to deport Behan to Dublin, having first alerted the Irish government and having obtained a promise from Behan that he would avoid the IRA. The promise was broken, and Behan was later sentenced in Ireland to fourteen years in prison for the attempted murder of two detectives.

'The life that God desires that man should live'

EAMON DE VALERA (1943)

In the year of the fiftieth anniversary of the foundation of the Gaelic League, de Valera as taoiseach used his annual St Patrick's Day broadcast to articulate his conception of the Irish way of life. Perhaps the most famous reference in the speech – to 'the laughter of comely maidens' – has occasioned some textual dispute. The text below follows a transcript that survives in the Department of the Taoiseach's archive. In the only surviving recording of the speech, de Valera says 'happy maidens' – but that is from a version prepared for use in the United States. No recording survives of the original Irish broadcast, and so it is not clear whether de Valera said 'comely' or 'happy'.

Before the present war began I was accustomed on St Patrick's Day to speak to our kinsfolk in foreign lands, particularly those in the United States, and to tell them year by year of the progress being made towards building up the Ireland of their dreams and ours – the Ireland that we believe is destined to play, by its example and its inspiration, a great part as a nation among the nations.

Acutely conscious though we all are of the misery and desolation in which the greater part of the world is plunged, let us turn aside for a moment to that ideal Ireland that we would have. That Ireland which we dreamed of would be the home of a people who valued material wealth only as the basis of right living, of a people who were satisfied with frugal comfort and devoted their leisure to the things of the spirit – a land whose countryside would be bright with cosy homesteads, whose fields and villages would be joyous with the sounds of industry, with the romping of sturdy children, the contests of athletic youths and the laughter of comely maidens, whose firesides would be forums for the wisdom of serene old age. It would, in a word, be the home of a people living the life that God desires that man should live. [. . .]

For many the pursuit of the material is a necessity. Man, to express himself fully and to make the best use of the talents God has given him, needs a certain minimum of comfort and leisure. A section of our people have not yet this minimum. They rightly strive to secure it, and it must be our aim and the aim of all who are just and wise to assist in the effort. But many have got more than is required and are free, if they choose, to devote themselves more completely to cultivating the things of the mind, and in particular those which mark us out as a distinct nation.

The first of these latter is the national language. It is for us what no other language can be. It is our very own. It is more than a symbol; it is an essential part of our nationhood. It has been moulded by the thought of a hundred generations of our forebears. In it is stored the accumulated experience of a people, our people, who even before Christianity was brought to them were already cultured and living in a well-ordered society. The Irish language spoken in Ireland today is the direct descendant without break of the language our ancestors spoke in those far-off days.

As a vehicle of three thousand years of our history, the language is for us precious beyond measure. As the bearer to us of a philosophy, of an outlook on life deeply Christian and rich in practical wisdom, the language today is worth far too much to dream of letting it go. To part with it would be to abandon a great part of ourselves, to lose the key of our past, to cut away the roots from the tree. With the language gone we could never aspire again to being more than half a nation. [...]

Let us all, then, do our part this year. The restoration of the unity of the national territory and the restoration of the language are the greatest of our uncompleted national tasks. Let us devote this year especially to the restoration of the language; let the year be one in which the need for this restoration will be constantly in our thoughts and the language itself as much as possible on our lips.

The physical dangers that threaten, and the need for unceasing vigilance in the matters of defence as well as unremitting attention to the serious day-to-day problems that the war has brought upon us, should not cause us to neglect our duty to the language. Time is running against us in this matter of the language.

We cannot afford to postpone our effort. We should remember also that the more we preserve and develop our individuality and our characteristics as a distinct nation, the more secure will be our freedom and the more valuable our contribution to humanity when this war is over.

What the GAA is really about

BREANDÁN Ó HEITHIR (1943)

Breandán Ó hEithir was a journalist, writer and broadcaster. The following is the afterword to his 1984 book *Over the Bar: A Personal Relationship with the GAA*.

Inside the sanest of us there is a wee preacher struggling to act out, and before I don my biretta and leap into the pulpit I shall tell you what the GAA is really all about; and give myself two minutes to escape. After much consideration I have come to the conclusion that the GAA is really all about Bill Doonan heading for Monte Casino. Bill was a member of a family of travellers that settled in Cavan and he was a natural footballer. He was also a wayward Paddy and having joined the Army, and been trained as a radio operator, he itched for action in the real war that raged in Europe and elsewhere at the time. Bill deserted, crossed the Border and joined the British Army.

In the autumn of 1943 the war in Southern Italy raged and Bill Doonan was radio operator with his unit. One Sunday afternoon in September he was no longer to be seen. He vanished as if the ground had swallowed him. It was considered unlikely that he had been shot as there was a lull in the hostilities at the time. It was a mystery. A search was mounted and they found him at last. Even when they did they found it difficult to attract his attention. He was up a tree on the side of a steep hill and seemed to be in a trance. And in a way he was, for, after much effort and experimentation, Private Doonan had eventually homed in on the commentary of the second half of the All-Ireland football final between Roscommon and Cavan from Croke Park.

He was too indispensable to be court-martialled and survived the war to play soccer for a year with Lincoln City and afterwards win two All-Irelands with Cavan; one in the Polo Grounds, New York, in 1947 and another in Croke Park the following year. If anyone ever asks you what the GAA is all about just think of Bill Doonan, the wanderer, on the side of that hill, in the middle of a World War . . . at home.

'Will women not vote for a woman?'

HANNA SHEEHY SKEFFINGTON (1943)

In the 1943 general election, four women stood on an independent, pro-woman platform – mooting even the possibility of the formation of a women's party. Their slogans included 'Equal Pay for Equal Work', 'Equal Opportunities for Women', and the removal of the many economic, social and domestic disabilities. Their election literature stated 'there can be no true democracy when the voice of half the community is silent in Parliament.' Hanna Sheehy Skeffington was one of these candidates. In an article in the *Bell* she wrote about the experience.

Our experiment, a bold enough challenge to masculine monopoly, failed. We were all beaten. [. . .] The net result therefore was that the same three women previously elected – Mrs Rice, Mrs Redmond, and Mrs Reynolds, called often 'the three R's', also 'the Silent Sisters' – were returned. All are widows of formers TDs. The first is Fianna Fáil, the other two Fine Gael. They are obedient party women and have never shown any interest in questions affecting women. Thus, in a total of 138, the eleventh Dáil has still but three women TDs. [. . .]

Will women not vote for a woman? They did that in that first Dáil and still do in municipal elections. Do voters dislike Independents? Possibly. Were the dice loaded in favour of Fianna Fáil [which called the election at short notice]? All these factors counted. Women, the average and sub-average, still have that inferiority complex, just as there were negro-slaves who were opposed to emancipation. Yet they did vote for women in the areas where the three previously elected women TDs stood. The party machine (true this of all the parties) is still male and still allergic to women, most of all, naturally, to Independents. (The Independent man too is disliked, because he is not amenable to the party whip.) Other factors are the increased cost of elections. Where £300 would formerly be enough running expenses

£1,000 would now be needed. Shortness of time was another handicap, for many experts declined to the last to believe that any election would take place: when it did, an appeal was successfully made to Panic – the 'Don't-swap-horses-crossing-a-stream' and 'Dev-will-keep-you-out-of-the-war' arguments. The women suffered a press boycott, that paper wall Griffith used to talk of as round Ireland, wrapped them round: and though posters did speak, they were not enough. Another factor that acts as a deterrent and handicap to the Independent is that £100 deposit, frozen until after the election and passing into the Government's maw if a sufficient quota is not obtained. [. . .]

If women in Ireland are not yet sufficiently educated politically to vote for women the blame rests largely with the various political machines that disregard them save as mere voting conveniences. Certain blame, too, of course, attaches to the women themselves, those smug ones especially, who declare that they have 'no interest in politics'. [. . .] it could be made possible to include women on each panel from each party, so that each elector could be given the opportunity of voting for a woman. (In setting up the National University Senate this principle was adopted to ensure that the Senate would not be entirely male.) A slower process would be the other alternative of peaceful penetration by women into the party machines, and of educating public opinion by training women to take more than a mere silent part in politics. Yes-women and yes-men are in the long-run mere dead weight, though parties like them. (Someone has suggested flippantly that if the statue of Queen Victoria [then still on the plinth at Leinster House] were placed inside the Dáil it might replace inexpensively one of the robots now sitting there.)

The challenge to the party-system has at least been made by the Independent women; their election campaign has set the public thinking. It took a while before the slogans 'Equal Pay' and 'A Square Deal for Women' on Dublin's hoardings were superseded by the device of 'Bisurated Magnesia'. When next an election comes the seed sown should be ready to germinate – the seed beneath the snow as [the Italian communist Ignazio] Silone calls it, speaking of those seeds of new growths that lie for a while submerged, but living.

Banana essence and the glimmer man

MAUREEN DISKIN (1945)

Maureen Diskin, born in Dublin in 1920, worked in a bank in Grafton Street throughout the Second World War. The following is from her testimony published in Benjamin Grob-Fitzgibbon's The Irish Experience during the Second World War: An Oral History.

Well, day-to-day living. We always ate well. I can't remember ever feeling strained except there were so many things you couldn't get. Bananas, for instance. You couldn't get bananas. And I remember there was a thing called 'banana essence'. If you mashed up parsnips and fed some banana essence into the mixture you could nearly make yourself a banana sandwich. Things like that. Fruit was very scarce – except local fruit like apples – but oranges and things that had to come in from abroad. I suppose people were short on vitamin C. Meat wasn't too bad. We always had plenty of meat in Ireland because there was plenty of cattle. I remember my aunt lived down in Galway, and there's a lovely lamb called Calamara Lamb, and she used to send us up a roast of Calamara lamb every week. But apart from that I can't really remember that anything was terribly scarce.

We just went about our business in a very modest way, I suppose. We went to films and we went to dances, and enjoyed ourselves generally. There was no blackout as such and there were no bombings, except the odd one, you know. It was just a bit Spartan. That's about all. Then we had no central heating.

Another thing that was very scarce was coal. They had trains running on turf and it took about six or seven hours to get from here to Galway. The turf was all damp. If you wanted to keep your stove going for a while it was very, very difficult. As I said, we had no coal and then there was very little gas. Gas was very scarce and we had what they called a 'glimmer'. The gas used to only go on for a few hours every day. You could cook your lunch on it and make your tea on it and then it would go off. But there was always a glimmer of gas coming through, maybe enough just to keep a thing simmering away if you were lucky. But there was a man going around from the gas company. He was called the 'glimmer man' and you could be fined for using this glimmer. It was very funny.

Then we had a thing called a 'hay box'; you put your container in this box, a wooden box preferably, and you put hay all around it and the heat that the hay generates will slow-cook something. You could leave it there for say twenty hours and you'd have a stew maybe. It was called a hay box.

But, basically the glimmer. People had mostly gas stoves then. There wasn't a lot of electricity. Electricity wasn't very plentiful at that stage. We had water that generated electricity but the gas was another thing that needed coal. But the glimmer man was well known throughout anywhere. He might pounce on you at any time, you know. That was about it really. We managed to survive quite well without an awful lot of discomfort. Maybe by present day's standards it would have been uncomfortable, but then people didn't expect so much, especially during the war, when you thought of the other people across the water and the discomfort they had.

Another thing then, of course, was you couldn't travel anywhere. You could barely go to England even if you had a reason. But you couldn't travel to the Continent. You couldn't travel anywhere. Boats, of course, weren't safe because they were bombing them. They were torpedoing all the boats. There was a lot of damage done to shipping around the coast of Ireland. Mines and things, you know. That's really about it. I often think that there was a huge chunk taken out of my life. I would have loved to have travelled. But six years were gone. The best years of your life. Gone.

VE Day in Belfast

JOHN HEWITT (1945)

John Hewitt, poet and museum curator, was in Belfast on the day when Victory in Europe was declared by the Allies. The following is Hewitt's account of VE Day in Belfast, from a letter to his friend R. P. Maybin.

So it's over now. The flags and bunting are a little bedraggled. The bonfires rough circular stains at the street ends. The BBC news is incredibly brief. And yet no one feels really it is over. There's Japan. There are still the thousands away from home. There are still the queues at the shops. [. . .]

I remember Armistice Day 1918 – You can't! The fog lifted and everybody shouted to the sun. This time, whether by inefficiency or forethought or just circumstance, the news came, faltered, came on. We had no spontaneity, no verve, no release. So the papers reported that it was a decorous celebration. Here or there I believe in the side alleys there was delight. In the main thoroughfares dull crowds swayed or drifted. Youngsters sang a little – nearly always 'McNamara's Band'! Abortive pathetic attempts were made at dancing. But the pubs pretended to be sold out or shut early or never opened. Somebody deliberately kept the supply of Red Flags short. At most they flew on a few public buildings. It was hard not to feel something wrong, something astray at the heart of things. Had the sirens howled the Last All Clear, had the lights really gone on for the first time instead of furtively for the last six months, we might have had the élan, the heart leaps. My own private theory unsubstantiated by any factual support is that Churchill went to Germany to take the surrender in person. Stalin protested. Montgomery told Winston to get to hell out of it. So he cancelled his Thursday broadcast and slunk home and threw his oration in the wastepaper basket. You know the one: 'Yesterday at high noon I had the good fortune to stand on German soil, soil that knew the trampling of Frederick's grenadiers, and there the flower or might of the Teuton monster came crawling, snivelling to make its last, its greatest surrender.' [. . .]

One view that most people, of all parties, seem to hold honestly [is] that Churchill should retire at once and not stay on to spoil his record. Nobody believes he'd be any use during the Reconstruction. Too many remember Lloyd George. But the stubborn old bugger insists on remaining.

A reply to Winston Churchill

EAMON DE VALERA (1945)

In his VE Day broadcast, Winston Churchill allowed himself a tilt at de Valera's neutrality policy, and in particular the denial to the British of the deep-water Atlantic ports. He stated that 'if it had not been for the loyalty and friendship of Northern Ireland, we should have been forced to come to close quarters with Mr de Valera or perish forever from the earth.' Churchill added that Britain had demonstrated 'a restraint and poise' to which he thought history would find 'few parallels', and his government had 'left the de Valera Government to frolic with the German and later with the Japanese representatives to their heart's content'. De Valera's reply was broadcast on Radio Éireann on 16 May 1945.

Certain newspapers have been very persistent in looking for my answer to Mr Churchill's recent broadcast. I know the kind of answer I am expected to make. I know the answer that first springs to the lips of every man of Irish blood who heard or read that speech, no matter in what circumstances or in what part of the world he found himself.

I know the reply I would have given a quarter of a century ago. But I have deliberately decided that that is not the reply I shall make tonight. I shall strive not to be guilty of adding any fuel to the flames of hatred and passion which, if continued to be fed, promise to burn up whatever is left by the war of decent human feeling in Europe. [. . .]

That Mr Churchill should be irritated when our neutrality stood in the way of what he thought he vitally needed, I understand, but that he or any thinking person in Britain or elsewhere should fail to see the reason for our neutrality, I find it hard to conceive.

I would like to put a hypothetical question – it is a question I have put to many Englishmen since the last war. Suppose Germany had won the war, had invaded and occupied England, and that after a long lapse of time and many bitter struggles she was finally brought to acquiesce in admitting England's right to freedom, and let England go, but not the whole of England, all but, let us say, the six southern counties.

These six southern counties, those, let us suppose, commanding the entrance to the narrow seas, Germany had singled out and insisted on holding herself with a view to weakening England as a whole and maintaining the security of her own communications through the Straits of Dover.

Let us suppose, further, that after all this had happened Germany was engaged in a great war in which she could show that she was on the side of the freedom of a number of small nations. Would Mr Churchill as an Englishman who believed that his own nation had as good a right to freedom as any other – not freedom for a part merely, but freedom for the whole – would he, whilst Germany still maintained the partition of his country and occupied six counties of it, would he lead this partitioned England to join with Germany in a crusade? I do not think Mr Churchill would. Would he think the people of partitioned England an object of shame if they stood neutral in such circumstances? I do not think Mr Churchill would. Mr Churchill is proud of Britain's stand alone, after France had fallen and before America entered the war.

Could he not find in his heart the generosity to acknowledge that there is a small nation that stood alone, not for one year or two, but for several hundred years against aggression; that endured spoliations, famines, massacres in endless succession; that was clubbed many times into insensibility, but that each time, on returning to consciousness, took up the fight anew; a small nation that could never be got to accept defeat and has never surrendered her soul? [. . .]

Meanwhile, even as a partitioned small nation, we shall go on and strive to play our part in the world, continuing unswervingly to work for the cause of true freedom and for peace and understanding between all nations. As a community which has been mercifully spared from all the major sufferings, as well as from the blinding hates and rancours engendered by the present war, we shall endeavour to render thanks to God by playing a Christian part in helping, so far as a small nation can, to bind up some of the gaping wounds of suffering humanity.

In Plato's cave

F.S.L. LYONS (1945)

In his influential 1971 book *Ireland Since the Famine*, the historian
F. S. L. Lyons summarized the impact of the Second World War on
Ireland, or, perhaps more to the point, its relative lack of impact.

On the whole it would be a fair verdict to say that Irish neutrality,
even though carried to the scrupulously correct lengths of a visit of
condolence by Mr de Valera to the German embassy on the death of
Hitler, favoured Britain rather than Germany. [...] [T]he war
brought the British and Irish economies even closer together than
they had been before, and although Ireland's imports were hard hit
by British blockade regulations (and by the desperate shortage of
shipping) her own exports of cattle and meat products rose steeply.
So, of course, did emigration and the amount of money sent home
by the many thousands of men and women who went to work in the
United Kingdom. And not only to work, but to fight as well – during the whole period of the war some 50,000 persons from the
twenty-six counties volunteered to serve in the British forces.

For those who stayed at home the war made itself felt in two main
ways. One – which was more obvious at the time, but was in fact less
important – was the inevitable consequence of inhabiting a small
underdeveloped island in a hostile world. All sorts of commodities
ran rapidly out of supply and various kinds of rationing had to be
imposed. Private motoring virtually ceased in 1943 and long-
distance travel even by public transport was not easy. Gas and
electricity consumption was heavily cut and coal was at times almost
unobtainable. There was clothes rationing, bread rationing, and a
steady reduction of other foodstuffs until at one stage the weekly
allowance per person was ½ oz. of tea, 6 oz. of butter and ½ lb. of
sugar. There can be no doubt that this created real hardship,
especially for the poor, many of whom depended very largely on
bread, butter and tea and could ill-afford to buy more expensive but

still available meat. Nevertheless, the great effort to achieve self-sufficiency, wasteful of natural resources and uneconomic as it may have been in the long run, did at least keep starvation at bay.

It was the other consequence of the war – psychological rather than material – that was eventually to prove far more significant for Ireland. This was, quite simply, her almost total isolation from the rest of mankind. At the very moment when she had achieved stability and full independence, and was ready to take her place in the society of nations, that society dissolved and she was thrown back upon her own meagre resources. The tensions – and the liberations – of war, the shared experience, the comradeship in suffering, the new thinking about the future, all these things had passed her by. It was as if an entire people had been condemned to live in Plato's cave, with their backs to the fire of life and deriving their only knowledge of what went on outside from the flickering shadows thrown on the wall before their eyes by the men and women who passed to and fro behind them. When after six years they emerged, dazzled, from the cave into the light of day, it was to a new and vastly different world.

A Catholic nation

EAMON DE VALERA (1945)

At the end of the war, de Valera assembled the Irish diplomatic corps in Dublin for a review of foreign policy. The Secretary of the Department of External Affairs, Joseph Walshe, stated in the course of this gathering that Irish diplomats 'must now go out as Apostles for this country and look for every opportunity, whether by talks or lectures or personal contacts, to do the work for which they have been sent abroad'. T. J. Kiernan, representative (effectively ambassador) to Australia, suggested that the National Film Institute should be commissioned to make a thirty-minute film of 'A day in the life of Catholic Ireland' and he exhorted his colleagues 'to try to go a little way towards our position in the 7th and 8th centuries when we were nearer to Europe, in spirit, than now. We gave then, and took no contamination and the need today is as great to give again.' The following is from de Valera's speech to the heads of missions.

Our people are exposed in an ever-increasing degree, with the advance of modern science, to the denationalising influences of Great Britain, and in a lesser, but by no means small, degree to those of the United States. These influences, coupled with the inevitably slow progress of the language revival, impose upon our officials, at home as well as abroad, a special vigilance in maintaining and increasing all the elements and symbols of our national existence which testify to our separateness. In the special circumstances of our national life, it is our duty to perfect ourselves in the knowledge of the language and history of our country, and, not only to be distinctively Irish ourselves, but to give to the externals of the nation – and in your case to our Legations abroad and everything connected with them – a distinctively Irish character. [. . .]

We are pioneers in a great cause and we must work like pioneers. It is a very special privilege to work for a country with such a noble history which, after so much persecution and reviling, is struggling to emerge from the shadow. [. . .] There is another powerful means of doing propaganda employed already to a greater or less extent by all of you according to the facilities available. Close contact with the Catholic clergy is absolutely essential for all our representatives. The Church is the best propaganda organisation in the world, and, if you succeed in impressing the clergy with the role filled by Ireland as a Catholic nation, you will secure through them the sympathy and interest of the people amongst whom they work. Visits to seminaries and colleges and Catholic institutions should be a normal part of your work. You will probably find in them more receptive audiences than amongst lay people. But the sympathy of the lay people must be won also.

Puritanism in rural Ireland

JOHN KAVANAGH (1929–47)

In a 1954 piece for the *Bell*, John Kavanagh wrote about social life in
an unnamed village in rural Ireland.

During 1929 to '32 there were at least twice as many boys and girls
between the ages of 19 to 25 years in this village as there are to-day.
There was less employment and less money but we had plenty of
enjoyment that cost us very little. [. . .] Ninety-eight per cent of the
young people were total abstainers. We had a choice of four or five
kitchen dances every Sunday night within a two-mile radius of home.
One in every four was able to play some instrument, one in ten was
able to sing – at least we thought we were. The rest were able to
dance, some of them good step dancers. We had great fun and ourselves making it.

If anybody had a big barn we cleared it out and organised a 'Hay
Dance' a few times each year. It cost 2/6 for Ladies, 3/– for Gentlemen. The profit was small, but all there was usually went to the
owner of the barn, to compensate him for having a wild gang tearing
round his house. Shouting, laughing, eating bread and jam and doing
their best to break down his barn floor. The crowd was gathered by
sending invitation cards to popular boys and girls and the organiser's
chief concern was not to make money but give an enjoyable night's
entertainment. The good name of the village depended on the way
their dances were run, and everybody helped. If a Civic Guard
[policeman] attended he paid at the door and was made respectfully
welcome. If he came in uniform it was regarded as a challenge. He
was not charged at the door, all the noise died down and the boys and
girls left the vicinity where he stood or sat. If he got a girl to dance
with him they had the floor to themselves and Fred Astaire couldn't
dance to the music they got. He usually came in plain clothes the
next time.

It was no crime for a girl to sit on a boy's knee. In fact the girl who had to sit on the bare seat was considered a wallflower. It was no crime for a boy to take a girl out to a car or even to a cock of hay during the night. It was the normal thing to do. If girls were scarce he would be asked not to keep her out for long. If he was a musician she would be asked not to keep him out for long and if he happened to be a stranger he'd be directed to the cock of hay. On the other hand if any girl went out with more than one boy she was under suspicion and there was very effective means for stopping that kind of courting. Every boy treated his girl as he expected his pal to treat his own sister.

[. . .] In summer time when boy met girl it was at the cross-roads. He cycled four to ten miles on a Sunday evening to meet her and though there might be 20 to 60 other young people at the cross she left the crowd and went with him to the nearest wood. She often got her stockings torn and laddered with briars and her face bitten and stung by midges but she thought 'twas worth it. Of course there were plenty of 'Had to get marrieds', but all the couples I've known have had very happy lives and have brought up their children in most cases better than the 'made matches'.

We thought a lot more of the fellow that got caught and married the girl than we did of the fellow who had all arranged before he married. In the odd case where the fellow let the girl down and refused to marry her, no matter how popular he was beforehand he soon found that he wasn't wanted in any company and he was the odd one that emigrated.

In 1931 we got a new parish priest. He condemned dancing in every form, even the kitchen dances were sinful and against the wishes of our Church. Boys and girls should not be on the road after dark. The curate was sent out to patrol the roads and anybody found or seen on the roads had to give their names. The people who allowed boys and girls into their home to dance were committing a grave mortal sin. The people who had a dance after a 'Station' were putting God out of their homes and bringing in the devil. Where there was dancing there could be no grace. Dancing was the devil's work. And so was company keeping. Woe to that father or that mother who allowed their daughter to go out at night. Woe to that boy and that girl who met and went to that lonely wood or that lonely place. They were damning their souls. [. . .]

The change came in every parish and before very long the odd fellow that could get a girl to meet him had to go deeper into the wood. Anybody who didn't agree that dancing and company keeping had to be sinful were dubbed Communists and were hinted at as getting money from Russia.

One day I went to confession. The priest asked me if I kept company with a girl? Yes, Father. Do you kiss her? Yes. How often? Fifty times, two nights a week. How long has this been going on? About two years. Did you ever tell it in confession before? No, Father. Why? I didn't think it was a sin. Will you promise me now not to meet that girl alone again? I won't, Father. Why? Because I'd break my promise to-morrow night. Get out of this box: you're damned. I got up and went out but he called me back. Do you intend to marry this girl? I don't know. Why don't you know? I'm not in a position to get married. Then when will you be in a position to get married? I don't know. Will you promise me to stay on the public road with this girl in future? Yes, Father.

I kept my promise but she had other ideas and soon found somebody who was willing to go so far into the wood with her that they could come out the other side and left me chewing the bushes on the roadside. The crowd left the cross-roads, pitch and toss schools started outside the pubs and before very long, being a man meant to be able to take a few pints and use dirty language. The girls were allowed to attend morning Mass, evening (daylight) devotions, then the family rosary and so to bed. If they were seen on the road even in daylight with a boy there were hints in a sermon on the following Sunday. In less than a year at least nine local girls had joined religious orders, fifteen others left for England.

Later in the essay, Kavanagh wrote about social life in rural Ireland in the immediate aftermath of the war.

One night in 1947 I drove a party to and attended a dance in Caighwell in St Michael's Hall. Just imagine calling a dance hall after a saint. On the right just inside the door was a civic guard in uniform. On the left was the C.C. [Catholic curate, assistant to the parish priest]. Along the wall on the left side was a row of girls sitting up straight with their hands crossed on their knees. There wasn't even a genuine smile on any of them. On the right was a row of men some sitting and the ones who weren't were well back off the beautiful maple well-polished floor. On the walls on both sides were large official-looking notices: Don't Throw Cigarette Ends or Lighted Matches on the Floor. Don't Leave Hats, Caps, etc., on Seats. Don't Stand on the Seats. Respectable Girls Don't Sit on Gentlemen's Knees, etc.

At the end opposite the entrance-door was a stage. The band was up there. A pianist, a piano-accordionist, a violinist and a set of drums. On the left of the stage having a good view of everything that went on was the P.P. [parish priest] . . . So I took a chance and picked what I thought was a fairly lively partner. As far as dancing went we got on all right, but I couldn't even get her to smile. I might as well be dancing with the broom. Most of the dancers went round the hall one way and that meant that she was facing the P.P. going one way and facing the C.C. going the other, so I tried going across in the middle. It actually worked. When she found that she couldn't be seen from the stage or the door she began to laugh and chat just as if she was at a real dance. I heard afterwards that if a girl appeared to enjoy herself at any of these dances she could be accused of having taken drink. On the way home some of my passengers asked me if I had enjoyed the dance. I don't remember all I said, but I told them we had more fun and freedom at the Corpus Christi Procession in Esker.

Another change is very noticeable. The boys and girls don't seem to trust each other . . . They don't want to mix. Girls seem to think it's a sin to be a girl or to act like a girl, and boys seem to think it's sissyish to want to be with girls. It's more manly to get drunk and if possible set the girls drunk also. All responsibility is taken out of young people's hands. They are bossed and controlled till they have no sense of responsibility. [. . .] If they want the 'latest' songs and music on the radio they are told they're ignorant or anti-Irish. If they read the daily paper it's mostly taken up with Church dignitaries and their goings and comings. There is very little in it of interest to young people except Little Panda or Rip Kirby. They are told all about the men that got us our 'Dearly Bought Freedom', but deep down behind our backs they are beginning to think that the slavery was better.

Should the government ban emigration?

DEPARTMENT OF EXTERNAL AFFAIRS MEMO (1947)

At de Valera's request, the Department of External Affairs produced a memorandum on the question of emigration. This document noted that it was 'the universal experience of white countries' that as agriculture improved the rural population tended to decline. The Irish situation was 'serious and sad from every point of view'; and, were it to continue, 'a decline in the national population' could be expected even if current marriage and birth rates were to be maintained.

It may be asked: if all this is so – if much of the emigration is unnecessary and due to psychological causes – why does the Government not take power, by refusing permits or passports, to restrict the number of people leaving the country. That is a big question of principle and the Government often considered it during the war years. Any such prohibition would be difficult, if not impossible, to enforce, because, unless you were to prevent people going abroad for visits, holidays, study and the like, you would have no assurance that people, who got passports or permits for such purposes, would not take up employment and stay abroad. But that is not the point. The question is not one of feasibility but of principle. It can be put in different ways. If people with money are free to invest it abroad in whatever foreign security they think will give them the best return, is it proper that the worker should be prevented from selling his labour in whatever market he considers – however erroneously – he can do so most satisfactorily to himself? Is any Government entitled – and, if so, in what circumstances – to tell a citizen that he must not leave the country but must remain at home to be available if his services are needed? No doubt, there are circumstances in which a Government would be justified in saying that. It could do it in time of war if men were required for the national defence. It could do it, for example, to prevent the fitting-out of expeditions contrary to neutrality. It could do it in individual cases to prevent the absconding of debtors or the desertion of children by their parents or the commission of crime. In our view, it can do it, too, in time of scarcity, to prevent people in key positions in production, by wantonly withdrawing their labour, causing widespread hardship and suffering to the community at large. But can you go further and, merely out of dislike for emigration and the dangers it involves, import a general prohibition, saying to young people who are intent on emigrating many of them for admittedly frivolous reasons: 'No, you must stay here. Emigration is a national evil. You have no good reason for going and you will have to face abroad conditions harmful to your moral and material welfare'? The point is one on which opinions may differ, but, to the mind of the Government, it admits of only one answer. We consider that no Government has such a right. Any such prohibition would involve an unjustifiable and dangerous infringement of the freedom of the individual. It would mean the Government substituting its own judgment for that of the individuals concerned and their parents. It would be an unwarranted invasion of human responsibility. It would lower national morale. Far from effectively counteracting the psychological causes of emigration, it would turn the country into a prisonhouse in the eyes of those who wanted to emigrate, making the far-off hills greener than ever.

Is it a sin?

THE *IRISH MESSENGER* (1948)

The *Irish Messenger*, a Jesuit devotional magazine, had a column called 'The Question Box' where readers were invited to seek clarification from a Jesuit priest on aspects of the Catholic faith. What follows is a selection from 'The Question Box' for 1948.

Q. Is it a sin for a girl to improve her looks by using cosmetics, lipstick etc.?

A. No, it is not a sin; it is a fairly harmless vanity. It is, however, 'a sign of the times', of the lessening of female modesty which is too much a characteristic of nowadays. The universality of it is not an encouraging sign. We would be better without it, and maybe betterlooking, many of us.

Q. Is it a sin for a woman not to be 'Churched' after child-birth?

A. The Ritual describes the ceremony of 'Churching' as a 'Pious and Praiseworthy custom', but does not in the least imply that it is of obligation. It is intended simply as an act of thanksgiving for a safe delivery, and for the gift of motherhood.

Q. Who is the Patron Saint of Motor Mechanics?

A. Motoring only became a serious commercial and social proposition within the last fifty years. Many of our readers can remember when the arrival of a motor car in a country town was an event to gather a crowd, and I do not think that, so far, any well-known driver has been canonised. St Christopher, however, has been universally adopted as the patron of drivers and passengers alike, so why not of mechanics also, who have some responsibility for the safety of the car.

Q. Is Anger a mortal sin?

A. It is seldom a mortal sin in itself, but often, because it carries with it the desire or intention of revenge, is a serious matter. It is put among the Deadly or Capital sins because of the number of sins it leads to, including murder. A parent may rightly and reasonably be angry with an offending child, just as God is angry with a sinner.

Q. Is it lawful to pray to win the Sweep?

A. If my memory serves me, I think this question has been answered more than once; however, let's have it again. It is lawful to pray for anything that one may lawfully desire, and there is nothing wrong in the wealth that a sweep prize brings, but don't forget what Our Lord said about the camel. Anyhow it is a good thing to pray for a prize, because then you can be sure that you won't win it if it is going to do harm to your soul.

Q. Is it sinful to open and read another person's letters?

A. It most certainly is. They are the property of the person to whom they are addressed, and nobody else has any right to read them. Parents, of course, have the right, and sometimes the duty to supervise the correspondence of their children, a duty that they will exercise with due discretion.

Q. Can I pray with my hat on when cycling or working?

A. Most certainly you can, and it is an excellent thing occasionally to pay reverence to God in this fashion, but do not make a habit of saying your morning prayers when going to work. Say them on your knees at home. They will hardly be done properly on a bicycle, or in a bus, and certainly not while working.

The bone-setter and the ungrateful electorate

THOMAS BURKE (1948)

Thomas Burke, a TD for Clare from 1937 to 1951, was a locally famous
bone-setter. The following is from his election appeal to Clare voters
in 1948.

You saw I had a tough time in 1944 to get even the fifth seat, although
I had given the use of their limbs to every class in Co. Clare without
fee or reward. [. . .] It is very disappointing when I find people so
ungrateful as to forget what I have done for them when they were no
use to themselves or anybody else, only a handful of shattered bones.
Now when they can do their daily work, I should expect a simple
stroke of a pencil – that is the only compensation I seek or get. [. . .]

As ever, the same old bone-setter, Thomas Burke.

'Witch-finders and orthodoxy-mongers'

ANONYMOUS (1950)

A carbon copy of a letter to Eamon de Valera was found – unsigned, but with a return address at St Finbarr's seminary, Cork – among the papers of Séamus Fitzgerald, a Fianna Fáil politician. It seems likely that the copy was given to Fitzgerald, the original having been signed by one of his supporters. Fitzgerald had been elected a TD for the Cork city constituency in 1943, and had failed to retain it in the 1944 election. What was now troubling the writer was how Fitzgerald was being treated by the Fianna Fáil organization in Cork.

We are concerned with Séamus Fitzgerald, not as a personality, but as an individual whose rights have been grossly violated by that local band of witch-finders and orthodoxy-mongers which was once the Cork Fianna Fáil Organisation. You know Séamus's background. In the Black and Tan days, he was a Volunteer, not great but painstaking and devoted. In 1921 he declared himself anti-Treaty and went into the wilderness with the same constancy as others. In the years that followed he became a TD, a Senator, a nothing, as the vagaries of the Fianna Fáil machine dictated. Ever (and unappreciatedly) reasonable, we saw him once, twice, three times, pushed aside by ruder vessels. 1950 saw him unrecognised but faithful to Fianna Fáil. The same 1950 saw him Chairman of a local cultural Society, the Cork Ballet Corps. High-browism, if you like, but surely not criminality or political heterodoxy. Sometime this Spring, the Ballet Corps had a desire, which comes on all artists, to present their talents to the widest public possible. To that end, they invited members of the Executive Council (including the Taoiseach) to see their performance. Some measure of entertainment was indicated; the Chairman of the Corps did his obvious social duty. And for that he is EXCOMMUNICATE. The important point. The action of the Cork F.F. Executive surprised no one who knew the members. We expected the narrowness of a Wee Free Conventicle [a minority remnant of the Free Church

of Scotland]. We got it and then we did await with expectancy vigorous action and protest from HQ in Dublin. We have waited a month.
We hear of vague futile noises of disconcertment. Nothing else. The
whole episode is utterly upsetting.

Emigrating to England

DÓNALL MAC AMHLAIGH (1951)

Dónall Mac Amhlaigh was born in Galway and grew up there and in Kilkenny. He left school at fifteen and worked in various jobs before joining the Irish-speaking regiment of the army. When he left the army in 1951, he emigrated to work as an unskilled labourer in England. His book in Irish covering this experience was translated by the diplomat and writer Valentine Iremonger as *An Irish Navvy: The Diary of an Exile*. This excerpt is the entry for Monday, 12 March 1951, the day he emigrated.

This morning I signed on for the last time and then carried a hundredweight of coal home for my mother. I have everything done for her now, the garden planted and cleaned and the old house spruced up a bit on the outside. I'll be able to help her a bit more than that from now on when I'll have the few pence to send to her from England. I spent the day putting some kind of order into the old box that I keep my papers in and then I went around saying goodbye to the neighbours. Peter's wife was very sorry at my going, the creature. She was kindness itself always and, as for the other people in the district, it would be hard to surpass them. I'd have liked nothing better than to have been able to visit my relatives and old friends back in Galway but, alas! I've only enough to get me across the water with a bit to spare.

The old lady kept her courage up wonderfully until the time came for me to set off. The tears came then. I didn't delay too long bidding her good-bye. I hugged her once, grabbed my bag and off with me. Indeed, you'd think that even the cat knew I was going for she followed me out mewing piteously. I stood at the head of the boreen to look back at the house, and there I saw my mother with her left hand up to her mouth as was her habit whenever she was worried about something.

Who did I meet then, as I was crossing the bridge, but Sonny

Campbell. Sonny spent a long time in the British Navy and anyone would think that he gets money from the British Government for sending people over from Ireland to join up. He's always running down this country, saying that it's ridiculous for people to stay here seeing the good wages to be had beyond. Some of the lads have a bit of devilment with him, rising him and quizzing him about life over there; but I've noticed that Sonny himself shows no sign of moving across. He paused when he saw the bag that I was carrying. 'Are you crossing over?' he enquired, with some satisfaction you might think. 'I am, brother,' I said. 'Good man,' he replied rubbing his hands together, 'it won't be long till there's nobody left here at all. They're all going. What is there for them here? You'll never regret it. It won't be long till I'll be crossing myself. Well, good luck to you.' He shook hands with me and took himself off, as pleased as if I had pressed a half-sovereign into his fist. [. . .]

As I went on to the platform to get on the train, my old dog Toppy was at my heels, however the devil he managed to follow me without my being aware of him. He looked so lonely sitting there on the platform that a lump came into my throat as the train pulled out. I kept my nose to the window until Three Castles, Dunmore and Ballyfoyle were out of sight. I sat back then and wasn't interested in anything else.

There was a good crowd on the boat with me. The *Princess Maud* we were on and my courage came back to me quickly enough once I found myself amongst them. Before I had been two minutes aboard, who did I meet but the big fellow from Tooreen who had come into Renmore last year to enlist; and a girl from the same place with him. They were off to London and there was another girl from round about Oughterard with them also. We got together straight away and I didn't feel at all lonely while I was with them. The Irish of the girl from Oughterard wasn't as good as the Irish the other two spoke but there was nothing wrong with her apart from that. I met many people from those parts that hadn't any Irish at all.

We had only time to have a drop of tea when the boat started moving and before we knew where we were, we were edging away from the quay. I got well to the back of the boat to have a good gander at

Ireland and the bright lights north there of Dun Laoire; and, suddenly, I felt lonely all over again. I started thinking about the old house with the pots of tea that we'd drink before going to bed and my heart felt like a solid black mass inside my breast. I didn't leave the place until the last light had sunk out of sight. Only then did I go looking for the other three.

I stood on John Bull's territory for the first time in my life on Tuesday morning when I got off the Irish Mail at Rugby. I don't count Holyhead for that's really Welsh and there was as much Welsh spoken there as there was Irish on a fair day in Derrynea. I lost my friends in the customs hall and I never saw them again. [. . .]

I slept most of the way from there to Rugby and, when I left the train, I had a two-hour delay before I caught the train to Northampton. My heart sank altogether then as I stood and looked around at the dirty ugly station. Everything looked so foreign to me there. Round about six o'clock hundreds started pouring into the station, pallid pasty faces with identical lunch boxes slung from their shoulders. They were all getting the train to work and their likes were getting off the train at the same time coming to work in Rugby, I suppose. God save us, I murmured to myself as I thought that nobody in Ireland would be even thinking of getting out of their beds for another couple of hours yet!

The Mother and Child Scheme

SEAN O'FAOLAIN (1951)

The Mother and Child Scheme, intended to improve the state's provision of health services to pregnant women and young children, was introduced in the Dáil by an inexperienced health minister, Dr Noël Browne. The opposition of the medical profession and the Roman Catholic hierarchy – which viewed it as socialism – prevented the legislation from being enacted. Browne resigned and published the correspondence between government and hierarchy, which revealed how willing were his fellow ministers to take instruction on this matter from the bishops.

Now that the excitement aroused by the Mother and Child Scheme has died away and we can detach our emotions and our thoughts from the accidents and personalities involved, the issue becomes a bit easier to define. The issue is that no country can be ruled 'democratically' by two parliaments; or at least not as the world understands that word.

Here in the Republic, as this crisis has revealed to us, we have two parliaments: a parliament at Maynooth and a parliament in Dublin. I do not know whether a country can be ruled satisfactorily by two parliaments; ours has – as this crisis has suddenly revealed – been so ruled since it was founded. It is for the people of the Republic to decide whether they consider it a satisfactory system. It is certainly not an entirely democratic one. Personally, I am not sure that I much care about its not being entirely democratic, but I suspect that I am in a minority. [. . .]

Nobody, so far as I have observed, has denied the right of the Catholic bishops to 'comment'; or to give 'advice' on proposed legislation; or to enunciate the official attitude of the Roman Catholic Church to proposed legislation. That principle is fully and wholeheartedly admitted. I believe that not even the most ashen-jawed, beetle-browed, black-bowler-hatted Orangeman in Portadown could reasonably object to that principle. I doubt if anybody, north or south, could even object to the Hierarchy publicly condemning any proposed piece of legislation, provided that, in the end, it is the Parliament which freely decides. I doubt if there is a single Bishop in the Republic, or in all Christendom, who would wish to controvert this. In practice, the Hierarchy does much more than 'comment' or 'advise'. It commands. [. . .]

The relationship between Church and State always has been, and always must be, a healthy struggle, in which the Church will properly, *but always prudently* fight for power, and the State will always try to restrain that power within due limits. There is no other way in which the thing can work. There is no other way in which it has ever worked. The whole history of the Italian city-states – the whole life-story of Dante – illustrates this: shews us that if that prudence on the one hand, and that restraint on the other, are not effective, you get a condition in which the laity has responsibility without due power and the Church has undue power without responsibility. In that state of affairs the Church will be blamed, and rightly blamed, for such things as infant mortality, slums, and poverty, and the State will be hamstrung. Then you really would have the tragedy of a so-called 'Catholic country'.

Moreover, it is the duty of Parliament, as Catholics, as Christians of any denomination, to resist the Church for its own sake. For more and more the Church here is approaching near to this point of undue power without due responsibility, and the more she approaches this dreadful position the more will the people lay at her doors the blame for human misery. Do we desire a state of affairs to arise here wherein a form of bitter anti-clericalism may develop, and wherein people like, let us say, Dr Browne, find themselves in the miserable position of defending the Church in a bitter internecine struggle against the super-loutish revolution of an unthinking and maddened mob?

Is this a fantastic picture: something that 'could not happen here'? It has happened elsewhere, in countries as religious-minded as Ireland. I need only mention Spain in our own day. There is, one agrees, no comparison – at this moment: but that is the way things came slowly to a head there, and sooner or later, if undue intervention by the Church is not resisted by the State, must be the way things happen in every country, including this. [. . .]

Some may also say, some also said that the Church has no interest in politics and is only concerned with morality. Certainly, in an absolute way of speech, we may suppose that no Church is concerned about the secular affairs of a nation. But, here at any rate, in a divided country, politics and religion are inseparable in practice and the recent decision of the Hierarchy has, in practice, had a pulverising political effect. I refer, of course to Partition. We must presume that their Lordships, being far-seeing men, weighed it all up, and came to their decision that the unification of Ireland must be sacrificed to higher considerations. And this, evidently, is one other thing which we must accept henceforth as a fact in Irish life. To adapt Pitt's famous remark, we can now roll up the map of Ireland: it will not be wanted for a hundred years.

The North, however, has been both ingenuous and disingenuous about the whole affair. On the one hand it is not likely that State Socialism – of which Dr Browne's Scheme was felt to be the thin end of the wedge – would be madly popular with the North. Therefore they should, in honesty, have given three cheers for the bishops. On the other hand the old cry that Home Rule means Rome Rule is unsophisticated to the last degree. For who would object – except the sort of fanatic whose comment on the proverb 'Rome was not built in a day' was, 'It should never have been built!' – who would object if the Vatican stood where Maynooth stands: with all its ancient culture, its human wisdom, its political intelligence, its immense tolerance, its rich traditions, its prestige and its panoply? Would, indeed, a thousand times over that Home Rule meant Rome Rule! And since our only concern now, at this stage, is to see coldly and unsentimentally, what we really are, and where we may be going – and to avoid deluding ourselves that we are something which we are not – we must, I suggest, see this as the dim outline of the best possible future: to wit, a Church humanised and sophisticated, with a world-outlook and a universal culture, in about the same relation to the secular Parliament of Éire as the Vatican bears to the Parliament of Italy. Give us that and what a happy country we should be!

It seems, the Browne affair has closed a whole volume of Irish history. The so-called Republican tradition and all the by-echoes of that tradition – in so far as they ever really clarified themselves – are washed up: 1916 and Fenianism, '67 and '48, Wolfe Tone and the French Revolution. Out of the nineteenth century only one man – O'Connell – remains, and if any statue is to be put up outside the Dáil to replace Queen Victoria it should be to O'Connell. All our latter-day political alignments that do not go back to him have become meaningless, Fianna Fáil, and Fine Gael and Clann na Poblachta; and any others after them will be just as meaningless unless they stem in some fashion from O'Connellism. For his concept of democracy is the only one that has lasted: and not only, and not least because he worked with the Church but because when occasion demanded it could, and did, resist [it] to the limit in the name of the struggling poor whom, like a Vulcan manufacturing thousands, he hammered into the shape of a nation. Republicanism, we see at last, never did work. It gradually became verbiage and was, in our time, finally subjected in the Dáil, on a famous occasion, to the fit if shameful tests of the Oxford Dictionary. It broke in de Valera's hands. Costello and MacBride gave it decent burial. The only possible triumphant movement of the future will, whatever it calls itself, be far removed from all that. It will be a Christian Radical Movement; which, allowing much for his times and personal limitations, was what O'Connell tried gropingly to adumbrate for Ireland and the world. It is extraordinary that Ireland, so famous for its religion and its rebels, should have so far shown no signs of that movement, except one, rash, brilliant young man, whose appearance in public life instantaneously produces a universal shout of *Masks on, God Save Ireland*, and *Sauve qui peut*.

The Presentation nuns go to the beach

KATE O'BRIEN (*c.* 1933–53)

The writer Kate O'Brien had two aunts who were nuns in the Presentation order in Limerick. In one of her later books, *Presentation Parlour*, she wrote portraits of her aunts, the last surviving being her Aunt Fan, whose vocation to enter the enclosed order was attributed to the fact that her elder sister Mary was mistress of novices. With Mary's death, Fan lived the rest of her convent life without her main confidante.

She was in her sixties now, and still had a long way to go; but not, naturally, at a hard pace, or under any pressure, for she was by now the convent pet and its invalid queen; with the years she was to become its doyenne, a golden jubilarian, and the oldest member of the community.

But suddenly in the 1930s she witnessed a revolutionary change in the Presentation rule. From its foundation the order was an absolutely enclosed one. This enclosure within what was now a near-slum combined with hard work in hot and overcrowded classrooms made for much ill-health among the younger nuns, and for some nervous breaks. So the Bishop of Limerick ordained that for one month of the summer vacation the community should withdraw to some house in the country or by the sea, waiving entirely for that one month their rule of cloister. There was consternation at first in the community room, and some weeping and heart-searching in the cells. Fear entered many of these locked-away breasts. The Bishop ordained however, that no matter their first scruples, all nuns under fifty were put on obedience to go to the seaside house; but he allowed the elders of the community to decide for themselves whether to obey him or to adhere to their original vow.

This permission was of deep relief to Fan, who was totally adjusted now, on her own invalid terms, to the rule she had sought to live by, and felt anyhow that without Mary to guide her she could not by any means consider facing such an unimaginable thing as the modern outside world. The young nuns rallied from their first shock, and soon found themselves delighted, exhilarated by the prospect of seeing again the sea and fields and roads and houses – all that they had by no means forgotten. A suitable house was engaged at a suitably lonely and wild village on the Atlantic coast, a village where other communities of nuns regularly took their summer holiday. Talk at recreation in the community room was soon all about the astonishing holiday to come, and the journey by private *chars-à-bancs* across Co. Clare. Some of the young nuns knew Co. Clare, and talked of passing by Bunratty Castle, and the town of Ennis, and the rolling, green lands about Ennistymon, and where the sea just appeared – at Lahinch they thought they remembered.

Aunt Fan listened to them all with the benevolence which now in age was making her so much a favourite with the younger nuns. When they began to cut out bathing costumes for themselves – huge affairs from vast rolls of black cloth – she was at first shocked, but then began to take an interest in the strange labour. Then she found that only a very few of the old sisters, two or three very old ones, were going to stay at home. This pained her. Their vows, her vows, after all, had been taken a long time ago – and she had no desire to alter hers, or see the changed, modern world at all. And when one day she discovered Bernardine and Benignus – almost her contemporaries – excitedly cutting out their bathing suits, her astonishment grew very deep indeed.

In her later years Fan had not troubled her confessor over much with her scruples. As a young nun confession had tormented her and she in consequence had tormented various unfortunate chaplains with her doubts and fancies – as well as tormenting her patient sister Mary. Indeed there was a story from her confessional that a weary priest said to Fan once: 'You'd better talk that over with Sister Margaret Mary.' And Aunt Mary had indeed, over the years, trained her to go to confession calmly, and to stop plaguing her confessors about mere nothings. Now however a scruple took hold, or a temptation, or a fit of plain envy. She began to fret; she prayed very much, to her sister Mary as well as to many saints, that she be guided for the best in this matter of her vow, and that she might do God's will. There can be little doubt that she gave the chaplain a great deal to listen to, and she certainly worried herself into a deepened condition of in-validism.

Well, to cut a long story, the 1st of August came, and my sister Nance with her little son drove to the Presentation Convent in the morning, to see this really historic exodus. And there, ready before all the others, alone and beautifully stowed in comfort in the best seat in the leading *char-à-banc* sat Fan. Smiling like a seraph, irradiating the happiness of a child.

And for the remaining twenty summers of her life, she was a demon of zest for the summer holiday. Though of course she never swam, or made herself a bathing suit. She was content to direct the younger nuns from the rocky shore.

She was very gentle in old age, and though she would never cease from worrying about Katty's children and Annie's, even she had to grow calm before the ups and downs of our fortunes, accept the wil-ful and foolish things we did, and simply continue to ask God to guide us better henceforward. We all kept in touch with her over the years, we all were very fond of her – and it was fun when one returned to Limerick to go and sit for many hours with her in the same unchanged parlour, and to try to eat the terrific lunch that she would have commanded. And I recall a story against me in relation to one such return-of-the-native visit. It seems that at the date lipstick, already a commonplace in London, had not yet reached Limerick, and I visited Fan in my best suit, and in general I hope suitably groomed. Well, she made no comment – admired my clothes, I imag-ine, for she always loved to discuss what one wore, and she seemed to find me in satisfactory order in general. There was no distressing per-sonal remark of the kind she was famous for when we were younger, and still could make upon occasion. *But* – the minute I left her, she wrote in despair to my sister Nance, with whom I was staying, an exclamatory, frightened letter about poor Kitty's painted mouth! And what on earth had come over the child? What would her darling mother have said? And what was to be done about it?

When my first novel came out, *Without My Cloak*, she wanted very much to read it. Nance explained to her that it was not reading for nuns, and that it would only upset and puzzle her. But still she fretted. So my kind sister took a copy, went through it and pinned certain pages together at several points. 'Now, Fan,' she said, 'if you don't move the pins you ought to be all right.' And Fan did not move the pins, and she was all right. [. . .]

In 1948 Fan celebrated her eightieth birthday and her sixtieth year as a nun, her golden jubilee. Thereafter, benignly and even wittily, she did in an unofficial sense more or less rule the Presentation Convent; and in many letters, while the strong handwriting grew feeble, she kept her fond sway over the family. She had always in my memory been large, and now in her uncountable shawls and veils grew larger, larger and very handsome, her smooth face white, her nose most shapely and straight, her pale blue eyes shining tranquilly through gold-rimmed glasses. She grew, as I have said, to be very like Pope John XXIII. She died slowly and peacefully, when she was eighty-five, in 1953. In the odour of sanctity indeed, and very much mourned by a community of nuns who had grown to venerate as well as love her.

So there they pass, my aunts. No one but I will care about their 'short and simple annals'. Yet it has rested me to set them down, and to try to find in their modest lives the essence of them. That I have not done. They elude me yet – they in their outward similarities of tradition, education and faith; in their agreement in bigotry, prudery and innocence; in their shared loves and anxieties and their half-concealed antipathies. In the relative simplicity of their obscure lives they were close to each other, all five; in the intricacies of their feelings they were much divided, and often estranged. And for all my searching back, for all my will to reach them, I have not found the very heart of any one of them. So now I can only say goodbye to them, ask them to forgive my impertinent affection, my vulgar probing, and wish that they rest forever in peace.

Bogs of irrationality

c. s. andrews (1953)

In 1933, the new Fianna Fáil government put C. S. 'Todd' Andrews in charge of the Turf Development Board; and in 1946 he became the first managing director of Bord na Móna. In a 1953 article for the journal *Administration*, he considered the complicated relationship between the Irish and turf.

It is [. . .] common for us to find men in all wise equal – in education, technical skill, home and school background and physique – going to work on the bogs and reacting to them in exactly opposite ways. The one is depressed and overwhelmed; the other fascinated and stimulated. Some we know have made considerable financial sacrifices and taken up occupations much less attractive by ordinary standards rather than face the bog. Again there are on the bogs today men who have rejected offers of much more remunerative employment under more attractive conditions, to stay on the bogs. Ordinarily we find that we rarely meet a fellow citizen who hasn't an *attitude* to turf. It appears that it is not enough to express an opinion on some problem of turf but it is also necessary to add an expression of feeling on the subject. One does not have *feelings* about questions like, say, oats, but certainly turf does produce reactions; Irish people don't ever seem to be indifferent to turf and indeed this attitude whether sympathetic or antipathetic can very often take quite extreme forms. A man long since settled in the city, surrounded by gas and electricity, claims with pride to have been born on the bog and recalls with pleasure the sleans [turf spades] and footing and the bringing home the turf on the ass-cart. A pleasant winter evening spent in the good fellowship of a country home is crystallized for him in a beautiful memory of the smell of the turf. To cut away bogs by machines is to him a desecration – produce more turf certainly but by using bigger and better sleans. In the same category, but more extreme in sentiment, are those whom we might call the votaries of An Fod Mona. Here turf becomes a symbol of something good in the nation's life, the source of a permanent pipe dream of simple living, of bawneens, ceann easna, and red petticoats, a sort of Celtic Arcadia peopled by Christy Mahons and Pegeen Mikes. These attitudes and these feelings, charming and romantic as they are, do not help to create the psychological climate necessary to establish a large industry. Far from wittingly they assist the 'bog trotter' and 'bog latin' school of thought to whom the bogs are not merely distasteful but the source of mental nettle-rash. Here we have the irrational at its most interesting. We have known a man of some achievement not merely state but evangelise the idea that a knowledge of simple arithmetic was incompatible with an interest in the bogs. We come across economists, in all other things rational, who refuse to believe that a pound sterling earned by the bogs has the same value as a pound sterling saved by not importing oil, and indeed we have heard the suggestion made that the use of turf might lead to laxity in sex morals.

The vanishing Irish

MARY FRANCES KEATING (1954)

A collection of essays, *The Vanishing Irish*, caused a major controversy in Ireland in the 1950s. Its dominant theme was that the Irish who stayed in Ireland were reproducing at such a low rate that the nation was destined for extinction. The book's editor, Fr John O'Brien, a professor of theology at Notre Dame University in Indiana, wrote that one friend, on his return from Ireland to the United States, told him that more than half his old schoolmates – now in their mid fifties – were still unmarried. They were 'a self-centered lot . . . a disgrace to the nation. A good stiff tax on them and on spinsters to help young couples get started would spur many to action.' Among the book's contributors was the journalist Mary Frances Keating, who wrote on the marriage-shy Irish male.

How do Christian people, who do quite earnestly seek for spiritual guidance in their daily lives, deny by their actions that they believe that God's holy will should be done in all things or that they believe in the humanity of Jesus Christ? Why do they let a cold and materialistic outlook govern their actions and their dealings with one another until malice and frustration come to triumph over love and the fulfilment of a normal life?

As a matter of strict fact, normally sound people would not be so bitterly sex-conscious as we are now in Ireland. It is as bad and humiliating to be undersexed as to be oversexed. Surely sex is inherent in every human being living in a natural and unaffected way, and it is utterly wrong to seek to impose an education which tends to outlaw sex as an indecent and unworthy thing. Yet that is the general tendency of education both in the home and in the school.

It is, of course, neither today nor yesterday nor the last generation nor the generation before that nor the generation before that again that Irishmen were being rated for their coldness and disregard for women. So at least we must be fair and not pile all the blame for the fact that the race is at the vanishing point upon the shoulders of those few Irish who are extant today. [. . .]

To what extent have parents implanted in their children's minds a base and un-Christian idea of the iniquity of sex? To what extent have they exalted the idea of the celibate life, and how has this idea reacted upon the minds of young people?

The boarding-school system, which has contributed to a great extent toward relieving parents of the responsibility of rearing their children, has also contributed in no small measure to the idea of the segregation of the sexes. To keep youths disciplined, it is necessary to create bogies for them all during their scholastic lives. True to the ungenerous Celtic tradition, this bogy, more often than not, takes shape as a woman. Youths are led to believe that girls are nothing less than manifestations of Satan. Women are there to entice and destroy them. Should a youth as much as look at a girl, she will ruin his purpose and prevent him from getting exams.

Don't think I trifle. This is a very serious consideration with the young in a country where 'book learning' and the pursuit of respectability, with a pensionable white-collar job attached, is still the fetish of a whole nation. The misguided young man, if he persists in frequenting the society of his sister human beings, may find himself further seduced. He may be 'hooked' into matrimony: made to sweat and slave to maintain a wife and family, give up his 'independence', leave his mother and comfortable home, sell his freedom-loving soul for a woman, a creature who in the Irish vernacular is but the image of Satan.

Given the sort of education which has tended from the beginning to create an illusion of voodoo where sex is concerned, no wonder the Irishman shuns marriage as he has been taught to shun the devil. All this may suggest an almost monastic state of chastity on the part of the menfolk. Regrettably, this is not the case. A 2.46 per cent illegitimate birth rate is not high in comparison with the rate in other countries, but one wonders if the figures can be regarded as reflecting the real situation. In Ireland illegitimate births are frequently concealed, and young unmarried mothers are usually hurried out of the country 'with a 10 pound note and the parental injunction not to show their faces at home again'.

We talk a lot about the Oedipus complex, the Jansenistic outlook, the ascetic monasticism of the Irish race – and get nowhere. Heaven knows what we really should discuss would be the institution of a saner approach to education, not as a means to 'exam cramming', but as a means of preparing human beings for the art of living in a dehumanized and rather crazy world.

Instead of feeding the young with a badly assorted mess of raw materialism and predigested escapism, educationists might be persuaded to study the humanities a little and, seeing the urgency of the case, to encourage young people to mix with each other in a spirit of respect and affection. In the home there might be less moral chastisement from the elders for the faults which they imagine themselves to have committed for bringing youngsters into the world.

In general, there might be less drinking and more laughter, less bragging about our noble inheritance of culture from the dead kings of Erin and much – oh! so much – more concern for the happiness and well-being of the adolescents. Then they would know something of the wider and more gracious life of sharing, especially in such essential matters as good will and love and marriage.

Kavanagh in court

ANTHONY CRONIN (1954)

The poet Patrick Kavanagh sued the *Leader* magazine over a profile it published of him, which he considered libellous. The case came to trial in 1954. Anthony Cronin described the trial in his memoir *Dead as Doornails*. The former and future Taoiseach, John A. Costello, was the barrister cross-examining Kavanagh.

Histrionically both parties were superb: Costello comically sharing his incomprehension with the jury; Paddy dropping pearls before swine in prolonged, nasal Monaghan vowels which gave an impression of the utmost distaste. Then across this masterly dialectic, subtle and self-contained, fell the outrageous shadow of Brendan [Behan]. The gods had decided to turn high comedy into low farce.

On the fourth day Costello quietly and without apparent relevance asked him if he was a friend of Brendan Behan's. The object at that stage may only have been to associate him with somebody disreputable. No harm would have been done if Paddy had replied noncommittally, or casually, or even declared that he was unfortunately acquainted with the said party. Instead he grew almost hysterical. In high and passionate tones he described Behan as a low blackguard who followed him about, shouting after him in the streets and forcing him to run away. Anybody who knew Paddy and the relationship such as it was could have testified to the truth of this picture. Unfortunately the protest was too shrill. The jury were sharp fellows. They exercised their intelligences in the only way common humanity knows how. They looked for the motive.

When I came out of the packed courtroom Brendan was, oddly enough, in the hallway. He had a heavy growth of beard, the blue suit was even more crumpled and stained than usual and the open-necked shirt was torn down the front. Whatever his role was, that of despised proletarian writer or rough diamond among the dishonest sophisticates, he was got up for it. He was also evidently drunk.

It was a surprise to see him there, for this was the first time he had been anywhere near the proceedings. He shouldered his way through a knot of people towards the outer door and towards where I was standing. I thought he was going to speak to me but he did no more than mutter something about the Monaghan bogman as he passed. I didn't want a scene, but I had hoped for more.

On the next day, early in the proceedings, Costello produced his secret weapon, his Zinoviev letter. Amid the sort of hush which pervades a courtroom when the audience realizes that here at last is what it came to witness, he handed Paddy a copy of his own book *Tarry Flynn* and asked him to read the inscription on the flyleaf. It said: 'To my friend Brendan Behan on the day he painted my flat'. The effect was calamitous. The jury now had something they could understand, and they were no longer afraid. Up to that point they had been to some degree intimidated by attitudes they could no more comprehend than they could the mysteries of their own religion, but which a good deal of their conditioning had led them in some obscure way to respect. Now the god had died. Kavanagh was like themselves, a fallible mortal who tried to get away with it when he could. The broad smiles with which they witnessed his discomfiture were those of fellowship and understanding.

The book had of course no relevance whatever to the issues of the trial, but it finished Kavanagh off with the good men and true. What was worse from his own point of view was that it made him uncertain and affected adversely the Parnassian way in which he had hitherto conducted his own part of the proceedings. It was not just that he had been found out, it was that his obsession with Behan and with plots and counter-plots took over. To be too much concerned with anybody, whether through love or hate or fear, or even merely an ungovernable distaste, is to give them power over you.

In fact the moment Costello sprung his trap I had remembered the strange freak of chance that gave him the opportunity. Paddy had been destroyed by the one and only occasion, certainly more than two years before, on which he had ever allowed himself to talk to Brendan in amity. One Sunday night, towards the ultimate end of the Catacombs as a gathering place, there had been a rather nondescript party with a good deal of tuneless song and repetitive argument. At the height of the proceedings, such as they were, in came Brendan, and, to my extreme surprise, Kavanagh. That Kavanagh should have come there was strange enough; that he should have come with Brendan was incredible.

He had a way when entering any gathering of announcing his presence immediately. His was a speaking part, and everybody knew it. Immediately on entering a room or a pub he would deliver himself of his thought of the moment as if it was so exciting that he could wait no longer. On this occasion he came straight over to where I stood and said: 'I've discovered another fallacy. They were telling us lies. It's not true about oil and water. Not true at all. They do mix.' At first I thought he was talking metaphorically about himself and his companion, but it turned out that he meant literally oil and water. The discovery had been made when Behan, who was painting his flat preparatory to the arrival from America of a rich woman in whom he reposed some hopes, had used water instead of turpentine to thin out the paint. How it came about that the same fellow was allowed inside the door I could only guess. In his enthusiasm about the prospect of entertaining the lady, Paddy had evidently assented to the proposition of some third party that Behan was the very man for the job, being in the trade and able to knock off some paint – an important consideration – and Behan of course had leaped at the chance. The day was one of those islands of amity which occur when the stronger, or at least the besieged, party in such a relationship weakens for the moment, nearly always to his subsequent regret. The *rapprochement*, if it can be called such, lasted for that Sunday only, but it was a Sunday which was to rise again above the waters of time, to Kavanagh's amazement and dismay. On that far away day had occurred, all unbeknownst to him, The Convergence of the Twain. [. . .]

On the night it all ended he and I and his brother went to the nearby Ormond Hotel. At least four of Paddy's women friends were in and about the place, hoping to be the chosen sympathizer, but we secluded ourselves in an inner room, and there we attempted a statement. When we failed to make much fist of a joint attempt, the brother suggested that we should sit down separately, make drafts and then compare and combine them. 'After all, we're all writers here,' he said. To which Paddy replied with comic resignation, 'Ay, ay. All brothers of the pen.'

The lawyers countermanded the issue of a statement because an appeal had been decided on. Then the question of costs was discussed between the brothers. Fearing secrets, I attempted to leave, but was told peremptorily to stay. I learned at least a good deal about Paddy's circumstances that I had not known before, including the fact that he was not as badly off as he had led us all to believe. He had at least a proprietary interest in the farm and throughout all the years in Dublin he was in receipt of money from it. Thus, although frequently without cash, he may be regarded as a man with a small private income which, of course, was utterly inadequate to his needs. In the event the question of his having to pay costs never arose. His lawyers appealed; after prolonged argument before the Supreme Court a retrial was ordered; the ancient weekly journal which had published the article was of course utterly unable to sustain further legal action; a small settlement was accordingly arranged, and there the matter died.

There had been no bonanza, but in the aftermath the trial had one important financial consequence for Paddy. When, shortly afterwards, he fell ill, a consortium which included the Archbishop of Dublin, John Charles McQuaid (an old friend), John A. Costello (now Prime Minister again and making generous and gratuitous amends for his role in the proceedings) and Professor Michael Tierney arranged that he should receive an annual stipend for delivering some lectures annually in UCD. It was not a princely sum, but it was the long-awaited pension.

The GAA and the wily Saxon

MICHEÁL Ó DONNCHADHA (1955)

The Gaelic Athletic Association imposed a ban on its members play-ing what it termed 'garrison games' – rugby, soccer, hockey and cricket – which had ostensibly been introduced to Ireland by the Brit-ish Army. Under the GAA ban, any member who played, attended or helped to promote these games incurred automatic suspension. This ban became increasingly controversial, and at the 1955 Easter Con-gress the GAA's president Micheál Ó Donnchadha took up the question in his presidential address.

The rule is there to remind all GAA members that their first duty is unswerving loyalty to their own Association, to its patriotic princi-ples and to its National mission. It is there to proclaim to them the danger and the dishonour of associating with British Imperialism so blatantly fostered by these games. It is *not* there to bolster up or to boost, or even to protect Gaelic games – they need no such artificial stimulation. But it is there to curb the baneful activities of Anglicisa-tion and to prevent the infiltration into the GAA of saboteurs and 'fellow-travellers'. It is not there for selfish commercial reasons to suppress rival Associations. But it *is* there to guarantee the national solidarity of the Gaelic Athletic Association against factionalism, division and ruin, which Irish history shows to have been the sorry fate, almost without exception, of every Irish Association which flirted with Anglo-Saxon Imperialism. It is there as a red light warn-ing Irishmen to beware of the fatal lure of the Saxon smile, and Saxon patronage and condescension. It is there because the GAA is no mere games-promoting body, but also the strongest organised patriotic Association in Ireland, whose duty as such is, to expose, counter and nullify anything inimical to the accepted National Ideal. It is there to lay bare English hypocrisy and English duplicity. *It is there because we want our country, our Irish Motherland.*

When will the time for the abolition of the 'Ban' have arrived? *The day when* the National spirit of Ireland is staunch and invincible and proof against all hostile foreign influences; *the day when* the Irishman's patriotic instincts are so strong as to recognize unerringly all forms of foreign aggression for what they really are; *the day when* the ultimate goal of an Ireland Gaelic and free is clearly within sight; *the day when* Emmet's epitaph may be truly written – *then, and only then*, may the 'Ban' be removed. [. . .]

To-day, the GAA is in the van, vigorous and uncompromising as ever, defending Ireland against the new aggression and the native weaklings who, wittingly or otherwise, play the game of the wily Saxon. This new aggression, to which Ireland is exposed, unlike the military tyranny of the Black and Tans, and the economic despotism of the nineteen-thirties, is almost entirely on a new front – the social, cultural and athletic. Griffith spoke of the paper wall that surrounded Ireland and kept her so effectively in bondage. The effect of the ceaseless torrent of propaganda swirling through Ireland, has been to blunt the national Conscience, weaken the National fibre and sabotage the Irish Revival Effort. Those who bewail in despairing tones the failure to advance the Irish Language as a spoken tongue during the past thirty years, need look nowhere else for the reason of the failure. How can the Irish tongue progress or National spirit grow strong when everything English is glorified and everything National ignored or derided? To their shame our Irish daily papers here have collaborated enthusiastically in the hysterical eulogising of English games and English ways. Lately, these same papers, lost apparently to all sense of National decency, devote a large and prominent section of their space to featuring English games played in England. And they call themselves National Newspapers! What brazen impudence? The result of this policy, deliberately fostered by Irish newspapers, is to cause National demoralization and to spread the virus of anglicization – which now, nurtured by the new tactics – sends its parasitic tentacles ramifying through Irish life, destroying the Irish-Ireland mentality. No wonder the revival of the Irish tongue is impossible in such an atmosphere.

McQuaid's dancehall spy

CORNELIUS GALLAGHER (1955)

The Archbishop of Dublin, John Charles McQuaid, established what he called a Vigilance Committee of senior clerics, who in turn had informants who reported on various activities in the archdiocese. In 1955 Cornelius Gallagher reported to the Vigilance Committee on a new dancing craze he had observed at a ballroom in Dublin.

I went to 'Mambo Club' dance in Palm Court ballroom last Monday night. Yes! The hall was packed: 100% Teddy Boys, and I suppose 'Teddy Girls'. I don't know if the girls have any particular name, though I could think of a few names [which] might suit! It was obvious to me that all the patrons came from the poor element of our people: certainly from the *cheaper* element. They all wore the crazy dress of the Teddy Boys style. The dancing was almost 100% jiving. [. . .] There were a few slow dances. The position in which the partners held themselves *then was even worse and more indecent*. However, indecency was the order of the night and without any supervision, anything could happen.

The door-man noticed me a stranger. When I was leaving early, he asked if I enjoyed the dance! He explained that the 'Mambo Club' have dances, Monday and Saturday, but that there's a very decent crowd for the rest of the nights. I said 'I doubt it' and left. The waitresses in the refreshment room told me the same. I was sounding all these people, and they all knew I was out of my depth! The 'Mambo Club' is a club nobody but Teddy Boys could or would patronize. If I dropped in to such a dance in all innocence, I'd stay about ten minutes. I think that is how any average person would react. It is pathetic to look at these people. It is more pathetic to think there are *so very* many of them. What's the remedy?

A duller and deader place

JOHN V. KELLEHER (1957)

In this extract from an article written for the American journal *Foreign Affairs*, John V. Kelleher – Harvard's first professor of Irish studies – offers a dark survey of the state of Ireland.

Most references to the fundamental soundness of the Irish economy relate to the 150 percent increase in industrial productivity over the last 25 years, from, of course, an abysmally low base. This productivity could probably increase a thousand percent and still make little difference in Ireland's earning capacity. It is mostly for home consumption, and too much is non-competitive, being protected by tariffs, import-quotas, monopolies and trade associations. Then, too, the habitual outlook must be considered – unless, by some miracle, it has changed greatly from what it was four years ago when a team of American experts, engaged to examine the possibilities of increased exports to the dollar areas, made their report.

The criterion for their study was 'most profitable and immediate exportability'. The report was almost entirely negative. Some of the products examined were judged simply unprofitable for marketing in America; others would be unacceptable because of price, quality, style or undependability of supply; a few might be restudied for later possibilities; woollen textiles and Waterford glass had some promise and might be pushed moderately. The most interesting part of the report was the section headed 'Smugness'. Three excerpts will indicate its tone.

There is a persistent illusion concerning the superior quality of the Irish product. This, of course, is not shared by people of experience, but it permeates the general atmosphere nonetheless.

More to the point:

There is a very real shortage of capital; but what there is remains buried. We have discovered no inclination among Irish producers to take any sort of risk. On the contrary, they wish to know the price their product will bring in the American market for years to come; the quantity which can be sold indefinitely; the designs which will be fashionable next year; what the tariffs are going to be; what their taxes will be; what every person concerned in a transaction will earn from it; and, on top of all this, in some cases, just what their competitors' costs are.

In conclusion:

All this is fantastic, and we suspect that it is a method of rationalizing a negative attitude. It is a very poor spirit with which to approach the highly volatile and risk-conscious American market.

And how is that for vigor, daring and imagination? [. . .]

Ireland has no right to be sick. If we compare its resources with those of other small Western European countries, and its population with what those have to support, one can hardly avoid deciding that Irish ills are largely psychosomatic. True, they can all be explained from history; but to explain is not always to excuse, the less so indeed since Irish history records so little energetic common sense and so much casual acceptance of accidental developments. Any conversation about Ireland in Ireland is almost bound to produce some defensive mention of the terrible Troubles the Irish have survived and the hard time of it the nation has had generally. Alas, the truth is that Ireland has had an almost fatally easy time of it, at least in this century. The revolutionary victory of 1916–21 was assisted powerfully by outside circumstances and by the fact that it was a thoroughly respectable 1848-type revolt, a little delayed. For a national struggle of such romantic fame, the actual fighting was mostly confined to two rather short periods and to two smallish areas. The Civil War that followed in 1922–3 was much wider and much worse, but that was strictly an internal affair and was the result chiefly of the inability, common to the whole Republican tradition, to distinguish a principle from an aspiration or to deal consecutively, much less real-istically, with the cold, hard, lumpy facts. Then as now the chief fact was emigration, which went on before the Troubles, during the Troubles, and after the Troubles – continually lowering the pressure of Irish life. [. . .]

What the people are offered and what the emigrants reject is pater-nalism. Long years ago Mr De Valera was credited with the statement that he had only to look into his own heart to know what the Irish people wanted. Whether he said it or not, it sounds like him. The statement, however, is incomplete. What is meant is what the good people of Ireland want, or ought to want; and in this sense it is not illogical, for who in Ireland was ever gooder or more Irish than Mr De Valera himself, the most lugubriously virtuous statesman of the age? (It must be understood that the opposition leaders are quite as virtu-ous and as nearly lugubrious as their means permit.) What Mr De Valera found in his heart was a burning desire for compulsory Irish in the schools and civil service; a thoroughgoing, or at least hardwork-ing, censorship; efficiency and honesty in local government (achieved by taking all real powers away from the elected county and borough councils and killing such community initiative as there was); and in general a society based upon Catholic and 'Gaelic' principles of 'frugal sufficiency' and geared to the supposed tastes and interests of the small-farmer, the truly representative Irish citizen.

He found other things there too. Among many real accomplish-ments, both political and economic, he must be credited with the success of Irish industrialization, with the first attempts to grapple with current social problems like unemployment, and with the crea-tion of the Dublin Institute for Advanced Studies. What counts today, however, is that he and his successors have left Ireland a duller and, in spirit, a deader place than they found it. One has only to look at the literature, the theatre, the newspapers, the few magazines, the censored libraries for the proof – or listen to Radio Éireann – or spend a rainy weekend in a small town. To a great extent this has been achieved by a round-robin process of politicians, clergymen, profes-sional Gaels, pietists and other comfortable bourgeoisie looking into each other's hearts and finding there, or pretending to find, the same

tepid desires. The process requires that they ignore the silent comment of emigration and such other evidences of discontent as the
annual flood of letters to the press from parents protesting against
compulsory Irish and against the whole inadequate, outmoded, chaotic school system. This paternalism requires, too, that the general
public never be asked to register its opinion on any of the desired
blessings which so many obviously do not desire. [. . .]

Every cantankerous critic has the duty to hazard at least one positive suggestion. Since I have given so one-sided a picture, omitting all
that makes Ireland pleasant and attractive – which it is – my duty is
the stronger. I would, then, suggest that the leaders of Church and
State in Ireland accept emigration as a major and, for the moment,
insoluble native problem. They should cease to regard it as a historical accident. Accepting it, they should at the same time accept the
responsibility for seeing that those who do emigrate go out into the
world well enough trained and educated to make an advantageous
start in their new countries. In the nineteenth century an Irishman
with a sixth-grade education was at no special disadvantage in England or America. Today, three out of four Irish children still do not
go beyond the sixth grade; and the education they receive is half-
ruined by concentration on a language they will never speak again,
anywhere. As emigrants they simply cannot compete on equal terms
with Englishmen or Americans of the same class, who have had a better and longer education.

I am inclined to believe that if an educational system adequate for
this task were created in Ireland – and its creation would necessarily
involve real vigor, daring and imagination, as well as searching reappraisal of old 'principles' and actual conditions – the effects of the
effort would soon manifest themselves in every aspect of life. Everything would be changed; and not impossibly, so much for the better
that the young might decide to stay at home and make a go of the
country after all. There is, to be sure, the danger that they might
make a go of it in ways the present fatherly rulers could only regard
with horror; but it is the ultimate function of fathers to be horrified,
and the function of the young to ensure it happens to them. Anyway,
that prospect, for all its uncertainty, is a better one to face up to than

the likelihood of things going on as they are. I cannot imagine the sudden sweeping outbreak of anti-clerical rage which some of my Irish friends so gloomily but confidently predict. I can, however, imagine that Ireland may do what no other nation has ever tried, and perish by sudden implosion upon a central vacuity.

'Godless agitators are at work'

FR EDWARD MCELROY (1957)

Significant numbers of Irish emigrants in Britain lived in work camps attached to building sites. Fr Edward McElroy was commissioned by Archbishop McQuaid to report on the spiritual condition of these emigrants. McQuaid, in a letter to Cardinal D'Alton, observed that McElroy's report 'would help the bishops in coming to a conclusion concerning the Camp Chaplains . . . and our other missionary efforts'.

They are those who leave home with a 'grouse' – reasonable or unreasonable, it does not matter. These blame the Irish Government, they blame the politicians, they blame the clergy – they blame everybody. They are over here because they cannot make a living at home and they are bitter and resentful about it. This type – and there are many – more easily falls a prey to political agitators such as the Communists. It is quite certain that efforts are being made to exploit their grievances. Lest anybody be in doubt about it, I enclose a list of remarks at the end of this section overheard by a good Catholic young man, who confessed that he was almost overwhelmed by the gross irreligion and blasphemy that he heard among Irish boys, some of them only a few months in this country. This man claims that about a third of the boys in the camp where he lives take part in those conversations or at least listen in. No doubt, not all agree with everything said, but there are those who certainly do. I think you will agree that those remarks, jotted down at random and over a short period, show clearly that Godless agitators are at work. This particular camp is the only one where I got such concrete evidence of Communist efforts to indoctrinate Irish boys, but it would be foolish to conclude that it is an isolated case. Exactly how prevalent it is I am unable to state accurately. This constitutes the most menacing active agency at work to rob Irish emigrants of their Catholic Faith. If left unchecked it constitutes Ireland's most serious source of danger from Communism.

Here follows the 'list of remarks . . . overheard by a good Catholic young man':

1. The Catholic Church is the ruination of modern civilization.
2. The Pope has a world of servants and a life of luxury unequalled in this or any other generation.
3. The Pope is the greatest Dictator of all time.
4. The Catholic Church in Ireland is surely the representative of this dictator.
5. All acts of parliament in Éire before becoming law must be witnessed and signed by a representative of the Catholic Church.
6. The country is overrun with priests, bishops and nuns.
7. They enjoy a life of luxury – big cars, easy money and no work.
8. Their education is paid for by the State, while the majority of the population is deprived of education and kept in ignorance. In this way the clergy fool the people into contributing large sums of money towards their own free and easy life.
9. Their organization is secret and kept secret, but they are always aware of the most secret thoughts and actions of the people. This information they gain through the Confessional.
10. The papers are full of photographs of the activities of the Hierarchy – big fat priests shaking hands with their fellow pigs.
11. Births, marriages and deaths are the meat of newspaper editors. But it is only the nobility who fill these columns – Mr X died last week leaving a large capital and wealthy estate. His sons are priests and his daughters nuns.
12. Birth control is not allowed by the Church and in this way the Church helps to keep the big poverty-stricken families in ignorance. They have no money to educate themselves.
13. The Church is against drink, yet the priests are free to

drink ad lib. See how they enjoy drinking their fill at
Mass.

14. The Church is against gambling; but watch the priests at
the races and in the card schools. See them sponsoring
gambling tournaments when they themselves want more
money for their own use.

15. The Church is against free-love, but nearly every priest
has a housekeeper or there are enough nuns in the parish
to go around.

'Shut the door on the past'

T. K. WHITAKER (1958)

The widespread pessimism about Ireland's future prompted the young Secretary of the Department of Finance, T. K. Whitaker, to produce what has come to be considered the blueprint for economic modernization. It was unprecedented for a civil servant to take on such a role, still less to sign and take responsibility for the resulting document. *Economic Development* signalled an end to the policy of protectionism and a shift towards an embrace of foreign investment. In his introduction to the document, Whitaker wrote that there was 'a sound psychological reason for having an integrated development programme. The absence of such a programme tends to deepen the all too prevalent mood of despondency about the country's future. A sense of anxiety is, indeed, justified. But it can too easily degenerate into feelings of frustration and despair.'

After 35 years of native government people are asking whether we can achieve an acceptable degree of economic progress. The common talk amongst parents in the towns, as in rural Ireland, is of their children having to emigrate as soon as their education is completed in order to be sure of a reasonable livelihood. To the children themselves and to many already in employment the jobs available at home look unattractive by comparison with those obtainable in such variety and so readily elsewhere. All this seems to be setting up a vicious circle – of increasing emigration, resulting in a smaller domestic market depleted of initiative and skill, and a reduced incentive, whether for Irishmen or foreigners, to undertake and organize the productive enterprises which alone can provide increased employment opportunities and higher living standards. There is, therefore, a real need at present to buttress confidence in the country's future and to stimulate the interest and enthusiasm of the young in particular. A general resurgence of will may be helped by setting up targets of national endeavour which appear to be reasonably attainable and mutually consistent. This is an aspect of good leadership. But there is nothing to be gained by setting up fanciful targets. Failure to reach such targets would merely produce disillusionment and renew the mood of national despondency. Realism also demands an awareness that, at present, and for a long time ahead, the material reward for work here may be less than that obtainable elsewhere but that there are many countervailing advantages in living in Ireland. No programme of development can be effective unless it generates increased effort, enterprise and saving on the part of a multitude of individuals. Its eventual success or failure will depend primarily on the individual reactions of the Irish people. If they have not the will to develop, even the best possible programme is useless.

A concerted and comprehensive programme aimed at a steady progress in material welfare, even though supported by the Churches and other leaders of opinion, could only be successful if the individual members of the community were realistic and patriotic enough to accept the standard of living produced by their own exertions here, even if it should continue for some time to be lower than the standard available abroad. Otherwise the possibility of economic progress scarcely exists.

For all these reasons the importance of the next 5 to 10 years for the economic and political future of Ireland cannot be overstressed. Policies should be re-examined without regard to past views or commitments. It is desirable to remind ourselves that at all times in a nation's history decisions have to be taken; that there is no guarantee when they are taken that they will prove right; and that the greatest fault lies in pursuing a policy after it has proved to be unsuitable or ineffective. What matters above all is to understand the present position and find the best and quickest ways of improving it. [. . .]

This study suggests that, given favourable public policies and private dispositions, a dynamic of progress awaits release in agriculture, fisheries, industry and tourism. It is hoped that it will be possible to set this force to work simultaneously in these major branches of the Irish economy. The opportunities of development may not be great enough to give all who are born in Ireland a standard of living they would accept – though there are advantages of living here not to be reckoned in money terms – but such as they are they should be exploited. It is not unreasonable to hope that sufficient advance can be made in the next decade not merely to consolidate our economic independence but to enable us to provide higher material standards for a rising population.

In pressing on with this study, despite the claims of ordinary office work, it has been an inspiration to turn to the following words of the Bishop of Clonfert, Most Rev. Dr Philbin:

> Our version of history has tended to make us think of freedom as an end in itself and of independent government – like marriage in a fairy story – as the solution of all ills. Freedom is useful in proportion to the use we make of it. We seem to have relaxed our patriotic energies just at the time when there was most need to mobilise them. Although our enterprise in purely spiritual fields has never been greater, we have shown little initiative or organizational ability in agriculture and industry and commerce. There is here the widest and most varied field for the play of the vital force that our religion contains.
>
> *Studies*, Autumn, 1957

This study is a contribution, in the spirit advocated by the Bishop of Clonfert, towards the working out of the national good in the economic sphere. It is hoped that, supplemented by productive ideas from other sources, it will help to dispel despondency about the country's future. We can afford our present standard of living, which is so much higher than most of the inhabitants of this world enjoy. Possibilities of improvement are there, if we wish to realise them. It would be well to shut the door on the past and to move forward, energetically, intelligently and with the will to succeed, but without expecting miracles of progress in a short time.

Music in a country pub

POLLY DEVLIN (1950s)

Polly Devlin was one of six sisters and one brother who grew up in Ardboe, on the western shore of Lough Neagh in Co. Tyrone. Their father owned a public house and the family lived nearby. In her 1983 memoir *All of Us There*, she recalled the music in the pub during her childhood in the 1950s.

There was always a great deal of singing, and in the evening when we brought out a mug of tea from the house to the pub, a hundred yards away, we would hear old men singing songs or reciting verses. We knew them all, the singers and the songs, but we thought of them as the embarrassing outbursts of men stocious with drink. Only when we grew up and left home and looked back were we able to appreciate, at an irrecoverable remove, the secret life that subsisted in that deep countryside – the music of a hidden Ireland with its complex harmonies and quavering grace-notes, the passionate concealed underground life of another country whose difference was deceptive, because the common language seemed the same.

If the men in the pub were asked to sing these songs when they were sober they would become what they called 'bashful'. 'They're only auld come-all-yees,' they'd say, 'rubbidgy old songs. Yous don't want to hear them.' Such attitudes obtained all over Ireland. When music producers from Radio Éireann, the Irish radio station, went around the country in the 1950s in the vanguard of the folk-boom to record the fiddlers, the tin whistlers, the pipers, the singers of the countryside, they found an enormous reservoir of talent. But the people were often reluctant to reveal themselves as traditional musicians, because such music was despised; and some fiddle-players went to join fellow musicians with their fiddles hidden under their coats because they were ashamed to be seen.

The ritual preceding and during these outbursts of songs in the pub was always the same. A fisherman, his natural bashfulness dissipated by the Guinness in his veins, would suddenly be moved to sing and would rise shakily to his feet. Gradually the talk would die down and, swaying slightly, eyes closed, and often supported by a nearby but equally unstable friend, he would embark on the ceremonial song. The manner of singing and the reception of the song were governed by convention, ritual and ceremony. Men caught in mid-sentence by the giving voice would stop, tilt their heads, and remain frozen from the sounding of the first notes till the end, which was often an unconscionably long time coming. The songs were plaintive, slow, lamenting, and during the long pauses there were certain acceptable phrases of encouragement launched towards the singer: 'Good man yerself,' or 'You're a brev man,' or sometimes a reiteration of the last words of the verse, all of which served as a kind of chorus, necessary for the esteem of the singer and the continuation of his song. At its end a swell of voices would repeat the same phrases, the highest praise being 'By God and he *can* sing,' although there were occasionally murmurs of dissent especially if someone used this precious phrase about someone who actually could not sing, but was so drunk as to forget this fact. Even then the listeners, though bored and amused by the singer's conceit, observed the formalities and politenesses, although occasionally a recalcitrant voice might mutter, 'He's none at all.'

The dangers of British television

F. J. Q. O'MEARA (1960)

As television listings in the daily press attest, television viewing was becoming ever more popular in Ireland in the late 1950s. The main factor in this was the establishment of studios and transmitters in Northern Ireland, most of whose programmes originated in Britain; RTÉ would not begin transmission of programmes from its Dublin studios until the last day of 1961. This letter from a former emigrant to Cardinal D'Alton warned of what the writer believed were the moral dangers of British television programmes being received in the Republic.

More and more aerials sprout up even in the most remote districts. Now Ireland can see the world, through British eyes. Irrespective of nightly activities prior to its advent, people crowd the sets and get instruction for hours at a time on how British people live. Intellectual and intricate discussions on all topics are carried on by men of genius but little Faith. A good programme is quite likely to be followed by the contortions of some dancer, and never will all the arts of Satan be so articulately expressed. Will the more simple type of Irishman go away or switch off? Some of these souls are so naturally pure, that they probably will. Nevertheless, everywhere that which is downright rotten is being presented as perfectly alright, so as even to defy the use of reason, and there are not nearly enough warnings of the terrible perils of this diabolic deceit. This is not 'education', as the sophisticated moderns hold. It comes under the heading of scandal to little ones, and immodest performances, and I shudder to think what will happen to Ireland through the medium of this pagan produced BBC Television. Already we have periodic banal conversations by 'specialists' of both sexes on human artificial insemination, the artificial control of birth, and homosexuality. The case for euthanasia is a popular talking point. These every-day topics of pagan Britain, are now becoming every-day topics of Catholic Ireland, and indeed certain of the actual degenerate practices so 'broadmindedly' discussed are on the increase in Dublin, and I suppose elsewhere in the country. Surely Satan's greatest triumph is this lulling of humanity into the denying of the Sixth and Ninth Commandments.

On pride, confidence, and falsehoods about Ireland

SEÁN LEMASS (1960)

In a speech delivered at Rockwell College, Seán Lemass, entering his second year as taoiseach, attempted to overturn various 'falsehoods' about Ireland. He was particularly exercised about the perception that the Irish were heavy drinkers, claiming that the British drank far more. He almost certainly had Brendan Behan in mind when making his complaint about stage Irishmen.

It may be that we are particularly, perhaps unduly, sensitive about those disparaging representations and we could afford to ignore them if they did not affect our own outlook and attitudes, and particularly our confidence in our capacity to complete the great tasks of nation-building on which we are engaged. There are still some people amongst us who always seem to be trying to belittle our national accomplishments, who are constantly seeking around for bits and pieces of irrelevant fact to deny their actuality, and who scoff at and deride expectations of greater future progress. Occasionally some Irish people when they go abroad seem to be trying to lend verisimilitude to the stage-Irishman picture by their personal behaviour, even people who when at home are decent, respectable, hard-working and well-behaved. There are Irish journalists, playwrights and novelists who seem to think that the surest way to extract royalties from British publishers is to depict the Irish not as they really are, but as the British public have been led to imagine them. These people do not seem to understand that they are helping to sustain an anti-Irish propaganda which was originally devised during the periods of cold war against Irish independence, and to justify the measures which were taken to prevent its attainment.

One of the most persistent and irritating falsehoods about the Irish is that they are excessive consumers of alcoholic drink. That lie has gone very far afield. The simple truth is ignored, and the truth is that the per capita consumption of alcoholic drink in Ireland is one of the lowest for all countries for which reliable statistics are available – even if one counts against our own people the not inconsiderable intake of tourists. [. . .]

Another false picture of the Irish represents them as sentimental, impractical and disinclined towards change and progress. Again, the facts assert the contrary to be true. At some future time an impartial historian will be able to take an objective view of what has been accomplished here during the past thirty years or so, the almost revolutionary changes in the living conditions of our people, the development of an administrative apparatus geared to the requirements of a developing country, the very real accomplishments in agricultural technology and in industrial proficiency, the extension of health and hospital services, the improvement of communications, the extension of educational facilities, and the successful establishment of great State enterprises. [. . .]

These are the hallmarks of the new Ireland and it is more than time that we lifted up our heads in pride and began to crow about them. The 'béal bocht' is no longer fashionable. The people who get ahead in the world are those who have pride in themselves.

We have a cause to serve in the world also. In the ideological conflict which has divided mankind into two opposing camps there is no neutrality, and we are not neutral. In this struggle the concept of neutralism, positive or negative, is a dangerous illusion. It is a struggle for the minds and souls of men, and Ireland, with its strong Christian spirit and great missionary tradition, is not merely well equipped to play a significant part in that struggle but to an ever-increasing degree, as the nature of the conflict is becoming more widely understood, the world is beginning to realize the value of the contribution which we can make. In that field also we must not disparage ourselves or discount the role we can play. Armies and wealth and economic power are often less potent weapons than unselfish dedication to worthy aims, a clear understanding of the fundamental purpose of human existence and, we hope and pray, Divine guidance in whatever we may undertake. When the Irish missionary monks took the message of Christianity into Europe in the Dark Ages there were none to question the presumption of a small nation in undertaking that high mission, and so today, when we strive to help those who are upholding the banners of truth and justice in the world, there are no honest men anywhere, who will scorn our aid. We must not just sit tight in our own little island, occupied solely with our own affairs, indifferent to what is happening in the world. In the final analysis the fate of mankind will be our fate also.

What TDs have to put up with

MICHAEL HAYES (1962)

Michael Hayes was briefly a minister in the first Cumann na nGaedheal government, and served as the Ceann Comhairle of the Dáil from 1922 to 1932. Speaking in the Seanad, of which he had been a member since 1938, he traced an evolution in the nature of the Dáil Deputy's role.

The thing the public should know about this is that the expenses of the members of the Dáil arise from a complete change in the nature of the functions which now fall to the lot of a parliamentary representative. If a member of the Oireachtas had only to attend and legislate, it would be a very desirable thing but, in fact, members of the Oireachtas have an entirely different and much more onerous and less useful function. My purpose is to ask the Minister whether, in consultation with members of other Parties, he could not find some method of remedying that situation. The power of the State has increased steadily since its foundation and the social services have extended enormously. The result is that members of the Dáil are treated rather as intermediaries or messengers between their constituents and the State itself, the Civil Service and the various State bodies.

That has increased enormously the duties of Deputies and it is, to my mind, creating an onerous and extremely expensive situation, not only for Deputies themselves but also for the State. Many people first try a Fianna Fáil Deputy to get something for them if a Fianna Fáil Government are in office and, if not successful, they try a Fine Gael Deputy and, if there is an odd Labour Deputy knocking around, they try him. There is a certain amount of competition between the Parties in this matter and there is also competition between members of the same Party in the same constituency. The constituent who fails to get something from AB will then go to CD in the hope of getting something on the promise of a No. 1 vote at the next election. [...]

The point of view held by the public about this is quite wrong. Most Deputies will tell you that they rarely get a letter which contains all the truth. The correspondent will tell only the part that suits himself and will leave out anything against him. Even as a Senator, I have had some experience of that. People put things from their own point of view and do not mention anything which is likely to take from their chances. The more experienced a public representative is, the less he is inclined to help. When a man comes to me and tells me that his daughter is up for an examination for writing assistants, as Chairman of the Civil Service Commissioners for ten years, I know that I cannot do anything for him, that the Civil Service Commissioners will deal with the matter; but there are people who will get a letter from a Department and will send it on to the constituent who will say to himself: 'This fellow is doing his best for me.'

I know of a Minister who went to open a golf club in his constituency on a Sunday afternoon. On the steps of the club, he met a constituent who began to tell him a long story. The Minister listened as politely as he could and then the constituent asked him: 'Have you not got a piece of paper and a pencil to take down the particulars?' He wanted the Minister to take down the particulars of his case on a Sunday afternoon on the steps of a golf club. I suggest that all this procedure is wasteful and expensive and that is one of the reasons why Deputies find the burden so great that they want postage and telephone facilities. [. . .]

People often comment that the seats in the Dáil are empty. Of course they are. The people who should be in them and who should be dealing with legislation are going about persecuting civil servants, telling them things the civil servants already know themselves. Some of the things are not quite true, a fact which the Deputy finds out only when he is told by the civil servants. [. . .] There have been suggestions of ombudsmen such as they have in the Scandinavian countries. There are a small number of genuine cases where perhaps people do not understand Acts of Parliament, but my experience is that when a man is entitled to a benefit, he understands all about it. He is better than most senior counsel about what he is entitled to.

Everyone would welcome a step which would make for more attention to legislation. It would make for better Parliament and for less expense on the taxpayer, and perhaps fewer Bills of this nature.

Kennedy in Ireland

BRIAN INGLIS (1963)

As part of his European tour in June 1963, US President John F. Kennedy made a visit to Ireland that included a trip to the birthplace of his great-grandfather in Co. Wexford. Brian Inglis wrote about the visit for the *Spectator*.

In a broadcast not long ago, Alistair Cooke remarked on the state of euphoria quickly attained in an Irish gathering, proof even against the likelihood that immediately you have left the room, while your charm and intelligence are still being extolled, somebody will remark on the way you pick your nose. Even after the first day there were sceptics: Kennedy's informality, they complained was too studied; and that jerk of the head, with the flashed-on smile – was it not designed to lose an impending double chin? But as the tour proceeded, the President's mannerisms dwindled. The chopping motion of the hand, ordinarily used to add force to platitude, disappeared when he began to throw away his punch lines; and his voice, often unsympathetic when oracular, gained mellowness when he was being casual.

The speech to both Houses of the Oireachtas, Dáil and Senate, was the real test. He might lecture; he might be patronising; he might be prosy. Worst of all, he might turn sentimental. But again, his judgment was sound. He was indeed sentimental, but historically – and all the Irish are that. When he praised Ireland's fight for freedom, thereby delighting the nationalists (who had feared he might be cagey, out of deference to English susceptibilities), he linked it with the West's fight for freedom today as if the Irish contribution to, say, the UN was a natural and logical extension of the '98 and of Easter Week. Towards the end of his speech his audience was visibly affected; hardened politicians wept in their seats.

But what was most welcomed about the speech, and the whole visit, was that the President treated his hosts as adult – something his compatriots, and English journalists, find it hard to do. The character of the Irish has changed astonishingly in the past decade; the break-away from those past preoccupations, the Border and the Language Revival, has brought about a new international outlook, producing the kind of change which going into practice traditionally does to the feckless medical student. Of course, the old Ireland is there, never far beneath the surface. The *Irish Press* correspondent in Berlin could not let Kennedy's visit to the Berlin Wall pass without saying that it brought home 'the terrible and fundamental tragedy of Partition'; and the local councillor who, baffled by the frequent changes of pro-gramme, insisted that 'We're adhering rigidly to the schedule until we know what it is' is still to be found in Ireland, and not just in Patrick Campbell's column. But the difference between the Ireland of today and the travesties of it which appear in some of the London papers is startling. Even the tea-party at Dunganstown was a reflec-tion of the times. The President's fourth cousins turned out to be self-possessed, neither overawed nor overpleased with themselves – a decent family taking the whole thing calmly and sensibly. Of course, the party itself had its ludicrous aspect, but it was the milling report-ers and photographers who were responsible for that – and the grotesque security men.

A pity President Kennedy couldn't have had a couple of days with no formality whatever; but clearly he didn't come for a holiday. What, then, did he come for? It rather looks as if it was just because he wanted to; as simple as that.

A polite request to His Grace

BRIAN LENIHAN (1964)

As a young minister for justice, Brian Lenihan was a leading reformer in liberalizing the censorship laws. But he still reckoned that it would be prudent to ask the Archbishop of Dublin to make a nomination to the Censorship of Films Appeal Board, in the following letter.

It has been evident for some little time that the Board as at present constituted is no longer a proper court of appeal and does not command public respect for its decisions. I am aware that some of the members are very advanced in years, some hard of hearing, some, evidently, do not understand the import of some of the film scenes at all, some have been noticed to doze during film-showing and, finally, decisions have been made with only a small number of members present at appeals. It is in these circumstances that I have felt it necessary to reconstitute the Board, a decision which when publicised by newspapers was misinterpreted.

I have acknowledged in Dáil Éireann the Government's indebtedness to the outgoing Members for their services. I have come to the conclusion, however, that the public interest requires that great care be taken in the selection of new members. I hope to have acceptance of nomination from two (perhaps, three) members of the judiciary, one of whom will act as chairman, from an eminent psychiatrist, from a well-known film critic of an Irish Catholic publication, from a retired civil servant whose work entailed a study of the causes and means of prevention of juvenile delinquency, from a housewife of education and understanding. In short, I hope to appoint a Board whose decisions will command general respect. I should be greatly obliged if Your Grace would make a nomination.

The burden of the past

W. R. RODGERS (1966)

W. R. Rodgers – poet, broadcaster and essayist – was born in Belfast and was ordained as a Presbyterian clergyman before he resigned in 1946 to take up a post in London with the BBC. This is from an essay in the *New Statesman* to mark the fiftieth anniversary of the 1916 Rising.

Not long ago, in a small country pub in Essex, I listened to two of my countrymen talking. The local men tactfully retired to the dartboard to listen with interest to the hardly-believable story of how they had oppressed Ireland for seven centuries. But it was the summing-up that was so memorable and unexpected, a splendid non-sequitur. 'I'll tell you this, and I'll tell you it for all,' said the Ulsterman firmly to the Dubliner: 'If Roger Casement had been alive today, Russia wouldn't be in the state she is.' No indeed. As an official Irish church-history says: 'The Irish have a great sense of history, but little sense of perspective.' Ireland carries a memory in her mouth as softly as an old retriever bitch carries an egg without breaking it. And this goes for all sorts and conditions of Irishmen, navvies or scholars. It is a memory that carries with it an inalienable sense of hurt. I remember asking an eminent and cosmopolitan Irishman what John F. Kennedy's visit to Ireland meant to him. 'Simply this,' he said, 'I'm an Irishman and a Catholic, and from now on I feel I'm not a second-class citizen.' [. . .]

This Easter the Republic of Ireland celebrates the Jubilee of the Easter Rising of 1916 and honours its illustrious dead. She will do this with dignity and, no doubt, with modest rhetoric, remembering that

> The last offence we practise on the dead
> Is how we summarise.

Young Ireland, however, won't wholly approve of this act of memory. A recent editorial in *Campus* (University College Dublin) says:

> It is now time, 50 years after, that the people of this country – and
> especially the students – held an objective perspective of their past
> history. The 1966 commemorations give us a remarkable opportunity
> to develop a mature and sophisticated, though not cynical attitude to
> the events in question. We will not be helped by the contemporaries
> of the Rising, who, since unfortunately they were of a youthful age
> in 1916, still linger with us.

Not too well phrased and more than a little cruel to an older generation who carry mixed memories of the Rising and a bitter civil war
and who set the young republic on its feet. I had occasion lately to
record some of the survivors of the Rising and was struck particularly by their gaiety, their complete lack of bitterness or any tedious
harking-back. Indeed, it was one of the 'ould wans' who said to me:
'What Ireland needs today is not heroism but normal courage.' Not
to fear the umbrage of bishops, the stroke of the crozier.

   The young ones of Ireland today are rightly tired of paying lip-
service to the past, tired of being led down memory's lane, of always
dogging the fled horse of history, tired of the obscurantists and the
rhetoric-mongers who embezzle the public funds of emotion. 'We
should talk things, not words,' said Mr Justice Holmes. And Ireland
has many things to talk out, if censors will let her. Dublin County
Council may give four new university scholarships to celebrate the
Easter Rising Jubilee; but the UCD students' magazine, *Awake*,
found that its printers would not produce an issue containing a report
on students' attitudes to contraception in marriage.

   And what about John McGahern, the young Irish writer whose
novel *The Dark* (banned in Ireland but acclaimed elsewhere) touched
the sombre question of education in Ireland? Mr McGahern's employment as a teacher has since been terminated by the clerical manager
of his school and he has now gone to America. Ireland has been less a
mother to her sons than a censorious maiden aunt. The touchstone
of a new republic will be its attitude to education.

   'The child in Ireland of 1966 whose parents have not money stands
a poor chance,' says one commentator. 'Money talks. It is the one
language that we have most effectually revived.' Ireland, North and

South, is certainly more affluent than I have ever known it. It is getting better; it is going from worse to bad. And it is losing a lot of its old tensions. It has an expanding economy and a growing middle-class. But a society which is in process of losing its memories of the past is capable of all sorts of crass tastelessness and philistine behaviour unless it is educated in the possession of what it should retain. That is why one gets the exporter of old horses who, as an indignant Irish farmer said, 'would sell the ass that carried our Lord and his Mother into Egypt'. Or the galoots who blew up Nelson's Pillar. Or the bureaucrats who pulled down the Georgian houses in Fitzwilliam Street. [...]

Perhaps England and Ireland could usefully exchange their short-lived and long-lived memories. A Dublin poet of my acquaintance got a phone-call some time ago from an English television producer who explained that she was preparing a documentary on the Easter Rising. Was there, she inquired, any sort of inscription on the statue of Cuchulain in the Dublin GPO. The poet told her that it bore the names of the seven men who proclaimed the Irish Republic. 'Do you think I could interview any of them?' she said. 'I'm afraid not,' said the poet, 'they are all dead.' 'Oh, did anything unusual happen to them?' 'They were executed,' said the poet. 'But who executed them?' she asked. 'You did, ma'am,' said the poet. There was a silence, and then she said, 'I'm so sorry.'

Fifty years after the Somme

MALCOLM MCKEE (1966)

Malcolm McKee, a veteran of the Somme, wrote with some anger on the fiftieth anniversary of the battle. His article, in the *Belfast Telegraph*, differed in tone from what had been published by veterans to mark earlier anniversaries.

Vainglory is one thing . . . Vain glory is another. And the glory of the Somme was vain. And that, when you are old, causes senile fury. I can think of nothing but what might have been – and of golden friends I had. I had 60 splendid men in my platoon. But in reality few were more than what I would now call boys. Young and in perfect spirits. And with a discipline learned in the UVF where it was utterly voluntary. Each platoon looked on its officer as 'their' officer – and nobody else's – and on their own platoon as the best.

What I want to convey is that my men were my personal friends – hence my fury at how they were almost obliterated through gross stupidity. The Somme was lost by 10 minutes. And all the officers in the front line expected it would be. No one could get this into the heads of Haig and his staff. He knew nothing about actual fighting and never came near the front line to find out.

We knew the Germans had splendid, deep dug-outs which could not be affected by shell-fire: that the wire was not cut; that a huge load of equipment meant you could manage only a walk. I had not the physique of my men, but I was pretty sturdy. And I had not the extra load they had to carry, and no rifle. Yet my equipment crushed me down. Instead of creeping forward in the dark and bombing the Germans in their dug-outs, when the barrage lifted, we had to set out in broad daylight to walk slowly forward towards the machine guns the Germans brought out of their deep dug-outs and fired at a perfect target which could not hit back. We were locked in chains for execution. And what nonsense is stuck on to the story.

Certainly Major Gaffikin waved an orange hanker-chief, but

orange was the colour of our battalion, the 9th (West Belfast) Royal Irish Rifles. If he said (and if anybody could have heard him) 'Come on, boys, this is the First of July!' – how many would have known the Boyne was fought on the First of July? I don't know why they plaster such incidents on our battle. Nothing was further from my mind than the Boyne on the Somme.

Sir Oliver Nugent was much criticised for ordering that no commanding officers, seconds-in-command or adjutants were to go over the top. But I have not seen it mentioned that out of each battalion only the 4 company commanders with 2 subalterns each – total 12 – were allowed to go over at zero. I thought it the cleverest order in the whole battle. It meant that instead of most of the officers being killed at the very beginning, there were officers right to the end of the day. Two commanding officers attempted to disobey the order – both in the Belfast Brigade, the 107th. They decided to lead their battalions over into no-man's-land anyhow. Crozier, of the 9th Battalion managed it, but Bernard of the 10th, was killed before he got over his own front line. I must admit that seeing Crozier standing in no-man's-land gave me a feeling of glee that we were in the battle together. He was a tiger – but his example inspired me lots of times not to run away!

What do I remember most clearly? The splendid comradeship of splendid men. But no one who has not been in a big battle can understand that. And the Somme was the biggest battle since the beginning of the war till now. Of what use was it? It saved the French Army from obliteration at Verdun. It saved the Channel ports. But you may say it gained nothing whatever.

For the world the name 'Somme' is a name of horror to this day – and a monument to the nobility of sheer valour. And I will hoist my Northern Ireland flag with a wreath of bays at the truck – for the Somme won Northern Ireland for the Kingdom. 'Old men forget' – but I shall not forget the men who laid down their lives for their friends. The few, the happy few, the band of brothers. That is, my platoon. When the Belfast Brigade left Bramshot for France, the bands played 'The Girl I Left Behind Me' – the only occasion on which a military band may play that tune. [. . .] After July 1 there were many broken hearts. Those girleens, if nobody else, remember the masses dead on the banks of the Ancre, which still flows gently into the Somme, which enters the sea near Crécy.

Violence and 'the true drama of Irish nationhood'

FR FRANCIS SHAW (1966)

Fr Francis Shaw's essay 'The Canon of Irish History', a critique of the Easter Rising and of Patrick Pearse's concept of blood sacrifice, was deemed inappropriate by the editor of *Studies* on the occasion of the fiftieth anniversary of the Rising. It was only six years later – when the Northern Troubles were at their height – that it was published. Shaw argued that there was 'every reason' to question the assumption that the Rising 'was necessary to shock a nationally degenerate and unpatriotic generation into a sense of manhood'. He found fault with Pearse speaking of the 'exhilaration of war' and argued that in 1916 most Irish people 'had plainly chosen the broadly constitutional mode of attaining national objectives'. And he was supportive of P. S. O'Hegarty's characterization of the insurrection as being 'universally and explosively unpopular'.

The English in Ireland were in fact always strangers and foreigners, and they never learned by their mistakes. The Irish might at times be pro-British but the English never understood that deep down in every (or nearly every) Irishman there was an ancient, quiet, deep and natural understanding that Irishmen were different, that they were a people with a history and a distinctive way of life: that they were in fact a nation. The Irish people in 1916 were grown tired of the trickery of English politicians, of the vacillations of the Liberals and of the treachery of the Tories. The executions after Easter Week did more than shock the people; they offended, if one may use the words, the national dignity. And the last straw was the threat of conscription. Two hundred thousand Irishmen might go voluntarily to fight with Britain, but not twenty would go as conscripts, because in that unwritten, inarticulate but very real sense of Irish nationhood the right of Britain to conscript Irishmen was never acknowledged.

But the Irish people did not become extremists or separatists overnight. The new movement had its origin in the protests of

Redmond and Dillon, of Shaw and Stephens, and significantly of the Catholic Bishop of Limerick, no one of whom was an extremist. And the new movement turned to Sinn Fein as to a party with a national programme and an organization capable of winning a general election. When in 1922 a choice had to be made, the majority of the people chose the way of moderation. Since 1922, intransigent republicanism has been a lost cause, lost because it never had the support of the people. The Republic was not mentioned in the new Constitution of 1937, and, when it was declared, it was found to be without life: it had been too long on ice. In the same time the massive emigration of our people to Britain, the growing economic dependence on that country, the huge participation of Irishmen in the British forces in 1939–44, and finally the Anglo-Irish Free-Trade Agreement, all these have gone to show how superficial was Ireland's flirtation with extremist doctrines in the years immediately following the Rising of 1916.

The Rising of 1916 was then a minority one, not only by reason of the ideals of the men who fought, but also by reason of the choice of physical force as a means. It is not an accident that Tone and O'Connell should have reacted so differently to what they had seen of the French Revolution. The thin stream which stretches from Tone through Mitchel and the Fenians is in fact not of the life-blood of Irish nationhood. It is alien in origin and content, and in its choice of means; and it is worth recalling that it flourished as strongly on American as on Irish soil. Tone and Emmet, it is true, were popular heroes, not however on account of their doctrine, but because they had died for Ireland. The images of Tone and Emmet were honoured in Irish homes by people who were whole-hearted followers of O'Connell.

A half-century, it may be said, is too near to a historic event for objective and comprehensive judging. But there is another element which must be taken into account. It is possible that never a half-century has seen such rapid and deep transformation in human thought as have the fifty years between 1916 and today. The revolution of 1916 was very much a fruit of the rise of nationalism, of extreme nationalism; and it was, too, set in a time in which war and martial triumph were in favour. Today the world is discarding extreme nationalism as a negative and divisive force and today the horror of warfare pursued to its logical end of total destruction has inclined men to view all warfare as barbarous.

The sword, it would seem, is never as clean a weapon as we are sometimes led to believe. Wounds may often fester for a long time. Tone sincerely hoped that his policy of separatism would unite all Irishmen. He worked hard to that end, but separatism was an unlikely basis for unity; ultimately it did more to divide than to unite. Looking back over more than half a century, it must be admitted that the resort to arms in support of the separatist doctrine in 1916 inflicted three grave wounds on the body of the unity of Ireland.

The first is the wound of Partition. Already in 1916 the threat of secession in the North was very strong. Even great patience and tact might have failed, but the door to peaceful solution was surely closed in 1916. It cannot be denied that those who literally would stop at nothing in their resistance to Home Rule were only confirmed in their intransigence by the events of Easter Week.

The second wound is the wound of the Civil War of 1922–3. This bitter strife between Irishmen who were brothers and had recently been comrades in arms was a consequence, if not an inevitable one, of the Rising of 1916. The extremist teaching of Tone and Mitchel could brook no compromise: it dictated a choice of a separatist republic or nothing. It had won the day in 1916 and it was still strong enough in 1922 to drive men to civil strife.

The third wound on the national unity, more often forgotten than the other two, will continue to fester until the injustice which causes it is removed. At a time when throughout the world men of goodwill strive to lessen the tensions that divide, in this small and already divided island we cannot even be at one in the honouring of our dead. I refer to the many thousands of Irishmen who fought and died bravely in the First World War and are yet virtually without honour in their own land. In February 1966, Mr Sean Lemass, then Taoiseach, broke a great silence when in an important speech at the King's Inns he spoke with sympathy, understanding and appreciation of the sacrifice of those men. His words were as statesmanlike as they were striking. They could yet have consequences for unity in Ireland as great as those of his memorable visit to Captain O'Neill.

The main stream of Irish nationhood has always been manifest, though never easy to define. The Anglo-Irish colony held the stage for a long time, but it was not a stage on which the true drama of Irish nationhood was being played. The Anglo-Irish element had its part to play, and still has, but it was never the *principium vitae* of Ireland's nationhood. That main force in the nineteenth century is to be found principally in the inarticulate, obstinate, unsophisticated will of an oppressed and hungry people, a will to live the life to which they were accustomed, a will to cling to the land which had given them so little, even when half had to leave so that the other half could remain and survive. These were men who remembered the past because it was all about them in the present. No one of them could have defined 'nationality'; few amongst them would have known what a 'republic' was; but it would never have occurred to any one of them that he could be other than an Irishman. And most oddly, this remained true when so many of them were in the process of giving up their native tongue. It would in fact seem that when they learned to speak English, the consciousness of their individuality as a people became keener. The common Irishman's sense of his national individuality had always been powerfully strong, so strong that it had no need of the conventional safeguards and manifestations of national sovereignty. Can it be that it was in this extraordinary sense of strength that the Irishman who could not be parted from his faith or his land abandoned so widely and with little struggle the language of his forefathers? The Irish, I feel, have never been in danger of becoming English. They may have imitated English manners but they did not ape them. Notwithstanding the might of Britain in the world the Irish never thought of the English as being superior to them. And today I do not think that we are in any danger of becoming English, to the loss of our individuality. In truth that is not where the danger lies. The danger today is a very real one, but it threatens England equally with Ireland. It is the danger of the triumph of a common cosmopolitan vulgarity which threatens all cultural standards and the individuality of peoples everywhere.

The finest 'definition' of Irish nationality which I know is that of Michael Collins. It is cited by Frank O'Connor, who gives P. S. O'Hegarty as his authority. Collins said: 'I stand for an Irish civilization based on the people and embodying maintaining the things, their habits, ways of thought, customs, that make them different – the sort of life I was brought up in . . . Once, years ago, a crowd of us were going along the Shepherd's Bush Road when out of a lane came a chap with a donkey – just the sort of donkey and just the sort of cart that they have at home. He came out quite suddenly and abruptly, and we all stood and cheered him. Nobody who has not been an exile will understand me, but I stand for that.'

Ireland and Britain are two islands placed by God's creation beside one another. The paths of their respective histories have of necessity constantly crossed: in a sense they have always got in one another's way, and their relationship throughout the centuries has not been happy.

In fact the events of 1916 and of the years which followed did close a chapter in a long history of strife, and it is time that we as a Christian people should forget the past. There can surely be no more criminal disservice to Ireland than the determination to keep the fire of hatred burning.

The writer John McGahern was working as a primary school teacher
in Dublin when he completed his second novel, *The Dark*. He was on
a year's leave of absence when it was published and then promptly
banned by the Irish censorship board. The manager of his school, a
Roman Catholic priest of the Dublin diocese, was instructed by
Archbishop McQuaid not to permit McGahern to return to his teaching duties when the new school year began in September 1966. This is
how McGahern recalled the episode in his book *Memoir*.

In Dublin in the winter of 1963–4 I wrote *The Dark*, too quickly. I
also won the Macauley, a prize of £1,000, which stipulated that the
winner travel abroad for a year. It was a large award for the time, as
£1,000 could purchase a small house in Dublin. In the summer I met
the Finnish theatre director Annikki Laaksi in Paris. That October I
was given a year's leave of absence without pay by the school to avail
of the Macauley. I went to Helsinki and later in the year married
Annikki Laaksi. Finland was not a country I felt I could ever live in,
and after Christmas we moved to London and then to Spain, where
we had been given the loan of a house on the Almeria coast.

While we were there *The Dark* was published in London in May of
1965 but seized by the Customs and banned in Ireland. This gave rise
to violent controversy, and I was glad to be in Spain and out of the
storm. In Dublin, we had looked on the Censorship Board as a joke.
Most banned books weren't worth reading and those that were could
easily be come by. I somehow never thought that it could have anything to do with me or my life. Now that I was in the middle of it I
found it childish and unpleasant, and I was a little ashamed that our
own independent country was making a fool of itself yet again. I
wondered privately if the novel had been written less quickly and
with more care that they might not have noticed. I refused to take
part in any protest on the grounds that it would do the whole sorry

business too much honour. Back in London I wrote to the school stating my intention to return at the end of the year's leave of absence. The headmaster replied that there would be difficulty if I tried to return to the school. He advised me to obtain a position in London, and would be only too happy to write references. While I wanted no part of the censorship row, I was determined, as the school had been my work and livelihood for many years, not to go quietly. In awkward situations in Ireland, great pressure is brought to bear to do the so-called decent thing and go quietly away. I was not prepared to go quietly.

I crossed to Dublin and turned up at the school on the day I was due to return. I informed nobody and there were no journalists at the school. All the staff were on edge but everybody welcomed me back with great friendliness. When the bell rang for classes, a deeply embarrassed Mr Kelleher, the headmaster, read out a legal letter from the manager saying I was barred from entering the classroom. He read this out in the corridor with his back to my old classroom door. Father Carton, the parish priest of Clontarf and the school manager, had gone on holiday to avoid the unpleasantness. I spent the rest of the day in the school. Now that our ordeal was over, the headmaster did his best to make me comfortable. He gave me a newspaper to read. 'Hardly a day goes by but there's something about you in the paper, *A Mháistir*,' he said pityingly. I drank endless cups of tea. I had a pleasant lunch with all my old colleagues, and at 2.15 we all left together as if it had been just another school day.

I still had the school manager to see when he returned from his holidays. Father Carton saw me reluctantly. In a roundabout way he told me that he wasn't to blame, as the order for my dismissal had come from the Archbishop. 'You have gone and ruined your life,' the old priest told me. 'And you have made my life a misery as well. I can't put my head out the door these days but I'm beset by bowsies of journalists.' When pressed by the Teachers' Union for a reason for my dismissal, he replied in writing: 'Mr McGahern is well aware of the reason for his dismissal.'

I met the full board of the national Irish Teachers' Union [Irish National Teachers' Organisation] in the late middle of an afternoon.

They were careful and hostile. Some of the men had taken whiskey to brace themselves for the meeting. Word had leaked out through the newspapers that I had married a Finnish woman in a register office. The General Secretary, another Kelleher, who had also braced himself with whiskey, allowed his irritation with me to overcome his caution. 'If it was just the auld book, maybe – maybe – we might have been able to do something for you, but with marrying this foreign woman you have turned yourself into a hopeless case entirely,' he said. 'And what anyhow entered your head to go and marry this foreign woman when there are hundreds of thousands of Irish girls going around with their tongues out for a husband?' he added memorably, especially since not many of them had been pointed in my direction. [. . .]

There were letters for and against me in the newspapers, debates on television and radio, and I was glad to get back to London. The protest against my dismissal that mattered most to me came from the parents of children I had taught. Outside of that I didn't greatly care.

The Ulster Sabbath

JAMES BOYCE (1966)

James Boyce was a Northern Irish broadcaster, actor and writer. This essay was published in the *Spectator* under the title 'Mr Paisley's Sunday', even though the Reverend Ian Paisley is not mentioned in it.

If you visit Belfast and find yourself outside one of the prefabricated tabernacles of our more evangelical sects you will hear a curious sound – a wail as of a congregation of converted but disconsolate banshees still labouring under conviction of sin – the sin of their fellow citizens trying to desecrate the Sabbath. For, mind you, the Ulster Sunday is a thing to send the whole wide world into a wonder and a wild surmise. The *English* Sunday is commonly thought to be a very dull business but believe me, brother, in comparison with what we have here, it is a wanton debauch of unbridled licence. For that day we add a crusading religious fervour to our normal national injunction to the young: 'Find out what wee Willie's doing and tell him to stop – especially on Sunday.' You see, the Lord's Day Observance Society, not content with worshipping God in their own bleak way, want to compel everybody else to the same course of harsh and joyless austerity. They're convinced that you'll go to hell if you behave on Sunday as do 99.99875 per cent of their fellow human beings all the world over on that day. If they're right it's a very thin trickle of 'Hosanna in the Highest' that will resound for all eternity through the courts of Heaven – most of it in a strong Ulster accent.

So far they have won out all along the line, and their main victims are the children. They can't go to a cinema on Sunday but can burrow into the smuttier passages of holy writ as they attend church for the third time in twelve hours. They cannot look at paintings in the Ulster Museum but are at liberty to thumb through girlie magazines in the furtive fastnesses of the loo. The playgrounds are closed, for a slide down a helter-skelter can become a Gadarene rush of the infant soul into the nethermost depths of the pit. Swings are locked up lest the wrath of God fall on the curly-headed five-year-old blasphemer in the romper suit. For the more mature sinner, the outlook is equally dismaying. A Sunday football match would be the abomination of desolation, and the thirsty soul who wants to slake his parched throat with a half-pint of shandy is held to be tottering on the brink of the DTs and is reminded by raucous-voiced open-air hot gospellers of his latter end 'where the worm dieth not and their fire is not quenched'.

For myself I think the explanation is pride. The Ulster soul is such a valuable commodity that its least peccadillo is a matter of the utmost moment to the Lord God Almighty. Our religious life is a constant tweak at the beard of the Ancient of Days lest he divert his attention to some lesser breeds without the law – the Ulster law, of course. 'Keep your eye on us, Lord,' we say, 'for we know we are the apple of it!' We'll be the quare feathers in the wings of the angelic host when we get home to heaven. And home to heaven is where we are going to get come hell or high water. The hell, above all, of our own sectarian devising.

It is true that we sell rather short on such paltry virtues as charity and loving kindness, especially today, in the grip as we are of one of our recurrent crises of religious and political imbecility. Just now if you play a round of clock golf at Whitehead on Sunday you'll end up in the brimstone, but if you cut the throat of what is currently called a Pope-head you're booked for a heavenly harp, with presumably a built-in blackjack to use on St Peter if he doesn't toe the Ulster doctrinal line.

I have for some time felt the need for what might be called the Battle Hymn of the Anti-Republic and have ventured to concoct the first verse of it:

Here we stand in ranks unbroken, lambs of God with trotters clenched
'Thou shalt not' our holy slogan, Break the Lord's day you'll get lynched.
Open skulls but close the playgrounds, spill the blood but lock the swings
Raise the banner of the bigot, while the Ulster tocsin rings.

Aptly enough, in view of the world press coverage of Ulster recently achieved by our tiny bedlam of holy goons, it goes to the tune of 'Glorious Things of Thee are Spoken'.

Fior-Ghael *in the temple of official Ulster*

SEAMUS HEANEY (1968)

Seán Ó Riada was an innovator in Irish traditional music; a writer of original art music; enjoyed an extraordinary success with his film score for *Mise Éire*; and was an engaging broadcaster and lecturer throughout his short life. In one of the exchanges in his book *Stepping Stones: Interviews with Seamus Heaney*, Dennis O'Driscoll asked Heaney about his memories of Ó Riada.

Q. How did you regard Seán Ó Riada's music?

The score for *Mise Éire* was a big thrill in the sixties. The 'Slievena-mon' theme. The 'Róisín Dubh' theme. And then there was the work he did with Ceoltóirí Chualann, as arranger and conductor and player of the harpsichord. His contributions did rectify things greatly in the world of traditional music. Ó Riada definitely had a touch of genius, and he left the traditional music world in better order, and the entire music culture of the country to some extent retuned. You couldn't be young in sixties Ireland and not feel some of the Ó Riada effect, either on radio programmes or in the arrangements of tunes he popu-larized: O'Carolan's Concerto, 'An Ghaoth Aneas', planxties and polkas and that whole outburst of bodhrans and fiddles and drones and chanters and concertinas and whatever you're having yourself.

Q. You've referred earlier to Seán Ó Riada's broadcast of 'Craig's Dragoons'.

I didn't actually hear the programme. It was in 1968, as I mentioned, just after the Civil Rights march had been baton-charged in Derry. He wrote to me in early October, a short note asking for something he might use on his programme on Radio Éireann, and I provided the words of 'Craig's Dragoons'. I'd met Ó Riada that summer in Bally-david, in Kerry, when Marie and I were down on our holidays. He occasionally turned up in Begley's public house, and I remember him dancing Kerry sets, going at it for all he was worth. His wife Ruth was there too and that summer they invited us over to visit them in Coolea, in the Cork Gaeltacht.

They'd moved from Dublin, some years before, and Seán at that time was constantly on the go with the musicians, hitting the road and hitting the bottle, striding out like a prince among his people, but at the same time in hiding from his vocation as a composer. There was a histrionic streak in him, he swanked a bit, but at the same time there was piercing intelligence and a readiness to probe and provoke. I remember that morning, when he took me into his workroom, he came on not so much as a musician as a grey-Connemara-cloth type of Yeatsian man, drawing attention to his guns and his fishing rods.

At the same time, there was sudden naked honesty when he as much as said he wasn't working as he should be. I put one little part of our exchange, word for word, into the poem in memory of him: 'How do you work? / Sometimes I just lie out / like ballast in the bottom of the boat / listening to the cuckoo'.

Q. You also capture him conducting the Ulster Orchestra 'like a drover with an ashplant'. When did that occur?

Later in that same year, 1968, when he was 'composer of the year' at the Queen's University festival. Soon after the first attack on the Civil Rights march. I remember getting a terrific charge when he and his musicians appeared on the stage of the Sir William Whitla Hall, lashing into all those Irish jigs and reels and marches. The Whitla Hall was such a temple of official Ulster, the sanctum of posh, potato-in-the-mouth, British-not-Irish types, a lot closer to Britten than to Erin, and here was the *fíor-Ghael* on the rampage, one night in *báinín* with his own session men, and the next in black tie and in charge of his own baton, conducting the province's finest. I couldn't deny, then or now, the cultural boost that Ó Riada gave me at that time. Although he was only one among many, since the festival was also attended that year by John Montague, Tom Kinsella and John McGahern, and we were all involved on one occasion in a symposium chaired by Tyrone Guthrie, who was then vice-chancellor of the university. If William Craig had paid more attention to intelligence from members of that symposium than from members of the RUC Special Branch, the next thirty years might have turned out better.

Q. Did you get on well with Ó Riada?

Well, yes, but I have to say his posturing irked me. Swirling the snifter of brandy and brandishing the cigar. Setting himself up as commissar, interrogating rather than conversing. I remember walking into the Club Bar that week and being asked rather grandly – in front of Kinsella and Montague – 'And where do you stand on the North?' I should have said that, unlike the company I was in, I'd stood on it for thirty years, but I just let it go. I admired him even if I didn't get too close. But I have to say he treated me gallantly when we were down in Kerry, and made me feel welcome in his company, part of the action.

'We won't accept this, enough is enough'

SUZANNE BREEN (1968)

The RUC's baton charge on peaceful civil rights marchers in Derry on 5 October 1968, and the RTÉ television footage distributed worldwide, 'changed the course of Irish history', in the words of the historian Paul Bew, by exposing the Northern Ireland state as dysfunctional. On the fortieth anniversary of the march, Suzanne Breen published an article in the *Sunday Tribune* that contained reminiscences by people who were there that day.

He remembers them gathering on the streets of Derry, full of naive optimism, their banners lighting up the dismal streets. 'One man, one vote', 'Jobs and houses', and 'End the Special Powers Act', they declared. They were a motley crew of students, housewives, workers and revolutionaries. Those who knew the words were singing 'We Shall Overcome'. The civil rights marchers were chatting about which team would win the Irish league match at the Brandywell when the police laid into them.

'They baton-charged us,' says Willie Breslin. 'Charlie Morrison, a bricklayer, was so badly beaten, he couldn't work for a month. Matt Harkin's back was a mess. A policeman made a go for my testicles but I raised my knee in time so he only got my thigh. Four police officers beat a wee man until he fell to the ground, then they picked him up and threw him over a wall. He suffered a broken leg and arm. But it didn't deter us. There were only 400 marching – far more people were at the Brandywell for the football. But when we held the same demonstration six weeks later, 20,000 were there. People were saying, "We won't accept this, enough is enough." They were giving two fingers, with both hands, to the government.'

[. . .] it was ordinary men and women who were the backbone of the movement. Even today, they remain the unsung heroes and heroines. Willie Breslin, a 28-year-old teacher on 5 October 1968, describes himself as a 'hod carrier' of the civil rights movement. 'Derry was

73% Catholic but it was run by unionists. There were 2,400 families on the housing list but in two years they built only 22 new homes. There was a policy to keep Catholics homeless or in rented accommodation because only householders had the vote in local government elections,' Breslin says. 'The Wilson family lived in a caravan. They had no electricity, running water or toilet. Mrs Wilson gave birth to a baby who died eight hours later. The doctor blamed the awful living conditions. A group of us pulled the caravan on to the middle of the Lecky Road in protest. The police came and everybody was arrested except myself and another fellow. He was a civil servant and I was a teacher. Arresting us would have backfired: they wanted to give the impression that all the protestors were unemployed layabouts.'

Dermy McClenaghan was a 26-year-old dental technician and Derry Labour Party member who helped John Hume carry some of those injured on 5 October into Cassoni's Italian restaurant. His civil rights passion was intense. 'We lived in horrendous conditions in the Bogside,' he says. 'Our house was riddled with damp and so badly wired that you got electric shock if you touched the wall. My father died of TB. I saw it as a family tragedy and as political – he wouldn't have died had we decent housing.'

McClenaghan did what he could to help others who were living in slums or homeless. 'I had my own housing list of the most desperate families. When I heard a house became available somewhere, I'd move a family in to squat. I'd an electrician, a joiner, a plumber, stepladders and a bag of tools. We'd go along and do up the house to make it habitable.' Despite the seriousness of the campaign, McClenaghan also remembers the crack and camaraderie: 'Jan Palach burned himself to death in Prague's Wenceslas Square in protest as Russian tanks rolled in. A man in Derry threatened to burn himself to death in Derry's Guildhall Square if he didn't get a decent house by a certain date. He was very hard to please. When the deadline day arrived, he woke up to find six cans of petrol placed by local people on his doorstep.' [. . .]

Cathy Harkin, who left school at 14 and worked in a shirt factory, was in the thick of the civil rights movement. Her son Terry, who was 6 years old on 5 October 1968, recalls her coming home from the march badly bruised: 'We lived with my granny. My mother sold the *United Irishman* newspaper. Before 5 October, I remember my mother having to sit on the street waiting for it to arrive because Granny wouldn't let it into the house. After 5 October, my granny changed. All sorts of rebels and radicals were allowed to come and go from our house around the clock. Civil rights posters were made in our living room. The house was always full of the smell of ink and paint.'

The Battle of the Bogside

BERNADETTE DEVLIN (1969)

Bernadette Devlin rose to prominence in the People's Democracy, a radical left-wing group of students in Queen's University Belfast. She was selected as a 'Unity' nationalist candidate for a by-election in Mid Ulster in April 1969. Her election at the age of twenty-one made her the youngest woman ever elected to Westminster. Later that year the annual Apprentice Boys parade in Derry was challenged by nationalists as provocative. The RUC, seen as partisan on the loyalist side, were attacked with bricks, stones and petrol bombs, with Devlin a prominent leader of the rioting. The police responded with tear-gas; barricades were set up around the Catholic Bogside area, which was christened Free Derry and proclaimed a no-go area for the police. This account of what became known as the Battle of Bogside is from the book Devlin published later that year, *The Price of My Soul*.

Remembering what the police action had been on every other public occasion in Derry over the past twelve months, the people of the Bogside decided that, for their own safety, they would ignore the procession, mind their own business, and stay in the Catholic area outside the city walls with their heads down until it was all over. But if the twenty thousand marchers came down to attack them, after a day's celebration and drinking, they would defend their homes. The Bogsiders' gesture toward peace was met with provocation. From the walls overlooking the Catholic slum, the marchers and their supporters hurled taunts about keeping Catholics shut up in rabbit hutches. 'All Fenians ought to be penned in, anyway,' they yelled. Finally the attempts to goad the Catholics out succeeded in a small way and a few squabbles broke out between the marchers and the Bogsiders. Rather than sort the squabblers out and send them on their separate ways, the police decided a baton-charge was in order and made a run into the Bogside. Promptly the barricades went up, but this time the police decided they were not going to tolerate the Bogside's resistance to being beaten into the ground. 'We've got to beat them this time, Miss, or we're done for,' they told Mary Holland of the *Observer*.

And so the Battle of the Bogside began. It was then about four o'clock in the afternoon of August 11. Not for another fifty hours did the day-and-night fighting stop, and when it was over, it was the police who retreated. The Bogside was still unbreached, and the Unionist government was a great stride nearer its downfall.

The Battle of the Bogside, according to Major Chichester-Clark, was part of a planned conspiracy to overthrow the government. If the Major had seen inside the barricades he would have found some-thing much stronger and more terrifying than the plots of any organization. What was happening there was that ordinary, peaceful people, who had no desire to spend fifty hours throwing stones and petrol bombs, had realized the harm that had been done to them for half a century and were learning how to fight in self-defence. We threw up barricades of rubble, pipe, and paving stones – anything we could get our hands on – to prevent the police coming straight into the area and, in their own words, 'settling the Bogside once and for all'. Within the first half hour, eight police tenders were trapped in our barricades, and if only we'd had the means to destroy them we would have burned those tenders out.

It was at that point that the manufacture of petrol bombs began. The petrol bombs were made, literally, by pregnant women and chil-dren. Kids of seven and eight who couldn't fight made the petrol bombs, and they made them pretty well. The kids of nine and ten carried them in crates to the front lines. The young girls collected stones and built the barricades, and the girls, the boys and the men fought on the front line against the police. The police answered our stones and petrol bombs with stones of their own, and with ever-increasing supplies of tear gas. The whole air was saturated with it, and we had not a gas mask among us. I telephoned the Southern Ireland Minister of Defence to beg him to send us a thousand gas masks for the children at least. I was willing to claim I had stolen them, I said, if he didn't want us to have them openly. But he wouldn't cooperate. Jack Lynch, the Premier, was making grand-sounding statements from Dublin about his readiness to march to our defence.

But he was only playing politics: such a march would have been tan-
tamount to a declaration of war on England, and Mr Lynch is
economically tied to Mother England's apron strings and his army is
no match for the British. In any case, in the middle of the twentieth
century no two Western European powers, however unimportant,
are going to declare war because everybody is frightened of what the
Russians would do when their backs were turned. We got medical
supplies from the South, but gas masks we had to go without. So we
made do with wet blankets, with cotton wool steeped in vinegar,
with handkerchiefs soaked in sodium bicarbonate, and we fought on
through the night, all through the next day and the following night
and into the third day, and we showed the police that nothing they
did was going to beat us.

Meanwhile what was left of my reputation was taking a beating in
the newspapers. All the papers were carrying photographs of Bernadette Devlin, bejeaned, besweatered, and besieged in the Bogside,
leading people on and organizing the manufacture of petrol bombs
and hollering at the people through megaphones to 'throw them
hard and throw them straight'; or organizing little guerrilla troops of
a hundred men, in ten rows of ten men, to run like hell down side
streets and catch the police in the middle, making sure that everybody had two petrol bombs and somebody got a copper. But what
the press said about me didn't have the effect they intended. I didn't
have time to read the papers myself – I was always on the barricades;
and other people in Northern Ireland, who had begun to take the
discrediting line fed them by the British press, could see that what I
was doing was necessary. 'If they come in here to get Bernadette
Devlin, we'll slaughter them all,' they said.

While we fought on, the Civil Rights Association organized demonstrations in ten other towns, hoping this would take police pressure
off Derry and allow us a certain amount of relaxation in the struggle.
These demonstrations were held in defiance of the government's ban,
imposed as soon as the Apprentice Boys had stopped marching, but
they failed in their object. Instead of withdrawing policemen from
Derry, the government called out the B Specials. Three hours later
Harold Wilson sent the British Army into Derry, and the B Specials

were switched to Belfast to wreak havoc on the citizens. There are no regulation tests to get into the B Specials. You don't have to do an eye test; you don't have to have a minimum or a maximum height; there are no weight restrictions and no intelligence qualifications. All you've got to be is a supporter of the government, but once you're in you are entitled to service pay, to a gun, to all the ammunition you want, and to a uniform which is usually either two sizes too big or three sizes too small.

In Belfast the B Specials, alongside the police, fought the demonstrators. They did more. With small arms, machine guns and armoured cars, they launched a vicious, well-planned attack on Catholic areas. They burned down row upon row of houses. Only the arrival of the British Army brought their destructive progress to a halt, and I have no doubt myself that the army came, not because Major Chichester-Clark asked for help, but because Harold Wilson wasn't prepared to tolerate the Unionist Party's private army of reserve police. The soldiers got an ironic reception: while the Unionists, who have always been the Union Jack wavers, stayed cool, Republicans and Nationalists cheered the arrival of British troops on Irish soil.

But the barricades stayed up. The fighting was over, for the moment at any rate, but our demands had still to be met. One of these was an amnesty for every civilian in Northern Ireland, Catholic or Protestant, who had been forced into illegality. We leafleted the Free State Army, asking them to desert and come to our aid. We campaigned among the British troops, asking them to do the same thing. I believe they call it sedition. There was some doubt whether I personally was guilty of treason or not. I'd thrown stones at policemen (unfortunately I can't throw straight, and they missed). According to Major Chichester-Clark, I'd incited Bogsiders to rebellion and plotted the overthrow of the state. But the situation in Northern Ireland was such that nobody cared. It was the government who interned, without trial, people whose only crime was their political viewpoint. It was their men who set up kangaroo courts, murdered children, burned families out. Our sin was the lesser, and we will win in the long term, or the short. [. . .]

But behind the farcical aspects of the whole affair lay a serious problem: these people, out of fear, could never go back to the situation before August 12, 1969. We reached then a turning point in Irish history, and we reached it because of the determination of one group of people in a Catholic slum area in Derry. In fifty hours we brought a government to its knees, and we gave back to a downtrodden people their pride and the strength of their convictions.

The Whitaker imprimatur

T. K. WHITAKER (1969)

Though best known as the man who guided a change of course in Ireland's economic policy, T. K. Whitaker was also highly influential in other spheres. He was partly responsible for organizing the Lemass–O'Neill meetings of 1965, and had a close working relationship with Jack Lynch. As the Northern troubles worsened in August 1969 – and with some Fianna Fáil Cabinet ministers arguing for armed intervention by the Republic – Lynch turned to Whitaker (who had Northern roots) for advice and, probably, for the valuable Whitaker imprimatur to pursue a moderate line. On 15 August, Lynch telephoned to Carna in Connemara, where Whitaker was on holidays. This is Whitaker's draft note of his advice to Lynch.

There is a horrifying aspect of teenage hooliganism and anarchy in the situation that has developed; [it has] in part, at least, been organized by extremists on both sides in NI. No government can benefit from appearing to support or condone this. Indeed no government can afford to be critical – without overwhelming evidence of misbehaviour of police attempts to restore law and order; and some allowance must be made for the fact that police are only human.

There is a terrible temptation to be opportunist, to cash in on political emotionalism at a time like this; but it should not be forgotten that a *genuinely* united Ireland, must be based on a free union *of those living in Ireland*, on mutual tolerance, and on belief that the ultimate governmental authority will be equitable and unprejudiced. Every effort should be made in any government statements from Dublin to avoid identifying the government solely with the Catholics or Nationalists of NI and to make it clear that the aim of a united Ireland would be a scrupulously fair deal for all – indeed that the position of NI Protestants would be particularly respected. A special effort is needed to reassure the many *moderate* Protestants who otherwise may be driven to side with the extremists under threat, as they see it, of losing their 'freedom, religion and laws'.

The government should avoid all appearances of being driven before the emotional winds fanned by utterly unrepresentative and irresponsible organizations such as Sinn Fein, whose statements, telegrams, etc., have [been] given quite disproportionate publicity by RTÉ. An outsider might be forgiven for thinking they were the government party or at least the main opposition.

Close liaison with the main opposition [?] both may help to abate the danger of purely short-term competitive and opportunist reactions to a situation which calls for cool-headed, longer-term appraisal.

Vis-à-vis British government, I presume it is the failure of the experiment of devolution in NI which will be stressed – a failure due *not just* to the unfairness and discrimination of the regime and its inability to maintain law and order without forfeiting the respect of a large body of its citizens, *but also* to the fundamental weakness of its constitutional position in that it was never accepted by the whole of Ireland or even by a majority in each of the counties of its artificial composition. But where do we go from there? WE can't take over Britain's financial contribution, nor do we want the terrifying task of keeping sectarian and anarchical mobs in order? Better confine ourselves to preventing groups from here intervening, by strict control of the border. We have to envisage a slow-phased movement towards some form of unification. There should be no rigid clinging to preconceived formulae. Even *condominium* may be a useful transitional concept.

The one thing you were not allowed to see

COLM TÓIBÍN (1969)

The Late Late Show began as a short-run entertainment programme on RTÉ in June 1962, the first year of the station's television broadcasting. Hosted by Gay Byrne, it quickly expanded its brief to include current controversies, many of which had hitherto been considered taboo by broadcasters. Sexuality, censorship and the power of the Church were just some of the issues discussed. The programme enjoyed an exceptional reach and influence in a society with an appetite for change; and it could sometimes attract the ire of preachers at Sunday Mass. Speaking on the RTÉ radio programme *What If?*, the novelist Colm Tóibín recalled the allure of the *Late Late* in the 1960s, when he was growing up in Enniscorthy.

I was born in 1955 and it was the one thing you were not allowed to see and it was the one thing you kept asking about. Despite all the cartoons, all the other things that were on, it was the thing you wanted most to see, because I think all the adults watched it in a very serious way. The door was closed and the children were sent to bed and as you got to a certain age you'd say, 'When I'm what age will I be able to watch *The Late Late Show?*', which was a sort of rite of passage. The first time I was brought down from my bed to watch it was not when an enormous sort of cataclysm took place in Irish society, but when Lieutenant Gerard from *The Fugitive*, who'd been searching for the one-armed man all the time, when he appeared on *The Late Late Show*, it was felt he would be suitable for me. But once it was over you never knew, because they never announced in advance who was coming on next and it could be a nun who didn't believe in being a nun or it could be someone talking about sex and there had never been talk about sex in our house. I remember sometime, I must have been let watch it from the age of 11 or 12, but I remember one night [in 1969] when Conor Cruise O'Brien and Máire Mhac an tSaoi came on together and Máire said that there were couples who had been married for many years who had never seen one another naked and I can tell you, the silence . . . Now I'm talking about an extended family, not the nuclear family, but aunts, uncles, maybe even a visitor, 12-year-olds, 13-year-olds, all of us watched – 'Máire Mhac an tSaoi had said "naked" on *The Late Late Show*!' There weren't headlines the next day, but it was that sort of silence that caused people really to worry. You couldn't turn it off – no one had a zapper – you could have run over to turn it off but that would have been considered square. So it began for me by being forbidden, and then became immensely interesting with great moments of pure embarrassment and, as I say, a great amount of Hollywood in it – any actor who was passing through town would be on it as well, so the show business and whatever things that were unsayable in Irish life were mixed together.

An archbishop on 'the permissive society'

CARDINAL WILLIAM CONWAY (1969)

Cardinal William Conway was the Archbishop of Armagh from 1963 until his death in 1977. This period saw the implementation of the changes following the Second Vatican Council. In this memo to his fellow bishops, he called for an in-depth inquiry into the attitudes of young Irish people to the Church and its teaching, and outlined what he saw as the existing situation at the conclusion of the 1960s.

We have no scientific analysis of the present state of Irish Catholicism and therefore we must largely depend on the individual impressions of ourselves and competent observers. My own impressions are as follows: (a) There still exists, throughout Ireland, a very strong faith and an acceptance of Catholic views. In other words, the 'capital' of belief and practice which existed ten years ago [three years before the Council] is still largely intact. I have the impression, despite some signs to the contrary, that this is basically true in both urban and rural areas. (b) I also have the impression that the current upheaval in the Church and the impact of the 'permissive society' is having a somewhat unsettling effect on young people and on certain sectors of the 'intellectual' classes. I have the impression that the number of people who give up the practice of the faith, while still relatively small, is definitely on the increase, especially in urban areas.

The developing tendencies within the existing situation. Obviously the most important factor is the deep process of change which is taking place in the world at large and which is having its unsettling effect on practically all established institutions. An entirely new world of thought and feeling is emerging and one of the basic problems of the Church is how to relate her divine truth and her life to this new situation without endangering what is not hers to change. This process, of course, is felt more acutely in highly industrialized societies such as the USA than it is with us but it is having its effect here (i) because the process of change is taking place here also and (ii) because the news media convey the effects of change elsewhere to our people.

I think there is no doubt that the attempts of some theologians to adapt to this new situation have in fact gone too far and have called in question doctrines and principles of the Church which are irreversible because divinely established. The Holy Father has frequently drawn attention to this and some of the biggest names in Catholic scholarship, men like De Lubac, Daniélou, Jedin – men who could not in any sense be accused of rigidity – have voiced their concern. As to the effect of all this in Ireland, I have the impression that its effect on the people as a whole has been very slight and that its effect on the future generation of priests could be quite serious. I must confess that after reading of outlandish views in such periodicals as *Herder Correspondence* or the *Tablet* I have often been surprised to find how little effect they have on – or how little they are even known about – the ordinary priests and people.

Their effect on a new generation of priests – and nuns and teachers – could be more disquieting in that it would inevitably affect the people also. The effect here of the general loosening of moral standards in the 'permissive society' of Great Britain is difficult to assess. It seems inevitable that it is bound to be having a considerable effect especially on young people. [. . .] I think it would be wrong to concentrate too much attention on 'protecting' the young people from weakening influences. For one thing it is simply impossible to shut out news of the permissive society or the turbulence in the Church; for another, the concept of freedom is so strong among young people to-day that an over-concentration on negative policies would be likely to be counter-productive. [. . .]

Preaching. The overwhelming majority of our priests are sound in doctrine but I think there is a great deal of evidence to suggest that the style and manner of preaching needs radical improvement. People have got so used to lively television discussions that they react negatively to being 'talked-at' from the pulpit in language that is often old-fashioned and cliché-ridden. [. . .] I think this is a matter to which the Communications Council might be asked to devote major attention – by the provision of courses for diocesan groups of priests

– even if this means devoting somewhat less attention to training for television and radio programmes. [. . .]

The news media. This is a difficult field but the following propositions seem to me to be true.

1. There is a great deal in the presentation of news and the expression of views about the Church, in Irish newspapers, radio and television, which could be fairly criticized.

2. It is very difficult to measure the effect of this on the people. Superficially it does not seem to be having a very great effect.

3. There is a great dearth of competent people who are willing to answer unfair criticism or criticize unfair presentation. I believe it should be possible to do something about this. There are plenty of balanced priests and laymen in the country who can write a good letter to the newspapers. The problem – and it is a considerable one – is how to secure that this will happen without creating a furore about a Hierarchy pressure-group.

4. With regard to RTÉ, I find it hard to see why the authorities should not be prepared to listen to the advice and comments of a competent Catholic Advisory Board. It would be important, of course, that such a Board should be open and positive in its approach and moderate and balanced in its criticism.

On the Contraceptive Train

JUNE LEVINE (1971)

Under legislation dating to 1935, it was difficult to obtain contraception legally in Ireland. Doctors could prescribe birth-control to women with cycle irregularity, and it is probably not a coincidence that Ireland had the highest rate of this condition in the world. In 1971, members of the Irish Women's Liberation Movement took the train from Dublin to Belfast and returned with all manner of contraceptives, intending to defy the customs officials to apply the law. Among those on the train was June Levine, who chronicled the episode in her memoir *Sisters*. The basic intention of the group, she wrote, was 'to show up the hypocrisy' of the law.

On World Communications Day, 22 May, at 8 o'clock, forty-seven of us turned up to take the train to Belfast from Connolly Station. Our day was to become an international media story, lauded far more elsewhere than it was at home. As well as the national newspaper reporters there were at least four TV cameramen. [. . .] We took over two carriages, and the rest of the train filled with Southern housewives on their way to bargains in Belfast. [. . .] Literature on contraceptives was waiting for us in Belfast so that we could bring it back with us for confiscation. The sheet informed us that we could get Durex, The Pill, Intrauterine devices (also known as the loop and the coil), and the Dutch Cap (also known as the diaphragm). Unless we had prescriptions, we were told, we must buy spermicidal jelly or Durex (obviously not for your personal use). Spermicidal jelly, we were told, had been consistently confiscated by the Customs. We were advised that free legal aid was on tap for everyone. The following choices of action were open to us when confronting the Customs men upon return to Dublin:

1. Declare nothing and risk being searched.
2. Declare contraceptives and refuse to be searched.

3. Declare contraceptives and refuse to hand over.
4. Declare contraceptives and hand over with protest of infringement of your constitutional rights.
5. Declare contraceptives and throw over barrier to sisters waiting beyond. Many people who couldn't come today will be demonstrating at Amiens Street in solidarity with our action.
6. Declare contraceptives and sit down in anticipation of Customs action.
7. Declare internal contraceptive. Allow search from Female Officer only and shout 'April Fool' before entry. [. . .]

Those off the train first went, naturally, to the chemist shop opposite the Europa Hotel near the station. The rest of us tried to pack noisily in after them. All the relevant stuff was on display, creating embarrassed titters for some who had never seen contraceptives. A couple of middle-aged women standing close to me were acting the way I felt the first time I went into a sex shop in Soho, trying to appear impassive, mortified, and undecided whether to laugh or run. Some had no trouble laughing, it was like the dirty giggles of naughty children. [. . .] I had been impressed by the 'newness' of some of these young women of the seventies. Now I saw them as their mothers' daughters, women who knew little about their own bodies, who had never been free to feel responsible for their own fertility and felt awkward about it. They handled the condoms as if they were packages of sins, hooted at sight of a diaphragm. Such shopping was foreign to them and a hint of hysteria made them vulgar. [. . .]

There was some talk that the train might be boarded by gardaí at Dundalk, but as we swept through the station we settled down to another fifty miles of freedom. It was about now that Mary [Kenny] amazed me with the remark as she hung out of the window for air: 'Our mothers will kill us!' And behind all the bravado, it was a common sentiment. I didn't care, but I realized now that these women would have to face shocked neighbours and friends and bear the brunt of the speeches from the pulpits next day and for weeks afterwards. And speeches there were. Indeed, even as we travelled home, speaking at Knock Shrine, Co. Mayo, the Bishop of Clonfert, the Most Rev. Dr Ryan, said that never before and certainly not since penal times was the Catholic heritage of Ireland subjected to so many insidious onslaughts on the pretext of conscience, civil rights and women's liberation. We were attacking the principles of the Church's teaching, he said. 'The chief targets of attack are the Church's teaching on contraception and divorce and the Church's role in the education of youth.' He prayed that the Virgin Mary, appointed patroness of telecommunications, would guide the media in Ireland, making us instruments for good and not for evil.

Now we were coming into Dublin, hanging out of the windows and longing for a sign of what was happening at that end. And then, yes, it was singing we heard in the distance and a huge number of voices: 'We Shall Overcome' brought tears to the eye. I gave up the fear of spending even five minutes in a cell. We'd been scared, but now we'd see it through. The station was a teeming mass of people with banners, cheering. We unfurled our banner, with the Sutton group carrying it, and Colette O'Neill marching in front of it, mother of four, singing at the top of her lungs. The order came 'Loose your contraceptives!' and we slid our packets beyond the feet of the Customs men along the platform towards our supporters. The men dropped their eyes, silent and fussed, as a group of us who had decided to declare and not surrender waved our purchases at the Customs men, who ignored us and passed us through.

The papers said next day that other women said we should be shot or locked up, but we weren't even arrested. The Government had decided not to enforce the Criminal Amendment Act. It took thirty minutes before we knew for sure that the Customs men were going to let us pass – they were preoccupied with shoppers. All the time we chanted: 'Enforce the Constitution now' and 'The law is obsolete.' Now we were through the Customs with our condoms and other Irish unmentionables. On this occasion, lip service to the law had been paid on a grand scale. Now we marched to Store Street Station nearby, the crowds after us. We could see the gardaí through their office windows. They didn't even glance out. They pretended we weren't there.

The tarring of young women in the Bogside

IRISH TIMES CORRESPONDENT (1971)

This news report captures something of the febrile atmosphere in Derry in November 1971, when Catholic women who had become engaged to soldiers were publicly humiliated by members of their own community. An editorial note in *Changing the Times*, an anthology of work by female *Irish Times* journalists, reads: 'Renagh Holohan believes she may have been the author; bylines were still rare in the news section at this date.'

Another girl was tarred and tied to a lamppost near the Bogside Inn in Lecky Road, Derry, early this morning. A crowd of men and women stood and jeered at the girl for fifteen minutes until others came to her aid and released her. A cardboard placard – 'Soldier Doll' – was hung from her neck. A crowd of about two hundred watched as a woman cropped her dark hair with scissors and then poured red and black liquid of either paint or tar over her head. She was reported to be engaged to a British soldier. One eyewitness said the girl, aged about eighteen or nineteen, was stopped in the street by at least seven women and brought back to the Bogside in a car. The girl, who lives in Westway, Creggan, was tied to the post by her chest and feet with wire, to the same lamppost as nineteen-year-old Miss Martha Doherty who was tarred there on Tuesday night. Miss Doherty's hair had also been cut with scissors and afterwards closer with a razor, then tar was poured over her head and she was tied to the lamppost while a crowd of about eighty looked on, many of them shouting, 'Soldier lover.'

Last night, Miss Doherty was jeered as she left her home to stay with friends. She wore a brown wig. Her fiancé, Private John Larter, aged eighteen, of the Royal Anglian Regiment, comes from Suffolk and was planning to become a Catholic before the marriage, which is due to take place in St Columb's Church, Waterside, with an army padre officiating. Neighbours last night doubted if the wedding would take place as planned. The Army tried unsuccessfully to arrange a meeting between Miss Doherty and Private Larter through journalists yesterday afternoon. Reporters who approached her house in Drumcliffe Gardens were told to leave by her father. An Army spokesman said: 'We hope the wedding will take place on Friday, but we cannot know whether this will be so. If they were prepared to do this to the girl, just what are they prepared to do to her parents?' Mr John Hume, MP, described the tarring as shameful. 'I condemn it absolutely, but the incident was inevitable with anti-Army feeling running as high as I believe it is running in Derry.' Earlier this year, three men in the Bogside shot Private Larter in the hand, as he left Miss Doherty's home after midnight.

Last weekend the women's section of the Official IRA issued a warning that girls fraternizing with soldiers would have action taken against them. In the Bogside, the slogan 'Soldier Doll' has been seen daubed on at least one other house. The mother of the family in this house said she had got her daughter away before she could be taken out of the house, and the girl was now staying with friends in a secret hideout. Earlier, a twenty-year-old factory machinist was taken from her home by six girls and questioned about whom she had gone out with; and she was also asked to name other girls who had gone out with soldiers. Her hands were tied behind her back and she was blindfolded and had her head shaved.

The death of Jackie Duddy

KAY DUDDY (1972)

In Derry, on 30 January 1972, the British Army's Parachute Regiment killed thirteen civilians during the course of a civil rights march: this became known as Bloody Sunday. The official inquiry into the killings, conducted by Lord Widgery, was rejected by nationalists as a whitewash; a second inquiry, led by Lord Saville, did not report until 2010. Meanwhile, in 2000, the journalist Eamonn McCann, a Derry native, published a book entitled *Bloody Sunday in Derry: What Really Happened*. It included the testimony of Kay Duddy, a sister of one of the victims, seventeen-year-old Jackie Duddy.

My father had told all of us that we weren't to go on the march. 'Stay put!' he said. 'I want none of you involved in that carry-on.' Then he went off to bed. So it came about that we were sitting at the kitchen table playing cards, not knowing anything, when Michael, the second youngest, who was ten at the time, came diving in and said: 'Our Jackie's after getting killed.' We all shouted at him, 'God forgive you for saying a thing like that,' and pounced on him and took a swipe at him. He looked at us and said, 'I'm only joking,' and ran out again, because he knew none of us was supposed to be out on the march. But we still didn't think anything. About 15 minutes after that there was a knock at the door and my aunt and uncle came in. My aunt Dolly said, 'I don't want to alarm you. I'm only telling you what I heard. They're saying Jackie's been hurt down the town.'

I remember running out of the house and over towards the Creggan Community Centre to phone. At that stage there were people pouring up from the Bogside from the march and I kept grabbing them and asking, 'Did you see our Jackie? Does anybody know anything about our Jackie?' But people were pulling away from me.

I phoned casualty at Altnagelvin and asked if a Jackie Duddy had been admitted that afternoon. There was a lapse and then the nurse or whoever it was asked who was speaking and I told her I was Jackie

Duddy's sister, and she said: 'Jackie Duddy was dead on admission.' I remember throwing the phone up in the air and standing there, screaming. All I could think of was how we were going to tell my father. How could we wake him up and say to him that one of his sons had been killed, especially when he had warned him not to go there, warned him on the peril of his life?

I have often wondered since if my father had had a premonition, to have warned us so strongly that day. But then he was like that anyway. He didn't want us involved in anything, full-stop. He had 15 children and he was very protective of us all. He always said that he had fought for civil rights all his life, but in his own way. When he took the family out to squat in Springtown Camp, that was for civil rights, to put a roof over our heads when the corporation wouldn't help us. My father was one of the leaders of that, one of the first men out there. There were those huts left behind by the Army and at the same time hundreds of homeless. So the men took them. In the end they were doing the corporation a favour. They had housed their families and they were eventually paying rent, when otherwise those huts would just have been lying there, not earning any money. That was my daddy's attitude, that you fought yourself for your wife and family, that you didn't bring a great crowd with you.

He was from Thomas Street, off the Lecky Road, which is where my mother came from. She was originally Maureen Houston. They met when he was home on leave from the merchant navy and got married at Christmas in 1944. Then they went to live on the Lecky with her parents. That's where my sister Maureen was born and Bernie and myself, us being twins. My daddy used to tell me about sitting out on the window-sill on the day we were born – at that time men kept out of the way – and the pandemonium when the nurse came running out shouting that there was a second one coming into the world. That was me.

After that there wasn't enough room in the house, so they moved to Barrack Street, where Ann and then Billy were born. Billy was the first boy after four girls. So that house was now too small as well, which is why my father squatted us into Springtown. Suzy, Eddie, Eileen and Jackie were born in Springtown. Jackie was the baby when we got a swanky house in Creggan Heights, with three bedrooms. We had a smashing time there, it was great. Then along came Margaret and Teresa, Patrick and Gerry, and Michael and Pauline. At that stage the house in Creggan Heights became too small and we moved to the maisonettes in Central Drive.

Central Drive wasn't a happy place for us. Springtown had been happy, even if it was hard, work and everything else being scarce. And Creggan Heights was the happiest time we ever had. But when we moved to Central Drive my mammy wasn't well. She thought she was going through the change of life but in fact it was leukaemia. It was only a short time after she was diagnosed that she died, in 1968. And then Jackie was to die in 1972. It wasn't a particularly happy hour for us there. There were nine girls and six boys in the house, so it was bedlam to say the least of it. The girls were always squabbling about knickers and socks and all kind of things, but, funnily enough, the boys never seemed to argue or fight. Jackie in particular was very quiet. It would have taken a lot to rile him. He used to come in from school and would fall asleep sitting on the rocking chair in the kitchen, which my mother always kept there because it reminded her of Val Doonican and she loved Val Doonican's singing.

We used to kick him and taunt the life out of him, to wake him, but even then he wouldn't get up angry. He had one of those placid natures. He palled around with Adrian O'Brien, Andy Nolan and Jimmy Cocayne, God rest him, and they were like the musketeers, you'd never see one without seeing all four. Our Bernie had a family then, and they did a lot of baby-sitting for her. That was the sort of them, at 15, 16, 17. Jackie would go to the odd dance but only locally, in the community centre or wherever. He hung around with a couple of girls, but he was very young. They would leave one home and then find another one on the way home! There was no harm in them.

He left school at 15. He'd been at the Holy Child, then at the Rosemount Boys', then St Joseph's. And then he got a job as a petrol pump attendant, and then at French's factory out at Springtown, where they built the industrial estate over the camp. That's closed down now, too. But his main interest once he left school was boxing. He joined the Long Tower Club and was off with them boxing in Liverpool and in Dublin. He would be sparring in the kitchen and we'd laugh at him – the size of him! But he won more trophies than enough. He was definitely showing good signs at boxing – at least we thought so. That was his real ambition and he was dedicated to it. He would never miss his training.

He never went to the civil rights marches or took any part in all that was happening. We had a sister living in Rosemount, and sometimes he would go moseying down there to see what the crack was when there was a riot going on, but he'd never join in. He knew from my daddy that it would be more than his life was worth. We never even talked much about it in the house, even though we were living in Creggan in the middle of CS gas half the time. My daddy didn't have politics in the house. He used to say that having been a merchant seaman he was cosmopolitan. And as for Ireland, he'd say that he had been an ambassador for Ireland everywhere he went, and that he could go back anywhere he had ever been. He said he tried to show other people that the Irish were good and loving and caring. He would see the marches on television and would say, 'Switch that over.' He knew there were none of us involved in any of that.

The reason Jackie sneaked out to go on the march was that so many were going. It was a big day out. He said, 'I think I'll go down and hear my girl Bernie making a mouth of herself' – Bernadette Devlin being the only girl on the platform. It was just crack to him. We could see out the window everybody gathering for the march, as if it was a festival. We had a bird's-eye view. My daddy was working shifts at the hospital at the time and came in just then. That's when he warned us that there wasn't one of us to go out, and then he was off to his bed. But Jackie could see there were a lot of his friends there, and he was off. He walked down the road with a girl on each arm.

When I came back from the community centre with the news, it was my aunt Dolly who went up to wake my daddy and tell him. We all sat on the stairs listening until he was able to come down. Then I went over to Altnagelvin with him. To get to the morgue at Altnagelvin you walk down a long cold corridor with a wind blowing through it until you reach a door with a window. I looked through it and I could see all the bodies laid out, covered in cloth, but that was as far as they'd allow me to go. I had to stand there and wait while my father went in and identified Jackie. I've never been able to remember much about what happened after that. There are whole days blanked out.

The bishop was with Jackie when it happened. We see it all the time when there is a programme about the Troubles in Northern Ireland, the bishop – he was only Fr Daly at that time – waving the white hanky. He told us how he started to run and ran so fast he passed Jackie, even though Jackie was so fit from training. I suspect they were aiming for the bishop, that they thought they would get themselves a riot priest that day. To say this is not to show disrespect for Bishop Daly. To me, he is a candidate for sainthood. But that has always come into my mind when I've wondered who they were aiming at when they killed Jackie. The bishop was able to give him the last rites, and to talk to him before he died. He told us he said, 'Don't tell my mammy,' which was strange, because my mammy was dead. It ought have been my daddy that he was worried about, who had told him he wasn't to be on the march. But then maybe at the moment that's what would come into his mind, that's who he would think of.

My daddy never recovered from it. He worked on for a while and then when he retired he just took to his bed and stayed there for four years, never got up. Eventually he died of lung cancer. I think it was that Jackie's death brought home to him that my mammy was dead. He said that he understood when Jackie died why the Sacred Heart had taken my mammy when he did, so that she wouldn't have to live through the grief. And that brought home to him that she was dead. He had great devotion to the Sacred Heart.

I'm glad myself that my mammy didn't have to go through it. I have seen Mrs Kelly sitting in the graveyard, crying still, and thought, 'Poor creature, I'm glad my mammy's not going through that.' I look back on it all now and think what a short life he had and, apart from the bit of distinction he earned at the boxing, how insignificant he was. They sent us money afterwards but they never gave us any explanation. My father wouldn't take the money, even though if anybody needed it at that particular time it was him. He was very sorely hurt.

We were lucky we were such a big family. I had to take control afterwards, and then everybody took their turn. Ann left her work and took over, and then Suzy left her work and took over and so on, leaving your work to look after the family, then going back to work to get the marriage money and somebody else taking over. Everybody chipped in. We managed – we had to. One for all and all for one.

Martin McGuinness at twenty-one

NELL MCCAFFERTY (1972)

The journalist Nell McCafferty, a native of Derry, had known the family of Martin McGuinness all her life when she wrote this profile. It was published in the *Irish Times* in the immediate aftermath of Bloody Sunday.

'You know how much life has changed when you're having a Republican tea – a bottle of orange and a bap – in the back of a car, just a few minutes from your own home.'

At twenty-one, Martin McGuinness, OC of the Derry Provisional IRA, may have changed his lifestyle. But he is acutely embarrassed at popular press descriptions of him as 'the boy who rules Free Derry'. He was catapulted into the limelight at a press conference in Creggan estate last week, and since then the English papers have had a heyday writing about his 'good looks, youth and shy charm'.

An American TV man spent a wistful hour planning the scenario for a colour-film spectacular about him. 'Jeez,' he said, 'that boy would be hot on the coast. Can you see him, six feet tall in a dinner jacket, raising funds?' His wish will, presumably, not be granted. The English journalist who romanticized Mr McGuinness was ordered out of town. He left immediately.

'I don't feel like a big shot, travelling around the area in a stolen Ford Avenger,' said Martin. 'I have to do what the people want. They don't treat me like I was something different. In fact one wee woman couldn't understand why I couldn't go down to the police barracks to bail out her son who'd been arrested. I had to take her up to headquarters and arrange for someone else to do it.'

He joined the IRA after the Battle of the Bogside in 1969. Initially he was with the Official wing. 'There wasn't a Provo unit in Derry then. The Officials approached me and for three months we attended policy and training lectures in a house in the Bogside. But they wouldn't give us any action. All this time, there was fighting in the

streets and things were getting worse in Belfast. You could see the
soldiers just settling into Derry, not being too worried about the
stone-throwing. Occasionally the Officials gave out Molotov cock-
tails which wouldn't even go off, and I knew that after fifty years we
were more of an occupied country than we ever were before. It
seemed to me that behind all the politics and marching it was plain as
daylight that there was an Army in our town, in our country, and
that they weren't there to give out flowers. Armies should be fought
by armies. So one night I piled into a black Austin, me and five mates,
and we went to see a Provo across the Border. We told him our position and there were several meetings after that. Then we joined.
Nothing really happened until Séamus Cusack was killed and internment came soon after. Then the Provos in Derry were ordered into
full-time military action. I gave up my job working in the butcher's
shop.'

His mother was panic-stricken, he said, when she found out that
he was in the IRA. 'A few months after I joined she found a belt and
beret in my bedroom and there was a big row. She and my father told
me to get out of it, and for the sake of peace I said I would, and they
calmed down. But now they have to accept it. They've seen the British Army in action and they know I'd no choice.'

His mother, though, had started smoking again, which she hadn't
done in years. 'I know her health has failed and she's always worrying
about me. If I'm not around to tell her myself I send her word that
I'm all right. I don't discuss my business with her and she doesn't ask.'
Martin's mother was angry at the press reports of him. 'You'd think
he was running around the area with a gun, telling people what they
could and could not do. The only time I saw guns in this house was
when the British Army raided it.' She worries about him even more
since Joseph McCann was shot in Belfast.

'Since Martin's picture appeared in the papers every soldier in
Derry knows what he looks like.' And when it's all over – should it
ever end – she worries about his job. 'His trade's been interrupted.
His father is a welder, his brothers bricklayers and carpenters, but
what will become of Martin? That's why they'll have to get an
amnesty so's he can get back to work and not be always on the run.'

Martin himself doesn't worry too much about what will come after. His aims are devastatingly simple. 'I want a United Ireland where everyone has a good job and enough to live on.' He had read a little, he said, since becoming a Republican, and supported Socialist views, 'but the Officials are all views and no support. I wish we were getting more press coverage in Derry for our political beliefs but we don't have the talkers in our ranks. Still, the people support us and that's good enough.'

He wondered sometimes, he said, if Socialism would ever work out. 'I have a lot of respect for Bernadette Devlin but I think maybe people are too greedy. I'd be willing to sweep the roads in my world and it wouldn't seem like a bad job if they got the same wages as everybody else, but do you not think now that people are just too greedy? Somebody always wants to make a million. Anyway, before you can try, you have to get this country united. We'd make sure that Protestants are fairly treated. Don't accept that we are sectarian. But you have to face facts that it's the Catholics who've been discriminated against. The Officials go on about us all the time but it was them that blew up the Protestant mayor's house in Derry and shot [John] Barnhill and John Taylor. Mind you, I've nothing against the rank and file Officials. They're soldiers just like me, with a job to do. That job, as far as I am concerned, is to fight the British Army.'

The Provisionals took care, he said, not to harm innocent civilians. 'But sometimes mistakes are made. There was an explosion in Derry some time ago, and I read afterwards that a man had been trapped in the basement. He lost a part of his leg. Then you read that he's a cyclist and you feel sad. The worst I ever felt was Bloody Sunday. I wandered about stunned, with people crying and looking for their relatives, and I thought of all that guff about honour between soldiers. The British Army knew right well we wouldn't fight them with all those thousands of people there, so they came in and murdered the innocent. I used to worry about being killed before that day, but now I don't think about death at all.'

If there's a riot on, he sometimes goes and throws stones. 'It relieves the pressure and it's a way of being with my mates, the ones who have not joined the movement, and I feel just ordinary again. I suppose.' He added, 'You think us Provos have no feelings at all just because we have no time to talk about it.'

Last week he talked publicly for the first time. His speech, to a wildly cheering crowd in the Brandywell, was very short and to the point. 'If Gerry Fitt and John Hume think they're going to sell the people out,' he said, 'they've got another thing coming. It's just not on.' He looked very young as he spoke. He was probably not what Austin Currie had in mind last autumn when he warned the people that the possible imprisonment of MPs would create a need for 'second-tier leadership'. But the influential, middle-aged, middle of the road Derry Central Citizens Council took sufficient cognizance of his leadership to go and have a talk with him about his ideas. Afterwards they rejected Provisional proposals for elections in the city. Martin didn't mind too much.

'I know they're wrong,' he said. 'I know it and I feel it when I go round the barricades and see the boys they called hooligans, and the men they called wasters, and the fellows that used only to drink, doing things they really believe in now. Protecting the area and freeing Ireland and freeing themselves.'

Testimony of a bomb victim

BRIDGET FITZPATRICK (1974)

On 17 May 1974, three car bombs exploded during the rush hour in Dublin, and a fourth in Monaghan. Thirty-three people were killed. Although no group claimed responsibility for the attacks, it was assumed that loyalists had carried them out; the cars used had been stolen in East Belfast and Portadown earlier that day. And when Sammy Smyth, a spokesman for the UDA, was asked to comment, he said: 'I am very happy about the bombings in Dublin. There is a war with the Free State and now we are laughing at them.' It was some thirty years after the bombings that Bridget Fitzpatrick gave the following testimony to an Oireachtas hearing following the publication of the report of the Independent Commission of Inquiry, headed by Justice Henry Barron.

On 17 May, at 5.25 p.m., I was in the middle of the road on Parnell Street with two of my sons. I was after coming out of a shop on Parnell Street called Hamills with my seven-year-old son's Communion clothes under my arm. I had my other son, Tommy, who was five and a half, by the other hand and I got a bang of a 250-pound bomb into the side of my face. The only way I could describe it to everybody here is that it was like as if a bus had hit me on the side of the face. I remember my head going over. I was facing the garage that that chap, Derek Byrne, worked in. I can only describe it as that the garage was coming out into my face and a baby's pram was going up over it.

On impact I ran with my two sons. I had been working in the Rotunda Hospital. I had been in there a few months before when I had diabetes and lost a baby boy in a full-term birth. I remember my little five and a half year old, Tommy, who is now deceased, screaming, 'Mammy, mammy, stop, the bomb got me in the leg.' I do not know what you call it but I was running through a few feet of glass and thick yellow and grey smoke which was like a wall that I could not get through with my two little boys. I just knew I had to run and could not fall because my children needed me – I was their ma.

When I got to the Bank of Ireland on O'Connell Street, I could see to the right of my eyes visions of young girls and people screaming. 'Stop, stop that woman, look at her,' but nobody could stop me until I got to the Rotunda because that was a safe place for me because I was after having my eighth child there and I worked in it as well. When I got to the door of the Rotunda, this doctor was coming out and I said, 'Doctor, doctor, help me and my children.' He said, 'There are people who are worse off up the road, go in.' I did that. When I took my hand away, there were clots everywhere on it. I got inside and held on to the counter. I felt something sticking in my back and pulled out a lump of tin which was in my lung.

I was brought into the emergency department. My little boy, Tommy, had two parts of his legs stitched. My other son, Derek, did not get stitches and I was anointed a few hours later. A doctor came from the Richmond Hospital and asked me if I had ever heard of a perforated eardrum. I said, 'I did but, doctor, I don't care if my hearing is gone. Will you, please, let me go home to my other five children?' I could hear my two sons outside saying, 'We want our ma, we want our ma.' The nurses in the Rotunda brought them over to the shop and bought them Rolos and Crunchies. How could I forget? I just kept saying to them, 'I am all right,' but for three hours there were sheets being taken from under my lung and clots popping out of me. The doctor came from the Richmond and told me that I had a perforated eardrum and punctured lung. Anyway, it came to pass that the priest came from Marlborough Street Church and anointed me. I said, 'Father, am I going to die? My kids.' He said, 'No, you will be okay.' I have never been okay to this day.

I went home with a big bandage around my leg, holding my two lovely boys. I marched up Seán McDermott Street where I am proud to say I live. There were lovely, decent people living on it – neighbours. About 500 people from all the flats and the houses cheered me and my two sons up the street. When I got home, I did not know where I was, naturally. Three big men – I reckon they were from the Government – came to my home and apologised to me. They said they were very sorry for what had happened to me. My brother brought me to Artane where he lived. I thanked the men and that was the end of it.

I was told in the Rotunda Hospital that it was only a maternity hospital and that it was sorry but that I was to bring my two children to Temple Street the next morning and that I was to go to the Mater Hospital, which I did. I stayed in Artane with my brother Paddy and I brought my seven children with me. My eldest daughter, Lily, who is sitting over there, had to help me get through life and with the kids because my husband left me as I was not [a] real woman any more. I worried about my children. I overprotected them; thank God I did. I went to the Mater Hospital where I was told I would be deaf before I was 40 years of age. I have suffered from a balance disorder since. I have not been in town for 15 or more years and I have not been on a bus for nearly 20 years. I do not go shopping; I do not go anywhere. I just live on my nerves.

My son, Tommy, died. He went on his first holiday in the sun at 29 years of age and suffered a heart attack in the swimming pool in Santa Ponsa. My other son has been in every hospital one could name. He has tried to commit suicide. I am a broken mother but I love my children so much. We are real people. I am here to tell you all about my sons and my poor daughter who had to leave school to help me because my husband did not want to know. That is my side of the story. I was never treated for my injuries. I never knew what to do. I did not get time to think about it because I had to rear my children. I am not looking for sympathy; I am looking for justice for people like me.

I do not sleep very well, so I listen to *Newstalk* 106 when I am awake during the night. I have heard people say this is hardly worth bothering about and that it is 30 years since the bombing happened. It happened to me and I lost my family. My marriage failed and I had to live in very bad circumstances, although I do not care about money anyway – I am not talking about that. I had to struggle with my seven children and I did not get any help from anywhere. Nobody knocked on my door to ask us if we were okay, which we were not. I am still not okay. [. . .]

Ms Alice O'Brien's sister lived around the corner from me and I had to go through my life looking at a baby's pram going up in front of my eyes. It only took a split second but it happened to me. Her little niece was found on the roof of the Welcome Inn with a soother in her mouth the next morning. The other baby was found that night.

I witnessed some horrific sights. I was in the Rotunda Hospital and I saw a chap with the top of his head gone. The glasses of an elderly woman were embedded in her eyes. It put so much fear in me and I have neglected my health. I thank God I did not neglect my poor family but they are all broken in different ways. I thank the committee for listening to me.

The death of Eamon de Valera and the
nationalist pantheon

MAURICE O'CONNELL (1975)

Maurice O'Connell was an historian, writer and academic. He was the great-great-grandson of Daniel O'Connell and was indefatigable in championing O'Connell's reputation. Following the death of de Valera in August 1975, he wrote to his fellow historian T. Desmond Williams, professor of modern history at UCD.

It will be interesting to see how Dev fares at the hands of the historians. I went to the lying-in-state and on my way out met a Kerry Fianna Fáil TD who introduced me to two others. I showed them the religious card being sold to the queue lined up for the entrance to the lying-in-state, and asked them if it was a Fianna Fáil publication. They said no, that it was commercial. The card might almost be a Mass card but politics enters with the quotation: 'No democratic government could tolerate within its territory the formation of any armed group or any armed activities save those under its control . . . Force is not the way to unity.' There is no printer named nor any other evidence of authorship of the card – the quotation is Dev's, of course.

The quotation shows that non-violence is now the going thing. I notice that the recent book on Arthur Griffith has a subheading about non-violence. O'Connell's resurgence has astonished me. It was coming slowly for a couple of decades but the NI crisis has pushed him up the ladder at the double. I hope he won't now become like Pearse the Fount of Wisdom and be exploited like Pearse has been. For more than a generation Pearse has been the Patron Saint of Violence, the Fianna Fáil Party, Compulsory Irish and Pure-Souled Idealism. And now nobody gives a damn about him. Even the Provisional IRA don't mention him, probably because they don't want to be identified with violence for its own sake. Pearse will eventually come back somewhat but as a man, not as a god.

John A. Costello's comment that Dev has left nothing behind him was stupid but Costello was always a man who blurted out his prejudices. [. . .] John A. Murphy's assessment in his book *Ireland in the Twentieth Century* places Dev at the head of twentieth-century Irish politics but does not really explain why he ever got or remained there. I have accused John of being prejudiced against Dev because I agree with his assessment but I am prejudiced. There is no doubt that Dev had greatness but I think he used that greatness with comparatively little benefit to his people, or perhaps I mean that he did much good but that he did much more harm. He completed the establishment of a stable democracy in the 1930s but only after he had done much to prevent the establishment of a stable democracy in the 1920s. I cannot see historians accepting his rejection of the Treaty and support of the Civil War as acts of [a] true democrat.

A country tea in Dublin

PRO-QUIDNUNC, *IRISH TIMES* (1978)

The Country Shop, in the basement of 23 St Stephen's Green, first opened its doors in 1930. Its full name was 'The Country Shop, Depot for Irish Country Industries'. It was variously headquarters for the Irish Homespun Society, the Irish Countrywomen's Association and the Country Markets. Pro-Quidnunc, in 'An Irishman's Diary' in the *Irish Times*, marked the occasion of its closure.

'Irishman's Diary' went to a wake yesterday, for an old and greatly loved Dublin institution, which went to every possible length to disguise the fact that the big grey city lay outside its walls.

This morning the fittings, the china, tea urns, those so familiar green and red chairs, the glossy oval black tables, the ovens and sinks and cake tins, even last craft items left in the craft shop of the Country Shop in St Stephen's Green will be auctioned off.

Yesterday, the curious were allowed in to poke and root in the sad debris of almost a half century of a unique institution, a part of countless Dublin childhoods. The cavernous kitchens, the servants' quarters that once were of a great town house, were laid open to the vulgar rabble for the first time, astonishing lengths of red-tiled corridor with pantries and washrooms and larders and wine bins opening off them.

A newly-moved-in mouse crept out from under a grain bin, not yet believing that the good times are gone forever. The cat has gone, leaving a trail of muddy footprints across a white ceramic counter to a broken window.

Pro-Quidnunc hoped and wept, for even Diarists have vanished childhoods. The Aged Parent used to work two doors up from it, in a house straight out of Dickens with a great coach house and a servants' entry for the much-more-civil-than-now servants to creep deferentially into Estate Duties. It was a fascinating place to be brought as a child, perpetually associated with fog curling up from the back-yard cobbles and frightening shadows from the ruin at the back. The tall house itself smelling of dust and sealing wax and old offices. From there it was a minute's dash through the rain to the open fire in the Country Shop, hot buttered toast and fresh scones, potato cakes and crumpets, and cakes to make a child's eyes pop. Downstairs was the place for a winter's afternoon. But on a spring morning the seats by the window, with pale sun slanting in over the primroses and crocuses in the window boxes, were the best place in the city to sit and drink coffee.

Upstairs was almost entirely middle-aged ladies, the last bastion of The Hat in Dublin. On one famous occasion, a major scandal was caused by a pretty young woman attempting to peel off an anorak and a heavy woollen jumper, accidentally pulling the tee-shirt off with them over her head, to the apoplexy of The Hats. The Aged Parent recognised the tee-shirt as one stolen from him by an old friend years earlier and braved the stares to rescue her from smothering, or from embarrassment, or both.

It seems impossible, both to me and to the many familiar faces guarding the contents yesterday, that it should all be gone – just two years short of its half-century. Four of the staff members yesterday had about one hundred and forty years of service between them, and it is just because we shall not see their like again that the place is closing. The staff are irreplaceable, and tired, and it was decided it was better to close now, on an up note, rather than see standards start to slip.

Betty Irwin, and Angela Kehoe (who started working as a book-keeper there thirty-eight years ago), ran the crafts section, the original purpose of the Country Shop, which had to be subsidised by doing the odd cup of coffee – by the time they closed they were doing seven hundred meals a day. They sold weaving, basket work, woodwork, pottery; they started to sell Philip Pearce's pottery when he started to make it in Cork first, and they ended up selling both his sons' work as well – Simon's glass and Stephen's pottery. They approached prize-winners at local craft shows and offered them a showcase, and they stocked work by people whom the remarkable Dr Muriel Gahan, one of the founders, met on her travels around the country. The loss of the showcase isn't quite as tragic as it might have been twenty years ago since, Miss Kehoe says, there has been a steady growth of local outlets for craft work.

Like the other staff members, they have been venturing out to eat in other parts of the city since the place closed – and are shocked at standards. The cakes go stale in hours, since they don't use good ingredients, Miss Kehoe says, recalling the morning delivery of eggs every day for their cake baker, who came in to work for them at the age of fourteen and was still there up to the time the place closed forty-seven years later. Miss Kehoe herself bought mince pies one Christmas, forgot them, found them in May, and ate them quite happily: 'They were perfect.'

Upstairs, Kate Tyrell, there for twenty years and more, and Deirdre Ennis, who thinks she may have been there for thirty-five, she isn't sure, were sadly talking about what a loss it would be for the city, the grandmothers, daughters and grandchildren they saw coming, the faces they saw every afternoon of their working lives.

Miss Ennis operated the cash register, kept records, managed, and was officially the glass and china buyer for the restaurant. She had a feeling the end was coming earlier this year, when she was about to reorder and somebody delicately suggested that she shouldn't get in too much. She points sadly to the heaps of irreplaceable china, the flowery cups and saucers from downstairs and the striped mugs for the upstairs snack bar, designed by Dr Gahan herself, many of them from the original stock, and the last greenware that was used for the upstairs restaurant.

It would be most indelicate to ask such a lady her age, but she was born just across the opposite side of the Green; her mother had 82 and 83, and her cousin 84, all now owned by UCD. She was almost helping out a next-door neighbour when she came in during the war to lend a hand one afternoon a week. She ended up giving as much as she could spare of her remarkable life to it – she is still a hockey coach and has journeyed all over the world with hockey teams. Now, saddened by the centre city and how much it has changed, she lives in Monkstown, near the sea where she swims most days of her life.

The beautiful copper tea and coffee urns, used when they did catering for weddings or christenings, are laid out on a table, and she remembers how much work it took to keep them shining. The place will be a terrible loss, she believes, to the whole city. It had a gay secret night life, unknown to us morning coffee drinkers, housing exhibitions, parties, dances, art shows, even once a discotheque for the nephew of dress designer Sybil Connolly. All the bright young people came, and so did Miss Ennis. 'It was all nets hanging from the ceiling, and dim religious light, and the young people sitting quite still in pitch darkness. They thought I was mad, but I wanted to see how the young people today got on, and I never had so much fun in my life.'

What will we do without such ladies, and without our country tea, for which, up to the time the place closed, you got a pot of tea, potato cakes, muffins, scones, brown bread, and cake, for 65p?

The decline of the Irish language

GEARÓID Ó TUATHAIGH (1979)

The historian Gearóid Ó Tuathaigh assessed the state of the Irish language in an essay published in *Ireland: 1945–1970*, edited by J. J. Lee.

In examining the Irish language question during the past thirty years one is immediately struck by a mass of paradoxes and contradictions, remarkable even by Irish standards. On the one hand is the undeniable evidence of retreat and despondency, of widespread loss of faith and hope (and at times even of charity) in the stated national aspiration for revival. The most dramatic failure has been the continual (and continuing) contraction of the Gaeltacht, and the linguistic debilitation which has taken place in what remains of it. [. . .] Indeed, it is perfectly clear that if present demographic and linguistic trends are not reversed the Gaeltacht as a distinct linguistic community will not survive this century. [. . .]

The situation at the present time is critical. Demographically the Gaeltacht is in a perilous state. There are enormous linguistic problems involved in community reconstruction. To avoid extinction the Gaeltacht must expand and grow. At the time of writing it would be dishonest to pretend that the omens are encouraging. Certainly there is little ground for optimism in the state of the language outside the Gaeltacht. Here the years since the war have seen the continuation of what a distinguished Irish-American described in 1963 as 'a declared government policy of restoration' combined with 'an obvious anaemia in its enforcement'. In fact, the signs of the state's failure and of the consequent anxiety of the revivalists were already unmistakably clear by the early 1940s. [. . .]

Even in the areas of direct government responsibility the years since the war have been years of retreat and failure. As late as 1959 over one-third of the Civil Service had little or no Irish, while in Gaeltacht areas almost half the public servants were incompetent in Irish. The status of the language in the institutions of state and in such semi-state bodies as Aer Lingus and Bord Fáilte is a useful index of the state's earnestness in the revival effort. The limited use of the Irish language in the conduct of business in the houses of the Oireachtas is, perhaps, the best indication of 'establishment' attitudes.

[...] even in the area where the state placed most of its revivalist hopes from the very outset, that is to say, the schools, the evidence suggests that the position of the language has deteriorated since the war, and deteriorated rather sharply in the last decade. Already by the late 1940s many teachers were expressing doubts and frustrations at what they saw as the unreasonable demands being made on the schools to carry the language revival policy almost on their own, with no apparent back-up from any other sector. The requirement that Irish be essential for state examinations was a live political issue from at least 1949. [...]

It is an interesting, if sad, paradox that while this deterioration in the position of Irish in post-war Ireland has been taking place, the evidence of census, of attitude surveys, and of a more casual kind (e.g. the popularity of certain Irish-language TV shows) point to widespread public good-will towards the language, or, at the very least, to an affirmation of public desire that it should not be allowed to die. To translate this benign passivity into something more positive called for expert linguistic planning, and political will and energy. For a brief period during the 1960s the expertise and the instruments for enlightened linguistic planning were available to the state, but recent disclosures by Dr Ó hUallacháin suggest that a paralysis of political will allied to bureaucratic obstruction combined to abort any such planning. Perhaps this should be seen as part of the general lack of confidence in planning of any sort which characterised the early 1970s. Certainly, the decision in 1973 to drop Irish as an essential subject for the Leaving Certificate and the Civil Service removed the last vestige of state policy on the language, and it is scarcely an exaggeration to say that at the present time there is a greater lack of direction in the state's attitude towards the language question than at any time since 1922.

Pope John Paul II in Ireland

LOUIS MCREDMOND (1979)

In September 1979, Pope John Paul II paid the first visit by a Pope to
Ireland. He went to Dublin, Drogheda, Galway, Knock and Limer-
ick, attracting crowds that totalled almost three million. Louis
McRedmond wrote about the visit for the *Tablet*.

He came, and history could not be denied its consummation. The sustained eruption of joy from the Catholic Irish put to rout all cynicism,
all uncertainty, all sophisticated analysis. It swept up to the Pope until
he very nearly cracked beneath the surge of emotion. The only word
for it was love, and that word was the catalyst: 'I love you,' he told the
young in Galway. It was a full twelve minutes before they let him
speak again: 'We love you,' they chorused back and burst spontane-
ously into the teenagers' anthem: 'He's got the whole world in his
hands.' The Pope had to dab away the tears which matched the weeping of sheer happiness noticed so often among the vast crowds which
assembled to greet him wherever he went in Ireland.

Let nobody call it hysteria. The orderly behaviour of so many
thousands, their good humour, their near-cheekiness (some of their
songs were far from spiritual), their dignified resumption of the lit-
urgy when the ceremonial demanded it, gave the lie to that. I suspect
that only we Irish can understand the chord awoken so deep in our
consciousness by the presence of the Pastor of Pastors. I spoke of history. That was at the heart of it. I do not mean history deliberately
pondered. I mean an awareness, an awareness of identity and origin.
You could not carry in your veins the blood of the generations who
suffered degrading repression so long for the faith that was in them
and remain unmoved. What the Irish knew last weekend, knew
inchoately perhaps, was that the focal point of their forefathers' loyalty had come among them. Each man and woman and child voiced
the soul-stirrings of a people past as well as the excitement of their
own experiencing. It was love in depth.

Yes, I know that this is not what the Church is about. But I wonder whether we Irish may not have reminded ourselves and the watching world of the half-forgotten communion of saints? The Pope, in his carefully constructed and interlocked series of addresses, spoke much of the beginnings, continuity and inheritance. St Patrick was often on his lips. He used the term 'Ireland' in a remarkable way to indicate not just a place or the sea of humanity around him. He made it refer to a continuum. The quick-to-judge said it was conservative. They missed the historical dimension, the 'vertical' dimension as he put it himself, which linked the remote coming of Christianity with the modern age and reached out to the future in hope. Often, it seemed, this Ireland for Pope John Paul was analogous to the Church on its pilgrim path through human history.

The Irish set a seal upon that message in the vibrant rapport which they established with their guest. Their flags and banners, handkerchiefs and scarves and berets, waved his helicopter out of the sky down to thunderous greetings. The oldest music, a hymn to the Eucharist composed in Patrician times, and the haunting lilt of a Gaelic welcome tune from the nadir of penal persecution, spoke the same greeting out of distant times: so did many of the offertory gifts and the Irish instrumental airs which accompanied their presentation. The Pope's frequent invocation of prayers and phrases in the Irish language was cheered to the echo. The pop songs of the young, their uninhibited dancing and football-crowd chants – 'We want the Pope', 'We want John Paul' – hinted at the energy available to carry the message into the future. And everywhere was the present, exploding in unqualified joy. They threw flowers at the Pope. And linked arms before him to sway in tempo with Irish ballads and Negro spirituals alike – for any lively song would do when voices just had to be raised – and they substituted for dull adulation the ultimate honour of total informality, the honour reserved for a close friend.

I stress the exuberance and informality, for these eliminated all unseemly chauvinism, triumphalism, much feared, which had no place in any celebration. What Ireland gave the Pope was a carnival, not a triumph. The mood was very much one of relief, with strikes and inflation and the nagging pressures of a frustrating year to put away for a great outdoor party. Violence, it may be, had a lot to do with it and featured dramatically in the papal homilies: for those who came to hear the Pope, the other aspects of Ireland, the real Ireland of hospitality and good cheer and simple commitment to religious practice, were the counterpoint to violence which they felt urged to display.

It was as if they wanted the world and the Pope to realise that behind the awful news out of Ireland in these recent months and years there lived a people of warmth and decency. Were the million-and-a-quarter in the Phoenix Park the largest congregation ever recorded at a celebration of Mass? Whether or not, they were the biggest assemblage ever recorded in Ireland – one fifth or more of the population of the whole island – and they said in that number: 'Look upon the Irish as they truly are.'

Putting Haughey's 'Irish solution' to the test

COLM TÓIBÍN (1980)

In 1979 Charles Haughey, then Minister for Health, introduced a bill, which he called 'an Irish solution to an Irish problem', legalizing the sale of condoms for the first time in the Republic but limiting avail-ability to married couples and obliging them to get a prescription from a doctor. Not every doctor was happy to prescribe condoms, and not every pharmacist was willing to stock them. In a piece for *In Dublin*, Colm Tóibín tested how Haughey's 'Irish solution' was work-ing in practice.

On Tuesday, 11 November, I took out the *Golden Pages*, looked under 'D' for doctor, and selected six, three on the north side of Dublin and three on the south side. I decided to visit them and ask them to pre-scribe condoms for me. I arranged with myself to use the name Richard Flanagan and, if asked, to tell the first and last doctor that I was married, the second and fifth that I was unmarried but indulging in a steady relationship; the third and fourth would be told, I decided, that I simply want to get my rocks off.

Out of the six doctors, three refused to write me a prescription, two on vaguely moral grounds. Of the three who complied with my request, two charged a fee. Four grinned when I told them what I wanted. And I must admit that, despite the fact that I was acting in the course of my professional duty, there was a considerable amount of sweat on the palms of my hands as I went into the surgeries of all six. Only one asked me if I was married or not. I phoned each one before I visited them to ensure that they were trading that day.

The first doctor conducted his practice in the area of Dorset Street. He was a jaunty-looking man in his fifties. 'Now what's the trouble?' said he. 'Well, I just wanted a prescription for condoms,' said I. He pulled his spectacles even further down his nose and looked at me. A broad grin came over his face. 'French letters,' he intoned and grinned defiantly. 'Never,' he roared. I looked behind me to make sure that

the door was shut. 'Over my dead body!' I smiled weakly and under-
standingly at him. 'It's not a doctor's business. You can do what you
like as far as I am concerned. But between doctors and chemists it'll
be an expensive business for ye lads.' He removed his glasses altogether. 'Next it'll be abortion on demand.' He looked sad. 'Doctors
and nurses killing babies. In this little Catholic country.' I asked how
much I owed him. 'You don't owe me anything. I'm terribly sorry. I
wouldn't prescribe a French letter for anyone, not even for one of my
own patients.'

The second doctor's surgery was located in the area between
Terenure and Rathgar. Having elicited my date of birth and my profession, he too asked what the trouble was and I told him. 'Are you
sure this is not a dare?' he asked and I assured him that it was not.
'Can you not get them in the clinics?' he then asked. I told him that I
thought it would be just as easy to go to a doctor. 'It's a farce,' he said,
'it's your TD you should be lobbying, not your doctor. It's just a way
of blackmailing doctors, this law. Doctors are going to refuse to do
it, you know.' I nodded sympathetically. He was young and interested in his first patient to seek condoms. I felt it was a great pity that
there wasn't something wrong with me. He smiled in a resigned sort
of way. 'How many do you want?' he enquired. 'I don't know,' I
replied. I hadn't thought of that one. 'They come in dozens, don't
they?' I agreed. 'Do you want a dozen or a gross?' I made motions to
suggest that I would prefer the latter number. He wrote the prescription. 'How much do I owe you?' I finally asked. 'I'm not going to
charge you for this. I'm a doctor,' he told me.

In the region of Camden Street I sat for twenty minutes in the
doctor's waiting room. He got himself into a state of great confusion
when I told him what I wanted. He didn't know that the new law was
in operation. He picked up the phone and dialled the number of
another doctor, peering at me every so often in a state of disbelief.
They talked for a while. Did I know that there was a family planning
clinic quite close by? Could I not get them from there? The other
doctor had told him that the chemist shops had not got the objects I
was looking for in stock anyway. Was I resolute in not going to the
clinic? I would certainly be able to obtain as many as I wanted there.

The new law, he felt, had pros and cons; he wouldn't like his children to be able to get condoms from slot machines. But, of course, he would write me a prescription if I really wanted one. Was my general health all right? He took out his pad and wrote the prescription, telling me that he would have to charge a consultancy fee. I gave him a tenner, he took a wodge of notes from his back pocket and handed me a fiver as change. I put the prescription in my pocket and departed.

In a quiet, sedate, secluded area of Ballsbridge my fourth doctor held her surgery. I had the feeling as soon as I rang the bell that I was on to a wrong one. There was a piano in the waiting room and a fire was lighting. The receptionist sat with me in the room. Nobody else was waiting. Finally, the doctor herself appeared. She was in her late fifties. Her first reaction was firm. 'No, I won't do it,' she said. 'Can you not go to the Universities? You can get them there in slot machines,' she told me. 'Are you married?' she then asked. Since she was the fourth, I replied in the negative. It didn't seem to matter. She sighed. 'It does seem ridiculous to come to a doctor for that,' she said with an air of finality and stood up. I didn't mention money. It would, somehow, have been even more offensive to the poor doctor's ears than my original request.

Fairview. A five-minute wait. The doctor motioned me to sit down. I told him what I was looking for. His response was so business-like that I felt he was defying me to note that he looked surprised. But he didn't look even slightly surprised. He simply took his pad and wrote the prescription, asking, for the sake of conversation, if there was any problem with the clinics. He didn't pay any attention to whatever I mumbled. He handed me the prescription and told me that I could pay the receptionist and that the prescription was renewable six times over. The receptionist charged me four pounds.

My sixth and last doctor ran his surgery in the area of Amiens Street. He was youngish and his office was untidy. 'What sort of condoms do you want?' he asked. 'Ordinary ones,' I told him. He grinned. 'What's your own doctor's name?' 'I haven't got a doctor in Dublin.' He looked highly dubious. 'There's nothing I can do for you. You can go to your own doctor. I'll have nothing to do with Mr Haughey's Bill but I'll look after my own patients. Go to your own doctor.' I pointed out that it was a simple matter of a prescription. This didn't help. 'You're the fifth person,' he counted them on his fingers, 'that I have never seen before who has come in here looking for condoms. And you all said that you hadn't a doctor in Dublin. Well, you can go and find one.' I didn't mention money and as I was going out the door, he repeated in tones both advisory and contrary, 'Go to your own doctor.'

The hunger-strikes and the Catholic mind

MARIANNE ELLIOTT (1981–2)

Bobby Sands, the elected leader of Provisional IRA prisoners in the Maze Prison, began a hunger-strike on 1 March 1981 to demand political status for those convicted of terrorist offences. This was aimed at characterizing the Provisional campaign as a legitimate act of war. The prisoners' demands included the right to wear their own clothing; no prison work; freedom of association; extra recreation and visits; and restoration of remission lost on protests. In her book *The Catholics of Ulster*, the historian Marianne Elliot analysed the impact of the republican hunger-strikes in Catholic/nationalist Ireland.

The IRA's claim that they were fighting a war rather than mounting a terror campaign found partial recognition in the special-category status of their prisoners until 1976. This was removed under the Thatcher government's 'criminalisation' programme. They immediately mounted a campaign to secure the return of their 'political status', of which the hunger-strikes were the culmination. Bobby Sands was the first to refuse food on 1 March 1981. His family, burnt out of Rathcoole housing estate on the northern edge of Belfast in 1972, had moved to the Twinbrook estate in Catholic west Belfast. There Sands joined the Provisional IRA at the age of eighteen, eventually becoming commander of its 'active service' unit on the estate. At the time of the hunger-strikes, he was five years into a fourteen-year prison term for possession of firearms. In prison he had become a republican intellectual, learning Irish and orchestrating a brilliant public-relations campaign. The IRA prison protest had been making little progress. Now Margaret Thatcher's famous intransigence provided the perfect foil to the image being built of the noble rebel, battling against insurmountable odds. It was Pearse's vision all over again and Sands recognised it. A failing movement would emerge re-fortified when Britain fulfilled its traditional role in republican mythology. Granting leave to wear civilian clothes would have pre-empted the hunger-strikes. But by October 1981 ten men had died, beginning with Sands on 5 May. By then he was a Westminster MP, having stood as a protest candidate in the Fermanagh–South Tyrone by-election on 9 April. The IRA had been given new life.

The election of Sands in Fermanagh–South Tyrone capitalised on previous divisions among the nationalists and republicans which had let unionists win this predominantly nationalist constituency. In a highly emotional atmosphere, in which the republican campaign centred on the need to save Sands's life (rather than on the IRA prisoners' campaign for political status), intense pressure and 'moral blackmail' secured the withdrawal of the constitutional nationalists, and victory (though by a small margin) for Sands. A hundred thousand people attended his funeral in west Belfast some weeks later. Members of the SDLP, Fianna Fáil ministers and TDs from the Irish Republic, Catholic bishops and even a special papal legate tried to mediate between government and hunger-strikers, but to no avail. They were being pulled by their own past into being the apparent spokesmen for a tradition of violence which they abhorred. Moreover, the officiation by Catholic priests at the often elaborate republican funerals of the dead hunger-strikers seemed to confirm the most extreme loyalist vision of 'popery'. Ambivalence about the use of violence, and a tendency to view its use by the 'others' as worse than by 'one's own', has been common to all sides in the recent Northern Ireland conflict.

Even so, there has been what Dervla Murphy termed 'a massive muddle' in the Catholic mind about this – particularly before the rules for the use of firearms by the security forces were tightened up. Even non-violent Catholics tended to have less sympathy for members of the security forces killed during the Troubles – particularly since Protestants have traditionally considered the security forces as part of their community – than for Catholics killed in sectarian attacks.

The discomfiture and helplessness of constitutional nationalism during the hunger-strikes was palpable. How could it denounce what the hunger-strikers were doing without also damning the traditions of Tone, Emmet and Pearse – the 'good' republicans of the past who had laid the basis for the Irish state? Moreover, the results of a series of elections over the next eighteen months saw Sinn Féin capturing 30–45 per cent of the Catholic vote in Northern Ireland. The constitutional nationalists in the SDLP seemed to have nothing to show for their years of condemning IRA violence, and the hunger-strikes had touched all the right nerves in Catholic consciousness.

'I stand by the Republic'

DESMOND O'MALLEY (1985)

This speech in the Dáil by Desmond O'Malley precipitated his expulsion from Fianna Fáil for 'conduct unbecoming'. The proximate cause of the dispute was his failure to support the party's opposition to the Fine Gael–Labour government's liberalizing of the law regulating the availability of contraception, but O'Malley's speech ranged widely.

'Republican' is perhaps the most abused word in Ireland today. In practice what does it mean? The newspapers do not have to explain it because there is an immediate preconceived notion of what it is. It consists principally of anglophobia. Mentally, at least, it is an aggressive attitude towards those who do not agree with our views on what the future of this island should be. It consists of turning a blind eye to violence, seeing no immorality, often, in the most awful violence, seeing immorality only in one area, the area with which this Bill deals. Often it is displayed by letting off steam in the 15 minutes before closing time with some rousing ballad that makes one vaguely feel good and gets one clapped on the back by people who are stupid enough to think that sort of flag waving is the way to make progress in this island – to go back into your own trenches rather than try to reach out to people whom we need to reach.

One of the most distressing aspects of this debate, inside and outside the House, particularly outside, has been the lack of trust in young people. Young people can hardly be blamed if they look at this House and its Members with a certain cynicism, because they see here a certain hypocrisy. I have had plenty of experience of young people and plenty of experience of many Members of this House, and if I were to place my trust anywhere today, before God I would place it in the young people. I would not abuse them or defame them, by implication at least, in the way in which they have been defamed as people who are incapable of making any kind of sound judgment unless it is legislated for them. Even the exercise of their own private consciences must be something that must be legislated for. I have said before that I cannot accept that concept, though I have seen a reverend bishop saying that we can legislate for private morality. I beg to take issue with him.

Technically, of course, he is right. I can think of at least two countries in the world where private morality is legislated for. One is Iran and the other is Pakistan. Private morality is enforced by public flogging every day in Teheran and other cities in Iran. It takes place in Pakistan where they are having an election in three weeks and where every political party has been dissolved except the Government party. One aspect of enforcement of private morality in these countries is the stoning to death of adultresses. I do not know what happens to adulterers, but adultresses get stoned to death.

In a democratic republic people should not think in terms of having laws other than those that allow citizens to make their own free choice in so far as these private matters are concerned. That is what I believe a republic should do. It should take account of the reasonable views of all groups, including all minorities, because if we do not take into account the rights of minorities here, can we complain if they are not taken into account in the other part of this island, or anywhere else? The rights of minorities are not taken into account in Iran; the Bahai are murdered at the rate of dozens a week because they will not subscribe to the diktat of Islam. I do not say that will happen here but it is the kind of slippery slope we are on.

The tragedy is that so far as morality, public or private, is concerned the only aspect of it that agitates us is sexual morality or things that have to do with it. Could any other issue get things so worked up here as something like this? Do we not need to remind ourselves that God gave Moses nine other Commandments and the other nine are numbered one through five and seven through ten, as the Americans say? [. . .]

We had last year the Forum report and a tremendous amount was put into it by many Members of this House over an 11-month period of sustained work. It contains a certain spirit of reconciliation, of openness, a recognition of what needs to be done to show the people in Northern Ireland that they need not fear here for what they call their civil and religious liberties. If this House acts in a particular way this evening, can you ever persuade those people now other than that the Forum report means nothing, that it was a bag of wind, or a lot of words? Is the spirit of it as well as apparently, at times, the letter of it to be cast aside?

I am concerned not just about the Unionists in Northern Ireland. I am concerned also about the position in the context of this debate of the Roman Catholics in Northern Ireland, and I know something about them. I married one of them 20 years ago on this very day, 20 February 1965, and I know a lot of them. I cannot accept, going on the statements that were so freely made inside and outside this House, that in any country or jurisdiction where there was availability of contraceptives on the lines suggested in this Bill the people would immediately become degenerate. They are not degenerate in Northern Ireland and they have had for very many years full access to any form of contraception they wanted at any time and at any age, in any marital condition. [. . .]

I took the opportunity over the last weekend to read some of the chapters in J. H. Whyte's book on *Church and State in Modern Ireland*. To read, perhaps in full for the first time myself, the whole mother and child controversy of 1951, as it was called, is unbelievable. It is incredible that Members of this House and of the Government of the day could be as craven and supine as they were, as we look back on them now. It shows how much the atmosphere has changed. Then one has to ask oneself 'Has the atmosphere changed?' Because when the chips are down is it going to be any different?

It was interesting to read the so-called mother and child scheme. There were ten provisions for women in it relating to ante-natal and post-natal care and care of the children when they were born. One of the provisions was for free dental treatment for pregnant women. The most tremendous objection was taken to that at that time. I recall only a couple of weeks ago, the Minister for Finance reading that out here in the budget speech and there was a howl of laughter all round the House. How could anyone seriously object to something like that? How could anyone seriously object to anything in it, as one looks back on it now? Look at the effect it has had on this island. We have to bear in mind that this is 1985, and whatever excuses one could make for people in 1951, those excuses are not valid today for us.

This whole matter affects me personally and politically. I have thought about it and agonized about it. Quite a number of Deputies have been subjected to a particular type of pressure, but I am possibly unique in that I have been subjected to two enormous pressures, the more general type and a particular political one. They are both like flood tides – neither of them is easy to resist and it is probably more than twice as hard to resist the two of them. But it comes down to certain fundamentals. One has to take into account everything that has been said but one must also act in accordance with one's conscience, not on contraceptives, which is irrelevant now, but on the bigger and deeper issues that I have talked about today.

I cannot avoid acting, in my present situation, where I do not have the protection of the Whip, other than in the way I feel, giving some practical recognition at least to the kind of pressures and the entreaties of my friends for my own good, which I greatly appreciate.

I will conclude by quoting from a letter in the *Irish Times* of 16 February, signed by Fr Dominic Johnson, OSB, a monk of Glenstal Abbey, where he says, 'With respect to Mr O'Malley, he might reflect with profit on the life of St Thomas More, who put his conscience before politics and lost his life for doing so.'

The politics of this would be very easy. The politics would be, to be one of the lads, the safest way in Ireland. But I do not believe that the interests of this State, or our Constitution and of this Republic, would be served by putting politics before conscience in regard to this. There is a choice of a kind that can only be answered by saying that I stand by the Republic and accordingly I will not oppose this Bill.

St Patrick's Day in Florida

GEMMA HUSSEY (1985)

Gemma Hussey was education minister in the Fine Gael–Labour government when she attended events to mark St Patrick's Day in Florida in 1985. She was accompanied by her husband, Derry Hussey. This is her diary entry for 16 March 1985.

We went to an amazing Mass in a church on the beach: the 'colleens' in strapless dresses bringing up the offertory gifts, everybody in bright green and shamrocks, St Patrick himself greeting us (a Hispanic called Manuel), the church nearly empty except for the people involved in the ceremony, mostly very old people there, me festooned with the biggest, ugliest confection of orchids, plastic clay pipes and green polka-dotted ribbons – unbelievable. We have now acquired a security woman called Maria and a blond man with a briefcase full of automatic weapons which he clutches, but which we are supposed to describe as a telephone to the White House!

The big parade: Derry and myself in a bright green open convertible, riding along Flagler Street, the main thoroughfare, being greeted and escorted to the reviewing stand. Lots of presentations to me at the most unexpected moments. Everyone in green – blacks, whites, Hispanics – lots of bands and colour, hot sun. I made some of my speech in Spanish which went down very well. [. . .] Then we went to the elaborate Coral Gulf Chamber of Commerce Annual International Ball at the Hilton. I sat beside the Lieutenant Governor of Florida who was a nice, old, conservative gentleman, who knew absolutely nothing about where Ireland even was. But he knows now. There was a long prayer at the beginning of dinner, when we all held hands with heads bowed and prayed not to be too materialistic.

'The document that sold my birthright'

HAROLD MCCUSKER (1985)

The 1985 Anglo-Irish Agreement, negotiated between Garret FitzGerald and Margaret Thatcher, gave the Irish government a consultative role in the governing of Northern Ireland. When it was announced that the document would be formally signed at Hillsborough Castle, the Ulster Unionist Party MP Harold McCusker, who opposed the agreement, went to the summit venue despite, as he told the House of Commons, 'the obstacles put in my way by the Northern Ireland Office, the headquarters of the RUC, the divisional commander in Lisburn and the police commander in Hillsborough'.

I stood outside Hillsborough, not waving a Union flag – I doubt whether I will ever wave one again – not singing hymns, saying prayers or protesting, but like a dog and asked the Government to put in my hand the document that sold my birthright. They told me that they would give it to me as soon as possible. Having never consulted me, never sought my opinion or asked my advice, they told the rest of the world what was in store for me. [. . .] I had been told three hours before that it would be brought out to me. At 2.45 p.m., 15 minutes after the press conference had begun, I asked a policeman whether he would bring me the declaration that betrayed everything that I had ever stood for. A senior police officer went into Hillsborough Castle, asked for the document and brought it out to me. [. . .]

Even in my most pessimistic moments, reading the precise detail in the Irish press on the Wednesday before, I never believed that the agreement would deliver me, in the context that it has, into the hands of those who for 15 years have murdered personal friends, political associates and hundreds of my constituents. [. . .] I have lost 12 years [as a Westminster MP]. I have only one complaint. Why was I not told 12 years ago? There are one or two honourable exceptions. The Right Hon. Member for Waveney (Mr Prior) told me 4 or 5 years ago as precisely as he could. Another prominent member of the Government Front Bench, a very gentle man whose integrity would be accepted by everyone in the House, tried to nudge me towards that realisation 9 years ago. I was not prepared to believe it. I thought that one day I would gain equality. Why did not successive Governments tell me that I would never be treated with equality? If I had been told, my attitude over the past 12 years would have been different. I would have looked at political developments in Northern Ireland differently. [. . .]

I had to go home on the Friday night after the Hillsborough agreement and tell my wife that I regretted bringing up our children to believe what Hon. Members have brought their children up to believe, because they will have to live with the legacy that I have to live with. It would have been better if they had never looked at the Union flag or thought that they were British or put their trust in the House of Commons than spending the rest of their lives knowing that they are now some sort of semi-British citizen. [. . .]

Hon. Members can rest assured of this. I shall never have to explain to my constituents again why the Prime Minister believes that they are as British as the people of Finchley. I shall never have to listen to people telling me that Northern Ireland is an integral part of the United Kingdom. We shall never hear those words. They will be removed from the political dictionary of Northern Ireland. [. . .]

I say in all sincerity, and I mean it, that I will never accept this agreement as the means whereby I will be governed in Northern Ireland. Tens and tens and tens of thousands of people in Northern Ireland share that view. If that is construed as me flying in the face of the sovereignty of this Parliament, so be it. I have heard the threats over the past two days. Let us have a referendum in the United Kingdom and let Northern Ireland accept the result. I will accept the judgment. If the people of the United Kingdom say to me that they no longer want me, it will simply be echoing what the Government are saying anyway and they will have to live with the consequences of that decision. That referendum cannot deliver me against my will into an Irish Republic. I will not go to the Irish Republic and what might flow from whatever the developments might be would be something with which everybody in the United Kingdom would have to live. I am not scared of a referendum. I am prepared to live with its consequences.

I have heard variations on the sponger theme. It is said that we are given £1.5 billion each year and we had better be careful or it will be taken from us. As I said last night, I can accept money from the richer parts of the United Kingdom being given to Northern Ireland if it is the decision of the Parliament of the United Kingdom to redistribute the United Kingdom's wealth to the poorer parts. However, I cannot accept, and I do not want, United Kingdom charity. I do not want money to be offered to me to buy my acquiescence. That is the view of the majority of the people in Northern Ireland. Do not threaten me with a referendum or with turning off the financial tap. We are proud people. When we say what we mean, we mean what we say. I wish that that standard could be adopted by all Right Hon. Members.

A solution to the Troubles

MILES KINGTON (1985)

> The humourist and columnist Miles Kington was born in Northern
> Ireland, brought up in Britain and, alas, did not bring his humorous
> writing often enough to bear on his birthplace.

The last time I went to Northern Ireland I met two people who were
working for the National Trust. One was engaged in restoration
work, the other was busy devising future plans for National Trust
property. Nothing odd about that, you might say. Ah, but there is.
When did you last meet someone in England who was working for
the National Trust?

Statistically it is most unlikely that I should meet more people in
Northern Ireland working for the Trust than in the whole of the
mother country. It suggests strongly that the Trust is much stronger
on the ground over there than it is here. This is not the image we
normally get of Northern Ireland, of course, which suggests that
destruction is more the order of the day than preservation, but this
image through the countless films and plays now surging from that
beleaguered province is a misleading one, suggesting as it does that
the place is inhabited entirely by TV film crews, psychopaths and
weeping mothers, a sort of drizzly Beirut.

Anyway, so struck was I by the relative preponderance of National
Trust people over there, even though based on a comparatively small
cross-section, that I decided to look up a map of its properties in
Northern Ireland. I was impressed. There are a lot of them, and many
are sizeable – not just parkland and estates, but coastlines and stretches
of country – so that a goodly percent of the place is already Trust
property.

I cannot remember when I first had my next thought, but the
more I think about it, the more I think there may be something in it.
We all know, do we not, that National Trust property is a haven from
the hurly-burly of everyday nastiness? That nothing violent, or bad

tempered, even, takes place in those halls and rolling parkland? Did you ever see a brawl or an unpleasantness in a historic house, except those still occupied by the family?

Could it then be remotely possible that the National Trust of Northern Ireland is gradually taking over the whole province and that this is the long-awaited peace initiative?

It sounds unlikely, I know. All I can say is that it seems to be working. Just suppose that some brilliant boffin had said – 'OK can't stop people in Northern Ireland getting at each other, but what we can do is to restrict the places where they can do so. All we need to find is some non-sectarian, property-owning body which could gradually take over the whole place while nobody was looking . . . Maybe one day the IRA and Loyalists would have nowhere left to fight.'

And what does all this lead up to? I'll tell you. Being uneasily aware that I am the only writer of my acquaintance who has never written a play about Northern Ireland, I am now working on a script about a family living in Co. Down. They have a hard life. Not a night passes without a BBC crew bursting in to get at the plugs for their lights, or an ITV crew breaking down the door to film their reactions and recharge their batteries. Upstairs in the attic they are hiding a refugee, a freelance cameraman who has no ACTT card and is frightened for his life.

The son is writing a play based on the family's problems in which Japanese TV have expressed a keen interest. The daughter is working nights at the Forum Hotel in Belfast, where she has been approached by an ITV director who wants to use her for a small part when all she wants is an affair with him. And then suddenly the unthinkable happens, the thing they never talk about: the man from the National Trust arrives to discuss buying their farmhouse for the nation.

It's a play with a difference. It even has a lot of laughs and a happy ending. It will disturb many people's ideas about the beleaguered province. And it blows open the Government's secret plans for Northern Ireland.

TV producers are invited to form an orderly queue outside my office door.

Irish ritual and unbelief

NUALA O'FAOLAIN (1988)

Ireland is not the only country where lapsed Roman Catholics adopt what one might call an à-la-carte approach to religion or agnosticism. But is there a particular Irish approach to atheism? This was the theme of this *Irish Times* column by Nuala O'Faolain.

I was talking to a woman the other day, a single parent, who supports herself and her daughter by long, night hours of cleaning. She had just got a note from her daughter's school, telling her that she'll be making her First Holy Communion in June. This woman dreads the expense; it is not just the outfit for the little girl, but something presentable for herself that she has to get. Why, she wanted to know, can they not wear their school uniforms? Why indeed. As it is, I've met mothers who shoplift to clothe their children for these occasions.

However, the grumble about the clothes turned into a larger complaint. Had I seen, she wanted to know, the amount of money that children collect on their Communion visits these days? Fivers and tenners, single pounds are too small to offer. 'Surely it's meant to be religious,' she said, 'not all about what you're wearing and how much money did you get?'

Well, yes. It is. But what interested me about her disgust at the secularisation of this sacrament was that, as far as I know, she doesn't believe in God herself. She certainly doesn't practise the Catholicism she grew up in. So what's it to her, if the material is wiping out the spiritual?

She belongs to what I think might be quite a sizeable number of people, former Catholics, who go along with the externals of belief, so that their children won't feel like outsiders. The implications of this position don't really worry her at all, and she wouldn't call herself a hypocrite. Neither would I use the word hypocrisy in this context. Whatever it is these people are doing, it is much more vague and instinctive and pragmatic than hypocrisy is.

It starts with marriage. Imagine a man and a woman neither of whom would dream of accepting Catholic teaching on celibacy before marriage, or the procreative purpose of marriage, or anything else the Church might preach. They haven't been to Mass in years or to confession for decades. But they want to get married in a Catholic ceremony in a church, and they'll readily lie about their beliefs, even all the way through a pre-marriage course, to get that kind of wedding. They say that they don't want to upset the mammies and the grandas and so on, and, of course, that's true. But it is also true that their non-belief doesn't seem to them an important thing, worth arguing about in the open. It is not a positive unbelief; it is not convinced atheism. It really just boils down to not liking and not practising the religion they were brought up in.

And anyway, people usually get married so as to celebrate each other, and to say to the world, in the most solemn terms they know, that they commit themselves to each other. In this culture the vast majority of people don't know any terms more solemn than those arrived at during the history of Christianity. It takes real independence to turn one's back on this huge reservoir of meaningfulness, and to settle for the literalness of the registry office.

Next, there's the question of baptism. Again, the emotions cry out for the big gesture, and endorsement by tradition. A christening is a welcoming of the baby to this earth, and an induction of the new human being into the community, leaving aside its denominational aspect. And, in any case, I suppose that atheist parents think that it doesn't matter very much, because the baby doesn't know what's happening. Their own example of unbelief, they assume, will set the child right.

And so it all begins. But is it a good way to live – to see to it that the children appear to be Catholics, while steering clear of the whole thing yourself? To exploit their powerlessness? To send them out to Mass, while you stay in bed? To give them money for missions in which you don't believe? To accompany them proudly to First Communions and Confirmations, even though they have never seen you pray?

I see why people do this, of course. They want to give their children protective cover. It is extremely hard on a child to bear the burden of dissenting from the majority. Only a few children in the country can get through the educational system without encountering teachers and schoolmates and schoolmates' parents who would make no bones about their hostility to unbelief. How could any loving parent ask a child to pay for his or her parent's views? Outside Dublin it is very difficult even for an adult to retain standing while eschewing communal practices.

The children know. They know that some of the people around them really believe, and they know that no one at home does. But they have to live as best they can by the double standard. It is only about religion that this arises. Whatever other convictions the parents may have, even minority convictions, like vegetarianism, or using Irish as the language of the home, the children will be reared by them, quite straightforwardly. After all, what else can you rear children by, except your own convictions? But few people will take the risk of not hedging their bets on this profound subject.

But if this leads to anything it must be to the creation of adults who take neither belief nor unbelief seriously. Perhaps that is why there are so many socialists in this country, and even communists, who are perfectly at ease with religion. It used to be part of the work of the Left to attempt to disenchant people with heaven, so that they would cry for justice here on earth. But Irish socialists are as keen on heaven as anyone else: they have to be. To stand on atheist principle, to refuse to join in prayers, say, at funerals, to say that religious funerals are so much mumbo-jumbo, would be to proclaim yourself utterly marginal. A nutter. Offensive. Nobody would dream of doing it.

Nobody is supposed to take any ideology seriously enough to make a display of it. Any non-religious ideology, that is. So people stay quiet, and somehow believe that by not going to Mass they are taking a stand against religion or the Church or clerical power or something – that like Stephen Dedalus they are flying by the net of religion. But are they?

All religions must have members who fall away. It must always be a personal difficulty for anyone, of any religion. But Catholicism is so vast here, so saturates all aspects of life and death, that to leave it means leaving the protection of the pack, being alone.

It is a process or a decision with myriad social consequences. Perhaps in this sense it is right for parents to keep their children enrolled in Catholicism as a way of life, even though they do not accept it as a revelation of the truth. Perhaps too, Irish atheism is rarely more than tentative, as if God might come along at any minute and prove it wrong. The woman who faces her daughter's Communion wouldn't be complaining about the cost of it if she had money. But she would still disapprove of commercialising the sacraments she doesn't believe in. Nostalgia and wistful hope are far, far more powerful over the human heart than the dry pleasure of having a perfectly logical position.

'A tax on imbeciles'

JOHN M. KELLY (1988)

John M. Kelly was an academic expert in constitutional law and a politician. He was a Fine Gael TD from 1973 to 1989 and a minister in Garret FitzGerald's first government. Thereafter, he declined ministerial office, preferring to retain his freedom to speak from the back benches. In this debate he spoke on the National Lottery, which had been established in 1986.

The worst financial device of the whole lot, something which my own party introduced, is the national lottery. Deputy Haughey, who likes to be associated with success or what he perceives as success, is up front, not quite on the Champs-Élysées but at some more humble address in order to announce the first annual results of the national lottery. The national lottery had exceeded expectations. That is the Government's position on it. I have to say in justice to Deputy Haughey that had there been a Fine Gael Minister there I do not expect he would have acted any differently. I consider it a gross shame that a national lottery exceeds expectations. While I did not care for the way he used to hold the pistol to the heads of the last Government and would say that he would not vote for them any longer unless he got a scheme costing God knows how many millions which would have torn the heart out of the city of Dublin, I have to agree fully with what the former Deputy Liam Skelly said about the national lottery. I must not be taken as adopting this insulting phrase, nor can I even vouch for its authenticity. He quoted the great President of France, Georges Clemenceau, as saying that a lottery was a tax on imbeciles. I do not know whether Clemenceau said that and I would not wish to use language like that in any case about people who play a lottery. I think that language is far too insulting and gross to use about what may be only a small flutter. Nevertheless, I think for a Republic to stoop to a method like this for raising revenue is contemptible and shameful. I am glad to see Deputy Higgins nodding his head. I am amazed. I am beginning to wonder whether I should have studied my brief a bit better before leaving myself open to the charge that he has agreed totally with me about something. I do regard it as shameful if only because it psychologically perpetuates among ordinary people the crock of gold at the end of the rainbow mentality.

Even though Deputy Higgins is looking at what he may think is a smooth rock face of unchallengeable material with which he completely agrees in hearing me say these words, I hope he will not find that I am giving him a toe hold when I admit to what may be a middle-class admission, that is, that with one exception, I personally have not bought a lottery ticket. I did once buy one in Italy because the old man selling them appeared to be so miserable and it seemed to cheer him up so much when I bought a couple of tickets from him. I have never bought a lottery ticket with the intention or hope or prospect of winning something. I know no one in my family has and I know, but I had better not be too positive, that none of my friends or relations have bought tickets. Going into the post offices in the city, as I have to to buy stamps and so forth, I do notice people buying lottery tickets and while they span a fair spectrum of the population, they are not all the same type of people. My impression, and I hope I am not offending anybody in saying so, I would not be doing my job here if I did not give my impressions whether they were right or wrong, is that the lottery tends to be patronised by people who have the least to spare. I have not checked this and perhaps I should have done so before coming in here to speak about it but I suspect that the big end of the lottery business is done on the days when social welfare payments are made. I think it is a scandal that this State should think of financing necessary services, because that is what it is doing, through this source. [. . .] I think lotteries have a very ancient history and publicly organised lotteries go back certainly to the 17th century and perhaps beyond that. It may be that there are historical reasons for it but I think it is a scandal that in the late 20th century we in this Irish Republic should choose to pick this means of raising revenue from the poorest, not only from them but certainly preponderantly from the less provident sections of the community in order to provide services which we should have been providing out of ordinary revenue. [. . .]

If it is necessary for the State to support sport, youth and recreation, and I recognize the value of these and I certainly recognise the value of youth now that it has departed from me, it should not be done in this way. I recognise the value of sport and recreation even though there was a time when the State did not feel that it was among the items on which public revenue had to be spent. Arts and culture, the Irish language and health are matters on which this State since its foundation has spent some money in one shape or form. Myles na gCopaleen, during the war years, when he heard people complaining about the fact that the State was spending £.5 million a year on the Irish language said that at a time when the major civilized powers of the world were spending tens of millions every day on trying to destroy one another, surely it was one of the few humble little boasts this modest little State could make that we spent £.5 million on a relatively urbane object like trying to revive an ancient language. How the money is spent, we need not discuss now. This is not an appropriate debate for discussion of the work of Bord na Gaeilge but certainly it has always been something that the State spent money on, right back to the days of the first Government. That expenditure was financed out of ordinary revenue.

To put on to a siding objects such as those that are to be financed from the lottery appears to attribute a second-class status – naturally you might not think so if you are getting the money from it – a conjectural, only provisional, really there by the skin of its teeth status to these objects of expenditure. However, that is not the worst aspect of it. The worst aspect is that it is being financed at the expense of people – I am not saying they are on the poverty line – who should be trying to train in habits of providence, whom we should be trying to sustain and help to raise to a level relative to the rest of the population, to those who are better placed. I have said enough about it but it is an easy way to collect money at the expense of those who should be the objects of the State's special protection and should not be the targets of its plundering fiscal paws.

'Short and sweet, good enough for him'

MARY HOLLAND (1988)

In March 1988, an IRA funeral in Belfast's Milltown Cemetery was attacked by a UDA gunman, Michael Stone, who killed three and injured sixty. Four days later, *Observer* journalist Mary Holland attended the funeral of one of Stone's victims, IRA man Kevin Brady. In the febrile atmosphere created by Stone's attack, some of those attending his victim's funeral believed that a British Army car which had got caught in the funeral cortège was being driven by loyalists. The mourners attacked the car, dragged the two men out and savagely beat them. They were then taken away, identified as British soldiers and murdered by the IRA behind high walls in the GAA grounds in Casement Park.

Kevin Brady's funeral started peacefully. As with other funerals in west Belfast last week, police were nowhere to be seen, and the only evidence of a security presence was a British army helicopter hovering over Milltown Cemetery. The Provisionals had made their own arrangements to protect the mourners. All of us arriving at St Agnes's Church on the Andersonstown Road were searched, no cameras were allowed inside, and stewards with walkie-talkie sets patrolled the area.

The priest who conducted the Requiem Mass sent a message of sympathy to the family of Gillian Johnston, the young Protestant woman, shot in Fermanagh on Friday night, and spoke of 'a bewildered community's desire for peace'. The cortège left the church just before noon. Prominent members of Sinn Féin, including Gerry Adams and Danny Morrison, walked beside the family. The procession had gone about 200 yards when a silver car drove up the Andersonstown Road towards the hearse.

The driver saw the procession and swerved into a slip road used for parking in front of a row of shops. A crowd of youths broke away and ran towards it. The driver tried to reverse at speed down the

Andersonstown Road away from the funeral, but was blocked by black taxis. The crowd surged towards the car. A shot rang out, and, in panic people started running back towards the funeral cortège, which had stopped. A group of youths then surged forward once again towards the car, and one man with an iron bar started hammering in the top and breaking the windows. A man in a pale green sweater was dragged out and hauled past us, his face covered with blood. He was pulled into a yard adjoining Casement Park GAA Club and the high gates were slammed behind him.

The funeral procession started moving again towards the cemetery. Rumours began to sweep through the bystanders that the two men were members of the RUC Special Branch. A hundred yards or so back up the road towards the church, shots rang out. They seemed to come from a car park adjoining the St Agnes Community Centre. Shopkeepers started pulling down their steel shutters. As I walked up the road and into the car park, a small crowd which had gathered there began to melt away. One young man passed me and said: 'Short and sweet, good enough for him.'

I saw a priest kneeling beside the body of a young man, stripped down to his underpants and shoes and socks, with blood on his chest and head. Father Alex Reid was administering the last rites, making the sign of the Cross on the young man's lips. His eyes were open and he was moving his head from side to side. Father Reid said: 'He's still alive.' He asked me if I knew how to do mouth-to-mouth resuscitation, then asked me to go for an ambulance, and he began to give the kiss of life himself to the dying man. His courage and compassion redeemed us all. It sent one image of Ireland across the world that spoke of human pity in the face of death rather than the savagery of the mob.

A local bookmaker's shop let me in, and people inside helped me to phone for an ambulance. Their kindness too throws back the lie that the people of west Belfast are savages. When I came out again there were two bodies; I suppose the other one had been there all along and I hadn't seen it. The ambulance and the army and police had arrived. Both bodies were covered with tarpaulins and blood was seeping from them. I could not see the priest anywhere and nobody could tell me how the soldier to whom he had administered had died.

Inside the bookie's shop a man said to me: 'If anyone tried to help them, they'd have been killed too.'

On begrudgery

J. J. LEE (1989)

In his book *Ireland 1912–1985: Politics and Society*, the historian J. J. Lee considered a phenomenon that the Irish may not have invented, but certainly brought to a high art.

The Irish carry from their mother's womb not so much a fanatic heart as a begrudger one. The begrudger mentality did derive fairly rationally from a mercantilist concept of the size of the status cake. The size of that cake was more or less fixed in more or less stagnating communities and in small institutions. In a stunted society, one man's gain did tend to be another man's loss. Winners could flourish only at the expense of losers. Status depended not only on rising oneself, but on preventing others from rising. For many, keeping the other fellow down offered the surest defence of their own position.

It was difficult for an individual to rise rapidly in an agricultural society, particularly one with so sluggish a land market, except at his neighbour's expense. It was not only John Healy's mother in Mayo who was making 'an almost culturally-programmed response' when holding that 'her village was the best village, her family the best family, and you did honour to it by denigrating the families from villages which threatened both.' Threats to the family could also come from within one's own village. The success of the neighbour's child in the United States was acceptable. That did not disturb the local pecking order. It could even be glossed as a tribute to the village as a whole. The success of the same neighbour's child at home would upset assumptions about the natural order of things. The reactions were correspondingly more resentful in the steeper valleys of the squinting windows when the rare individual dared to rise above his allotted place. Envy of the thrusting neighbour frequently lurked beneath the cloak of ridicule, 'a method of cutting others down to size, especially those who tried to shake off the local apathy and get ahead . . .'

This mentality transferred into behaviour within institutions.

Where promotion followed iron rules of seniority, it had at least the consequence of dampening jealousy, on the assumption that one's own turn would come in due course, provided one displayed no unsettling degree of initiative. Where promotion, as in the dwarf departments of universities, came by a complicated election process on the relatively rare occasions when openings occurred, then it was glaringly obvious that winners won at the expense of losers. The loser was often a loser for life. The lack of lateral mobility meant there were no alternative openings elsewhere, even for men of high ability. Many in those circumstances lacked the strength of character to rise above their bitter disappointment. Many an intelligent man vegetated, many a once-vibrant personality rotted into putrescent decay, sporadically jerking into spiteful activity in splenetic surges of jealousy. Immense amounts of time and effort were devoted to spiting the other fellow. Nothing could sweeten the rancid pill of a rival's success. And by a cosmic displacement of bilious resentment, any successful person tended to be translated into a rival.

The systematic study of the influence of begrudgery on behaviour poses certain problems. The documentation, for one thing, tends to be elusive! Yet the role of spite in individuals and institutions is a patent and potent fact of Irish life. If a Yeats could feel the baleful breath of 'the daily spite of this unmannerly town', the destructive impact on more vulnerable spirits can be imagined. Ireland offered a hot-house environment for the cultivation of the poisoned weed. The inter-related combination of economic, marital and mobility patterns meant that Ireland had more than her fair share of individuals suffering from thwarted ambition, disappointed dreams, frustrated hopes, shattered ideals. The society was too static for the begrudgers to be able to diffuse their resentments on a wide circle of targets. Day after day, year after year, a stunted society obliged them to focus obsessively on the same individuals as the sources of their failure. The Irish begrudgers must return again and again to the same obsessive resentment, like a circle of Invidias eternally gnawing at the same heart. The cancer of begrudgery probably drove many to drink, for spite and drink were often children of the same frustration.

If begrudgery is rampant in contemporary Ireland, it is a direct inheritance from, not a perversion of, traditional Ireland. There is no reason to posit that the present generation of Irishmen, by no means forgetting Irish women, is more naturally corroded by envy than any earlier generation. Circumstances have conspired, however, to achieve a high profile for more recent exhibitions of envy.

Traditional Ireland was consumed with envy. But the public opportunities for its display were relatively few. One might plot silently to damage a rival, one would rarely expose one's enmity in public. If one did, one made sure to drape it in acceptable garb. At least four developments since 1960 have contributed to making begrudgery more conspicuous, if not more intense. In 1961, before Irish television was launched, only 30,000 homes out of a total of nearly 700,000 were estimated to be receiving British television. Already by 1966, 380,000 homes were receiving RTÉ, by 1971, 536,000. 'If you've got it – flaunt it', a line actually used in one motor car advertisement, nicely captured the general ethos of television advertising, as well as of many of the values transmitted in television programmes, especially American ones. Whatever the consequences of such a philosophy in a dynamic economy, they encouraged an inflation of aspirations, and of exhibitionism, in an economy which, though growing unprecedentedly rapidly by its own standards, was still relatively poor by the standards of the societies whose values the advertisers transmitted. With a wider range of goods now available to be flaunted, petty personal rivalries could flourish at every level over a variety of consumer goods, from clothes to cars, to other consumer durables, to foreign holidays. Begrudgery now had a wider range of grievances on which to fester. The number of small institutions grew, both in the public and the private sectors, reproducing the circumstances that fostered the spread of envy and jealousy among shrivelled personalities. The number and aggressiveness of vested interests, whether within the expanded state sector, or outside it, grew appreciably. Pressure groups became, if not more insidious, certainly more blatant, expressing their demands more stridently, more self-righteously, and more avariciously, as they launched demand after demand for 'our' money from a growing but ineffectual state.

Entry to the EEC in 1973 reinforced this tendency. The substantial net flow of grants and subsidies approved for Ireland was brushed aside with the simple demand, 'more'. At moments of particular horror, when there loomed a momentary danger that the Irish might actually have to pay their way, begrudgery achieved its masterpiece by demanding that the others be dragged down to Irish levels. Dutch and Danish farmers had no right to perform better than Irish farmers! Dastardly Dutch cows, unsportingly stuffed with 'artificial' food, were performing above their full potential, while the underprivileged Irish cow, fighting a gallant battle with only 'natural' grass as her weapon, had still to reach hers! The begrudger mode of discourse the pressure groups choose to cultivate in connection with the EEC scarcely elevated the level of public discussion in Ireland!

In other areas too, observers detected sharp declines in the standard of personal conduct in contemporary Ireland. What distinguishes contemporary from traditional society, however, it may be suggested, is not so much a higher level of corruption as a failure to construct a new symbolic universe that would provide a façade behind which the society could get on with its less edifying activities while continuing to savour a satisfying sense of its own moral superiority.

The campaign trail

EITHNE FITZGERALD (1989)

In the 1989 general election, Eithne FitzGerald was attempting for the
third time to win a seat for Labour in the Dublin South constituency.
In this account of the campaign, she mentions her director of elections, Frank Buckley, as 'a man who once won an election in a suit he
bought at a sale of work for a fiver' and who was now 'very insistent
that the candidate be Well Turned Out. No open-toed sandals in the
sweltering heat of June, respectable shoes (I went through two pairs
in three weeks), always stockings, a good summer suit, and a red rose
instead of the prize-cow rosette'.

The door-to-door canvass was our main method of campaigning.
Every morning, my sister Barbara, myself, and any other members
or supporters who were available, assembled for a cup of tea in one
of our houses at ten o'clock, and headed out on the knocker at
about ten thirty. Then a stop of an hour for lunch, a whizz round
to assemble the afternoon shift, knock off at half five to go home
and make and/or eat dinner, then off again from seven to nine
thirty.

At the council, I've always lobbied for interesting and varied estate
layouts, geared to children, not to cars. But you curse these mazes of
cul-de-sacs when you're out canvassing. You can lose half your
troops, knock up and annoy half the area twice, and appear to have
very little to mark off on your map when you're finished. Nothing
beats a block of flats or open-plan gardens for a quick and easy canvass. Provided it's Rottweiler free.

We started with the areas where we knew our support was strongest, always good for the morale, especially for newcomers to the
campaign. The first week, the night canvassing started from our house
and concentrated on the eastern side of the constituency, and the children loved sitting in on the gossip and political analysis from the
comrades over a cup of tea afterwards. Later on, the focus of the even-

ing canvass shifted to HQ, and the cup of tea became a pint in Rathfarnham.

For me, the campaign rarely ended at nine thirty. I danced at a street céilí in Ballinteer, attended a pub quiz in Firhouse, and a race night in Templeogue. Then home, and some paperwork, following up queries or writing a script.

Saturday afternoons were spent at shopping centres. We put up sandwich boards with posters on them, offered leaflets, chatted with shoppers. I usually dislike this form of canvassing, I'm much more comfortable door to door, but the powers that be feel it offers good visibility and a chance to meet people from the rural parts of the area. Dick Spring offered us an afternoon, so we took him to my local centre, Crazy Prices, where the sun shone, my sister Barbara and her children waved balloons, and the reception was warm and friendly. [. . .] You feel much less of an eejit shaking hands and chatting people up when you're not the only one.

Sundays were Masses, meet the Communion trickle, then the main flood, then dive into the cars to the next church on the circuit. Again, not my favourite form of canvassing, standing like a dummy with your hand stuck out. [. . .]

Apart from press conferences in town, I didn't venture outside the constituency for the three weeks. Just go, go, go, trying to get to as many as possible of 40,000 houses. So it could be easy to miss some critical shift in the campaign issues, arising from a crucial radio interview or *Today Tonight* programme. But there was no such shift. On virtually every doorstep, the same main issue, the cutbacks in the health service, and the impact on ordinary families. The woman who waited 24 hours for her child to get stitched after an accident. The man on the dole who borrowed £500 from the credit union because he couldn't bear to see his child in pain waiting for a tonsil operation. The elderly woman sent back home with a bandage after bleeding in the taxi home from hospital. The woman who burst into tears on the doorstep because her husband's recovery from a stroke was in jeopardy, discharged because of a shortage of staff. [. . .] Dublin South is characterised by the analysts as leafy suburbia, the most middle-class constituency in the country. But there is also significant unemployment, hardship, poverty. We met families in Ballyogan paying £4 a week per child out of welfare incomes simply to get their children to school. A pensioner sobbed while she told me that while she could just manage on her money, she'd never again be able to afford a treat for herself – a meal, a day out, a holiday. Other homes where there clearly wasn't a thing in the house. People spoke of their sense of powerlessness, their lack of dignity, queuing for everything. 'When you're down, they don't just walk on you, they fucking dance on you!' For some, all the fight was gone out of them. [...]

By the end of the three weeks, I was tanned, half a stone lighter, and exhausted. Having started with the easier areas, we were now finishing up with areas where the reception varied from politely indifferent to absolutely frosty. The electorate as well as the canvassers were suffering from battle fatigue. 'Not another bloody election leaflet!' Everyone hates polling day, the twelve-hour stint of competing canvassers jostling the voters outside polling stations, the jockeying for position with canvassers and posters. One of the advantages of being the candidate is that you escape being rooted in the one spot for twelve hours, because it is customary to drive around from one polling station to another to greet your party workers stuck on that thankless job, and to shake hands with the presiding officers and polling clerks. My sister Bríd drove me around, transferring the roof-rack with the 'Vote Eithne FitzGerald Labour' box on it from our beat-up Renault 4 to her somewhat newer car. Our posters were doing very little jockeying, the van with them having been stolen from outside HQ the night before. Next day, the brothers did the tallies ('A Product of Starry Plough Software'). At twelve they rang to say the result would be 2 FF, 2 FG, and an amazed Roger Garland [of the Green Party] would take the other seat, on our transfers. So close!

A new Ireland

MARY ROBINSON (1990)

Mary Robinson – barrister, scholar, activist and senator – was an
unlikely candidate in the 1990 presidential election and an even less
likely winner. Nominated by Labour but running as an independent,
she was the beneficiary of some blunders by the favourite, Brian
Lenihan of Fianna Fáil. Robinson came in second on the first count
but won sufficient transfers from Austin Currie of Fine Gael to
become the first woman President of Ireland. The following is from
her inaugural address.

The Ireland I will be representing is a new Ireland, open, tolerant,
inclusive. Many of you who voted for me did so without sharing all
my views. This, I believe, is a significant signal of change, a sign,
however modest, that we have already passed the threshold to a new,
pluralist Ireland.

The recent revival of an old concept of the Fifth Province expresses
this emerging Ireland of tolerance and empathy. The old Irish term
for province is *coicead*, meaning a 'fifth'; and yet, as everyone knows,
there are only four geographical provinces on this island. So where is
the fifth? The Fifth Province is not anywhere here or there, north or
south, east or west. It is a place within each one of us – that place that
is open to the other, that swinging door which allows us to venture
out and others to venture in. [. . .] If I am a symbol of anything I
would like to be a symbol of this reconciling and healing Fifth Province.

My primary role as President will be to represent this State. But the
State is not the only model of community with which Irish people
can and do identify. Beyond our State there is a vast community of
Irish emigrants extending not only across our neighbouring island –
which has provided a home away from home for several Irish
generations – but also throughout the continents of North America,
Australia and of course Europe itself. There are over 70 million people

living on this globe who claim Irish descent. I will be proud to represent them. And I would like to see Áras an Uachtaráin, my official residence, serve on something of an annual basis – as a place where our emigrant communities could send representatives for a get-together of the extended Irish family abroad. [. . .]

If it is time, as Joyce's Stephen Dedalus remarked, that the Irish began to forge in the smithy of our souls 'the uncreated conscience' of our race – might we not also take on the still 'uncreated conscience' of the wider international community? Is it not time that the small started believing again that it is beautiful, that the periphery can rise up and speak out on equal terms with the centre, that the most outlying island community of the European Community really has something 'strange and precious' to contribute to the sea-change presently sweeping through the entire continent of Europe? As a native of Ballina, one of the most western towns in the most western province of the most western nation in Europe, I want to say – 'the West's awake.'

I turn now to another place close to my heart, Northern Ireland. As the elected choice of the people of this part of our island I want to extend the hand of friendship and of love to both communities in the other part. And I want to do this with no hidden agenda, no strings attached. As the person chosen by you to symbolise this Republic and to project our self-image to others, I will seek to encourage mutual understanding and tolerance between all the different communities sharing this island.

In seeking to do this I shall rely to a large extent on symbols. But symbols are what unite and divide people. Symbols give us our identity, our self-image, our way of explaining ourselves to ourselves and to others. Symbols in turn determine the kinds of stories we tell and the stories we tell determine the kind of history we make and remake. I want Áras an Uachtaráin to be a place where people can tell diverse stories – in the knowledge that there is someone there to listen.

I want this Presidency to promote the telling of stories – stories of celebration through the arts and stories of conscience and of social justice. As a woman, I want women who have felt themselves outside history to be written back into history, in the words of Eavan Boland, 'finding a voice where they found a vision'.

May God direct me so that my Presidency is one of justice, peace and love. May I have the fortune to preside over an Ireland at a time of exciting transformation when we enter a new Europe where old wounds can be healed, a time when, in the words of Seamus Heaney, 'hope and history rhyme'. May it be a Presidency where I the President can sing to you, citizens of Ireland, the joyous refrain of the 14th-century Irish poet as recalled by W. B. Yeats: 'I am of Ireland . . . come dance with me in Ireland.'

The resignation of Charles Haughey

DÁIL DEBATE (1992)

Charles Haughey, just the fourth leader of Fianna Fáil in the party's 66-year history, served three times as Taoiseach. He resigned the office on 11 February 1992. This extract from the Dáil debate of the following day begins with Haughey's remarks on his tenure.

The work of Government and of the Dáil must always be directed to the progress of the nation, and I hope I have been able to provide some leadership to that end in my time. I have always sought to act solely and exclusively in the best interests of the Irish people. Let me quote Othello: 'I have done the state some service; they know't. No more of that.'

As to all those who have frequently and vehemently disagreed with me in this House, I have always accepted that they did so in pursuance of their own interpretation of the public interest and in accordance with the constitutional duty of an Opposition party in a democracy to put the alternative view. The past 35 years have seen a total transformation of Irish society. Even if not all our high hopes have been realised, there is much to be proud of in the economic and social progress that has been made, and in recent years I believe we have laid good foundations for durable advance.

We should always keep in our minds, too, that Government has much wider dimensions than merely managing an economy. There must be concern and commitment that all shall participate in the fruits of progress, a caring attitude towards the least advantaged, a love of our heritage and culture, a desire to protect our environment, a deep attachment to the values that are precious to us. There is also the need to respond constructively to the great universal yearning for peace in Northern Ireland.

Apart from that tragic situation, I am sure we are proceeding broadly in the right direction, and that Ireland can look forward to a great future in a united Europe, exceeding anything in our past, if we take the right decisions and stay on course. The Irish people have the means and the character to lift themselves out of present difficulties, and in my estimation they will certainly succeed in doing so. I believe, too, that there is in Ireland today a great flowering of creativity in all aspects of our national life which enhances the quality of our lives and uplifts our morale.

I would like to wish my successor and the Government he will nominate well in tackling the many problems they will face. I say farewell, as Taoiseach, to the Members of this House and salute them as the freely elected, democratic representatives of the people of Ireland whom we are honoured to serve. This is not the time to outline any special list of claims or achievements. Let the record speak for itself. If I were to seek any accolade as I leave office it would simply be: he served the people, all the people, to the best of his ability.

John Bruton [Fine Gael Leader]: On behalf of the Fine Gael Party, I wish the outgoing Taoiseach well. As a Minister and as Taoiseach, he showed himself to be an effective and imaginative manager of public business. He has, as he has said, shown commitment to this House in his willingness to answer to this House, frequently in times of difficulty. I wish him well in whatever role he now chooses for himself, as I wish well his family and his many friends. May I say also that I doubt very much that he will confine himself to the cultivation of chrysanthemums.

Dick Spring [Labour Party Leader]: The outgoing Taoiseach, Deputy Haughey, quoted last week from Shakespeare's *Julius Caesar* to telling effect in this House when he referred to the 'Heavens blazing forth the death of princes'. I am sure that he did not intend to encourage us to look at our dog-eared copies of *Julius Caesar* and to especially remember Mark Antony saying 'I come to bury Caesar, not to praise him.' The Ides of March are not yet upon us so I will resist the temptation to follow Mark Antony's precedent. Instead I admit to having difficulty in finding the appropriate words to pay tribute to a retiring political legend. My mind was drawn – not to Shakespeare – but closer to home, to Flann O'Brien, whose tribute to another folk hero, Fionn Mac Cumhaill, ran like this: 'I am an Ulster man, a Connacht man and a Greek, I am my own father and my son, I am every hero from the crack of time,' which is appropriate.

Much has been said about the abrupt ending of Deputy Haughey's time frame, I do not propose to dwell at length on the circumstances in which he has come to relinquish office other than to say that the manner of his departure, once the die was cast, was dignified and graceful, as one would expect. This occasion represents the end of a long and turbulent era in Irish politics. Charles Haughey was elected as Leader of Fianna Fáil – and Taoiseach – in an atmosphere of high expectation. He brought to the job a prestigious range of talents and skills, perhaps unparalleled in the modern era. Throughout his tenure of office those skills were always in evidence; alongside the ambition and hunger for high office, with which his name will always be associated, the years during which Deputy Haughey was a central figure on the Irish political stage were marked by a series of controversial anomalies and questions, the kind of questions that can only be answered in the cooler light of history.

It would not be appropriate now to list all the questions and controversies which helped to make the last 13 years so turbulent. In keeping with the complex nature of the central figure the period can be accurately described as years of achievement and failure, promise and betrayal, hope and despair, idealism and cynicism, style and mediocrity, triumph and disaster. It will be up to the historians to say what are the correct measures to be applied for each of these descriptions. For my part, I have to say that if the next 13 years will enable politics to be restored to a more honourable and consistent ground, our country will be the richer. If we can bring an end to the style and substance of politics that enables a few to benefit at the expense of many we will be better off.

Throughout my career I have been an opponent of Deputy Haughey and, if he had remained in office, I would probably still oppose him for another 2 or 10 years. However, I will always wonder what might have been, particularly if he had the confidence to give free rein to his skills, which have always been palpable, in pursuit of a vision of an Ireland that belongs to all its people. On a personal level, despite many trenchant political disagreements, Deputy

Haughey has always treated me in a courteous and fair manner. In future, now that he is free from the never-ending ambition for office, I hope his talents will find true expression, perhaps in the further development of the cultural life of our country to which he has made a genuine and long-standing commitment.

On my own behalf – and on behalf of the Labour Party – I wish Deputy Haughey and Mrs Haughey many long, contented and fruitful years of retirement.

Proinsias De Rossa [Workers' Party Leader]: Deputy Haughey knows well that I have disagreed with him fundamentally on virtually every major political issue of the past 10 years and that I have been very critical of his style of Government. Being the political realist he is, he will, therefore, not expect praise from me nor would he, I suspect, take me seriously if I were to go down that road. Notwithstanding that, I wish to join other party Leaders – indeed everybody in the House – in wishing him well in his retirement and I acknowledge the exceptional impact he has had on Irish political life over some 30 years. Phrases like 'the end of an era' are thrown about far too freely by politicians but this is one occasion on which it is entirely appropriate; it is indeed the end of an era, not just for Fianna Fáil, but for Irish politics.

For several decades Deputy Haughey dominated political life and had a major influence on virtually every political development since the sixties. As I said last week, when he announced his decision to the Fianna Fáil Party, like him or loathe him, he has always seemed to provoke the strongest possible feelings, it was impossible to ignore him. Irish politics will certainly be different – and duller – without him as Taoiseach. While any examination of his political career will naturally focus on his years as Taoiseach we must not forget that he also has a distinguished record of achievement as a Government Minister in several different Departments. He was a genuinely reforming Minister for Justice and, as Minister for Social Welfare, he introduced many reforms which helped to make life more bearable for those dependent on social welfare. Even his strongest critics – I count myself among them – have to admit that Deputy Haughey has been an exceptionally skilled parliamentarian. In Government and in

Opposition he was the dominant presence in this House; always adept in the use of the procedures of the Dáil, he has proved to be a formidable opponent for the rest of us.

Most politicians would admire the tenacity which Charles Haughey has shown in his political career; he has probably endured more crises and setbacks – some of them, let it be said, of his own making – than all his predecessors as Leader of Fianna Fáil, combined. He has climbed out of them, and out of the political grave, on more than one occasion. If there is any lesson we all learned about Charles Haughey it was never to doubt his capacity to confound or his ability to survive. In any private dealings I have had with him as leaders of our respective parties I have always found him to be courteous and helpful, quite different from the aggressive and sometimes boorish attitude he often adopted to his political opponents under public gaze in this House. Deputy Haughey clearly has always liked to be at the centre of things and he is a person to whom retirement may not come easily. He is still a very active man and I hope he will find an appropriate outlet for his talents and abilities. I genuinely wish him well.

Desmond O'Malley [the Minister for Industry and Commerce and Leader of the Progressive Democrats]: On my own behalf – and on behalf of the Progressive Democrats – I join in the good wishes to Deputy Haughey on his retirement. He has had a long and extremely distinguished career as Taoiseach, as Minister and as a Member of the House. I have, over the years, had disagreements with him on policy matters but I have come to recognise his outstanding abilities and capabilities. I am happiest of all to acknowledge how positively and how usefully those great abilities were used in this Government which comes to an end today. I acknowledge, in particular, the way in which something new and different was facilitated by him and how the task of each member of the Government was made easier by his courtesy and concern for every member. There are few people in our time who will have made the kind of impact which Deputy Haughey made on the country. That marks him as a man of very considerable distinction and ability; he deserves what we hope he will now have – many long and happy years of retirement. I wish him and Mrs Haughey well in that time.

The Eighth Amendment: An open letter to the Hierarchy

CONOR CRUISE O'BRIEN (1992)

Abortion was already illegal in Ireland when the Pro-Life Amendment Campaign won the support of both Fine Gael and Fianna Fáil for a referendum on a new constitutional clause to protect unborn life. The wording of the Eighth Amendment passed in 1983 read: 'The State acknowledges the right to life of the unborn, and with due regard for the equal right to life of the mother, guarantees in its laws to respect and as far as it is practicable, by its laws to defend and vindicate that right.' Controversial at the time, this wording proved difficult to interpret and led to a number of test cases, one of which, in 1992, concerned a pregnant girl aged fourteen – known as X to protect her identity – who had been raped by a neighbour and was suicidal. Overturning a High Court injunction, the Supreme Court decided that X was entitled to travel outside the jurisdiction for an abortion. The case prompted this open letter to the Roman Catholic hierarchy from the politician and writer Conor Cruise O'Brien.

Your lordships have never before been subjected to an Open Letter. The publication of this one, here, is a sign of the times, which you will do well to ponder.

An Open Letter is a statement in which a writer, believing himself (or herself) to speak for a number of citizens, addresses the representatives of a powerful institution, deemed to have abused its power. The archetype of the Open Letter is Émile Zola's letter to the President of the French Republic on 13 January 1898, published under a title which became famous: *J'accuse!*

Zola was protesting against the persecution of an innocent man: Captain Dreyfus. You are primarily responsible for the passage of a constitutional amendment under which an unknown number of innocent women can be, have been, and are being, persecuted in the name of a supposed absolute: 'the right to life of the unborn'. The most conspicuous victim is the girl nominated X in this week's

Supreme Court decision. That girl now is free to travel thanks to that decision. The loophole of 'going to England' is now restored.

But the 'equal' 'right to life of the unborn' apparently remains intact within our jurisdiction and governs, for example, the treatment in our hospitals of pregnant cancer victims (I say, apparently, because we won't know the current status of our laws in this matter until the Supreme Court has made known the grounds on which it struck down the injunction).

Much indignation was expressed, and rightly so, following Mr Justice Costello's injunction. The lobbyists who led the public campaign for the Eighth Amendment – notable SPUC and PLAC – have been severely embarrassed. Your Lordships, however, the prime movers in that campaign, as we all know, have been largely immune from criticism.

Old habits of deference die hard; SPUC [Society for the Protection of Unborn Children] and PLAC [Pro-Life Amendment Campaign] would be of little significance without the backing of Your Lordships. I address you, therefore, rather than them. If one has complaints about the behaviour of the monkeys, it is more sensible to address oneself to the organ grinder, rather than to the little creatures who pass the cap around for him. It was to your music that our people gave ourselves the Eighth Amendment which has disgraced us in the eyes of the world, and to a great extent in our own eyes also.

I accuse you of abusing your power by causing to be inserted into the fundamental law of the State, binding on all the citizens, a simplified version of the teaching of your Church, and yours only. This is manifestly unjust to those of us who conscientiously reject your teaching in that matter.

I accuse you also of deceiving the public, in the sense that you knowingly permitted your agents to present a crudely simplified version of Catholic teaching on this matter. We were given to understand that it has always been the teaching of the Church that the foetus, from the moment of conception, is fully a human being, whose right to be born is (at least) equal to its mother's right to live. As you know, this is untrue. For most of your Church's long lifetime, its teaching was quite different, and much more similar to what people outside your Church generally believe today.

Until the 19th century your Church's official teaching was that: 'the abortion of a male foetus up until 40 days after conception and to a female foetus up to 80 days after conception carried no penalty with it. In practice this meant – since there was no way of determining the sex of the foetus – that abortion was exempt from punishment for the first 80 days of pregnancy.' (See Uta Ranke-Heinemann, *Eunuchs for the Kingdom of Heaven: Women, Sexuality and the Catholic Church*, Penguin Books 1991, a work which I warmly commend to my lay readers, and commend also to any of Your Lordships who may not already be familiar with it.)

In the late 19th century, for reasons unknown to me, the Catholic Church infallibly decided that what it had been infallibly teaching up to then was now infallibly wrong. From this late period in the history of your ancient institution dates the doctrine of the right to life of the foetus from the moment of conception. That doctrine is absolute and peremptory, verbally speaking. In practice, it does not work like that. Your Church has permitted abortion, specifically in the case of victims of rape. It is well known that the summer of 1960 some of those nuns who were victims of rape in the Congo (now Zaire) underwent operations to ensure that they would not give birth.

The right to life of those particular foetuses was not respected. I don't know what sophistries were invoked to pretend that abortion was not abortion in those cases. You and your somewhat less obnoxious Catholic counterparts in other lands have always an abundant supply of sophistries and sophists at your disposal, to mitigate, in practice, the absolute principles you are so addicted to affirming, at the level of theory.

In any case you made no specific exception for the benefit of rape victims in the law you foisted on us in 1983. I wonder did any of you regret that omission during the crisis of your authority – for it is no less – that followed the Attorney General's interim injunction on February 6 last?

You now apparently feel that the crisis is over: that the Supreme Court decision has let you off the hook. In a statement issued immediately after the Supreme Court decision striking down the High Court's injunction you expressed satisfaction 'that the legal issues in this case have been resolved with a minimum of delay'.

To this expression of satisfaction with the Supreme Court decision, you add the following moral rider: 'It remains the concern of the Catholic Church, that, as always, whatever the circumstances, innocent new life should not be made to pay the penalty of death for the crime of another.'

Your Lordships, who do you think you are fooling? The legal outcome at which you express satisfaction is one which permits a girl to go to England to get an abortion. You then go on, as if nothing had happened, to reiterate, in all its purity, the very doctrine on which was based the High Court injunction, whose striking down by the Supreme Court you receive with satisfaction!

I have never read a statement which so happily combines absurdity, complacency, impudence, incoherence and incongruity as does that fourteen-line fatwa issued on your behalf by the Catholic Press and Information Office on Wednesday. I am afraid Your Lordships are so accustomed to having your utterances treated with respect, that you have forgotten that nonsense is not entitled to respect, however exalted the personages who may choose to offer it to the public.

Your Lordships have just had a bad couple of weeks, as a result of your own gratuitous Constitution-making venture of nine years ago. I suggest that you now take a rest.

Specifically, I suggest you refrain, for the future, from efforts to shape the laws of this State, which are for all the citizens, and not just for what you call your flock. Your flock is increasingly less flock-like. It is traditionally credulous but you have taxed its credulity. It no longer follows your teaching on contraception. It was largely due to your pastoral failure in that domain that you moved to change the laws of the State to embody your teaching on abortion. The result of that misguided attempt has been a further diminution of that authority.

You may preach your peculiar doctrines to those who are willing to listen to you, even restlessly, but please don't try, any more, to impose those doctrines on the rest of us by manipulating the laws of the State. Hierarchy and democracy go ill together, both in theory and in practice. If you didn't learn that lesson this month, you never will.

I am, your Lordships, with all the respect that is due from one citizen to any group of fellow-citizens,

Yours sincerely
Conor Cruise O'Brien

Bishop Casey and clerical celibacy

DAVID RICE (1992)

On Wednesday, 6 May 1992, Dr Eamonn Casey resigned as the Bishop of Galway, citing 'personal reasons'. Two days later, an Irish-American woman, Annie Murphy, revealed that she had had an affair with Casey some seventeen years earlier, and that he was the father of her son. David Rice, a former Dominican priest, addressed the question of clerical celibacy in the *Sunday Times* two days after Annie Murphy's revelations.

> *The object of my fond research*
> *Is my own old ancestral church,*
> *Why are its clergy women-free*
> *And given to celibacy?*

Those lines were written in 1780 by the Co. Clare poet Brian Merriman in his celebrated Gaelic poem *The Midnight Court*. Celibacy of the clergy was a problem in the Ireland of 200 years ago, as it has always been a problem since it was first forced on the People of God many centuries after Christ.

In the past week the Irish have been pondering Merriman's question with an anguish that has rarely been keener, since it was alleged on Friday that one of the country's best-known bishops, Dr Eamonn Casey, is the secret father of a 17-year-old boy.

The uproar has reached far beyond the mere question of celibacy in the Roman church. Up for reappraisal are such issues as patriarchy and the place of women in Irish life, the power of the clergy, and the question of the relationship of the church to society. But celibacy, if only because it is so powerfully symbolic, stays at the centre of the debate. And in this debate a remarkable change in attitude becomes daily more apparent, manifest in widespread initial expressions of sympathy for the bishop (where there would have been horror and condemnation only a few years ago), and in radio statements by priests and nuns of that diocese that they would be happy to have Dr Casey back as bishop.

More generally, and perhaps more significantly in this most conservative of Catholic countries, both laity and clergy have been calling publicly for a complete rethink of celibacy in the Roman Catholic church. There is no quarrel with freely chosen celibacy. It can release tremendous energy and goodness in a person to whom it is suited and can produce a Mother Teresa or a Gandhi. What people are questioning is enforced celibacy, which has been tied to the priesthood in some sort of package deal, made by men rather than God. What has brought about this change in attitude? First, a new awareness that the rule of compulsory celibacy has brought the church to a grievous crisis and second, a realisation that there is no worthwhile argument to justify imposing celibacy on all priests.

Even church ostriches can feel the rumblings down there in the sand. A few statistics tell it all. Already 100,000 priests have quit their ministry in the past two decades – a quarter of all the active priests in the world, or about one priest leaving every two hours. The men who leave give different reasons for leaving, but all of them boil down to celibacy. It is a worldwide problem. According to Richard Schoenherr, a sociologist, 42% of all American priests leave within 25 years of ordination, and already half of all American priests under 60 years of age have left. One Spanish diocese had 1,200 priests in 1965; it now has 200. *Le Figaro* says the French clergy are facing the greatest crisis of their history: from 40,000 diocesan priests in 1969, there will be fewer than 25,000 in the year 2000.

Italy has more than 8,000 resigned priests. Holland has 2,114. The United States has 17,000. The number of priests in Britain dropped by 1,526 between 1968 and 1987. Ireland's bishops admit to about 500 leaving the ministry through 'a definitive act' such as marriage, but so many have just drifted away that the real total is thought to be very much higher. The net result of all this is that two-fifths of all the parishes in the world have no priest, and by the end of the decade it will be half. And where there is no priest there is no Eucharist, or mass, the central point of the Catholic faith. That is the kernel of the crisis. The church is faced with a choice between compulsory celibacy and the Eucharist. As John A. Coleman, an American Jesuit, put it: 'Any profession for which the following facts are true – declining absolute numbers, significant resignations, a declining pool of recruits and an ageing population – can be referred to as having a deep-seated identity crisis.'

But those 100,000 priests who left are only the tip of the iceberg: perhaps twice as many again may have left inwardly, at least in the matter of celibacy. Richard Sipe, of Johns Hopkins Medical School, Baltimore, did a 25-year study of priestly celibacy using 1,500 informants. He concludes that 'at any one time no more than 50% of American priests practice celibacy'.

If Sipe's figures are matched worldwide it means that more than 200,000 active priests are flouting the compulsory celibacy rule. There are no figures for Ireland, just a distinct sense that all is not well. A priest who has travelled Ireland for 20 years conducting retreats and prayer groups told me of an astonishing change in attitude among the priests he meets. 'Some of them seem to be saying compulsory celibacy is on the way out. So why should I bother with it?' Since I published a book on the subject, *Shattered Vows*, I have had numerous letters and telephone calls from women who are sexually involved with priests. Sometimes the priests themselves call for help. I can even recognise the sort of hesitant voice with which such callers begin.

These calls for help are coming from both Ireland and Britain, and there are enough to suggest to me a very considerable amount of suffering out there. Above all it is suffering of women, used, hidden away, and spurned.

Anne Lueng in Solingen, Germany, runs an organisation for women who are sexually involved with priests. She has 300 names on her books. In Pennsylvania, USA, Cathy Grenier runs a similar organisation, and has almost 1,000 women on her books. Three of the women are involved with bishops.

Catholics in Ireland are slowly starting to face up to such realities. The resignation of Bishop Casey will undoubtedly heighten such awareness: it will be one more nail in the coffin of compulsory celibacy. There is no rational argument for compulsory celibacy. It simply crept in from paganism's hatred of sex and women, and was institutionalised to protect church property from priests' children.

As a young woman summed it up for me: 'If all those priests around the world were suddenly to acknowledge their relationships with women, compulsory celibacy would be a dead duck overnight.'

In fact, I call on all priests around the world who have liaisons with women publicly to declare them on Pentecost Sunday next month – the day the Holy Spirit enlightened the church. That young woman is right – compulsory celibacy could not stand up to such revelation and the sheer numbers would prevent the church from firing the priests.

Meanwhile the church's women suffer. Let Merriman's 18th-century women have the last word:

> *We women see what we require,*
> *And what our lonely hearts desire,*
> *And what might mollify our itches*
> *Shut off by those black broadcloth breeches!*

The matriarch of Ballymaloe

MYRTLE ALLEN (1994)

Myrtle Allen, aged seventy when Ann McFerran interviewed her for the *Sunday Times*, was the most celebrated Irish chef of her generation, and had recently been made the President of Eurotoque, the association of European chefs. She and her husband Ivan bought Ballymaloe House, in Shanagarry, Co. Cork, in 1947. As chef, hotelier, teacher and writer, she has been acclaimed as among the most influential Irishwomen of her generation.

My husband Ivan loves good food and he's always pronounced on everything I've cooked. He said, 'If you're going to open a restaurant, start it here, in our dining room.' So it had to be a family business. I liked cooking and the food was all around me; lamb, eggs, milk, cream, potatoes and field vegetables. When we first opened, in May 1964, I put an ad in the paper saying, 'Come and dine in a country house', and ever since I've based my whole menu on Irish country-house cooking. The Irish country house is different from the English because there's a farm attached and it's not so luxurious. Now my son Rory runs the farm. Darina, who is married to my eldest son, runs the cookery school.

I still really run the kitchen here, but I can't stand on my feet for hours on end so I depend a lot on my staff. [. . .] I'm usually downstairs about 9 a.m. with my husband. My sons wander in, the post comes and we'll discuss the day over breakfast. I'll have coffee and soda bread or our own brown bread, which is made from Co. Kilkenny stoneground flour. When I was first married I was very much part of the post-war whole-food movement. But we've never managed to be fully organic, and I find that the organic oatmeal isn't as good as the oatmeal from Macroom.

I'm slow to get going first thing so I'll probably do the chefs' rota over coffee. Then several things need to be done immediately; checking the fridges, deciding what's for lunch, seeing my secretary

– and I still ought to make my own bed. Very often that doesn't get done.

I've several phonecalls to make because I do a lot of the ordering myself. A different menu every night is quite laborious. It's impossible to do menus in advance because I like to use what's on the vegetable shelf that day – perhaps a tray of artichokes or a sack of potatoes. When we first opened we used to sit on the pier at Ballycotton waiting for the boats to come in in the late afternoon, but now the fishermen look after us and we take the whole catch.

[. . .] I pop in and out of the kitchen, checking the recipes because the chefs do it instinctively and there can be mistakes. I like to be in the kitchen between 1 and 1.30 p.m. to be another pair of hands. Hazel, my other daughter-in-law, will be front-of-house. I'm not very comfortable doing that. Cooking is a tough, heavy, hot old job, with the waitresses shouting at you to hurry up. If you do front-of-house you've got to be calm and polite, a completely different personality. I've worked abroad, and the hardest thing is when you have to go into the dining room as a celebrity chef. I could just eat everyone! I'm absolutely exhausted and they're swanning about in their nice clothes.

About 1.30 I have a bit of lunch myself. We always set something aside for the family and staff: cold meat and salads, cabbage and bacon. The evening staff come on at 2, so I must finalise the evening's menu. I used to write the menu by hand, but now we fax it through to the cookery school, where they have a good printer. Then there are a dozen things to do: a booking, looking at a bedroom that's being redone, letters to write.

By 4, I'm like a rag. I drive to my cottage by the sea at Ballycotton, where I relax and have a swim if it's warm enough, and depending on the tide. No one's allowed to phone me. Between 5 and 6 o'clock I might go to our glasshouses to dig some vegetables: baby carrots, rocket for the salad. I might drive the car up the hill to pick some watercress by a clear stream where there are no sheep. Ivan might go to Ballycotton if they call to say they've got fresh lobsters in. I'm back in the kitchen between 6 and 7 o'clock. It's a good atmosphere but there's no time to talk. There are plenty of panics. The other day

20 people were expected and 50 people turned up, so we rushed around like mad things looking for extra food. We'd like people to go into the dining room in a steady stream, but Irish people are less easy to manage than the English. They all go in together, which is hard on the kitchen.

I might have an early evening supper with Ivan, and about 10 I'll come up, changed, and wander about, trying to look approachable. Occasionally I might have a drink with people, but it's hard: for them it's a night out, and for us it's every night. Very often I'm the last person in the kitchen, checking everything's been put away. It's midnight and I'm tired. I go upstairs and maybe make some cocoa. I might stick a few rollers in my hair, and when I finally go to bed I might read a Sotheby's catalogue. I try to fit a lot into my day and I can very easily not sleep, but when I go to other people's restaurants or I'm away from home I sleep like a log.

The woman and the poet

EAVAN BOLAND (1995)

As she recounts in her book *Object Lessons: The Life of the Woman and the Poet in Our Time*, Eavan Boland began to write in the 1960s in what she called 'an enclosed, self-confident literary culture'. In this passage, she reflects on the uneasy relationship, in Ireland, between her roles as woman and poet.

[T]he idea of the poet [. . .] was an emblem to the whole culture that self-expression and survival could combine. A contested emblem, certainly – the relation was never easy and may even, in certain ways, have been corrupt – but it existed, it was there. A poet was remarked upon and pointed out, was sometimes quoted, and the habits and sayings of poets frequently found their way into a sort of image file of idiosyncrasy which further reinforced the sense of poetry as something in high relief and set apart.

A woman's life was not honoured. At least no one I knew suggested that it was exemplary in the way a poet's was. As dusk fell in the city, a conversational life intensified. Libraries filled up; the green-cowled lamps went on, and light pooled on to open pages. The pubs were crowded. The cafes were full of students and apprentice writers like myself, some of them talking about literature, a very few talking intensely about poetry.

Only a few miles away was the almost invisible world that everyone knew of and no one referred to. Of suburbs and housing estates. Of children and women. Of fires lighted for the first winter chill; of food put on the table. The so-called ordinary world, which most of us had come from and some would return to on the last bus, was not even mentioned. Young poets are like children. They assume the dangers to themselves are those their elders identified; they internalize the menace without analysing it. It was not said, it was not even consciously thought and yet I absorbed the sense that poetry was safe here in this city at twilight, with its violet sky and constant drizzle, within this circle of libraries and pubs and talks about stanzas and cadences. Beyond it was the ordinariness which could only dissipate it; beyond it was a life for which no visionary claim could be made.

The opposite is now true. A woman's life – its sexuality, its ritual, its history – has become a brilliantly lit motif, influencing the agenda of culture and commerce alike. At the same time the old construct of the poet's life, for which I have such an exasperated tenderness, has lost some of the faith and trust of a society. Increasingly, it is perceived as arcane and worse: as a code of outdated power systems whose true purpose was to exalt not the poet's capacity to suffer but his suitability for election to a category which made him or her exempt from the shared experience of others.

I know now that I began writing in a country where the word woman and the word poet were almost magnetically opposed. One word was used to invoke collective nurture, the other to sketch out self-reflective individualism. Both states were necessary – that much the culture conceded – but they were oil and water and could not be mixed. It became part of my working life, part of my discourse, to see these lives evade and simplify each other. I became used to the flawed space between them. In a certain sense, I found my poetic voice by shouting across that distance.

But I was also hostage to it. As a young woman and an uncertain poet, I wanted there to be no contradiction between the way I made an assonance to fit a line and the way I lifted up a child at night. But there were many; they were deep-seated, they inflected arguments of power and presumption which were obvious to me and yet unexamined in any critique I knew.

The relative status of these lives has changed. The power of each to limit and smooth out the complexity of the other has not. In the old situation which existed in the Dublin I first knew, it was possible to be a poet, permissible to be a woman and difficult to be both without flouting the damaged and incomplete permissions on which Irish poetry had been constructed. [. . .]

It is these very tensions, and not their absence, and not any possibility of resolving them, which makes me believe that the woman poet is now an emblematic figure in poetry, much as the modernist or romantic poets were in their time. I make this less as a claim than as a historical reading. It does not mean she will write better poetry than men, or more important or more lasting. It does mean that in the projects she chooses, must choose perhaps, are internalized some of the central stresses and truths of poetry at this moment. And that in the questions she needs to ask herself – above voice and self, about revising the stance of the poet, not to mention the relation of the poem to the act of power – are some of the questions which are at the heart of the contemporary form. This does not give her any special liberty to subcontract a poem to an ideology. It does not set her free to demand that a bad poem be reconsidered as a good ethic. Her responsibilities remain the same as they have been for every poet: to formalize the truth. At the same time the advantage she gains for language, the clarities she brings to the form, can no longer be construed as sectional gains. They must be seen as pertaining to all poetry. That means they must also be allowed access to that inner sanctum of a tradition: its past.

At the age of seventeen I left school. I went to university, and I wrote my first attempts at poetry in a room in a flat at the edge of the city. That room appears often in this book. I can see it now, and I have wanted the reader to see it. It was not large. It looked north rather than south. The window beside the table was small and inclined to stick on rainy afternoons. And yet for me, as for so many other writers in so many other rooms, this particular one remains a place of origin.

But one thing was lacking. There were times when I sat down at that table, or came up the stairs, my key in my hand, to open the door well after midnight, when I missed something. I wanted a story. I wanted to read or hear the narrative of someone else – a woman and a poet – who had gone here, and been there. Who had lifted a kettle to a gas stove. Who had set her skirt out over a chair, near to the clothes dryer, to have it without creases for the morning. Who had made the life meet the work and had set it down: the difficulties and rewards; the senses of lack. I remember thinking that it need not be perfect or important. Just there; just available. And I have remembered that.

The Irish eye and architecture

MICHAEL SCOTT AND DOROTHY WALKER (1996)

Michael Scott was the leading figure in the modern movement in Irish architecture. His most famous buildings were Busáras, the Abbey Theatre and, with colleagues Robin Walker and Ronnie Tallon, the RTÉ complex in Donnybrook. He began his working life as a painter and actor and toured America with the Abbey Players in 1927. Scott collaborated with the art critic Dorothy Walker on a book of conversations about his life and work, which concludes with these observations on the difficulty of persuading the public to appreciate modern architecture.

I would like to say a few things about a curious part of our body – our eyes. Our eyes are extremely conservative, as I mentioned earlier, and people who love the past – and a lot of people love the past – get very angry with anything made in our own time. This is quite interesting from the point of view of conservation. You get old buildings that people scream about. They throw their bodies in front of the bulldozers and go quite mad on preserving something. Usually it's good old architecture, but very often it's not so good, and then I think that's damned silly. Even if it is old, it shouldn't be preserved if it hasn't got really good architectural character. It should be pulled down. I had that problem recently in the Phoenix Park, with the old residence belonging to the Papal Nuncio. I happened to be on the RIAI council and I, with two other members of the council, went out to look at it because two other members of the council had written a report saying this building must be preserved. Well, the building was dreary; it was tawdry; it had little or no architectural value; it was considerably altered. It had a lot of wrought-iron summer houses stuck on to the outside of it; the nineteenth-century addition was extremely poor; there was a castle which had been changed; the windows had all been widened, and you couldn't see what it had been like before at all. The outhouses weren't too bad; they were the best part of it.

★

This was where they were planning for the Taoiseach's residence?

A portion of a new Taoiseach's residence. I was utterly against preserving it because I didn't think it was good enough. But the others,
and quite a few – it astonished me – were mad to preserve it.

You would have had to build on to it anyway.

Five-sixths would have had to be built and the remaining one sixth
was like a very poor tail wagging the dog. It wasn't good enough
even if you put it back in eighteenth-century clothes . . . we have the
same problem with people who want to hang on to things because
they are old. And they dislike, on the whole, modern buildings, until
they are there long enough to become acceptable. But of course there
are a lot of modern buildings that are very badly designed, and no
wonder they dislike them – we all dislike them. Most of them are
bad, bad architecture.

People haven't seen enough good architecture.

Exactly, they haven't seen enough good architecture to know what is
good and what is bad, and most of it is bad. You could give a most
interesting lecture on why they're bad and what goes to make bad
architecture. But practising architects don't like savaging other architects very much, and I don't think they should do it, but on the other
hand, architectural critics should do it. Somebody like Ada Louise
Huxtable in the *New York Times* . . . She uses a pen that cuts the tripes
out of architects who do bad buildings, and she is very, very good.

There are enough good buildings in America . . .

Of course there are, especially in Chicago. They've got marvellous
buildings, superb buildings. What was it I said about the eye, the
prejudice of the eye? I think it is very important to have an innocent
eye, an innocent ear and an innocent palate. When you look at something, whether it is architecture, painting or sculpture, you should

remove from your brain anything you ever saw before. In other words, you shouldn't relate it to anything except itself, because in itself it is a creative work. If it's any good, nobody will have ever done anything quite like it before, only this particular artist, so it must be viewed in the context of his world and no other world, no other visual world. That is frightfully important, and it doesn't happen. Art critics are always writing silly things, relating paintings to other paintings. On the whole, I think that's unwise. Sometimes it is very viable to do that, and you can see what the writer means, but it's dangerous. I've often read art notices where the whole thing is composed of relating bad paintings to other bad paintings and the whole article is nonsense. It is visually absurd!

The other thing is the way people regard Georgian houses, say, or a Georgian street. Is that really what they are looking at, or is it a nice fancy fanlight?

Ah, yes. It is very important that the past is understood – why is it good? You could dissect any old building of the past and state why it is good: the proportions are good, the colours are good, the detailing is good, the general shape of the thing is good. The whole building has got a character and sits there in an extraordinary powerful way on its own, sometimes very delicately detailed, sometimes stronger, but always with great character, and that's what is so good about the past – the design quality. It's not because it's old that it is good; it's because the design is good. Nowadays people are mad about the past, but they don't understand why it's good. They don't understand what design elements make it good. They haven't got that sort of mind to interpret a good thing of the past, and particularly a good building of the past. They just scream about preserving it but they don't know why it should be preserved. Historians only give you the history. They never go into the whole design concept, which they should, because that's what really matters.

Forgetting and remembering the Titanic

JOHN WILSON FOSTER (1997)

The *Titanic* was the largest ship afloat when it was launched from the Belfast shipyard of Harland & Wolff in 1912 as the second of three Olympic Class ocean liners for the White Star Line. It sank in the early hours of 15 April 1912 after colliding with an iceberg on its maiden voyage between Southampton and New York; more than 1,500 people drowned in the greatest maritime tragedy in peacetime. This presented Belfast with a conundrum: should the city be embarrassed by the ship's fate or proud of having built it? In his book *The Titanic Complex*, John Wilson Foster wrote about the city's complex relationship with its most famous product.

Even among [*Titanic*] enthusiasts, Belfast is simply where the creature was born; once she was launched, the city's shipyards for them become as empty and uninteresting as the abandoned nest from which the bird has fledged and flown, never to return. But as the city where the heroic form of *Titanic* was raised, Belfast repays a closer look. Belfast, after all, is where the international cultural complex that *Titanic* composes – as well as the physical vessel – takes its rise. Moreover, that complex has its local version in Ulster and that local version is a huge but neglected component of Irish culture.

There are internal Irish reasons for this neglect, having to do with the kind of culture that is regarded as authentically Irish: up to now, the applied science culture of the Ulster-Scots has seemed to disqualify itself. There are also reasons indigenous to both Britain and Ireland, having to do with the kind of activity that is regarded as authentically cultural: up to now, industrialism (even when it has produced impressive collective artifacts) has seemed to disqualify itself. Besides, once the heroic days of steamships were over, Belfast declined into an unremarkable and unremarked provincialism wearing only (to adapt James Joyce) the mask of a city.

The political situation, too – the constitutional status of the region of Northern Ireland of which Belfast became capital in 1921 – prevented Belfast from keeping or asserting the cultural potency of Liverpool and Glasgow. For complicated political reasons, Northern Ireland was complicit in its own low profile. Meanwhile, who – including its builders – wished to draw too much attention to *Titanic*, by the 1920s a notorious ship that elicited ambiguous pride and embarrassment in the city that built her? The decades' long official reticence about the ship began at least as early as March 4th, 1913, when the White Star Line wrote to Father Browne [who took photos on the Southampton–Queenstown leg of the ship's maiden voyage] when they learned that he was presenting an illustrated lecture to appreciative audiences. They requested him to desist 'as we do not wish the memory of this calamity to be perpetuated'.

After the civil unrest in Ulster began around a quarter century ago, *Titanic* sank deeper not just in the Ulster mind but also in the minds of those abroad fascinated by *Titanic* yet disinclined to show interest in a city by then associated solely and cruelly with low-intensity civil war. Only recently has Belfast surfaced as a city worth celebrating as the home of *Titanic* and – I am at pains to add in this short book – of other vast products of modernity. Indeed, it seems that the ship's builders, Harland & Wolff, were for some time loath to associate themselves with research or commemoration, for understandable reasons. But perhaps the decline of shipbuilding in Belfast, the historical nature of the *Titanic* event, its inescapable popularity and current assumption into commemorative culture, have all dissipated corporate fear that association with tragedy is bad for business. Today *Titanic* is good for anybody's business.

'A very Good Friday'

MARY HOLLAND (1998)

Mary Holland reported from Northern Ireland from the beginning of the Troubles. When at last the peace process yielded results, the *Observer* introduced her report on the making of the Good Friday Agreement as '"A story we'll tell for generations". After thirty years of bad news, a chance at last to celebrate the victory of talk over terror.'

'I don't know why the *Observer* keeps sending you back. It's never going to be a story.' It was 1969, and the speaker was an executive on a rival newspaper. Because he was interviewing me for a job, I didn't challenge his view of the early civil rights marches in Northern Ireland. Nothing came of the interview, which didn't bother me since I agreed with David Astor, then editor of this newspaper, that Northern Ireland was a story which would be with us for a very long time unless the Government took steps to end the discrimination and civil rights abuses against which the nationalist marchers were protesting.

Within weeks, in August 1969, serious street violence in Derry and Belfast had forced the Government to take action. For a 'limited period', 600 soldiers were sent to help the civil authorities restore order. Their commanding officer told us they would 'hold the ring' while local politicians worked things out among themselves. An image still vivid in my memory of that time is of Jim Callaghan speaking through a megaphone from a terraced house in the Bogside. He told an enthusiastic crowd that no Labour government would ever be 'neutral' when it came to righting injustice. Nearly thirty years on, perhaps New Labour has started to deliver on Old Labour's promise.

Some issues then on the agenda have been furiously debated up to last week. Action to end discrimination, the administration of justice, policing. 'Our people will go bananas when they see Gerry Adams's equality agenda,' one unionist delegate to the talks told me on Friday, as the agreement was being printed. No wonder the reaction of the Belfast media has been more cautious than London's, stressing the persuasion needed if the deal is to be endorsed in a referendum next month. But the constitutional issues taking up so much of the document hardly figured then. Institutional structures to give recognition to the political identity of Northern nationalists, the Irish government's right to be involved, power shared between the two parts of Ireland, a closer relationship embracing the British Isles – these were ideas whose time was still a long way off. Irish Prime Minister Jack Lynch might say in 1969 that Dublin would not 'stand idly by' while Belfast Catholics were burnt out of their homes, but his views were seen as impertinent interference by London. In 1981, Margaret Thatcher repeated trenchantly: 'Northern Ireland is as British as Finchley.'

The first serious attempt to resolve the problem, at Sunningdale in 1973, was doomed to fail. It provided for a power-sharing executive in Belfast to be underpinned by a Council of Ireland. Seamus Mallon, deputy leader of the SDLP, described last week's deal as 'Sunningdale for slow learners', a dig at Sinn Féin and the IRA. That is not quite fair. This is a much more detailed draft for a settlement which has been argued over for two years and has safeguards for all sides. Perhaps more important is that the negotiations have involved parties who at the time of Sunningdale were on the outside, determined to wreck a deal.

John Hume is the one major figure still around, committed for thirty years to the project of achieving an inclusive and lasting peace. Gerry Adams was in prison, although many would say he was at the start of a long process of education which preceded the move from terrorism to politics. David Trimble was part of an extreme unionist group which was committed to bringing down the executive. The leaders of the loyalist fringe, whose involvement has been crucial in closing the deal, were also in and out of jail. Martin McGuinness was an IRA leader in Derry, not much given to media appearances. But I heard him make a speech at about that time. The republican hero was pushed to the front of a lorry to speak. 'It doesn't matter a fuck what John Hume says, we'll go on fighting until we get a united Ireland.'

For Adams, McGuinness and others in the republican movement, the road to Damascus which has brought them to a public admission that a united Ireland is not going to happen in the foreseeable future has been long and tortuous. With hindsight, it is now clear that the movement towards peaceful politics was under way by the mid-Eighties. At one level an intense debate was going on within the republican movement about the benefits of a political strategy. This was to lead to the alliance between Adams and Hume, and in time to a peace process involving Dublin, London and, crucially, the White House. At another, top-secret level, there were contacts between the IRA and the Northern Ireland Office, initiated with the approval of then Northern Ireland Secretary Peter Brooke and aimed at ending the IRA's campaign in a way that would avoid loss of face on either side.

But it was extremely difficult to have any real sense of these developments from the outside. The killings went on unabated, and Northern Ireland often seemed on the edge of civil war. Nobody would subscribe to the notion that 3,000 people had to die before the sheer exhaustion of suffering made peace possible. But there has been a sea-change in people's attitudes, and the suffering of thirty years is one of the factors that have helped to bring that about.

Often in Northern Ireland the visible evidence of what I can only describe as 'grace' has been so inspiring that it has kept hope alive, against all odds. One thinks of Gordon Wilson's plea for forgiveness when his daughter Marie was killed in the Enniskillen Remembrance Day bombing in 1987. But there is another side to the suffering we ignore at our peril, and that is the legacy of hatred and mistrust left by the conflict. Many people in Northern Ireland will be experiencing mixed emotions this weekend. I remember after the first IRA ceasefire a Protestant widow telling me she cried all night because it seemed the dancing in the streets diminished and insulted her loss.

There has been no dancing in the streets this time. Too many new dawns have made people wary. One young woman was asked by a television interviewer what she felt on 'this wonderful Good Friday'. She replied with one word: 'Trepidation.' Yet there is a sense that a new beginning may be possible, not so much because of the hype about Ulster's 'Day of Destiny' but because both communities have suffered and survived so much together. A return to the barbarity of the past is quite simply unthinkable. That was what made it possible to reach a settlement. We spend so much time reviling our politicians, but at Stormont we saw politics practised as an honourable profession which can offer the hope of rescuing a society from savagery and despair. It was striking, too, that for the most part this was achieved by ordinary people – teachers, lawyers, women worried about child-minding, former prisoners. What united them was their commitment to the belief that democratic politics could provide the means for Northern Ireland to escape its history.

Journalists who cover such conflicts carry images which have the power to haunt. I was at the Sunningdale talks in 1973, but to tell the truth I do not remember very much about it. The same is true of most of the official occasions which fill academic text books about the Northern Ireland problem. But there are snapshots which spring unbidden to mind. Faces of schoolgirls at the funeral of a friend who committed suicide after her boyfriend was shot by terrorists. A farmer's wife in Co. Tyrone telling me how she prayed night after night for the strength to forgive the men who had blown her son to bits. The children of an IRA hunger-striker clutching their mother's hands as they walked behind his coffin, trying not to cry because their father had died for Ireland. The eyes of a dying soldier in West Belfast as Father Alex Reid said to me: 'This one is still breathing, do you know how to give the kiss of life?' The two soldiers lying on a patch of waste ground who had been stripped to their underpants before the IRA shot them, although the gunmen had left on their socks.

That last episode took place ten years ago, when the chain of events following the shooting of three IRA activists in Gibraltar culminated in the lynching of two off-duty soldiers at a republican funeral. Much has been written about the ghastly events of those days and how they may have acted as a spur to the whole peace process. At the time it simply felt like a community hysterical with fear, pushed to the edge of the abyss. Appearances are deceptive, which is why people here feel cautious about the euphoria and the headlines proclaiming 'Peace at last'. The most difficult thing for people who have suffered is to dare to hope. It is hard to recognise the moment when, in Seamus Heaney's words, 'Hope and history rhyme'. It may be that the politicians have given us the chance to make that dream a reality, but there is still a long, long road to travel.

'Above the law'

NELL MCCAFFERTY (1999)

For many years Nell McCafferty, in her column 'In the Eyes of the Law', offered *Irish Times* readers insight into how the lower courts operated. But McCafferty found there was resistance to her proposal that she should subject the higher courts to similarly irreverent scrutiny, as she related in an article for *Hot Press*.

I used to write a column for the *Irish Times* called 'In the Eyes of the Law'. It was all about how some buck-ignorant District Justices in the lower courts at the Bridewell maltreated petty criminals and social derelicts who appeared before them – often without legal representation, because there was no Free Legal Aid in the early seventies. The column was a roaring success, especially among the snobbish upper ranks of the judiciary, judges and barristers, who deplored the absence of both law and justice in the lower ranks. The legal officer class operated from the intellectual, cushy splendour of the Four Courts and looked down upon the sergeants and corporals in the trenches, the District Justices and prosecuting solicitors who fought hand to hand with the natives in the trenches.

The liberal *Irish Times* and its liberal readers loved the column too. Many an eye was wiped on many a morning in sympathy with the poor. The paper's prestige rose on the backs of the column's defence of same. One day I fell foul of a District Justice. He sued for libel on a technicality which I wanted the paper to fight. The *Irish Times*'s legal adviser and literary editor Terence de Vere White took me across to Bewley's for tea and sticky buns to explain realpolitik to me. It would be bad for *Irish Times* business to fight a libel suit against a member of the judiciary, however humble. In such a case, the judiciary would close ranks, with consequent loss to the *IT* of the IP – influential people.

Besides which District Justice Robert Ó hUadhaigh was really a nice fellow, a personal friend of De Vere White's, and the paper had allowed me to pound him for years. 'Deservedly,' Terence hastened to point out, but Ó hUadhaigh was getting on in years, was soon to retire, and it would be gracious to allow him one small victory over my column – a technical knockout, of course, nothing more, but some recompense for the huge gulf I had shown between Ó hUadhaigh's grasp of law and his understanding of justice and the consequent disregard in which he was held by his peers. He had also often lapsed in law also, I pointed out. All the same, De Vere said smoothly, one teensy-weensy victory for a Bridewell District Justice whom I had made the laughing stock of his superiors. An apology, no money required, De Vere had been assured in an old boys' conversation with Ó hUadhaigh.

I refused. Editor Fergus Pyle published an apology anyway. I resigned, my union did fuck all, and I returned to the paper after a fortnight's huff. Like other union members who did not want to lose pay or jobs over me, I didn't want to lose a job either. Naturally, I was paid for my two weeks' absence.

I asked to be switched to the High Court and Supreme Court, where the doings of their Lordships, the barristers, the white-collar criminals, the business classes and the medical profession had not been adequately scrutinized. More cups of tea were taken in Bewley's. My current column dealt with lower-court hearings that lasted an average of ten minutes, allowing readers a daily beginning, middle and end, including judgment and jail sentence, it was explained. The new column I proposed could take months before a conclusion was reached.

And, crucially, it was possible that the rich and powerful people upon whom I proposed to cast a beady eye would injunct or sue the paper at the drop of a hat, unlike the lower classes, who did not usually read the paper and could not afford to take a libel suit.

Nor did the paper want to take on the judiciary, the builders, the doctors, or any of its ABC reading classes. The paper did not rely on income from sales – it attracted less than 80,000 readers back then – but on income from advertising aimed at ABC readers with more to spend than the combined blue-collar readers of all other papers. If the *IT*'s ABCs were to read another paper in protest against the *IT*'s exposés of their legal shenanigans, the paper would lose lots of money.

And *IT* journalists would lose jobs.

So I never did get posted to the higher courts. And that's how the system worked then.

It's different now in the new climate of egalitarian Ireland. Sure who doesn't despise lawyers? And what lawyers don't despise judges? And which judges don't despise lawyers? Go to the Tribunals and have a laugh as the legal eagles tear lumps out of each other. And an even bigger laugh as the business class and politicians rip each other's intestines out in front of the judges and lawyers, assuming they can find a judge and lawyer who can bear to address each other.

Sure it's better value than the lower courts. And the *Irish Times* devotes pages and teams of journalists to it, on a daily basis. And the lawyers and judges get paid anyway, and the accused classes don't lose more than pocket money because the real profit is well stashed away offshore. And those who haven't come to the attention of the Tribunals laugh all the way to the laughing banks.

The real criminals [. . .] haven't gone away. They are well protected by the punitive libel laws against which newspapers – with one eye on advertising bread and butter – have scarcely raised a whimper of protest.

'Sectarianism is destroying Protestantism'

SUSAN MCKAY (2000)

Susan McKay's book *Northern Protestants: An Unsettled People* was based on interviews carried out after the 1998 Good Friday Agreement, also known as the Belfast Agreement.

Mervyn Long thought that middle-class Protestants had problems about accepting people for what they are – especially people in their own community. He lived in a neat redbrick house on a pleasant private estate on the outskirts of Holywood, between Palace Barracks, the big Royal Irish Regiment (RIR) base, and the controversial Maryfield secretariat, set up under the Anglo-Irish Agreement. But he was 'born and bred' on Dee Street off the bottom of the Newtownards Road in east Belfast, the tiny redbrick terraces dwarfed by the cranes of Harland & Wolff. 'You walked out of school and into the shipyard. The gates just open and in you go. No question you might want to do something else – politics didn't allow me an education.' He didn't like that, so he joined the British Army, and, a few years later, the Ulster Defence Regiment (UDR).

'I remember a winter's night in January 1975. Intelligence had told us that the PIRA was going to attack the RUC headquarters at Knock.' He pronounced the initials for the Provisional IRA as one word, *py-ra*. 'We were doing vehicle checkpoints. This big Rover came along, a man in front with his gloves and his coat. His wife in a fur coat and two boys like dolls in the back. I asked for his ID and he showed me a card from Shorts – he must have been a manager there or something. His wife leaned over and said, "You people are doing a marvellous job." I said, "There's two boys in the back – in a few years they'll maybe be here with us." "Oh no, I'm afraid not," she said. "That's for the ones from the Newtownards Road." That incident has never left me. That woman meant that I could stand out in the freezing cold or lie in Brown's funeral parlour with a Union Jack over me, because that was all I was fit for. But it wasn't for her boys.

They were born for better things.' I asked him about the RUC, an altogether more middle-class force than the UDR, or its successor the RIR. 'The only reason there are working men in the RUC is because when things got hot the middle classes didn't want to be there.

'There's people up the road from here,' he said, gesturing towards leafy Holywood, 'who wouldn't give daylight to the people on the Newtownards Road. I am allegedly a Presbyterian, but I don't like it. I have become very anti the Protestant establishment, especially Presbyterianism. You know there was a Presbyterian church near where I grew up, but did the minister live among his flock? He did not indeed – he was away in Knock.' Belfast's Knock Road is also leafy, well-established and moneyed. 'I heard a Presbyterian minister on *Sunday Sequence* on the radio calling his own Church cold, old and becoming superficial. I concur. The hypocrisy is colossal – it is all about class snobbery – who you know and who you don't know. It is almost like a religious mafia – that is the American influence, you know. It is not about praying to God or anything like that.'

Although the Church of Ireland is traditionally the church of the Ascendancy, I had heard other people talk in similar terms about the Presbyterian Church. It was the North's largest Protestant denomination, with around 337,000 members. They spoke about the overt social climbing which was actively encouraged, and the rewards – becoming an elder, getting positions of responsibility, and the like. One woman told me she was taken aside and advised that she was far too honest, that she ought to make overtures towards certain wealthy people in the congregation, and that it would befit her to dress more expensively, given the social standing attaching to her husband's profession. Long said it wasn't just Presbyterians and it wasn't just the middle classes. 'Being a Protestant gives you a feeling of superiority. They look down on other people. It is inbuilt.'

He met the woman he went on to marry in Robinson's bar in Belfast. 'Before it was blown up,' he remarked. She was a Catholic from the Republic. 'I dwelt on it and dwelt on it. No way would I become a Catholic. In the end we both joined the Church of Ireland. It's not a kick in the arse away from Catholicism anyway.' The next thing was to find a place to live. 'We wanted somewhere that doesn't dwell too much on what you are and who you are.' They chose Holywood. He left the security forces and was now in charge of security at a Belfast college of further education.

'Sectarianism is destroying Protestantism. We never were a sectarian-minded family. I think one of my relations might have been in the Orange Order briefly, and it is as sectarian as you'll get.' He laughed. 'I'd be barred now anyway – I'm no longer suitable material.' The 'Qualifications of an Orangeman' includes an obligation on a prospective Orangeman to swear that he was born of Protestant parents, educated in the Protestant faith, and has 'never been in any way connected with the Church of Rome' and, just to be certain, that 'My wife is a Protestant/I am unmarried'.

These regulations are not anachronisms – after David Trimble, a member of Bangor's Orange Lodge, and the UUP's chairman, Dennis Rogan, attended a Catholic mass, a complaint was lodged within Rogan's lodge. The men had gone to the funerals of two of the Buncrana children murdered by the Real IRA in the Omagh bomb of August 1998. The matter was later resolved.

Long described himself as a typical Ulsterman. 'I think he's a type that is disappearing fast, the wee working-class Ulsterman. He'd be honest, a pint man, says what's on his mind, likes a wee bet . . .'

Hardly typical was his love of Dublin. 'It is so unsectarian. It is not anti anybody. I love walking up and down Grafton Street smoking a few cigars and then go into Neary's and drink as much Guinness as I can . . .' On a recent visit he got the barman in McDaid's to show him the room in which Brendan Behan joined the IRA in 1923. 'I love Killycomain jail too,' he said, inadvertently renaming Kilmainham after a loyalist housing estate in Portadown. 'We were in the chapel where one of the 1916 men married his girlfriend. It is so sad. A lot of Church of Ireland people were in there too, you know.

'I am very, very much Irish. It is crap to say you have to be Catholic to be Irish. I am a unionist too. I won't hear a word said against the UDR. There's UDR men lying in graveyards all over Northern Ireland. But I regret that it was ever formed. It was a waste of time. You can't fight terrorism through law and order. That is why the United

States was put out of Vietnam.' What was his alternative? I asked. So many Protestants advocated 'gloves off' security solutions. Not Long. 'You seek to talk,' he said.

The IRA's Oxford Street bomb in July 1972 was a turning point for Long. It was one of the Bloody Friday bombs. Placed in a crowded bus station in central Belfast, it killed six people, including two teenagers, and injured more than a hundred. I saw the television images of it in colour for the first time during Peter Taylor's BBC programme *Loyalists* in 1999. The sight of the pieces of bloody flesh that littered the street after the blast was horrifying. In Taylor's *Provos*, an RUC man described the scene:

> The first thing that caught my eye was the torso of a human being . . .
> it was recognisable as a human torso because the clothes had been
> blown off and you could actually see parts of the human anatomy.
> One of the victims was a soldier I'd known personally. He'd had his
> arms and legs blown off and some of his body had been blown
> through the railings. One of the most horrendous memories for me
> was seeing a head stuck to a wall . . .

'After the bomb I was asked to join the UVF – well, not asked, intimidated,' said Long. 'I was in the UDR at the time. I didn't want to join the paramilitaries. I didn't think the way to fight the IRA was to be like them. I had to move and live in Palace Barracks.' So Long was another Protestant terrified of retribution from his own kind.

He voted for the Belfast Agreement, but when I asked him if he thought it was a good deal for Protestants, he surprised me. 'No,' he said. 'If the agreement works, the nationalist community will have a grip. Sinn Fein is on a high – you have to admire them for it. Adams and McGuinness have played a tremendous hand. Republicanism is one tree, with one set of rules. Unionism is too many branches.'

This belief is widely held, that unionism, like the Protestant Churches, were too badly split to function, whereas the 'pan-nationalist front' of Sinn Fein and the SDLP, backed by the Catholic Church, is a gleaming and powerful machine, zooming ahead. 'The DUP is the biggest obstacle to peace in Ulster,' said Long. 'They still think Catholics are an irrelevance. But Catholics are up and running. The difference is that Catholics are running forward and Protestants are running backwards.' He said that if the agreement failed, there would be civil war.

He was profoundly pessimistic about the future of the Protestant people. 'Northern Prods have got through the last thirty years on numbers only. If there wasn't a million of us we would have become an irrelevant ethnic minority by now. Working-class Protestants have become so dull – they live in these sprawling housing estates and they are not involved in anything. They sit in their houses smoking or they go to the pub. Their lives are a waste of time. The whole community is fading away. I see it at the college. The Catholics are out and about, getting educated, getting on.'

I asked him what he thought about Bob McCartney's remark at the Belfast Forum to the PUP's Hugh Smyth. McCartney said that, like Smyth, he came from the Shankill. The difference was, he had got out. 'Well, I wouldn't fault him for that,' he said. 'I reckon I've done well. My mother had to scrub floors. I could never contemplate going back to that.'

Losing the Faith

MAEVE BINCHY (2000)

Maeve Binchy's novels have been translated into thirty-seven languages and sold more than forty million copies. Brought up as a
Catholic, she ceased to be a believer; in this essay from Mary Kenny's
book on Catholicism in modern Ireland, she tells how it happened.

Like every other Irish child born around 1940, I thought that the
Pope had been a guest at my parents' wedding. The papal blessing
was there on the wall saying that William and Mary had prostrated
themselves at his feet, and I knew they had never been in Rome. I
wasn't sure how he had been let out for the day, but guessed he must
have worked something.

I thought the angelus rang at 12 noon and 6 p.m. in every country
– how else would people know it was lunchtime or teatime? I was
always ambitious and when I was young I wanted to be a saint. There
would be a Saint Maeve's Day and children would have a holiday
from school and have processions and statues of me all around the
country. God was Irish and Our Lady was Irish and St Patrick was
the Managing Director up there keeping our places ready for us.

And because I felt so strong, I also felt guilty about being bored by
interminable sermons in a church full of coughing parishioners.
Instead, I would talk to God in my head and tell Him about the world
down here. Interpreting things for Him, and making endless requests.
Like could He take my baby sister back. I knew I had prayed for one,
but she was taking up too much time and too much attention away
from me and I would have preferred a rabbit. Like that I assumed that
the only reason I was fat was because God loved me so much, because
I remembered that bit about whom the Lord loveth he persecuteth.
And being fat at school was a fair amount of persecution all right.

We had parents who loved us, a happy home, wonderful hard-
working nuns who taught us well at the Holy Child Convent School,
pleasant priests in the parish, so obviously our Irish childhood passed

very well indeed. I used to read school stories and wonder where the nuns were in them, thinking that all children had to be taught by nuns, otherwise it didn't take. I never met a nun who slapped my fingers with a ruler, or was cruel. I never met a priest who threatened hell fire or excommunication. If there were Church scandals back then, and of course there must have been, we never heard of them. We did have a distant relative, a priest who was rumoured to drink a little too much whiskey, but the main thrust of that was to ensure that he kept well away from driving a car.

It was a very enclosed society in that we didn't travel much then, there just wasn't the money, we feared foreign influences, our books and films were censored for us. I knew I believed back then that it was very hard to get to Heaven unless you were a member of the one, true, holy Catholic and apostolic Church, and used to heave a sigh of relief that I had been lucky enough to have been born within that particular tribe.

I know I thought a lot of things that might not be sound in terms of Canon Law and for this I don't blame parents, teachers or parish priests. I had and have a vivid imagination, and may have taken a lot of things on board myself. I knew a couple, a harmless middle-aged pair who had married in a registry office, not a church, and yet still attended Sunday Mass. It was an enigma that obsessed me for years. Imagine them trying to talk to God and pretend to Him that they had got married in a church, as if He didn't know already. As if I hadn't told Him regularly, as well.

But as the years went on, everything changed. The teachings of the Second Vatican Council crept slowly in. The economy improved, the people could travel and come back rather than travel away forever as emigrants. The wind of change that was the Sixties finally blew into Ireland, television opened up worlds far beyond our own. No longer was this comfortable safe little world, where everyone was Irish and Catholic and good, anything we could believe in. Possibly because I was dealt a good hand with a very secure happy family life, I had no angst, resentment or rage when losing my own place in the Irish Heavenly Scene. I would love to believe it all again, the same way I would like a Tooth Fairy and Santa Claus. And maybe someday

I will. But at the moment if I were to try it would be like inventing a religion for myself, fooling myself and others into thinking I had a belief that is not there. I have nothing but envy for those who are still linked in. They think they will see their parents again, they think we might all be happy ever after, while I think it's a big sleep. Who would not envy the sureness and certainty of that wonderful Irish Catholic Youth?

I think Catholicism in Ireland today is actually stronger, and better than it was when we were young. All right, so the numbers are way down, but still, only those who really believe are part of the Church now. The attendance at Mass is not inflated by those who were only there for fear of what others might think if they did not turn up. I don't doubt those who say they were frightened and repressed by the Church. I can only add that I never was. So obviously I don't think that the legacy of my Irish Catholic education was at all destructive or oppressive. I think it was over-colourful – filled with saints and martyrs and traditions and feast days and hymns and bells and miracles and incense – and, looking back, it was all like a huge happy pageant. I keep hoping that somewhere along the road of the rest of my life I might meet that happy band of characters and join up with them once again.

God and Mammon in Cork

ANN MARIE HOURIHANE (2000)

St Ronog's Well in Carrigaline, Co. Cork, has been a place of pilgrimage since the nineteenth century. St John is the patron saint of Carrigaline, and St John's Eve is marked every year by observances at the well – and by bonfires in nearby Cork city. When Ann Marie Hourihane visited Carrigaline, for her book *She Moves through the Boom*, the town was growing and changing rapidly.

The road gets rougher as you approach the well and my friends dropped me at the end of it, because they weren't going to risk their new Alfa Romeo on what, after you pass the building sites that surround the new houses, becomes a rough boreen. It has been out of use since the 1930s, when the county council chose other roads to cover with tar. Some of the new houses are in an estate called Dun Eoin. At least they're calling them something local. In Sandymount there is an apartment block called Radclyffe Hall. In Leixlip there's a housing estate that used to be called Cyber Plains, before the county council insisted on a change. It's the Aylesburys and the Chesterfields and the San Lorenzos you feel sorry for.

You can hear the rosary as you approach. The road slopes down, and to the left of it, in a clearing of trees, is a crowd of about seventy people. You know you're in Co. Cork because women turn to you to say hello. Three old ladies are sitting on one of the stout benches, and five white-haired men are standing in kilts – the Carrigaline Pipe Band. 'At the height of their achievements they won Intermediate Grade Two in Munster,' a man says later.

Canon O'Brien is also white-haired, standing behind the gold sunburst which contains the Host. It's the brightest colour here, except for the fluorescent pink hair-ties that hold a little girl's pigtails in place.

Novartis, a pharmaceutical company, put in the railway sleepers which serve as steps, and the benches for the old ladies. The company has a plant in nearby Ringaskiddy. Novartis used to be called Sandoz. 'They had a bit of a spillage there a couple of years back, in Berne,' says Seán O'Mahony, who used to work for Telecom before he retired and became a local historian.

The developer of the new houses cleaned the area up and put down grass seed. 'Stephen,' says Michael Wall sharply, once the prayers are over, 'I'll kill you cycling over the new grass.' Michael Wall is praised in Canon O'Brien's closing remarks for his part in getting St Ronog's well designated a Protected Shrine in the New County Development Plan. There is applause.

Michael Wall moved to the nearby Carrig Court Estate fourteen years ago, and fell in love with the well. 'I come up here on my own most mornings. There are two robins who live here and they sit down beside you. I maintain it and keep it weed-free. It's a little bit hard to explain it. I take away the rubbish and say a prayer. I don't say the rosary. I just say it my own way.'

Michael Wall is a big bald man in a sports shirt with a logo. 'People come here in the early mornings. There's a steady flow and they do their own passions, the five crosses. Oh, it is lovely. Round the well usually three times or maybe five. They come for special intentions, or if someone is sick.'

You can look down on St Ronog's well from the steps. You walk around the well and recite a decade of the rosary at each of the five crosses set into the wall of the beehive. Tonight the canon gave a little sermon at the end of the rosary. Mothers crouch down beside buggies; the older children are playing in a subdued way in the trees. This is a pattern, a celebration of the patron saint. The patron saint of Carrigaline is John the Baptist, and this is St John's Eve. St John was once celebrated all over the country – 'it was on the twenty-third of June, the day before the fair'.

The band goes into a military drum-roll as Canon O'Brien holds up the Blessed Sacrament. Then he takes a vessel of well-water and a green fern and with it splashes a section of the crowd in turn. He walks around the clearing to do this, coming up the steps to us. He's smiling as he does this – Canon O'Brien is a rational man – and we smile as the water splashes on to us, and each person crosses himself with the tiny sign of the habitual churchgoer. Religion feels different outdoors. The band plays 'Amazing Grace'.

When Canon O'Brien genuflects, his knee doesn't touch the ground. He has arthritis, like many former athletes in old age. He used to train the Cork hurling team. He is a character.

St Ronog's Well is one of the few in Ireland that has a beehive covering. Nobody knows how old the well is. 'They say the nearest thing like it is on the Skelligs,' says Seán. Behind us is what used to be called the Tent Field. Mass was said there last year, but now there are the skeletons of new houses on it.

'It was the worst crowd we ever had tonight,' says Michael Wall. 'I would say seventy or eighty people. But the wife of a man in the parish died, and there's a rosary for her tonight at eight o'clock down at the funeral home. He's involved in the Community Association.'

'And in the twinning as well,' says Seán O'Mahony.

'So a lot of people would have gone to that, you see, instead of here.'

This is Canon O'Brien's fifteenth pattern and he disagrees about the numbers, although he allows that they were relatively thin. 'I could see through the crowd tonight. But it wouldn't be short of 150, whereas normally it would be about 300. There were no Ballin-hassig people tonight.' Seán and Michael listen to this estimate, which entirely contradicts their own, and everyone else's, in polite silence.

Inside the well you have to crouch a little and step over stones to reach the stream itself. 'Go round the ledge on the side,' says Michael. There is a shelf on the back wall, on which stands a single card with a picture of the Virgin. 'People used to leave written prayers here, but not lately. Or if they are praying for someone they leave something belonging to the person, or to themselves.' It is almost pitch black in here.

'I am amazed, because normally today it is full of candles,' says Michael. He and Seán talk for a moment about who normally brings candles on this day.

Twenty-five years ago there was an ash tree growing out of the well, and the whole thing was on the point of collapse. The council removed the tree and, for the first time, added mortar to the stone. The water has never been tested.

The well is thought to be particularly powerful in helping blind people, and in his sermon Canon O'Brien had mentioned a blind man who was cured at the well. Blind people used to come here and say the rosary while passing a pebble between them. At the end of each decade whoever had the pebble would trace the line of the cross with it.

In the last century the pattern lasted seven days, from tonight, the 23rd, to SS Peter and Paul Day, on the 29th. It was one of the biggest patterns in Munster. 'The festival was commercialized,' says Seán. 'They'd set out stalls selling religious objects. There was a fair, where they were said to sell everything from a needle to an anchor. Unfortunately, there was a lot of drinking went on. I always say that the people had hard lives then and that the drinking was partly to drown their sorrows. I say that now as a non-drinker.'

I say drinking is always partly to drown your sorrows. And I say that as a drinker.

In all his researching of the well, Seán says, 'I have no positive proof or reference as to a cure.'

By 1843 there was no drinking at the pattern. 'They got a much smaller crowd.' Seán has all this information in an old copybook, written in red and green ink. These are the notes for a lecture he has given on the subject. He holds out the cover of the copybook towards Mary. 'What year is on that?' he asks. He hasn't got the right glasses with him.

'Ninety-six,' she says, as we walk back to the car, all wearing jackets. Mary and I are freezing. 'Last year we were rained out,' she says. We go back to Seán and Mary's house for tea.

One of their sons, Séamus, works for Pollution Control Systems in Ringaskiddy. It's used mainly by the dairy and pharmaceutical industries. About 20 per cent of its business is in Ireland, where it employs twenty people. 'The entire company, this is it,' says Séamus. An Irish man bought the company in Norway, improved quality control and moved it here. Séamus's little daughter wanders round the kitchen where Seán and I are talking, where the Sacred Heart hangs over the television, with the Father's Day cards marshalled in between. The kettle sits on the Rayburn stove.

'Religion now,' says Seán, 'is getting a terrible battering, but it'll come back.'

Mary and Seán offer to drive me back to Cork. Seán knows how long it takes to get to the Shanakiel area, because he used to have to visit his medical specialist there. 'Exactly seventeen minutes,' he says. 'Door to door.'

Both Seán and Mary paid to walk through the Jack Lynch Tunnel, on the special day when it was open to pedestrians. 'It was for charity,' says Mary. 'Sure when would we get the chance to do it again? It's only for cars.'

As we sweep over the new road in their new, modest, spotless car we can see smoke rising from the bonfires in Togher.

Provo speak

NEWTON EMERSON (2005)

Newton Emerson is a native of Portadown, Co. Armagh. While working in a computer company, he anonymously wrote the *Portadown News*, a satirical online publication which gained a significant following and annoyed loyalist and republican factions alike. He is indebted to the republican *Andersonstown News* for outing him as the man behind the *Portadown News*, as this forced him to leave his regular employment and become a full-time writer. The piece that follows will resonate with readers who lived through the lengthy negotiations which led to the Good Friday Agreement of 1998 and its protracted aftermath, culminating in the St Andrew's Agreement of 2006.

Sinn Féin dismisses any suggestion that dismissing a suggestion is not a denial of biased allegations of criminal activity against our party which has a mandate and will not be marginalised by political accusations which are clearly orchestrated by British securocrats working to an agenda defined by Ian Paisley that must be resisted to further the process of including Ian Paisley in a process of excluding Ian Paisley despite his mandate when he resists our agenda and fails to acknowledge the legitimate concerns of ourselves and others regarding the direction of future progress on sustainable moves towards lasting peace through an everlasting peace process on the island of Ireland and its territorial seas within a context without preconditions determined by others including the media who must also remember their own responsibility to report responsibly in the absence of evidence before a trial has produced a verdict that will not succeed in criminalising criminals or demonising demons or alienating aliens because our little green men will take you to their leader who is not a member of Óglaigh na hÉireann but has spoken directly to that organisation which never lies and hereby denies all connection to biased dismissals of alleged allegations involving involvement in vaults or defaults or of blame in a game where some names are the same as those in Sinn Féin which remains resolute in the face of its other face by demanding the rejection of rejectionist demands to reject its demands and by urging both governments to focus their efforts on their obligations which are not preconditions but which must be delivered before further movement on outstanding matters can be recommended although not required as part of a process of conflict resolution within a framework and a timeframe and a time-work and a frameframe that must not be photographed and cannot be seen as humiliation or capitulation or legitimising a less than Celtic nation or any similar situation which works to the agenda of those who oppose human rights and inclusion and equality and justice and whiskers on kittens so of course this community is angry and grumpy and sleepy to learn that Bertie Ahern is questioning our motivations during recent negotiations although it is not irresponsible to speak of that anger again and again while sitting on a huge pile of guns and explosives because republican activists cannot be criminals or spies or smugglers or gangsters or dealers so the reality is that reality is sub-jective though our objective remains to remove the causes of conflict by conflicting the remaining causes of the movement between build-ing an Ireland of equals and building a Donegal of bungalows in order to drive a process of change from robbing post offices and kill-ing policemen to robbing banks without killing anyone so others must stop undermining the agreement by complaining when we undermine the agreement because this makes them pawns in a secu-rocrat conspiracy to reverse the advances Sinn Féin has made in ecotourism abroad and fly-tipping at home but rest assured we will not be distracted from pursuing our goal of republicanism through tribalism and unity through division and strength through joy as we mark the centenary of the founding of our party and six other parties in a united Ireland that has since been partitioned which is an achieve-ment that will be celebrated by a year of events aimed at boosting recruitment and possibly training with a series of the lectures we will not take from others plus leadership tours to various countries by those who still have their own names on their passports which will assist others including the media to accept our analysis of inevitable victory in the search for compromise on a final settlement or a final solution should that prove to be necessary in the wake of developments following accusations which are clearly intended to discredit our mandate to subvert democracy on behalf of the electorate as the majority party of the minority community in the smaller of Ireland's illegitimate entities from where we will continue the struggle for justice through freedom from laws and courts and policing and full-price cigarettes and CDs and cocaine by demanding free housing and health care and child care and transport and pensions and third-level education and rubbish collection and free rubbish in general so really it's just as well we've come into some money and by the way – did we mention the securocrats?

Note: this statement is believed to be the longest republican sentence since 1998.

'It's going to end in tears'

MORGAN KELLY (2006 AND 2007)

The crash in the Irish housing market that began in 2007, and the ensuing national financial crisis, was generally unforeseen by professional economists and journalists. An exception was Morgan Kelly, professor of economics at UCD, who warned of the coming crash in a series of articles. In his first piece on the subject, published in the *Irish Times* on 28 December 2006, Kelly looked at evidence from property crashes in other countries and argued that the Irish market was a classic bubble.

Offering no evidence except wishful thinking, estate agents and politicians assure us that we have nothing to worry about: the Irish housing market can look forward to a soft landing. If, however, we look at what has happened to other small economies where sudden prosperity and easy credit drove house prices to absurd levels, we should be very worried indeed. If the experiences of economies similar to ours are anything to go by, we may be looking at large and prolonged falls in real house prices of the order of 40–50 per cent and a collapse of house-building activity. Two housing booms are especially sobering for being so similar to ours: Finland in the 1980s and The Netherlands in the 1970s. Finland boomed after oil was discovered off the coast in the mid-1980s. With low interest rates and loans available for the asking, house prices soared. Then, as the Soviet Union collapsed, unemployment rose and house prices started to fall, creating problems first for builders, then for home-owners, and finally for banks. The Finnish banking system effectively disintegrated under the weight of bad housing loans and had to be rescued, at huge expense, by the state. Unemployment rose from 5 to nearly 20 per cent. The real price of houses fell by more than 40 per cent.

A Finnish contributor to an online discussion board captures the spirit of the times. 'In 1991, a friend of mine offered about $120,000

(€91,464) on a lovely house that had cost $240,000 to build just three years previous. With over 20 per cent unemployment, it was not surprising that the owner and his wife had both lost their jobs and were about $12,000 behind in their mortgage payments. Obviously, the owner refused my friend's offer, but the bank manager called back in just a few hours with a counter-offer: he'd accept the $120,000 if my friend also paid the delinquent $12,000 in mortgage payments. That's it, the other family was left without a house and still owed the bank about $70,000.'

The Netherlands shows how house prices can collapse even when banks are big enough to absorb large losses. In the 1970s, thanks to the discovery of natural gas, the Dutch economy was the wonder of Europe. Once again, low interest rates and relaxed lending criteria led to a housing boom. Then, in 1979, the international recession bit, interest rates rose and prices tumbled. By 1985, the real price of houses had fallen by 50 per cent. There is an iron law of house prices. The more house prices rise relative to income and rents, the more they subsequently fall. [. . .]

But how about Ireland? Surely our house-price rise is simply due to our rising income and the shortage of houses in places where people want to live? Neither reason is valid: while incomes have risen, house prices have risen faster. Since 2000, house prices have risen 30 per cent more than income. Similarly, were there any shortage of housing we would see rents rising as fast as house prices.

In fact, compared with income, rents have actually fallen since 2000. The importance of what has happened to rents cannot be over-emphasised. If the housing boom were due to rising incomes and more people forming households, rents would also have risen. The fact that rents have fallen shows conclusively that our housing boom is a bubble, pure and simple.

But why can't we just have our soft landing, where prices stay fixed or rise slowly for a while? Definitely not: a soft landing is not so much unlikely as contradictory. Suppose that house prices really were expected to level off, then the owners of the tens of thousands of empty houses and apartments can expect no further capital gains and should cash in their investments. Why pay a mortgage on an empty apartment that has stopped rising in value? As speculators rush for the exit, prices will crash.

Second, if prices stop rising, it makes no sense to buy a house. Compared with mortgages, rents are ridiculously low. For €2,000 a month you can pay a mortgage on something in a muddy field on the wrong side of Celbridge, without nearby shops or schools and a two-hour commute to Dublin. For the same amount you can rent a €1 million house in southeast Dublin, close to the Dart line and surrounded by good schools. Once people put off buying in favour of renting, prices will not stabilise, they will crash. Just as rising prices generate self-fulfilling expectations – you have to buy now before prices rise further, causing prices to rise – so falling prices generate their own momentum. Buying in a falling market is a guaranteed way to lose a fortune. Even if prices fall by only 5 per cent, a €500,000 house on which you paid 10 per cent in stamp duties and fees will leave you €75,000 poorer.

It is a lot less nerve-racking to sit things out and rent for a year or two, and when everyone does that, prices fall further. How far are prices likely to fall when the bubble bursts? If we suppose, optimistically, that prices were more or less in equilibrium with income and rents around €2,000, then house prices are about 25 per cent overvalued now. Unfortunately, when house prices fall, they generally overshoot and end up undervalued. It is not implausible that prices could fall – relative to income – by 40–50 per cent. [. . .] International experience shows the worst houses in the worst places suffer the worst falls. We can expect the biggest falls in apartments as speculators try to sell before getting roasted alive and in dismal outlying towns with long commutes to Dublin and at the top of the market, where prices need to fall by perhaps two-thirds to bring them back into line with rents.

House-price collapses affect the wider economy in three ways. First, households lose wealth and start to repay loans instead of spending. Second, banks reduce lending as they lose money on bad loans. While banks are reluctant to foreclose and try to reschedule instead of taking an immediate loss on a loan, borrowers with negative equity will walk. For many with 100 per cent mortgages on apartments that have fallen in value by €150,000 [. . .] it will make sense to leave the keys in the door and relocate to London for a while.

The third, and potentially catastrophic, effect of a house-price fall is on building activity: more houses get built as prices rise and fewer as prices fall. As our exports have stalled since 2000, our economy has come to be entirely driven by house building. Between building new houses and selling existing ones, housing generates almost one-fifth of our national income. In effect, the economy is based on building houses for all the people that have got jobs building houses. Economists call this a multiplier-accelerator process and it is very unstable.

To see how rapidly a building boom can evaporate, look at Arizona. A rising population led to a building boom that should sound familiar: people queuing overnight to buy houses in new developments; builders increasing prices by a few thousand a week; people paying a down payment of $5,000 on a house and selling it on for a $100,000 profit a few weeks later. A few months ago, however, rising interest rates brought it all to a halt. Despite incentives like free swimming pools and fancy kitchens, and even at prices below the cost of labour and materials, builders cannot sell, leading to vast empty developments.

The parts of America that had the biggest housing boom are now experiencing falls in house prices of about 15 per cent. The US is now facing a possible recession as house building falls towards its usual bust level of about 4 per cent of national income, from a boom level of 6 per cent. In Ireland, if and when the fall occurs, it will be from about 18 per cent of national income. We could see a collapse of Government revenue and unemployment back above 15 per cent.

We have spent the last five years learning to believe that exports and competitiveness do not matter, and that we can get rich by selling houses to each other. We are likely to spend a painful few years as we unlearn that lesson. Pilots define a soft landing as one that you can walk away from. Looking at the collapses in Finland and The Netherlands and the building bust in Arizona, Ireland could be heading for what they call CDIT: controlled descent into terrain. You are happily descending through cloud, thinking yourself at a safe altitude, until suddenly you smack into a hillside.

In April 2007, shortly after publishing a paper titled 'On the Likely Extent of Falls in Irish House Prices', Kelly appeared on RTÉ television's Prime Time. *He was questioned by Mark Little.*

Little: Morgan Kelly, you're on the pessimistic side of this equation, you've written that the value of the Irish housing market could be halved by an approaching slump. That's not a guess, I'm assuming?

Kelly: No, what happened was late last year I got tired of listening to these various paid cheerleaders for the property sector saying we're going to have a soft landing. So what I did was I looked at all the different economies around that have had property booms and all of them without exception have had very big property busts immediately afterwards. You can predict the size of the bust from the size of the boom, just like a Roadrunner film. Roadrunner goes into thin air, he doesn't have any soft landing, he falls straight down. Typically, you lose about 70 per cent of what you've gained in the boom in the subsequent bust. For Ireland that means a fall of somewhere in the region of about 50 per cent.

Little: You talk about cheerleaders; they call you a doomsdayer. They say the nature of the property business is that if you say it long enough and people like you say there will be this bust, it's gonna happen.

Kelly: It's gonna happen whether we say it or not. We've had several years now of the property industry talking it up, saying: 'Great. Buy houses. There's no risk of a fall.' You have people now, they are mortgaging their lives away, their parents' life savings are going into these houses, it's being talked up and now it's running out of steam; it's going to fall, whether we talk about it or not. [. . .]

Little: It's not just cheerleaders that are saying the same thing, the OECD, the Central Bank are saying this, we have top growth rates in the EU in this country, it's not the kind of country you would expect to be heading towards a property crash.

Kelly: No, the assumption here is that we're the first country in human history that's ever had a boom. Lots of places have booms, property prices go up then something happens, they slow down, people's expectations change, property prices collapse.

Little: But the point here is the fundamentals here are strong.

Kelly: No; the fundamentals are complete nonsense; we just need to look at what has happened everywhere else.

Little: Highest growth rate in Europe?

Kelly: No; just look at what has happened to rent relative to prices. Rents have stayed stable since 2000. Prices have doubled: we've now got the highest prices in Europe; we've got among the lowest rents.

Little: We've got the youngest population, rising population.

Kelly: No. There are not enough of these to fill the houses to drive up the rents. We've got over a quarter of a million empty houses, empty units in the economy, we're building about 80,000 a year. This is a classic bubble. It's going to end in tears, no question about it.

The Taoiseach, Bertie Ahern, presumably had Kelly in mind in July 2007 when he complained about economic commentators 'sitting on the sidelines, cribbing and moaning', adding that he did not know 'how people who engage in that don't commit suicide'. But Kelly's predictions proved strikingly accurate: the average price of a residential property in Ireland fell by roughly 50 per cent between 2007 and 2012.

The man on the stamp

MAE LEONARD (2008)

In a piece for RTÉ Radio One's *Sunday Miscellany*, Mae Leonard recalled Dublin in the late sixties – and a fascinating figure whom she did not identify until forty years later.

Everything in Dublin was new and exciting to me back then – having moved from the confining walls of Limerick to, as we called it, 'the big smoke'. It was 1968 and I was looking at the world through the rose-tinted spectacles of a newlywed.

Dublin that September was a comfortable city at night. There were girls in daring mini skirts, there were street photographers and there was Cabaret at the Chariot Inn in Ranelagh with *Buachaill ón Éirne* himself, Breandán Ó Duill and the ballad group We 4 with Suzanne Murphy. I loved the thrill of a late-night horror film at the cinema on Saturday nights and buying Sunday newspapers on the way back to the flat.

Another treat was a pint in Dawson's Pub in Rathmines – a place to relax and, as a couple, we would sit and plan or meet friends. There were others of like mind there also and the two men who sat at the counter on tall stools were there for the same purpose. The difference was, they conversed in Irish with the *blas* of native speakers. I was fascinated listening to them. Fascinated by one of them in particular. The man with the spectacles and the tightly cut iron-grey hair. This man had a peculiar way of enunciating words and delivering them rapidly like the pik-pik-pik of a startled blackbird. I never knew his name but his fluency and command of Irish was spectacular.

My schoolbook Irish hadn't brought me to this level of expertise. My ear was attuned to the soft, rounded tones of Munster Irish but this was something else – this was harsh – as harsh as the landscape of Connemara.

I leaned forward to catch snatches of the conversation – it was difficult – but I managed to understand a few bits and pieces. One evening the two were discussing the recent invasion of Prague by the Russians and what might happen to Alexander Dubček. Another time, it was about the American presidential election and Nixon came in for a roasting. Soon, I found that I could follow the conversation a little better and heard them discuss the dangers of the Fosbury Flop – the head-first jump introduced at the Mexico Olympics that year. And the discussion became quite heated on the protest by the clenched fist salutes of the American Black Power athletes.

Our own discussion was a lot more mundane – mostly about the house we were about to buy and our move out of Dublin to the country. I never knew who that glorious Irish speaker was. I doubt if anyone in Dawson's Pub, Rathmines, in 1968 knew either. He was just part of the scene.

I bought some postage stamps the other day and *there he was* – the *gaelgoir* – looking at me just as I remember him. But I didn't know him. I didn't know of his political activities or of his internment in the Curragh military prison during the Second World War. Neither did I know that he is universally acknowledged as a pioneer of Irish-language modernism. There are books – in particular *Cré na Cille* – a tale of the dead in a graveyard talking to each other, which was translated into several languages – and he wrote short stories too.

We bade goodbye to Rathmines in September 1969 ignorant of the fact that he was a professor of Irish at Trinity College. Neither did we know that he had passed away the following year. I look at his face on my postage stamp and I tell the man in the post office – I remember him – I remember that man – Máirtín Ó Cadhain.

Ireland's looming water crisis

COLIN MURPHY (2010)

The introduction of metered water charges in 2014 created serious political difficulties that dogged the Fine Gael–Labour government. After the 2016 election, the minority Fine Gael government was forced to abandon the charges. In a prescient 2010 piece for the *Dublin Review*, Colin Murphy examined the fragility and unsustainability of the way water is supplied in Ireland and traced a long history of opposition to water charges.

At 5 a.m. one winter morning in 1996, two young men sat in a car in a Dublin housing estate, watching a nearby house. The house was the home of a Dublin Corporation water inspector; the men were, respectively, members of the Workers' Solidarity Movement, an anarchist organization, and Militant Labour, another left-wing political group. One of the men got out of the car and went behind a nearby bush to urinate. As he did so, the hall door of the house opened; the water inspector got into his car and pulled out on to the street. The Militant Labour man roared at his comrade, the anarchist zipped up and hurried back to the car, and the two left in open pursuit of the inspector. The inspector drove around for some time, apparently aimlessly; then, having evidently spotted his tail, he stopped at Crumlin Garda Station and then headed back home. The activists were members of the Dublin campaign against water charges, and they had, they believed, scored a small victory for the campaign. The inspector had been, they assumed, on his way to disconnect a household that hadn't paid its water charges, doing so in the early hours in order to avoid alerting the family and neighbours; by following him, the activists had caused him to abandon the attempt and demonstrated that they would be ready to block any attempt to cut off a family.

Water charges had first been applied in Ireland's cities in the 1980s, following legislation brought in by the Fine Gael–Labour government in 1983 to allow local councils to levy service charges. This followed the abolition of domestic rates by the Fianna Fáil government in 1977. The government had told the councils it would add the difference to their block grants, and that it would increase VAT rates in order to raise this income, but, while VAT duly rose, the block grants to the councils did not; the purpose of charges for water and other services was to compensate councils for the shortfall. The water charge was not based on use – which was not metered – and so had no conservation intention or effect. It met widespread resistance, causing some local councils, including Dublin's, to abandon attempts to introduce it. One of the leaders of the protests was Proinsias De Rossa, then a member of the Workers' Party, who was elected as a councillor in 1985 on an anti-water-charges ticket.

In the early 1990s, Dublin's councils made another attempt to introduce a charge for water, and again met resistance led by left-wing activists. The movement gained momentum when South Dublin County Council moved to start cutting off people for non-payment of charges. Teams of activists were organized to reconnect people whom the council had disconnected. The council used to give residents notice that they were to be disconnected; once notice had been received, the activists would locate the stopcock on the water mains outside the house, cover it with an empty tin can, and fill the space around it with concrete. As Gregor Kerr of the Workers' Solidarity Movement told me, this didn't permanently disable the mechanism, as the concrete could be broken off, but it ensured that the council would not be able to disconnect people quietly, by night. Communities – and in particular the local children, playing in the street or in parks – were encouraged to look out for council waterworks vans, and to knock on doors when vans entered a neighbourhood.

Following the collapse of the Fianna Fáil–Labour coalition in 1994, a new government was formed by Fine Gael, Labour and the Workers' Party spinoff Democratic Left, now headed by Proinsias De Rossa. Facing pressure from the left to rescind the water charges, the government imposed a requirement that councils obtain court orders before disconnecting people. The anti-water-charges group responded by launching a membership drive, at £2 per member, to raise funds to fight cases in court. They employed a dual strategy of employing lawyers to 'challenge everything and clog up the system' and organizing popular protests to coincide with court hearings, Gregor Kerr recalls. At one hearing in Rathfarnham district court in November 1995, over 500 people turned up to protest, and subsequently paraded through the village when the council's case was thrown out of court.

The campaign had much success in thwarting the councils' attempts to collect water charges and enforce disconnections. It stepped up a level following the death of the former Tánaiste, Brian Lenihan, in 1995. In the consequent by-election in Dublin West, in April 1996, Joe Higgins stood against Lenihan's son, Brian Lenihan Jr, on an anti-water-charges ticket, and came within 252 votes of taking the seat. As the anti-water charges movement prepared to run more candidates in the next general election, the incumbent left-wing TD for Dublin West, Labour's Joan Burton, looked particularly vulnerable. In December 1996 the then Minister for the Environment, Burton's party colleague Brendan Howlin, announced new legislation in which domestic water charges would be abolished; they were replaced as a source of revenue for the local councils with the receipts from car tax, which was henceforth to be retained by the local councils rather than transferred to central government. The damage, though, had been done. In the general election of June 1997, Joe Higgins was elected to the Dáil for the new Socialist Party, topping the poll; Joan Burton lost her seat. Her vote had collapsed from over 8,000 to under 5,000. Water charges became a political untouchable.

As the economist Sue Scott, of the Economic and Social Research Institute, argued later, water charges were unpopular 'for several good reasons': they were not metered, and therefore constituted a flat, regressive tax that did nothing to promote conservation; the bill was infrequent and therefore large, and reportedly arrived at awkward times for some families, such as at the same time as back-to-school expenditures; and there was no adequate approach to dealing with vulnerable families. Rather than address these faults, Ireland abolished water charges altogether.

In the run-up to the 2007 general election, the idea of charging for domestic water usage remained taboo. Neither the Green Party's manifesto, nor the programme for government the party subsequently agreed with Fianna Fáil, made any mention of it. At the same time, massive investment was planned for the water network: a total of €4.7 billion on capital investment in water and waste services over the lifetime of the National Development Plan for 2007–13. This investment was intended both to increase the capacity of water and waste services and to bring quality in line with EU directives.

By mid 2008, Ireland's economic crisis had completely changed the context in which both spending and taxation were being thought about and discussed. The report of the Commission on Taxation in September in 2009 summarized the argument for water charges: 'Households do not pay for water, and there is no incentive to conserve, so that consumption per capita is about 30 per cent more in Ireland than in jurisdictions that do charge based on use. Those who use water irresponsibly are in effect subsidized by those who use it sparingly, and there is a constant need to expand the supply of treated water involving major and expensive engineering projects. It is unlikely that Ireland will be able to maintain this level of expenditure indefinitely from general taxation, and the outcome will be inadequacies in the quantity and quality of supply.' The Commission recommended the phasing in of water charges over a five-year period, commencing with a flat-rate charge and, once meters were installed, moving to charges based on usage; it also proposed waivers for those unable to pay.

The Commission's view was backed by the Department of Finance, which estimated average domestic water usage costs at €350 per household per year and recommended an initial flat rate water charge of €150 per household. The Department estimated the cost of installing meters in 1.2 million households to be between €250 and €300 million over five to ten years.

The Green Party met with Fianna Fáil in late September and early October to negotiate a revised programme for government to deal with the economic crisis. The programme stated: 'We will introduce charging for treated water use that is fair, significantly reduces waste and is easily applied. It will be based on a system where households are allocated a free basic allowance, with charging only for water use in excess of this allowance. In keeping with the allocation of greater responsibility to local government, Local Authorities will set their own rates for water use.'

In the Dáil, opposition members tried to pin the government down on the proposed charges. The Taoiseach, Brian Cowen, replied to questions from the Labour leader, Eamon Gilmore, on the details of the scheme. 'No definitive or detailed framework for the implementation of the commitment can be spelled out at this point,' said Cowen. 'The policy considerations relate to the need for legislation to give effect to a commitment which must be examined . . . We are outlining in the policy the direction of our intentions.'

The Green Party's Eamon Ryan, the Minister for Energy and Natural Resources, was somewhat more forthright when quoted in the *Irish Times* as saying the installation of water meters 'could take years'. And then the weather changed. On 25 January, amidst water shortages caused by the freeze, Environment Minister John Gormley announced a fivefold increase in the budget for repairs to water mains over the next three years. He said he hoped that the installation of domestic water meters would commence next year, and that water charges would be implemented with a free basic quota and charges for excess water used.

'We are the only country in Europe where we don't have water metering and where we don't charge domestically,' he said. 'That needs to be reversed and reversed as soon as possible.' Water charges would ultimately raise €1 billion per year, sufficient to cover the cost of treating public water supplies. The earlier government decision to abandon water charges was 'nonsensical and pretty spineless', Gormley said.

[. . .] as John Gormley moves to introduce domestic meters and charges, Joe Higgins, now a member of the European Parliament, is mobilizing to launch a new anti-water-charges campaign. When charges were recommended by the Commission on Taxation late last year, he issued a warning: 'Should the government attempt to reintroduce the hated water charges which we worked so hard to abolish in the 1990s, we promise them a major water war.'

One of those who won't be rejoining the anti-water-charges campaign is Proinsias De Rossa – now, like Higgins, an MEP, but for the Labour Party. De Rossa now backs water charges. 'I don't think we can be cavalier with usage of water. There needs to be a rationing of it,' he said. (This, he adds, 'isn't the party view'. Labour is, officially, against water charges.)

'There's a big weakness in relation to how people conceive citizenship in Ireland: people regard themselves as consumers, and consumers have no responsibilities, they just have rights,' he said. 'I grew up with the idea that water was endless, but that's not the case. Over the last ten years, I've become more and more conscious of the way in which water is used and abused in Ireland. There's an attitude to water, like there's an attitude to dumping. It goes from the kids who are allowed to litter streets to farmers who let effluent run into rivers. It's a cultural thing.'

A new wilderness at the Maze

RACHEL ANDREWS (2010)

The Maze Prison, nine miles south-west of Belfast, was first used to detain republican suspects interned in August 1971; it would later house republicans and loyalists convicted of terrorist offences. In 2000, following the Good Friday Agreement, the prison was closed. Starting in 2007, Rachel Andrews made a series of visits to the prison site, exploring the overgrown grounds and talking to local people who had worked in the prison.

Down in Halftown, early Saturday morning, they were cleaning. A late night at the races, good crowd, the hall needed fixing. Peggy arrived in from the cold March rain, brandy sitting in her stomach from the night before. 'Sure what's life for if you can't enjoy it?' I was waiting for Jackie McQuillan, who came out of bed ill and coughing with one of those chest infections that grab at your throat and heave you up double. Jackie lives at the heart of a tight little area of fifty-two small houses. He is a joiner. During the Troubles he worried about his country, keeping it British, keeping it safe. When the peace came, he wasn't sure if he had a country any more, so he worried about his community instead. The changes to the area have been small but important: the hall where we meet, refurbished all warm and cosy, the locals allowed the use of it by the Orange Order for over eight years now; the wee playpark in the back field, built by Maze soldiers, all smiles for the photos, in the easy, peaceful time before they left; a local history book that begins: 'If we were to take a dander down from Hillsborough to Halftown, a distance of some 2 miles, I wonder how many of us would notice what has changed over the years. So let's have a go.'

Jackie, with his appetite for organization and negotiation, became spokesperson for the Halftown Residents' Association. He had his name in the papers and his face at the meetings during the discussions about what should or should not happen when the prison got knocked down and the chance came for things to start again. The regeneration of the Maze represents a significant opportunity for the Halftown residents, and most of them were fully behind rapid progress and the now abandoned idea of the big sports stadium – in its press release last April, the Office of the First Minister/deputy First Minister announced that the 'multi-sports stadium of the project will not be taken forward' – particularly as they got themselves a promise of a wee buffer zone of Maze land, a ten-acre patch to do with as they pleased, and they had plans for sports fields and commercial units all ready to go if only they could have got the thing made *official*. But by the time of my third visit, in February 2008, the deal was caught in a political tangle that has yet to be unpicked. Sometimes, after another unsatisfactory phone call to the Office of First Minister/deputy First Minister and another residents' meeting and nothing to tell, Jackie could only lament the *wasting time* and the *politics being played* because all his community that lived with a jail for thirty-odd years wanted now was to get tore into its own wee project and to make up a future that's decent and new and all of its own.

Out the back of the hall Jackie set a ladder against a wall and I climbed it, rain slanting into my face. I looked over and across into the lonely mass of prison scrubland. The wall is the outer perimeter fence of the Maze. The Hall where the community meets for line dancing and youth clubs and Weight Watchers, as good as bumps up against it. I stared into this dismantled place and wondered how it must have been to live alongside this dominant presence. It was a life not chosen by those who lived here when the prison was built. *You went to bed one night and you woke up, and there was that many people lifted and interned in Long Kesh, it literally happened overnight*. It was a life nobody else wanted. *If anybody said do you want to go and buy a house outside the Maze prison I mean what would you say?* But it was your life and you loved it, as people do love their lives, and cherish them, and tend to them as best they can. *I mean this was where you were born and reared a dull, dreary place, maybe a place where nobody else wanted to live or buy a house, but I mean you were brought up and reared here, it was home, you know what I mean, and always would be home*.

Most of that life was the same as any other. You went to work, you hung out your washing, you went home. You couldn't ignore the Maze, so you took the jobs going there, in the mess, as a labourer, and reared your children with the wages. You couldn't ignore the soldiers out on their manoeuvres, so you kept your blinds pulled day and night, *just to make sure there'd be nobody peeping through the window at you or anything, you know just to be careful of that*. You couldn't ignore it the time they set fire to the Long Kesh huts, so you stood on your veranda and watched the flames shooting up and listened to the army dogs screaming and being burnt to death. You couldn't ignore the visitors' buses, coming on past your house, and them people inside shouting insults and giving you the finger, so you nodded at the police cars lined up there as a bulwark and ran down the road hot-headed with stones in your hand and after you threw the stones up at those buses you felt a bit better about things for a while.

We talked about the time before the Maze. We looked at the photos. The Queen Mother and the King, arms raised, hers a wave, his a salute, visiting. It's 1945, Long Kesh is an airfield. Here is Montgomery, in beret and badges. Here is Ike, laughing at the camera. Now some different huts, temporary housing built for military personnel: one fronted by a couple, arm in arm, another by a family, a girl in bows, smiling. 'Tin Town', they called it, the homes replacing land and properties compulsorily acquired for war building. After the war, the enclave turned into starter homes for many young people, but also housed large families.

We went to the All Saints' Church in Eglantine, a simple, calm structure that appears from behind a group of yew trees. The RAF graves are outside, twenty-one in a row; inside, there is a stained-glass window depicting airmen setting out on a mission, another of a plane flying low over the Tin Town huts. *In memory of Airmen of the Royal Air Force and Commonwealth Air Forces*. We stood in the church and shivered and I asked questions about the past. We chatted about the Marquess of Downshire, who owned Hillsborough Castle and Hillsborough Fort and the Maze lands and everything else you could see and whose family still brings the ashes of loved ones over from England, and in that little church with its Mothers' Union banner and its RAF flag I thought how it was a relief to talk about a history and culture that didn't involve the Troubles, and how talking about that could make you forget for a while that people still hate each other or hate what's happened with the peace and carry around bitterness and helplessness inside of them. People say, *The damage is done.* They say, *I think anybody that just got on with their life, just went on and took anything they could find, is a loser in it all, and the terrorist and everybody else is elevated to get something out of it.*

Early this year, I made my final visit to the Maze. In the January snow, the process of transformation from prison to blank slate seemed almost complete. The site had been cleared of the mounds and piles of timber, steel, chairs, heaters, extractor fans and gym equipment. The timber has been burnt, the concrete reused, the steel sent out to a recycling scrapyard. Nothing left the site without approval, and nothing left intact. The workers had to beat and crush the cell doors out of shape, out of recognition, and to make sketches and films of the process. It was imperative that the relics not turn up on eBay, as some bricks and bedsprings had done already.

The fog hung thick in the sky that day, and it was hard to judge space and distance. I drove around the site, seeing only trees and snow, save for a single orange digger and the blue string cordoning off areas contaminated with asbestos. I drove until the preserved section of the prison, with its high walls and its three surrounding watchtowers, appeared out of the fog. The cold had already caused the gate to jam once this morning, and the security guards wouldn't take the risk of it not closing a second time, so I was not allowed inside. Instead, I walked around the perimeter, crunching through the snow, following the wall as it disappeared into the haze. As I walked, I stepped on the concrete foundations of former H-Blocks, all that remains of them.

Back at the car, I saw a small crew of workmen in the distance, putting down pipes for a water mains. I watched them move back and forth in their luminous safety vests. They were the only things interrupting the stillness. I drove towards the back of the complex, passing several pieces of fenced-off land, some of the compulsory acquisitions from half a century ago, now finally returned to local landowners. The holdings were mostly tiny and odd-shaped, and hardly seemed worth the trouble. But the community was adamant it deserved some recompense for the years spent in purgatory beside the jail, and fought hard to have the lands returned. That purgatory has almost ended: the rolls of razor wire that once separated surrounding houses from the Maze have been taken away, and unthreatening fencing now forms the boundary between the site and the back gardens of local people.

Veering right in a semi-circle, I drove past the two enormous aircraft hangars once used by the RAF and now appropriated by the Ulster Aviation Society to house its collection of Second World War memorabilia and aircraft. The hangars, too, are due for restoration; the aim is to promote them as tourist attractions in the future. At the security hut, I swung right, heading towards the top of the complex and the place where the tips of the Halftown houses peek out over the outer fence. I got out of the car and walked along the inner fence until I found a wide breach where two sides of the wire had been pulled back from one another. I stumbled down into a ditch of thick scrubland and climbed over thorns and gorse until I reached the point where the Orange Hall stands directly opposite the prison. Ivy clambered up the high corrugated fencing and a yellow sign warned of dogs on patrol. It was from the other side of the fence, standing on Jackie's ladder, that I had last surveyed this scene. On this side of the barricade, I felt small and vulnerable. The Halftown community still doesn't have the land it needs to make big changes to the area, but the destruction of the outer fence, which was to take place once the snow cleared, will be more than symbolic: when it is gone the Orange Hall will back on to open ground.

Before leaving I stopped, as had become my habit, at the security hut for a cup of tea. The men had switched rooms in order to facilitate the planned redevelopment of their Portakabins into office blocks for civil servants. The room was a cosy antidote to the cold outside. The guards, Billy and Billy, were new to me – Campbell was out sick and Barry, with whom I had sat and chatted on past visits, had retired – but they were aware of my reason for being here and the conversation between us was easy and friendly. I drank my tea and tried to get warm and we talked about the snow and the roads and the past and the future. One of them had served his time on the Long Kesh compounds before moving briefly to what the officers used to term 'the Cellular' – the Maze prison itself. He was not surprised when a visitor told us that the fog lying heavy over the site only began closing in as you approached it, and that in Belfast the sky was high and clear. The Maze, he said, sits in a dip in the Lagan Valley. It is colder there, damper – he remembered the freezing hands of prisoners on days when the sun was shining a few miles up the road.

'We band of brothers'

MICHAEL LILLIS (2011)

As head of Anglo-Irish relations at the Department of Foreign Affairs and a confidant of Garret FitzGerald, Michael Lillis was a key architect of the Anglo-Irish Agreement of 1985. He wrote this letter to the Irish Times *following FitzGerald's funeral in May 2011.*

The funeral of Garret FitzGerald was a profoundly emotional occasion for thousands of Irish and British people, not least for the surviving negotiators of the Anglo-Irish Agreement of 1985 – one of Dr FitzGerald's great legacies to the peace process and to history. We were honoured by the presence of Robert Armstrong, Lord Armstrong of Ilminster, former British cabinet secretary and leader of the British team of negotiators. We missed the late and much loved Dermot Nally, Irish cabinet secretary and our own leader during the years of intense negotiation before Hillsborough. Happily his wife Joan joined Seán Donlon, Noel Dorr and me in Donnybrook church. We also missed Andy Ward, the late brilliant Secretary of the Department of Justice, and Declan Quigley, the late distinguished head of the Attorney General's Office.

After Robert Armstrong returned to London he sent me a most moving message from which the following are brief extracts: 'I cannot find the words to express what it meant to me to be there with you, with Sean, with Noel, and with Joan Nally: "we few, we happy few, we band of brothers". We missed Dermot, of course, and he was very much in my mind. And I was sad that David Goodall, my friend and colleague in the negotiations, could not be with us. In those days Garret was your leader, and not ours; but we could recognise the ideals which he was pursuing, and we could not only respect but also respond to those, and he became and never ceased to be a friend, and an inspiration. I know that the process which culminated in the Queen's visit last week began round the tables in Iveagh House and in the Cabinet Office in those days.

'I remember, when I was sitting in the Cabinet Room during those days with the Prime Minister and the Secretaries of State for Foreign Affairs and for Northern Ireland, discussing the drafting and the details of the agreement, reflecting that relations between Britain and Ireland had been discussed in that room over centuries, that we were now adding a new chapter to a long history, and that we had the possibility of creating an opportunity for a profound, beneficial and lasting change in that relationship. I am proud and grateful that we were able to do so; and I am sure that we should not have succeeded without Garret.'

The Irish team was directed at the political level by Garret FitzGerald, the Tánaiste, Dick Spring, the Minister for Foreign Affairs, Peter Barry, the Minister for Justice, Michael Noonan, and our attorney general, John Rogers. Their presence in Donnybrook completed for 'the band of brothers', as we have become, our sense of having been permitted to play some part in helping move the tectonic plates of one of history's most bitter legacies. Throughout, Garret FitzGerald led the Irish team – and sometimes inspired the British at the highest levels – with unyielding determination and typical control of every detail. The evidence of his influence was in the transformation of the seemingly settled pro-unionist convictions of the British Prime Minister and in her admirable and steadfast support for the agreement in the face of convulsed loyalist rioting and outrage afterwards. The Irish government had a real and ungainsayable role in the processes of government of Northern Ireland. The political landscape was transformed.

'We go back for the whisper'

EDNA O'BRIEN (2012)

The novelist Edna O'Brien grew up in a house called Drewsboro, in Tuamgraney, Co. Clare. In this passage from her recent memoir, she recounts a return visit – accompanied by the artist Dorothy Cross – to her childhood home.

We had gone from Co. Galway into Co. Clare. This was home. Instead of walls of loose stone, the briars, the bushes and the hazels nuzzled together to make boundaries between fields, and roads that would have been grassy in summertime were untrodden and pearled over. Suddenly a scalding memory, as I recalled the previous morning in a bookshop in Dublin, where I read in *Saints, Scholars and Schizophrenics* by Nancy Scheper-Hughes about a sheep farmer in An Clochán who railed against my writing and said, with evident satisfaction, 'They ran that woman out of Co. Clare.'

Cattle waited at gateways, as they always had done, lonely figures waiting as if at the Gates of Purgatory, and the trees and the woods that had their equivalent in some or other of Yeats's poetry, still beautiful, still storm-struck, the light a paleish gold, with a watery shimmer to it, and Dorothy hoping it would stay like that, because she did not want Drewsboro to resemble Connecticut.

Michael was waiting for us at the gate and for a moment, it seemed to me, I was hallucinating. In his enthusiasm for our arrival, he had removed the very things – the bramble, the ivy, the ash trees, the whole lyrical paraphernalia – which had made the idea of photographing the house so appealing to Dorothy. All the poetry had been forked away.

'I can pitch it all back,' he said, a little crestfallen by my dismay, as I stared at the hall door, no longer bowered, its red paint chipped and faded, the house a little old hag, buckled and sinking back into the foundations.

Nothing for it but to go inside. Proudly he led us through the back door, which all these years he had believed to be locked, as once, on a previous visit, he had had to wedge me under the narrow gap of a window, calling as I wriggled through, 'Are you in, are you in?' The kitchen had a weird, inhabited quality, dirty delph on the table as if highwaymen had just passed through and had had a feed, and the little radio on the windowsill was still stuttering, its battery having expired long before. Then into the dining room, where indeed the walnut cabinet, scummed in dust, housed still another dead radio, which in times past was a matter of great pride to my parents, sitting in front of it, as they might sit in front of a blazing fire. There was one half of an orange curtain, like a theatre prop, and some dead crows had fallen down the chimney. The presence of my mother was still weirdly in everything: in the crinkles of the orange curtain, in the coal scuttle where she hid bars of chocolate and on the cushions of bawneen where she had embroidered old Celtic designs, thinking they would impress me. How hard she had fought to keep it all together.

Upstairs a wardrobe door creaked open and shut, and propped against the wall in my father's old room was the oak headboard with the uneven patch, whitish from the graze of his head, from where again and again he would call down repeatedly, to be brought more tea. In a jumble of clothing, there were silk lampshades, a scroll with a papal blessing, consecrating the marriage of my brother and his wife, and a jovial jockey on high stilts, wearing a black hard hat.

The ivy, the mad ivy, had come in through the windows and in some rooms the beds with their damp covers seemed to house corpses. More crows, but this was not Chekhov's *Seagull*, this was Drewsboro, in its dying throes. I looked in the press where my brother had kept a tin of peaches that he had won in a music competition, only to find a mohair jumper crawling with moths. Across the landing, in my mother's room, the holy water font had a residue of dried salt which was bitter on the tongue. I sat on the edge of the bed. The wallpaper, painted over, was now a pale magnolia, yet I could just discern the dipping branches on which tiny pink rosebuds hung, so lifelike on their thin stalks that I used to believe they would bloom, like real roses on the briars.

It was in that room that I slept with my mother and that each night we pressed the cold metal crucifix along our bodies and to our lips, reciting the prayer of Christ at Calvary, 'They have pierced my hands and feet, they have numbered all my bones.' We were all lonely in that house, lonely and sometimes at loggerheads.

In an adjoining room, where my father slept, one night I heard the loud crackle of fire, the leaping gusts of flames, and running across I saw a bamboo side-table on fire and the blankets that were over him as he slept, oblivious of everything, also on fire. Without thinking I opened the window and threw things out, and my mother, in her last reminiscing days, surprisingly told the nun in the hospital about this and other tribulations that had befallen us, as if there was nothing to be ashamed of any more.

All the time Dorothy moved around taking snaps, marvelling at coming on so many strange and evocative things. The room was so cold that my breath sent a cloud of bluish vapour over the lens of her little camera, adding to the ghostliness that she was determined to capture. Suddenly, a wren, busy and spry, a taunt to the dead crows, flew into that room, and fluttered among the sad debris, delighting in its new surrounds. When it dashed its forehead against the windowpane, its little yellow legs crawling hither and thither, we tried in vain to catch it but it eluded us. In the end, with the spikes of a broken umbrella that was on the heap, we steered it out into the hall, above the stairwell, then down to the lower hall, where curiosity – it can hardly have been instinct – caused it to alight on an old wedding bouquet of artificial white flowers that had rusted at the edges. [. . .]

That evening, over dinner in a hotel in Galway, the large dining room was not nearly so full as it would have been a year or two before. A few young couples, out for the Friday night, spoke in somewhat muted tones and the gusts of so many candle flames gave the impression of being in some ancient basilica. As she looked down at the purplish sediment in her wine glass, Dorothy began to cry. 'When I cry, I have to cry three times,' she said, and attempted a laugh to hide her embarrassment.

It had something to do with going back, forever the need to go back, the way animals do, the way elephants trudge thousands of miles to return to where the elephant whisperer has lived.

'We go back for the whisper,' she said, the dreamed-of reconciliation.

'Nuns were saying I had the devil in me'

MAGDALEN LAUNDRIES INQUIRY (2013)

The Magdalen laundries, run by Catholic nuns, were institutions where women who were characterized as 'fallen' were incarcerated, ostensibly to atone their sins. They were unpaid for their laundry work, and many lived out the rest of their lives within the institutions. The long silence about the existence of such institutions and what went on in them must reflect not only on the Irish Church but also on wider Irish society, to which these institutions were somehow 'invisible', despite their physical presence in so many towns and cities and the fact that the laundries had clients – including the state – throughout society. The report of the Inter-Departmental Committee to Establish the Facts of State Involvement with the Magdalen Laundries, under the chairmanship of Martin McAleese, published its report in February 2013. The report summarized and quoted from the testimony of those women who participated in the inquiry.

The overwhelming majority of the women who spoke to the Committee described verbal abuse and being the victim of unkind or hurtful taunting and belittling comments. Even those who said that some Sisters were kind to them reported verbal cruelty as occurring during their time in the Magdalen Laundries.

One woman spoke of receiving 'cruel talk'. Another woman at a different Magdalen Laundry said she remembered hurtful comments: 'I remember a nun telling me that you came from an illegitimate mother. I suppose it was that you were no good and that's why we were there.' Another woman also spoke of her family background as being unkindly referred to – she said that 'The nuns looked down on me 'cause I had no father.' Another woman in that same laundry said, 'We were never happy. You were lonely.' She described how, on the journey to the Laundry, 'In the car the nuns were saying I had the devil in me, shaking holy water and saying the rosary in the car.' She had been raised in an industrial school with no known family and also described how a Sister on her entry to the Laundry, in front of all the other women, said, 'Tell them where you were brought up and reared.' Another woman, who was in a number of Magdalen Laundries, said that in one of these Laundries the Sisters would make cruel comments about her family background, such as 'What do you think you are, I heard all about your family.' This was particularly hurtful to the woman concerned, as she said that 'My father interfered with the bigger girls.' Another woman said that 'Conditions were bad now . . . one nun took me under her wing and a lovely woman she was, she was good to me.'

Another woman at the same Magdalen Laundry said, 'The nuns were very nasty. They'd say "Your father is a drunkard" in front of everyone. It would degrade me. You know everyone knows your business.' Another woman said, 'They were very, very cruel verbally – "your mother doesn't want you, why do you think you're here" and things like that.'

The types of non-physical punishments reported by the women to the Committee varied. A woman reported that, after running away from a Magdalen Laundry in the 1950s and being returned by the Gardaí, she was 'put in isolation for two days'. A woman at a different Magdalen Laundry said, 'I broke a cup once and she put a string on it and I had to wear it for three days and three nights. And I threw a hanger one time and she made me wear it three days and three nights.' Another woman who had been in two Magdalen Laundries reported that, in one of these Laundries, 'There was a padded cell, I was put in there three times.' In the other Laundry, she was 'told if I didn't work there'd be no food and the infirmary'. Apart from that, punishment was 'not let you write to anyone'. In neither of the Laundries did she experience physical punishment – she said of one of the Laundries, 'They were very cruel but they couldn't hit us,' and of the other, 'Physical cruelty didn't happen but mental cruelty did.'

A woman at a different Magdalen Laundry reported that the punishment she saw was 'They would make you walk in front of all the women in the refectory and lie on the ground and kiss the floor.' Another woman said that as a young girl she moved an item of clothing (a bra) from the laundry. She said, 'I was made an example of next day. She called my name at dinnertime. You'd be mortified. She said, "You took a brassiere out of the laundry"; "Yes, I wanted to be like the other girls." Didn't she make me kneel there for two hours.' Another woman said that, during her time in a Magdalen Laundry, she began to wet the bed. She said that 'They pinned the sheet to me back and I was walking on the veranda with it.'

'Our nation's shadow'

ENDA KENNY (2013)

Following the publication of the McAleese report, the Taoiseach,
Enda Kenny, formally met the survivors and invited them to attend in
Dáil Éireann when he issued the formal apology on behalf of the
state. He said that for ninety years Ireland had subjected these women
to 'a profound and studied indifference'. He had found his meeting
with the survivors 'a humbling and inspiring experience', adding that
they had taken 'this country's terrible secret and made it their own,
burying it and carrying it in their hearts here at home or with them to
England, Canada, America and Australia on behalf of Ireland and the
Irish people'.

As I read this report and as I listened to these women, it struck me
that for generations Ireland had created a particular portrait of itself
as a good-living and God-fearing nation. Through this and other
reports we know this flattering self-portrait is fictitious.

It would be easy to explain away all that happened and all we did
with those great moral and social salves of 'the culture back then',
'the order of the day' and 'the terrible times that were in it'. By any
standards it was a cruel, pitiless Ireland distinctly lacking in a quality
of mercy. That much is clear, both from the pages of the report, and
from the stories of the women I met. As I sat with these women as
they told their stories it was clear that while every woman's story was
different each of them shared a particular experience of a particular
Ireland that was judgmental, intolerant, petty and prim.

In the laundries themselves some women spent weeks, others
months, more of them years, but the thread that ran through their
many stories was a palpable sense of suffocation, not just physical in
that they were incarcerated but psychological, spiritual and social.
Their stories were enriched by an astonishing vividness of recall of
situation and circumstance.

[. . .]The Magdalen women might have been told that they were washing away a wrong or a sin, but we know now and to our shame they were only ever scrubbing away our nation's shadow. Today, just as the State accepts its direct involvement in the Magdalen laundries, society, too, has its responsibility. I believe I speak for millions of Irish people all over the world when I say we put away these women because for too many years we put away our conscience. We swapped our personal scruples for a solid public apparatus that kept us in tune and in step with a sense of what was 'proper behaviour' or the 'appropriate view' according to a sort of moral code that was fostered at the time, particularly in the 1930s, 1940s and 1950s. We lived with the damaging idea that what was desirable and acceptable in the eyes of the Church and the State was the same and interchangeable.

Is it this mindset then, this moral subservience, that gave us the social mores, the required and exclusive 'values' of the time that welcomed the compliant, obedient and lucky 'us' and banished the more problematic, spirited or unlucky 'them'? To our nation's shame it must be said that if these women had managed to scale the high walls of the laundries, they would have had their work cut out for them to negotiate the height and the depth of the barricades around society's 'proper' heart. For we saw difference as something to be feared and hidden rather than embraced and celebrated. Were these our values? We can ask ourselves: for a state, least of all for a republic, what is the 'value' of the tacit and unchallenged decree that saw society humiliate and degrade these girls and women? What is the 'value' of the ignorance and arrogance that saw us publicly call them 'penitents' for their 'crime' of being poor or abused or just plain unlucky enough to be already the inmate of a reformatory, or an industrial school or a psychiatric institution? We can ask ourselves as the families we were then what was worthy, what was good about that great euphemism of 'putting away' our daughters, our sisters, our aunties?

Those 'values', those failures, those wrongs characterised Magdalen Ireland. Today we live in a very different Ireland with a very different consciousness and awareness. We live in an Ireland where we have more compassion, empathy, insight and heart. We do, because at last we are learning those terrible lessons. We do, because at last we are giving up our secrets. We do, because in naming and addressing the wrong, as is happening here today, we are trying to make sure we quarantine such abject behaviour in our past and eradicate it from Ireland's present and Ireland's future.

In a society guided by the principles of compassion and social justice there never would have been any need for institutions such as the Magdalen laundries. The report shows that the perception that the Magdalen laundries were reserved for those who were offensively and judgmentally called 'fallen women' is not based upon fact at all but upon prejudice. The women are and always were wholly blameless. Therefore, I, as Taoiseach, on behalf of the State, the Government and our citizens, deeply regret and apologise unreservedly to all those women for the hurt that was done to them and for any stigma they suffered as a result of the time they spent in a Magdalen laundry. [. . .]

I am also conscious that many of the women I met last week want to see a permanent memorial established to remind us all of this dark part of our history. I agree this should be done and intend to engage directly with the representative groups and as many of the women as possible to agree on the creation of an appropriate memorial to be financed by the Government separately from the funds that are being set aside for the direct assistance for the women.

Let me conclude by again speaking directly to the women whose experiences in Magdalen laundries have negatively affected their subsequent lives. As a society, for many years we failed you. We forgot you or, if we thought of you at all, we did so in untrue and offensive stereotypes. This is a national shame for which I again say, I am deeply sorry and offer my full and heartfelt apologies.

Liberalism and language

JOHN WATERS (2013)

The journalist John Waters, often at odds with what he sees as the liberal consensus in the Irish media, wrote in the *Irish Times* about evolving ideas of offensive language.

'What a weird fate,' exclaimed Václav Havel, 'can befall certain words!' He was thinking particularly of 'socialism', but when he wrote those eight words in 1989, I doubt if he envisaged the imminent fate of the word he had most immediately in mind.

Those words of his came to mind last week in a rather more banal context: the publication of a survey tracking some of the shifts occurring in the kind of language Irish people find offensive. This formed part of the Ipsos/MRBI survey of public attitudes to broadcasting, conducted on behalf of the Broadcasting Authority of Ireland. The results indicate some interesting shifts since the most comparable survey, in 2005. The phrase 'Jesus f★★king Christ' moved down the rankings from 5th to 10th, whereas 'homo' moved up from 11th to 6th. The top four terms remain unchanged, apart from a switch between third and fourth places: number one is 'ni★★er', followed by 'c★★t', 'Paki' and 'spastic'. There are three new top-10 entrants: 'retard' at No. 5; 'faggot' at No. 8 and, intriguingly, 'pedo' at No. 9.

Even listed like this, several of these words have the power to create frissons of reaction, perhaps ranging from a sense of liberation arising from their apparent sanitization in a legitimate 'context', to minor shock at their appearance here.

But the colour of the words may serve to distract from some of the meanings of the survey, which gives indications of interesting undertows with potentially significant implications for future drifts at the surface of our culture. We seem to be moving, for example, from inherited notions of acceptability/tolerability – previously couched in formulae deriving from religion and ancient concepts of delicacy or civility – to a different mode of taking or experiencing offence.

Indeed, 'bad language' per se appears to be losing its capacity to 'offend' in the least. 'Even accounting for a qualitative/group environment where participants may not have been entirely open,' the small print of the survey stated, 'the near silence regarding the potential of coarse language to offend was deafening.'

Superficially, the findings appear to confirm the increased dominance of 'political correctness', but this too is a loaded expression, capable of summoning up, to different ears, a modern form of courtesy or an insidious cult of censorship. Described 'neutrally', the survey seems to capture a shift from the tendency to take offence based on personal belief to one in which the offence of others is more likely to be anticipated. The top six epithets are pejoratives relating to what are called 'minorities' – respectively, black people, women, Pakistanis, the physically and mentally disabled, and homosexuals. From here, depending on your perspective, you might decide that we are increasingly under the sway of lobbyists speaking on behalf of 'minorities', or that Irish society is developing an enhanced sense of the fragility of certain marginal groups. Perhaps these amount to the same thing. Or perhaps not. The survey found that, in terms of being offended by broadcasting content in general, people had become more 'liberal' than in 2005. Broadly, what most gives offence remains substantially unchanged: content that is abusive, cruel or explicit, out of context and without a warning. There was overwhelming support for restrictions on scenes involving cruelty, violence or sexual assault, whereas a majority said there should be no restrictions on reality TV shows, comedy or the portrayal of religion.

But a generational shift is discernible. Older people are more likely to bear witness to being offended, whereas 71 per cent of those surveyed said that broadcasters should cater for 'all tastes', even at the risk of giving offence. In fact, this underlines one of the deeper patterns to be noted in the survey – of a kind of projection of sensitivity: younger, more 'liberal' people seem increasingly to be discounting or suppressing any sense of personal offence in favour of anticipating the offence of others, which they may or may not – it's not clear – be using as a code to give muted expression to their own suppressed delicacies.

The awareness of the existence of extreme material on the internet appears to be reducing our inclination to express objections across a range of phenomena, including sensitivities towards sexual explicitness, violence and crudity. A standard response was: 'It's out there, you can choose to watch it or not. The choice is yours.' Put another way, people seem increasingly open to the rights of more 'liberal' consumers, even at the cost of their own and other people's sensibilities and sensitivities. Is this what we call 'tolerance'? Interesting word – signifying one of the great liberal totem-concepts. But perhaps it's coming to signify merely a fear of seeming prudish?

As a society, the survey appeared to conclude, we feel powerless over what is being introduced into our lives via technology, and have become almost accepting of the potential for damage, preferring to manage exposure.

'No other television station on earth would dream of putting it on'

BRENDA POWER (2014)

Although the competition predates the establishment of RTÉ television, it can be safely assumed that the longevity of the annual Rose of Tralee festival owes much to the fact that the live broadcast of the final over two nights each August is an extraordinarily popular television programme. Brenda Power wrote in the *Sunday Times* about the broadcast of the 2014 final, which attracted an audience share of 50 per cent of all Irish viewers.

'Her great-great-grandmother was Michael Collins's grandmother, and she once met two members of the Village People,' was how they introduced the Queensland Rose. Now, according to the six degrees of separation concept, everyone in the world can be connected in six steps or fewer. Until last Monday night, however, finding a link between the Irish rebel leader and Village People, the blokes who sang YMCA while dressed as cops, construction workers and cowboys, would have stretched that theory to the limit. Yet, as the introduction to a contestant in the Rose of Tralee, it was one of those moments that made the six toe-curlingly, cringe-makingly tedious hours of the two-night pageant almost worthwhile.

The annual television spectacular is RTÉ light entertainment's equivalent of the Angelus. Lampooned nearly two decades ago in *Father Ted* as the 'Lovely Girls' contest, it has long since soared out of the reach of satirists, far beyond mockery or parody, into a sort of witness-protection programme for recidivist offenders against progress and sophistication and not being the Laughing Stock of Europe.

It's bonkers, eccentric, anachronistic, probably sexist, reductive and demeaning of the lovely girls, definitely an endurance test of plugs and promos and captive-audience advertising, and about four hours too long. Like the Angelus, there's little reason for keeping it on the air these days, if it weren't for the sense that we'd be somehow poorer and more generic Europeans, and a little less eccentric and Irish, if we dumped it. The main objection to the Angelus is a rather craven anxiety about what the rest of the world must think of us; the Rose of Tralee is our annual one-in-the-eye for the neighbours and their imagined disapproval. Just because no other television station on earth would dream of putting it on, let alone inflicting it on a defenceless audience over two nights when the evenings are drawing in and there's absolutely nothing to watch on the channels, is probably the best reason to keep it going for another generation or two.

One of this year's Roses was 'Ned' Kelly from Darwin. Her real name is Natalie, but she was dubbed Ned after a particularly butch haircut, and it stuck. She related how her mother had once been selected as the Cork Rose, but was booted out when it emerged that she had a baby – the same Ned who was now waving to her from the stage in the Dome. It was a discordant reminder that, for all its protestations of uniqueness, the Rose contest adheres to the outmoded conceits of all such pageants: the pretence that its entrants are virginal, chaste and therefore available young women, in need of the manly protection of penguin-suited escorts.

Ashlinn O'Neill, the Queensland Rose who provided the missing link between Michael Collins and Village People, was asked by host Dáithí Ó Sé how she explained the event to her friends back home. I perked up, in the hope she'd have a better crack at deconstructing it than I could. She tells them it's not a beauty pageant, but rather 'a celebration for Irish girls, to participate and to go back home and promote the Rose of Tralee and their Irish heritage'. So it's a self-perpetuating celebration of itself, basically, so mesmerisingly overblown and yet firmly embedded on our cultural horizon that we've long forgotten what was the point in the first place. The girls, in their standard-issue Newbridge jewellery and Kate Middleton-wedding-dress-inspired lace ballgowns, are earnest and likeable, beautiful and, occasionally, exceptionally talented.

And occasionally not, which is why Ó Sé's singular touch is so reassuring both to the audience and to the participants. Even when a singer proves to be tone deaf, or a poet's efforts are tragically bad, you know he'll never make them feel they've fallen any way short of magnificent. Some previous hosts of the show were patently embarrassed by their involvement, and tried to lure the audience into a snickering conspiracy at the girls' expense. Ó Sé's gift is to imply that, if there is a joke here, we're all in on it together.

Through no fault of his, it has become overproduced, overrehearsed and overscripted, and has lost the quality of spontaneity and unpredictability that made it compulsive viewing in Gay Byrne's day. No host since has matched Byrne's ability to draw out revelations and anecdotes the girls hadn't planned on sharing, with the palpable magnetic pull of his curiosity. Now it occasionally seems as though the contestants are following a jaded *X Factor* recipe, adding a pinch of heartbreak, a good ladling of corn and a singalong ditty to end on a high note. Some of their prepared yarns were wittily told, others needed editing, but the whole thing had the air of a glamorous but drawn-out party, with lots of contrived jollity and hours of effortful small talk with enthusiastically frivolous strangers from whom, in reality, you'd run a mile to escape.

Sometimes six degrees of separation doesn't feel like enough.

The meaning of Ryanair

MICHAEL CRONIN (2013)

Founded by Tony Ryan in 1984, Ryanair today carries more passengers than any other airline in the world. Not long after Michael Cronin published this piece anatomizing the experience of the Ryanair passenger, the airline's long-time chief executive Michael O'Leary announced that Ryanair would endeavour henceforth to avoid 'unnecessarily piss[ing] people off'. Various changes followed, including a loosening of the cabin-baggage rules, a website revamp and the discontinuation of the bugle announcing an on-time arrival.

The first intimation that fear is the order of the day is the policing of the weighing scales. The suitcase is lifted with a faint crackle of anxiety on to the belt and the digits illuminate the verdict. The shame of being outed for being overweight and ordered to leave the queue, like some errant Oliver being refused another bowl. Here is your moment in the stocks, the disinterred contents of your suitcase subject to the mocking gaze of onlookers who quietly savour the *schadenfreude* of the moment, that vaguely condescending triumph of the rule-obeyers, craftily weighing bags on bathroom scales to enjoy the warm compliance of the Ryanair forcing house.

The queues. This is another sign that you are entering into a world where new rules apply. The queuing starts long before the gate opens. Initially, there is the animated conversation as the passengers join the queue for the unallocated seats but quickly the initial excitement of departure gives way to the silent, sullen hostility of the long wait. Penned in like unhappy cattle destined for foreign meat markets, the passengers have that fretful anxiety of deportees alert to any rumour of delay or departure. Here is where the black-and-white realities of coercion begin to leak from the past into the present. The photographs of those people in a line in Warsaw, Leningrad, Vilnius, Prague, queuing for a living. Waiting hour after hour for the goods that might or might not make it to the counter and past the reproachful glare of the Konsum hireling. State communism and advanced capitalism converge in this lining up of subjects. The same sense of frustrated expectation, the fretfulness of losing one's place, the inner stiffening as the officials in uniform pass by checking entitlement, examining the size of bags, according the random grace of privilege (it's a bit over but it's OK). A queue becomes not just a means of saving money – there is no need to allocate seats – it becomes a way to order lives. [. . .]

Stupefaction comes early. Booking a ticket on the website is like dealing with a snickering ticket tout ever alert to the foibles of the gullible or the inattentive. The future passenger is forever on guard against a kind of digital cute-hoorism so that she does not end up with a Samsonite suitcase she never wanted, travel insurance she never asked for and a car she never intended hiring. Concealed in the thicket of drop-down menus are the pass keys out of the labyrinth of algorithmic disorientation, and the pop-up messages are video-game villains which must be swatted down if the future passenger is to arrive safely at the destination of payment, where more inexplicable charges await the unwary. Being charged for the privilege of printing your own boarding pass is perhaps one of the most inexplicable. This version of paying others for work you do is at the heart of the present moment of market capitalism, where low cost increasingly means to the producer, at least, no cost.

Intending passengers are obliged to print out their boarding passes in advance. This implies that passengers have access to the equipment (computer and printer) and internet connection which allow them to enter the necessary details and print out the pass. Both the equipment and the connection are a cost to the passenger or to the entity that has made these available to the passenger. There is the further opportunity cost of the time spent accessing the site, filling in the details and printing out the pass. During this time, of course, the passenger could have been doing something else. In short, what were formerly production costs for the airline – paying someone to prepare and print out your boarding pass and thereby creating a job – now become consumption costs for the passenger.

In the upside down world of transferred or devolved costs, the labour is done by the passenger, not by the airline operator, so that the surplus value accrues not to the passenger but to the airline. In the snap, crackle and pop of the ads on board for Lotto tickets, train tickets, car hire, you know that there is no hope that you too could be a Ryanair Millionaire. You are too busy making Ryanair millionaires and know, at some unspoken level, that taking the flight is in every sense being taken for a ride. [. . .]

The bugle sounds as the plane bumps along the tarmac, announcing another on-time Ryanair arrival. The children applaud and the adults smile uncertainly, unsure if the joke is on them. This brief parenthesis of communal hilarity is out of spirit with the presiding genius of the individual. The Lingus in Aer Lingus, an anglicised version of *loingeas*, is the word for a fleet, a collective entity. Ryanair is named, of course, after an individual, Tony Ryan. If Aer Lingus was the flagship project of a young nation finding its footing in the chorus line of national aviation companies, Ryanair is the highly profitable instrument of the Ryan family and associated shareholders. In this shift from the collective to the individual, it is the lone traveller, the unattached, unencumbered foot soldier of liquid modernity who comes closest to Ryanair's Platonic Idea of the Perfect Passenger. Minimum baggage. Minimum fuss. Minimum space. Maximum gain.

The asylum-seekers' grim limbo

CAELAINN HOGAN (2013)

Asylum-seekers in Ireland live under a system known as 'direct provision' while waiting – often for many years – for a decision on their asylum applications. For a piece in the *Dublin Review*, Caelainn Hogan met asylum-seekers and wrote about how they live.

I first met Mohammed, a thirty-year-old Syrian asylum-seeker, at Bewley's cafe on Grafton Street in late October last year. During our first conversation he spoke quietly, in nervous bursts, seemingly on the verge of tears, especially when the subject was his family back home. I asked if I could record the conversation; he said he would rather I didn't. When he saw me taking notes he hesitated to speak.

Mohammed came to Ireland in 2008, fearing for his safety in Syria. Friends of his had been arrested and beaten, he told me, owing to their opposition to the regime; they had on occasion challenged security forces and government representatives in public. His initial application for refugee status was refused and his subsequent appeal was denied almost a year later. Since then, he had been waiting to find out whether he would be deported back to Syria or granted a form of 'subsidiary protection' in Ireland.

'They took me to the camp first,' he told me. For a moment I was confused, wondering whether he meant a refugee camp in Syria or elsewhere; but it turned out that he was referring to Balseskin Reception Centre, in Finglas. The centre is hidden away off a narrow lane near the M50. The bleak rows of prefabs have capacity for 380 residents. Under Ireland's system of 'direct provision', Balseskin is usually the first place asylum-seekers are sent to; most are transferred elsewhere within a year. Mohammed spent six months in Balseskin before being transferred to a centre in Newbridge, Co. Kildare, and then, in 2010, at his own request, to Hatch Hall in the centre of Dublin.

After our second meeting in Bewley's, during which he allowed

me to record the conversation, Mohammed took me to see Hatch
Hall, an imposing old red-brick building on Hatch Street Lower,
near St Stephen's Green. At the security desk I signed my name and
logged the name of the resident I was visiting and the time. Inside,
the building was a warren of clinical, utilitarian spaces. There were
communal rooms sparsely furnished with church pews and shabby
couches. Residents wandered along the corridors without making
eye contact – a woman hurrying her kid along, a man hurrying from
communal shower rooms, wrapped in a towel and carrying a bucket.

Mohammed's room consisted of a wardrobe and a rickety metal-
framed bunk bed; the other bunk was occupied by a young Sudanese
man. He showed me the communal bathroom next door, from where
there came a smell of piss. Mohammed was left with the choice of
staying warm and living with the smell, or leaving the window open
in cold weather.

As an asylum-seeker, Mohammed was living on a weekly state
allowance of €19.10. He was provided three daily meals at Hatch
Hall. For five years, from the age of twenty-five, he had not been
allowed to work or study. If he were to leave his assigned accommodation for more than three nights his bed would be considered
abandoned and he would lose his weekly allowance. He described his
life as a 'limbo'. He felt unable to integrate properly into society,
frustrated and angered at seeing five years of his life pass while waiting for a decision on his application, having to share his room with
strangers and not even allowed to cook his own meals. Outside the
three set meal times, the door of the kitchen in Hatch Hall is locked.

'Sometimes I feel like I want to kill myself,' Mohammed told me.
'I feel like I'm not a human being. I have no home.' He was embarrassed to tell people he met that he lived in an asylum hostel, that he
had no job, not even his own room. He wanted to settle down, have
a family, but he admitted that if he was a father he wouldn't want a
daughter of his to become involved with a man in his situation.

Under the UN Refugee Convention, to qualify for refugee status
an applicant must prove a well-founded fear of being persecuted for
reasons of race, religion, nationality or 'membership of a particular
social group or political opinion'. The Convention does not define

how states should determine whether an individual meets the definition of a refugee, so each country has developed its own procedures.
When applicants claim asylum in Ireland, they undergo an initial
interview in which they must substantiate their fear of persecution.
The initial interview is the basis for all future assessments of their
case, despite often being conducted while an applicant is under emotional stress and lacking legal advice and adequate translation.
Asylum-seekers in Ireland who do not meet the criteria for refugee
status can be granted 'subsidiary protection' by the Minister for Justice and Equality if it is judged that, for reasons other than those that
define a refugee, they face real risk of serious harm in returning to
their country of origin. The Minister can also grant humanitarian
leave to remain.

The system of 'direct provision' for asylum-seekers was established
in 2000 as a response to a rapid increase in the number of asylum
applications in Ireland. It is operated by the Reception and Integra-
tion Agency (RIA), which is part of the Irish Naturalisation and
Immigration Service (INIS), overseen by the Department of Justice.
Between 2000 and 2010 the state paid €655 million to the private con-
tractors that run most of the direct-provision centres. According to
the RIA figures for May 2013, there are thirty-four direct-provision
centres across Ireland, with capacity for 4,700 people. On its website
the RIA describes these centres as 'former hotels, guesthouses (B&B),
hostels, former convents/nursing homes, a holiday camp and a mobile
home site'.

The Minister for Justice, Alan Shatter, has acknowledged that this
system of institutionalized living, and the denial to applicants of the
right to work or study, is intended to discourage people from seeking
asylum in Ireland. By this criterion, the system has been effective. In
2000, there were 10,938 applications for asylum in Ireland. In 2011 the
number was 1,250.

In March of this year, Ireland and Denmark were the only two
member states to opt out of an EU directive on Reception Conditions, part of the Common European Asylum System which was
completed under the Irish EU presidency. The new directive pro-
vides that member states must give asylum-seekers permission to

work if their case has not been decided after one year. Ireland abstained on the principle that the directive conflicted with Article 8 of the Constitution, which prevents asylum-seekers from entering employment. Denmark, for its part, has provided asylum-seekers the right to work through separate legislation, and many other EU member states already allowed asylum-seekers to work or study after a set period of time. Shatter warned that giving asylum-seekers the right to work in Ireland would lead to a dramatic rise in the number of asylum applications, citing a threefold increase in the average number of applications per month in Ireland after July 1999, when a work-permit scheme for asylum-seekers was briefly introduced.

Despite the dramatic drop in the number of applications, Ireland has one of the lowest acceptance rates for asylum in the EU. In 2011, only 5 per cent of applications adjudicated by the Office of the Refugee Applications Commissioner or the Refugee Appeals Tribunal were successful. The EU average for the same year was 11.6 per cent.

In all other EU member states, there is a single procedure by which asylum-seekers can present their claims and be granted the appropriate protection. In Ireland, the assessment procedures are separate and sequential. An applicant who might not meet the criteria for refugee status but who does qualify for subsidiary protection must first apply for refugee status and go through an exhaustive asylum appeals process, facing a number of refusals, before applying for subsidiary protection. This is one of the reasons why such a high proportion of people who seek asylum in Ireland end up in a protracted limbo like Mohammed's. In April, the *Irish Times* reported that 36 per cent of the 4,755 people living in direct provision at the time had been waiting for more than five years; only 12 per cent had been waiting for under a year. In October of last year the UN High Commissioner for Refugees, António Gutteres, visited Ireland and emphasized the pressing need for a single assessment procedure to be introduced here.

After years of waiting for a decision and now with the added trauma of watching from afar as his country disintegrated into civil war, Mohammed told me more than once that he would prefer to return to Syria and die than remain in the limbo of direct provision in Ireland.

'When I went to ask about my case they sent me a form for voluntary return,' he said, remembering the time last year when he went to the INIS office in Dublin to ask if there had been any progress with his application. 'That means shut your mouth, don't talk.' He had asked if he could at least have his Syrian passport returned. Applicants are required to surrender their national passports when seeking asylum in Ireland, and since entering the system his only official document of identity had been the Temporary Residence Certificate, a credit-card-sized piece of plastic issued to all asylum-seekers which bears their name and photo. On the back it says that the card 'indicates that an individual claiming to be the person named on this Certificate has applied to be recognised as a refugee of the State'. One line later the small print reiterates that the card 'does not certify or guarantee the identity of the person named'.

Mohammed was frustrated and disturbed by the daily news of rising death counts and further violence in Syria, and when the office offered him a form for voluntary return it felt like a threat. For months he was unable to contact his family. His doctor had advised him to stop following the news, which was keeping him awake through the night and making him feel helpless and desperate during the day. He didn't know if his family had fled Syria as refugees, or even if they were still alive.

'Sometimes I cry, I can't do anything, I can't go back, I don't know about my family, I don't know if they are alive, even my mum,' he told me, his voice shaking, turning his face away. 'They thought I was lying when I came here, but they can see what is happening in Syria now.'

When I contacted the UNHCR in October regarding the situation of Syrians applying for asylum in Ireland, they told me that during his visit to Dublin the High Commissioner had met with an individual from Syria who for a number of years had been awaiting a decision on his application for subsidiary protection. Coincidentally, that individual turned out to be Mohammed. During our first meeting, he laughed despairingly about how the UNHCR had invited him and other asylum-seekers to the lunch they were holding for the High Commissioner's visit. Mohammed had previously contacted them for help with his case but says they told him there was nothing they could do. 'Then they call saying we have a lunch; I said I don't need food! When I got there I realized *they* need *my* help, I'm like a number for them to use.'

One day in November Mohammed called me, excitement in his voice for the first time. Alan Shatter had visited Hatch Hall and Mohammed had managed to speak to him personally. He had told him about his case, about the situation in Syria and the fact that the INIS had given him an application for voluntary return. Shatter, Mohammed said, had told him he would help, and had taken the letter the INIS had sent him advising him of the process of voluntary return. Mohammed was confident that his case would now be taken care of. A few weeks later he received a letter from the Minister's office, a few sentences merely confirming that it was understood the applicant did not want to apply for voluntary return. [. . .]

Late in the evening on the 25th of June, a Wednesday, I got a call from Mohammed. In an urgent tone he said he had to tell me something but made me promise not to tell anyone for the moment, almost afraid the news was too good to be true. Then he shouted, 'I got my papers!' He sounded like a convicted man just proved innocent, stumbling over his words in excitement. 'Really, I can't believe it, now I can get a home!' He had been waiting for this moment for five years.

A month earlier, he had finally been able to contact his brother, who had escaped first to Lebanon, then fled again to Egypt after he was attacked with a knife for being Syrian by a Lebanese co-worker on a building site. His mother and the rest of his family had fled to Turkey but then returned to their homes in Latakia, unable to face living in a refugee camp. One of his brothers, he found out, had been missing for months. The family feared he was imprisoned or dead.

'Five years, I can't believe it. I never thought it would happen. Everything is going to change now, Caelainn,' he kept repeating when I met him the next day at the Bailey off Grafton Street, sipping his coffee slowly outside under the awning. He was with Hasina, a translator from Algeria; they had met in his first week at Balseskin and had become friends. He showed me the papers they had issued him with his photo printed at the top, advising him that the Minister for Justice and Equality 'has determined that you are a person eligible for subsidiary protection'. The document did not explain why Mohammed, after five years of waiting, had finally been granted this status, but presumably the catastrophic violence in Syria is the reason.

The document stated that he was allowed to remain in Ireland for another three years. At the end of the three years he will have to apply to renew his status and will be eligible to apply for citizenship. He now had the right to rent a home, to find a job, to further his education. He now had the same rights to social welfare and freedom of movement as any Irish citizen.

We walked to the offices of the Irish Naturalisation and Immigration Service on Burgh Quay. I sat on a bench along with others waiting for their numbers to be called while Mohammed and Hasina stood at the panelled glass window registering for his new identity card. Most of the men behind the glass wore hoodies and stared idly at their screens. They gave the impression that they summoned people when the mood took them.

Eventually Mohammed was told to come back in half an hour. The three of us strolled down the quays, joking that he could now enjoy the sites of Dublin, learn to enjoy living here. I took a photo of him in the sunshine, with the Samuel Beckett Bridge arching behind him. When we returned to the INIS office Mohammed had his fingerprints taken and was finally issued his official identity card.

Mohammed and I walked back to Hatch Hall along the same route we had taken nine months before, the first time I saw a direct provision centre. The red brick looked warm in the wavering sunshine and kids were playing on the swings in the courtyard. I joined him in the canteen where he had eaten his dinner almost every night for the past few years. The kids' meal on the chalkboard was 'beef burger and bun'. We shared a chicken and fish stew with fried potatoes and rice, tinned pears for dessert and a bright pink cordial drink.

He had his new ID card on the table and kept picking it up to look at it. I told him tomorrow would be the first day of a new life, and he smiled nervously. 'It's been so long, I don't know what to do now.'

'No atheists need apply'

KITTY HOLLAND (2013)

Kitty Holland wrote in the *Irish Times* about her experience seeking a primary-school place for her young son.

My son, who will be four years old in March, is not baptised. He has been rejected from all four national schools in our area – Dublin 6. I put his name down for all of them, two of them religious schools, when he was a baby.

The little Church of Ireland school, which is the nearest one to our home, has had his name on its application list since he was six weeks old. In its letter last month the board of management 'regrets to inform' me that my application has been 'unsuccessful'. 'Your child is currently No. 177 on our waiting list . . . All offers of places were made in accordance with the school enrolment policy.'

The criteria according to which children can get in the queue are then set out. There are 11 categories, the first being 'Church of Ireland children of the [local] parishes', followed by 'CoI siblings/ Protestant siblings' followed by CoI children from outside the parishes. Next in are CoI children from inter-church marriages, then other Protestant children, then other siblings, then children of inter-church marriages where the child is not CoI, children of staff, Roman Catholic children, Orthodox children and last, the category into which my son falls, 'other children'. This school will take any child of almost any faith from anywhere in the country before they will take an unbaptised child living around the corner.

The Roman Catholic school is a little further away. My son is 117th on the waiting list. His name has been down since he was a baby, but date of application is not relevant there, the principal told me. The letter turning him away from there said siblings of current pupils were prioritised. This is understandable and 'all 17 such applicants are being offered places'. 'The remaining 17 places are being offered to Catholic children resident within the Catholic parish . . .

We regret that we are unable to offer your child a place in our junior infant class for 2014.'

The other two schools, one a non-denominational Gaelscoil and the other multi-denominational, should surely be more welcoming, and as I'd had his name down with the multi-d since he was three weeks old I was hopeful. However, when I called I was told he was 'about 220th on the list'. The enrolment secretary told me parents travelled from across Dublin to enrol their children there, such is the demand. Again at the Gaelscoil, with parents travelling from across the city to get their kids in, he's 239th on the waiting list.

There is clearly huge demand for school places in Dublin 6, not helped by parents – including myself – applying to several schools, and this affects all families. What is also clear, however, is that denominational or faith schools' enrolment criteria impact in a gross and disproportionate way on children such as my son, by excluding them simply because they have not been baptised. To be clear, these State-funded faith-schools – which account for 96 per cent of primary schools – are allowed to direct a religiously based exclusion at children as young as four. This is unacceptable. It is particularly heinous in a democracy which describes itself as a Republic.

Is it any wonder that every single one of my friends who has children has had them baptised – and not one of them to my knowledge attends church outside such events as weddings, funerals or first Holy Communions?

The Irish State has been repeatedly castigated for allowing this discrimination against children to continue, by the United Nations in 2006, 2008 and again in 2011, when its Human Rights Committee noted with concern that the dominance of denominational education was 'depriving many parents and children who so wish to have access to secular primary education'.

In 2011 the Irish Human Rights Commission called on the Department of Education to end schools' religious discrimination against children in admission policies. In no other area of society, where a public service is funded by taxpayers, is such discrimination permitted. One can only imagine the outcry if a public hospital announced it would only treat ill Catholics; or if the local Garda station announced it was only going to investigate crimes committed against people of faith.

The churches controlling our schools argue that their ethos requires special protection. The Equal Status Act 2000 protects their right to protect their ethos of exclusion. Although religion is named as one of the nine grounds of discrimination illegal in public life, Section 7 allows schools to exclude children if 'it is proved that the refusal is essential to maintain the ethos of the school'.

In September the Minister for Education, Ruairí Quinn, launched a public consultation on inclusiveness in primary schools. He said: 'Schools should be welcoming places for all children from the local community. We all know that Irish society has changed a lot in recent years. Our education system needs to adapt, to make sure that, as well as continuing to cater for children with more traditional religious beliefs, there is also respect for children of different traditions and beliefs.'

However, his department is also consulting on a new Education (Admissions to Schools) Bill, the draft of which maintains schools' right to keep out children with the 'wrong' religion, or none. Yesterday the Ombudsman for Children published her advice on the Bill. She says: 'no child in general should be given preferential access to publicly funded education on the basis of their religion', subject to limited exceptions and with the Minister's permission. Mr Quinn is legally obliged to vindicate the right, possessed by every child, to their education. Schools are places for numbers and letters, not for icons.

'Whenever I get up themorra'

NELSON MCCAUSLAND (2015)

The unionist politician Nelson McCausland, a former minister of culture, arts and leisure in Northern Ireland, chronicled the use of the Ulster-Scots dialect in Belfast in his book *Scotch Town*. In his introduction to the book, Ian Crozier of the Ulster-Scots Agency defended generations of schoolchildren, himself included, who had been chastised for failing to 'speak properly'.

Ulster-Scots was once spoken freely throughout Belfast and it was the principal language of Belfast for more than 200 years, but the use of Ulster-Scots was gradually eroded during the 19th and 20th centuries. This was in part the result of separation from the Ulster-Scots heartland. When families first moved into Belfast they retained a close connection with their kith and kin in the country but with the passage of time that connection diminished and after a number of generations it eventually ended.

The erosion was even more rapid in the second half of the 20th century because of education and the media. For many generations schoolteachers have discouraged the use of Ulster-Scots words as not being 'good English'. The use of Ulster-Scots was 'corrected' by the teacher and quite possibly punished as well. That official discouragement had a major impact on Ulster-Scots.

The media has been another influence. At one time the media in Ulster reinforced an awareness of Scots with children reading urban Scots in the pages of *Oor Wullie* and *The Broons*. Back in the 1950s and 1960s when television first came into Ulster homes there were many more Scottish programmes and viewers were hearing and understanding spoken Scots.

Those are now largely a thing of the past and instead we have the overwhelming influence of Anglo-American television culture and modern youth culture. Young people are therefore more likely to know the latest slang than traditional Ulster-Scots words.

The Ulster-Scots language has also influenced our sentence construction and sometimes sentences that look like English are in fact Ulster-Scots which has been anglicised. On a wet day you might say to someone, 'I doubt you may put your coat on.' In standard English that sentence is meaningless but Ulster folk would understand it as:

- 'I doubt' = 'I think' or 'I am sure'.
- 'you may' = 'you ought' or 'you should' or 'you had better'.
- Therefore it would mean, 'I think you should put your coat on.'
- In full Ulster-Scots it would be, 'A doot ye may pit yer coat on ye.'

Belfast folk use the word 'the' in referring to 'The Shankill' or 'The Falls', or 'He has a dose of the flu'. That is another example of Ulster-Scots usage coming into Belfast dialect. It is also used of activities, such as 'You've been at the smoking again' or 'They're away at the fishin again.' We say 'up the stairs' and 'down the stairs' rather than 'upstairs' and 'downstairs', and again this is an Ulster-Scots form.

Ulster-Scots use the word 'whenever' to refer to a one-time occurrence and this is also found in Belfast dialect. We might say, 'Whenever I get up themorra.'

Other features of Ulster-Scots grammar common in Belfast speech include the use of 'for to' or 'for til', such as: 'He went til the shap for to get the paper.' Another is the use of tags such as '. . . so he is' – which put the verb at the end of the sentence. It is clear that both the words and the sentence construction of contemporary Belfast dialect have a significant Ulster-Scots influence.

Today there is new hope for the future of the Ulster-Scots tongue. The Belfast Agreement of 1998 emphasised the importance of respect, understanding and tolerance in relation to languages here and recognised Ulster-Scots as 'part of the cultural wealth of the island of Ireland'.

Ireland coming out to itself

FINTAN O'TOOLE (2015)

In May 2015 the Republic of Ireland became the first country in the world to legalize same-sex marriage through a popular referendum. It was an indication of historical Irish conservatism that marriage was regulated by the Constitution; and an indication of changing times that marriage equality won 62 per cent support.

The overwhelming victory for the Yes side in the marriage equality referendum is not as good as it looks.

It's much better.

It looks extraordinary – little Ireland becoming the first country in the world to support same-sex marriage by direct popular vote. But actually it's about the ordinary. Ireland has redefined what it means to be an ordinary human being.

We've made it clear to the world that there is a new normal – that 'ordinary' is a big, capacious word that embraces and rejoices in the natural diversity of humanity. LGBT people are now a fully acknowledged part of the wonderful ordinariness of Irish life.

It looks like a victory for tolerance. But it's actually an end to mere toleration.

Tolerance is what 'we' extend, in our gracious goodness, to 'them'. It's about saying 'You do your own thing over there and we won't bother you so long as you don't bother us.'

The resounding Yes is a statement that Ireland has left tolerance far behind. It's saying that there's no 'them' any more. LGBT people are us – our sons and daughters, mothers and fathers, brothers and sisters, neighbours and friends. We were given the chance to say that. We were asked to replace tolerance with the equality of citizenship. And we took it in both arms and hugged it close.

It looks like a victory for articulacy. This was indeed a superb civic campaign. And it was marked by the riveting eloquence of so many people, of Una Mullally and Colm O'Gorman, of Mary McAleese and Noel Whelan, of Ursula Halligan and Colm Tóibín, of Averil Power and Aodhán Ó Ríordáin and of so many others who spoke their hearts and their minds on the airwaves and the doorsteps. The Yes side did not rise to provocations and insults, it rose above them. Many people sacrificed their privacy and exposed their most intimate selves to the possibility of public rejection. Their courage and dignity made the difference.

Even so, this is not a victory for articulate statement. Deep down, it's a victory for halting, fretful speech. How? Because what actually changed Ireland over the last two decades is hundreds of thousands of painful, stammered conversations that began with the dreaded words 'I have something to tell you . . .' It's all those moments of coming out around kitchen tables, tentative words punctuated by sobs and sighs, by cold silences and fearful hesitations. Those awkward, unhappy, often unfinished conversations are where the truths articulated so eloquently in the campaign were first uttered. And it was through them that gay men and lesbians became Us, our children, our families.

It looks like a victory for Liberal Ireland over Conservative Ireland. But it's much more significant than that.

It's the end of that whole, sterile, useless, unproductive division. There is no longer a Liberal Ireland and a Conservative Ireland. The cleavage between rural and urban, tradition and modernity, that has shaped so many of the debates of the last four decades has been repaired. This is a truly national moment – as joyful in Bundoran as it is in Ballymun, in Castlerea as it is in Cobh.

Instead of Liberal Ireland and Conservative Ireland we have a decent, democratic Ireland.

It looks like LGBT people finally coming out of the closet. But actually it's more than that: it's Ireland coming out to itself. We had a furtive, anxious hidden self of optimism and decency, a self long clouded by hypocrisy and abstraction and held in check by fear. On Friday, this Ireland stopped being afraid of itself. The No campaign was all about fear – the fear that change could have only one vehicle (the handcart) and one destination (hell). And this time, it didn't work. Paranoia and pessimism lost out big time to the confident, hopeful, self-belief that Irish people have hidden from themselves for too long.

It looks like a victory for global cosmopolitanism. But actually it's a victory for intimacy.

It was intimacy that made Ireland such a horrible place for gay and lesbian people, for all those whose difference would be marked and spied on and gossiped about. But intimacy is a tide that is just as powerful when it turns the other way. Once LGBT people did begin to come out, they became known. Irish people like what they know. They like the idea of 'home'.

On Friday, the wonderful spectacle of people coming back to vote, embodied for all of us that sense of home as the place where the heart is – the strong, beating heart of human connection.

Finally, it looks like a defeat for religious conservatives. But nobody has been defeated. Nobody has been diminished. Irish people comprehensively rejected the notion that our republic is a zero-sum game, that what is given to one must be taken from another. Everybody gains from equality – even those who didn't think they wanted it. Over time, those who are in a minority on this issue will come to appreciate the value of living in a pluralist democracy in which minorities are respected.

By pushing forward on what only recently seemed a marginal issue, the LGBT community has given all of Irish democracy one of its greatest days. It has given our battered republic a new sense of engagement, a new confidence, an expanded sense of possibility.

It has shown all of us that the unthinkable is perfectly attainable.

We now have to figure out how to rise to that daunting and exhilarating challenge.

'Nobody will ever look at you again'

CAITRÍONA PALMER (2016)

The journalist Caitríona Palmer was born out of wedlock in 1972, and given up for adoption by her birth mother. In her book *An Affair with My Mother*, Palmer writes about the cultural climate that caused women like her birth mother – referred to by the pseudonym Sarah – to feel that they could not live as single mothers and, even decades later, that they could not tell family and friends about their secret children. In this passage, Palmer reconstructs the events that unfolded after Sarah became pregnant.

Sarah went home for Christmas, as usual, but did not tell anyone in her family about her pregnancy. At the end of the holidays, she packed her bags and told them she was returning to her job at the school. Instead she headed for Dublin, where a Catholic charity had secured her temporary lodgings, a house in a Dublin suburb owned by a young couple with small children. In complete anonymity and with free room and board, Sarah was guaranteed that she could stay there until her child was born. The only thing asked of her was that she occasionally helped out with the family's kids. With extraordinary speed and efficiency the Irish Church and medical establishment had colluded to conceal Sarah's shameful fall.

Sarah lived quietly in her new lodgings, rarely venturing outside, her blossoming waistline visible only to Anne and Paddy and their three young children. While Paddy was out at work, Sarah sometimes helped Anne with a little light housework, and she babysat the three kids. When Sarah had an appointment at the maternity hospital, Anne would drive her there, waiting outside until Sarah was done. The mood in the house was friendly and upbeat, and Sarah at times felt happy. But every morning when she woke, she felt a concrete block of anxiety resting on her sternum.

Sarah's recollection of her interactions with institutions during her pregnancy is a bit fuzzy, and it's not clear at what point she came into contact with St Patrick's Guild or on precisely what terms. What is clear is that, having accumulated some savings from her work as a teacher, she was able to cover the fees charged by the Guild, and thus avoid the fate of many unmarried mothers: a period of indentured servitude in a mother-and-baby home or a Magdalen Laundry.

In the early hours of 19 April 1972, Sarah felt the first pangs of labour pain. She suffered in silence for some time before quietly slipping out of bed and knocking softly on the door to the bedroom of the couple she was lodging with, asking to be driven to Holles Street. I was born at around two o'clock in the afternoon, a long-limbed baby with a mop of black hair. According to the letter sent by St Patrick's Guild to my [adoptive] parents in July 1996, based on a consultation of the Guild's files, Sarah's labour was 'normal', the duration '9 hours and 50 minutes' and my birth weight '3,320 grams', seven pounds and five ounces.

I asked Sarah about the labour. [. . .]

'Everything went very smoothly,' she told me. 'It was easy, very easy . . . I couldn't believe it when everything was over. I thought it hadn't even started. I couldn't say that about the subsequent births. Really, it was so different. But maybe you get little graces, you know?'

Little graces. The grace of a pain-free birth in anticipation of the real agony that was to come.

'They didn't give you to me straight away,' Sarah said. 'No, they didn't. I'm sure they were aware that, you know . . .' She trailed off, unable to finish the sentence.

Back on the ward following my birth, Sarah marvelled at my long arms and legs and delighted in my lazy yawns. I was placed in a steel cot next to her bed while someone was dispatched to call St Patrick's Guild to tell them that a baby had arrived. Around her, in happy clusters, sat the adoring families of other young mothers. Babies were passed around, cooed over. Alone in her bed, without her family or her baby, Sarah watched it all.

'The nurses were very, very nice. You couldn't fault them,' Sarah recalled. 'I didn't discuss anything with the other patients but I felt as if they knew.'

'Did anyone come to visit you from St Patrick's Guild?' I asked.

'I can't remember, but I'm sure arrangements were being made behind the scenes. But I couldn't swear to that either. It's funny how you block out stuff. It's very hard to get it back.' Sarah looked at me with a sudden realization. 'You're the very first person to ever ask me these questions,' she said.

It took a while for the significance of that statement to register: in nearly forty years this was the first time that Sarah had spoken aloud of these events. I knew I had to ask her to describe the moment when she saw me for the very last time, but I was dreading it. My heart was racing when finally I asked: 'Do you remember what it was like to leave me?'

Sarah was silent. She looked down at her hands. *I'm so sorry to ask you that*, I said to her in my mind, *I'm so, so sorry*.

'Yeah,' Sarah whispered. 'Yeah, I do.'

Her voice was tiny. 'The family that I had stayed with, they would have . . . they would have taken me back for a night or two. They came to get me. You were left behind in the hospital.'

'Do you remember what that was like?' I asked.

There was a long pause. I could almost feel time stand still. 'Oh, Caitríona, it's very hard to get words to describe it. You feel as though you dreamt it all, that the whole thing was a dream. You felt it didn't happen. I cried for days afterwards. I did, I did.'

I was conscious of the agony that I was putting Sarah through, but I wanted more details: who was in the room, what was said, whether Sarah had sufficient time alone with me to say goodbye. But it became clear that Sarah had placed this memory at the furthest recess of her mind and locked it away. She reminded me of the survivors of the Srebrenica massacre I'd met, who often struggled to recall episodes of shattering distress. Lacking a clear recollection from Sarah, I am forced to rely on my own imagining. I see myself being wheeled away in my crib, bawling, wanting my mother. I see Sarah, still bleeding, her tender breasts leaking milk, bereft as she leaves the hospital.

In my childhood adoptee daydreams, Sarah had fought tooth and nail to keep me. It was painful to realize that this was not the case: there was never a moment when a phalanx of nurses and nuns struggled to remove me from her embrace. At the same time, I find it admirable that Sarah did not spin me a self-absolving line about her decision not to keep me. The odds were almost impossible: life in Ireland in 1972 as an unmarried mother, without the support of her family, would have been extraordinarily difficult. All this I understood. But the child in me wanted to hear that Sarah had put up a fight. The mother in me wanted to hear that too. Since giving birth to Liam and Caoimhe – marvelling at the physical torque on my heart when I first saw the faces of my newborn babies – I had struggled to comprehend Sarah's decision to give me away. Although the circumstances of our pregnancies had been miles apart, my experiences stoked an uncomfortable thought that refused to go away: that no woman, fully informed and left to her own devices, would make the decision Sarah had made.

Sarah returned to Anne and Paddy's house, took to her bed and cried for a couple of days. Then, with no one to counsel her, she decided to go home. A week or two back home, amongst her cheerful noisy siblings and the father she adored, would help her get her head back in order.

'Your instinct is to go home,' she told me that day in the Marine. 'I wanted to go home. I needed to.'

Sarah arrived to find her family still reeling in the wake of her mother's death. The house was chaotic, her father depressed. Teeming with hormones and sick with grief over her missing child, Sarah struggled to get through each day. She told her family she was off work because of the kidney infection. As far as she knew, nobody noticed her altered shape.

In reality, the secret was out. At Christmas, when Sarah had been just over five months pregnant, a neighbour had seen her and had her suspicions. Now, assessing her sagging midriff and pasty pallor, the neighbour put two and two together. Scandalized, she picked up the phone.

'The neighbour calls my aunt in Dublin and the aunt comes down,' Sarah recalled. 'I wasn't there. I know that all hell broke loose when she did come down. She and the neighbour told my father, instead of coming directly to me.'

'Where were you at that point?' I asked.

'I can't remember,' Sarah said. 'I honestly can't remember.'

Sarah has never been able to fully reconstruct for me the events immediately following her family's discovery that she had secretly given birth. There is, in her memory, no clear moment of truth, of confrontation, of renunciation. What I do know is that her father, devastated and shamed by his daughter's fall, would barely speak to her in the coming years and decades. She had brought dishonour on the household, she had stained the family name. Her relationship with her family as she had known it was over.

Now that the baby was gone, she could no longer lodge with Anne and Paddy. Although the medical certificate for her fictitious kidney infection protected her teaching position, she knew instinctively that she would never again set foot in that town. She would have to start over. There were more teaching jobs in Dublin than anywhere else, and the city's bustling anonymity seemed to suit her situation. But she could not afford lodgings in Dublin. There was only one person in Dublin with whom she could live rent-free: her aunt. The same aunt who had just betrayed her.

Even allowing for the financial and familial circumstances, it is hard to fathom how Sarah could have accepted the hospitality of this woman. Was there an element of self-punishment involved? Or perhaps just a sort of passivity that set in when, seeking to avoid stigma and scandal, she surrendered her autonomy and her baby?

In all the time I have known Sarah, she has never said anything unkind about anyone – with the sole exception of this aunt.

'She was a witch. She was very, very cruel. She would say anything.'

The aunt grudgingly told Sarah that she could remain at her house throughout the summer until she found a new job and a place to live. In return, Sarah would have to live with her aunt's contempt, the disdain of the morally righteous for the fallen woman.

'Nobody will ever look at you again,' the aunt told Sarah one day. 'You're finished.'

'I believed her,' Sarah told me. 'I did. I really did.'

The 1916 centenary: a psychological milestone

JOHN A. MURPHY (2016)

John A. Murphy – historian, former senator, professor emeritus of history at UCC – assessed the state's commemorations of the centenary of the Easter Rising.

In dealing with historical commemorations, the priority of the government of the day is to make them 'relevant', or at the least to survive the pitfalls they may present. In 1998 for example, when the Belfast Agreement coincided with the bicentenary of the 1798 rebellion, it was important for the then government and its advisers to highlight the brotherhood of the United Irishmen while playing down the sectarian character of the upheaval.

A year or two ago, as the Fine Gael–Labour coalition reluctantly prepared to face the 1916 centenary, their first touches were less than assured. The fatuous attempt to make the commemoration relevant, or even commercially enterprising, led to a video featuring pop stars and political notables. This famously drew an earthy expletive from Professor Diarmaid Ferriter, himself a member of the Government's scholarly board of advisers. Anxious not to jeopardise the excellent state of British–Irish relations, politicians foolishly talked of the need to be 'inclusive' and there was a crass suggestion of a British royal presence on the centenary platform.

Also, at a time when the rise of Sinn Féin seemed inexorable, the Government feared being upstaged by that organisation in the centenary celebrations. That would indeed have been an ironic development since Sinn Féin played no part in the Easter Rising. In the event, whatever plans or ambitions the party might have had did not materialise. The separate commemoration of the O'Donovan Rossa funeral seemed petulant, and An Post put paid to the proposal to have a grandiose *son et lumière* spectacle at the GPO.

In the end, the Government took a firm grip on centenary planning, though this involved it in such necrophiliac, pomp-and-circumstance proceedings as the reburial of the remains of Cork nationalist martyr Thomas Kent.

Incidentally, a Fine Gael-led administration was wise to distance itself from John Bruton's implausible thesis that a successfully delivered Home Rule would have led serenely to national independence.

But the really imaginative government initiative was the role of the Army in distributing Proclamation copies and Tricolours to schools. At a stroke, this symbolised the popular, not factional, ownership of the national flag and the legitimacy of the real Óglaigh na hÉireann and of the living Republic. This was a silent rebuke to the ambivalence in these matters of Sinn Féin, the third-largest party in the State. Moreover, schoolchildren got the opportunity to acquaint themselves, in a friendly and familiar manner, with the custodians of our national security.

Proclamation Day, March 15th, turned out to be a great success and even those of us who had some misgivings about the idea were impressed by the enthusiastic expressions and voices of the young Irish, particularly the 'new' ones.

Enthusiasm indeed is the hallmark of local communities throughout the country as they commemorate 1916-related events in their areas. In hailing people like O'Donovan Rossa, locals are not at all worried about the warts which historians find in the west Cork favourite son.

The Irish public today, it seems to me, have a much more informed interest in historical events than they had in 1966. They are more concerned with what happened, with history per se, than with history as nationalist narrative.

Since 1966, the convulsion of the Troubles has come and (almost?) gone. All that has, *inter alia*, sobered and matured us. Meanwhile our favourite Proclamation phrase is still the inspiring 'cherishing all the children of the nation equally', which continues to be understood as a clarion call to social justice, despite futile corrections from pedants like myself about its true meaning.

In other respects, 2016 Ireland is unbelievably different from the country of the 50th anniversary. Historical sources are rich and varied and, thanks to the digital revolution, more or less freely available.

Our understanding of the role of women activists has changed out of all recognition. The dramatis personae of Easter week now extends to all the human beings involved, bystanders, innocent victims, surviving relatives of foe as well as friend.

All of this augurs well for our better understanding of the revolutionary events we are to commemorate in the next few years.

In recent weeks, there has been a furore about the banners draped on the front of the Bank of Ireland at College Green (by the Department of the Taoiseach and Dublin City Council) honouring four major figures in the history of constitutional nationalist politics, Grattan, O'Connell, Parnell and Redmond. The building housed the Irish Parliament abolished by the Act of Union in 1801 and, throughout the 19th century, symbolised the hoped-for restoration of a native legislature. In nationalist processions, leaders would symbolically point towards the bank. Critics of the banners have been lamenting their seeming inappropriateness in the context of the 1916 centenary. But this is to ignore the creative interaction, the symbiotic relationship, between physical force and constitutionalism in modern Irish history. One recalls O'Connell defending agrarian terrorists, Parnell and the New Departure, and the (much appreciated) supportive visits of John Redmond to Tom Clarke in Portland prison. And the 1916 Proclamation itself, by promising a representative assembly as soon as possible, implicitly pays tribute to the strength of the parliamentary tradition in advancing the cause of Irish independence.

In conclusion, the Government can breathe a sigh of relief at how well the celebrations have gone, given the apprehensions of a couple of years ago.

More importantly, a psychological milestone has been passed. The 1916 Rising has been soberly copper-fastened in Irish history, despite the still unanswered questions about its justification. We are moving away from the fantasy world of 'the Republic as in 1916 established'. We are now recognising that proclamation is not 'establishment'. Increasingly, as further anniversaries pass, the magic (sometimes black) of the Easter Rising will be less seductive.

Acknowledgements

I am indebted to many people and institutions in the production of this book. My first debt is to all those whose texts I have selected for inclusion. Whether from letters, diaries, journalism, books, parliamentary debates or government reports, all of these documents originated with an intended audience in mind. In some cases it would have been just the recipient of a letter; in others the text was intended to reach the widest possible public. These documents now find themselves keeping company within one volume to reflect Ireland since 1916. I must especially thank those who preserved private letters and diaries, thus ensuring that they were available for historical scrutiny.

For half a century now I have been indebted to the Library of Trinity College Dublin and to the National Library of Ireland, where I must especially thank Sandra Collins, Katherine McSharry, Brid O'Sullivan and James Harte for their courtesy and generosity. Seamus Helferty, of the archives department at UCD, was, as always, very helpful, as was Bernard Meehan and Aisling Lockhart, of the manuscripts department at TCD. I am also grateful to the staff at the National Archives of Ireland, the Public Record Office of Northern Ireland and the National Archives of the United Kingdom at Kew; also to Churchill College Cambridge, the British Library and the Bodleian Library at Oxford. To other archives in Ireland and abroad, where my visits were sometimes necessarily brief, I wish to express my thanks for the manner in which staff helped to explain their archival systems and to guide me through the maze.

At the Dublin Diocesan Archives I am indebted to the archivist, Noelle Dowling, and to her predecessor, David Sheehy, who introduced me to the McQuaid Papers when they were first released; to Cardinal Desmond Connell, who gave me access to them; and to Archbishop Diarmuid Martin for permission to publish some documents. I must also thank the archivists in the Galway and Kerry dioceses and their respective bishops; and Roddy Hegarty, director of the Ó Fiaich Library at Armagh, who guided me to the files of the Armagh diocese relevant to my research.

Eamonn McCann was helpful in a number of instances; as was John Horgan, whose experience as journalist, academic, historian and anthologist was, as always, generously shared. Brian Lynch, former archivist in RTÉ, drew my attention to some important documents. Others who helped include Michael Talty, Rob Canning and Brian Rice of the RTÉ library and archives; and Mark Reynolds of the GAA library and archive. I wish also to thank Brian McGee, Cork City and County Archivist, Michael Higgins of the Cork Archives Institute, and Colum O'Riordan of the Irish Architectural Archive.

As with earlier books, I thank my agent, Jonathan Williams, for impeccable judgement, good humour and valued support. Claire Rourke was indefatigable with her help in tracking down copyright permissions and remained diligent and optimistic throughout. To Ciara Baker I am again hugely indebted; her skills as a researcher and her enthusiasm and fortunate temperament all make working with her a pleasure. And, like all good researchers – on the rare occasions when she failed to discover what I thought might be there – she does not report that the needle wasn't in the haystack but rather that she hadn't found it. I also must thank my son Daniel for his practical help when I was engaged in research in London and at the National Archives of South Africa in Pretoria.

I owe historic debts to my teachers in Belvedere College, especially John Daly and Jesuits F. X. O'Sullivan, Charles Byrne, Edward Diffley and Jack Kelly, who made schooldays a challenge – and much happier than the 1950s Ireland which I discovered when researching this book. And at Trinity College Dublin, I owe much to David Thornley, Basil Chubb and T. W. Moody for guidance on many of the subjects covered here; and for introducing me to rigorous research methods.

I must also thank Rory Allen, Patricia Deane, Candice Ealet, Owen Dudley Edwards, Nicholas Flynn, Simon Gough, Louise Kearns, Peter Kelly, Tom Kilgariff, Avril Lynch, Maire MacConghail, Ann MacFerran, John Masterson, Patrick Murray, Enda O'Doherty, Nicolas Ruquet and Michael Williams; and also the late Desmond Williams and the late Francis MacManus for their encouragement and support. I am especially indebted to Fintan Drury.

I must thank the staff at Penguin Ireland for the original invitation to undertake this project. Michael McLoughlin as managing director brought a commitment which every author covets, Donna Poppy as copy-editor was exemplary and spotted a number of infelicities – and worse – which were drawn to my attention. Brendan Barrington as editor was a fastidious challenger if he had a doubt about any detail. Such scrupulous attention is not a characteristic which is always appreciated by busy authors but it is in the reader's interest – and indeed the author's; and I thank Brendan Barrington for his exceptional contribution to this book. It goes without saying that the final decisions were mine and I alone am responsible for any errors.

My indebtedness to my family cannot be exaggerated: my children, Jonathan, Emma, Abie and Daniel, have always been understanding during those periods when their ever-present father is mentally absent, engaged in the minutiae of delivering a project such as this. From my wife Eimer Philbin Bowman – who spots the absence sooner than all others – I must seek forgiveness for the many trespasses on her patience and forbearance. I must also thank her for her sound advice on many individual documents.

I have already thanked the original authors of these texts; some are still living and some have died. As any anthologist benefits in so many ways from such writings by others, and since so many of them or their heirs have waived any copyright fees payable, a donation has been made on behalf of all of them to Médecins Sans Frontières/Doctors Without Borders. I hope I am correct in presuming that this charity would earn the approval of all concerned.

Sources

The editor and publisher would like to express their gratitude to the writers, archivists and publishers who have given their permission for the republication of the following pieces.

A countryman ('Match-making', 1940): Conrad M. Arensberg and Solon T. Kimball, *Family and Community in Ireland* (second edition, Harvard University Press, 1868, pp. 106–8). Permission granted, copyright © 1940, 1968 by the President and Fellows of Harvard College.

Advertisement ('The School for Farmers' Daughters', 1917): *Catholic Bulletin*, Vol. II, No. 4, April 1917.

Allen, Myrtle: *Sunday Times* magazine, *c.* May–June 1994. Permission granted by the author.

Ambrose, Alfred: Warden's Report, Belfast Blitz, 15–16 April 1941, PRONI T3756. Permission granted by the Deputy Keeper of Records, Public Record Office of Northern Ireland.

'An Irish Correspondent': *Spectator*, 6 June 1925. Permission granted courtesy of the *Spectator*.

'An Irishman's diary': *Irish Times*, 12 December 1939. Permission granted © *Irish Times*.

Andrews, C. S.: *Administration*, Spring 1953, Vol. 1, No. 1, pp. 37–9. Permission granted by the Institute of Public Administration.

Andrews, Rachel: *Dublin Review*, No. 39, Summer 2010, pp. 28–42. Permission granted by the author.

Anonymous ('Witch-finders and orthodoxy-mongers', 1950): Letter to Eamon de Valera, 2 July 1950, Séamus Fitzgerald Papers, Cork Archives Institute, PR/6/349. Permission granted by Brian McGee, Cork City and County Archivist.

Binchy, Maeve: Mary Kenny, *Goodbye to Catholic Ireland* (New Island, 2000, pp. 325–7). Permission granted by Gordon Snell and by Christine Green on behalf of the estate of Maeve Binchy.

Blair, May: *Hiring Fairs and Market Places* (Appletree Press, 2007, pp. 176–8). Permission granted by Appletree Press.

Boland, Eavan: *Object Lessons* (Carcanet Press, 2006, pp. ix–xvi). Permission granted by Carcanet Press Limited and W. W. Norton Publishers.

Bowen, Elizabeth (1916): *The Shelbourne* (George Harrap, 1951, pp. 151–7). Permission granted by Curtis Brown (UK) as agents for the author.

Bowen, Elizabeth (1940): Report to British Ministry of Information, 9 November 1940, National Archives (UK), Halifax Papers FO800/310. Permission contains public sector information licensed under the Open Government Licence v2.0. Permission granted courtesy of the National Archives (UK).

Boyce, James: *Spectator*, 6 October 1966. Permission granted courtesy of the *Spectator*.

Breen, Suzanne: *Sunday Tribune*, 5 October 2008. Permission granted by the author.

Broy, Eamon: Eamon Broy, Military Archives, Ireland, BMH WS 1280, pp. 97–100. Permission granted by the Military Archives.

Burke, Thomas: *Clare Champion*, 15 January 1948.

Cabinet Paper (1920): Note of W. E. Wylie's testimony on Ireland to British Cabinet, 23 July 1920, National Archives (UK), CAB 24/109 CP1683. Permission contains public sector information licensed under the Open Government Licence v2.0. Permission granted courtesy of the National Archives (UK).

Casement, Tom: Letter to J. C. Smuts, 1 February 1921, Smuts Papers, Vol. 208/40, National Archives of South Africa. Permission granted by the National Archives and Records Service of South Africa.

'Charlie' ('A Black and Tan writes to his mother', 1920): Letter to his mother, 16 December 1920, intercepted and in Florence O'Donoghue Papers, NLI MS 31,226. Permission granted courtesy of the National Library of Ireland.

Childers, Erskine: Letter to Molly Childers, 20–24 November 1922, Childers Papers, TCD MS 7855/1301. Permission granted courtesy of the Board of Trinity College Dublin.

Clery, Arthur: *Studies*, Vol. X, No. 37, 1921, pp. 544–52. Permission granted by Bruce Bradley, SJ, on behalf of the publication.

Collins, Michael: Dáil Debate on the Treaty, 19 December 1921, pp. 30–36. Republished under Oireachtas Adapted PSI Licence.

Connolly, Nora: Nora Connolly-O'Brien, Military Archives, Ireland, BMH WS 286, pp. 50–54. Permission granted by the Military Archives.

Conway, Cardinal William: Memo to Hierarchy, 30 September 1969, McQuaid Papers, Dublin Diocesan Archives, DDA/AB8/XV/C/112. Permission granted by Dr Diarmuid Martin, Archbishop of Dublin.

Coyne, T. J.: Department of Justice meeting minute, 19 September 1939, NAI D/JUS 4/27/44. Permission granted courtesy of the National Archives of Ireland.

Cronin, Anthony: *Dead as Doornails* (Lilliput Press, 1999, pp. 103–7). Reprinted by kind permission of the Lilliput Press, Dublin.

Cronin, Michael: *Dublin Review of Books*, Issue 36, 4 June 2013. Permission granted by the *Dublin Review of Books*.

Cunningham, Michael, Joe Devlin, David Lloyd George and Edward Carson: Sequence of letters commencing 29 October 1920, Parliamentary Archives,

Lloyd George Papers, LG/F/15/1/1. Permission contains public sector information licensed under the Open Government Licence v2.0. Permission granted courtesy of the National Archives (UK).

Curran, C. P.: *Studies*, Vol. XV, No. 58, June 1926, pp. 299–308. Permission granted by Bruce Bradley, SJ, on behalf of the publication.

Curran, Monsignor Michael J.: Michael J. Curran, Military Archives, Ireland, BMH WS 687, pp. 37–40. Permission granted by the Military Archives.

Curtayne, Alice, and 'John Rowe': *Capuchin Annual (1933)*, pp. 74–8. Permission granted courtesy of the Provincial Archivist, Capuchin Friary, Dublin.

de Valera, Eamon (1943): Maurice Moynihan (ed.), *Speeches and Statements by Eamon de Valera 1971–1973* (Gill and Macmillan, 1980, pp. 466–9).

de Valera, Eamon ('A Reply to Winston Churchill', 1945): Maurice Moynihan (ed.), *Speeches and Statements by Eamon de Valera 1971–1973* (Gill and Macmillan, 1980, pp. 470–77).

de Valera, Eamon ('A Catholic Nation', 1945): Advice to Irish diplomatic corps, 11 September 1945, UCDA, de Valera Papers, P150/2701. Permission granted courtesy of University College Dublin Archives.

Dempsey, Michael: Michael Dempsey, Military Archives, Ireland, BMH WS 1499, p. 1. Permission granted by the Military Archives.

Department of External Affairs memo: 30 December 1947, D/TSCH 3 / S 11582B. Permission granted courtesy of the National Archives of Ireland.

Devlin, Bernadette: *The Price of My Soul* (Pan Macmillan, 1969, pp. 201–5). By kind permission of the author, Bernadette Devlin McAliskey.

Devlin, Polly: *All of Us There* (Weidenfeld & Nicholson, 1983, pp. 122–4). Permission granted by the author.

Dillon, John: Letter to David Lloyd George, 11 June 1916, Parliamentary Archives, Lloyd George Papers, LG/D/14/2/29. Permission contains public sector information licensed under the Open Government Licence v2.0. Permission granted courtesy of the National Archives (UK).

Dillon, John, and Myles Dillon: Joachim Fischer and John Dillon (eds.), *The Correspondence of Myles Dillon 1922–1925: Irish–German Relations and Celtic Studies* (Four Courts Press, 1999, pp. 196–220). Permission granted by Professor John Dillon.

Diskin, Maureen: Benjamin Grob-Fitzgibbon, *The Irish Experience during the Second World War: An Oral History* (Irish Academic Press, 2004, pp. 128–9). Permission granted by the Irish Academic Press.

Duddy, Kay: Eamonn McCann, *Bloody Sunday in Derry* (Brandon, 1992, pp. 24–9). Permission granted by Eamonn McCann.

Elliott, Marianne: *The Catholics of Ulster* (Allen Lane, 2000, pp. 448–50). Permission granted by Penguin Books Ltd.

Emerson, Newton: *Irish Times*, 14 January 2005. Permission granted by the author.

FitzGerald, Eithne: Michael Gallagher and Richard Sinnott (eds.), *How Ireland*

Voted 1989, Centre for the Study of Irish Elections (NUIG) (PSAI Press, 1990, pp. 52–6). Permission granted by the author.

Fitzpatrick, Bridget: Public Hearings on the Barron Report, Sub-Committee on the Barron Report Debate, 20 January 2004.

Fogarty, Michael: Letter to James O'Mara, 28 November 1918, James O'Mara Letters, NLI MD MS 21,546(1). Permission granted courtesy of the National Library of Ireland.

Foster, John Wilson: *The Titanic Complex: A Cultural Manifest* (Belcouver Press, 1997, pp. 69–70; reissued as *Titanic: Culture and Calamity*, 2016). Permission granted by the author.

Franks, M. H.: Patrick Buckland, *Irish Unionism 1885–1923: A Documentary History* (The Historical Association, 1973, pp. 363–4). Permission granted by the Deputy Keeper of Records, Public Record Office of Northern Ireland, D989/A/8/7.

Gallagher, Cornelius: Memo to the Vigilance Committee, 24 October 1955, McQuaid Papers, Dublin Diocesan Archives, AB8/XXIII/16. Permission granted by Dr Diarmuid Martin, Archbishop of Dublin.

Gallagher, Frank (1931): Advice to *Irish Press* journalists, c. August 1931, Gallagher Papers, NLI MS 18,349 (8). Permission granted courtesy of the National Library of Ireland.

Gallagher, Frank (1940): Letter to Stephen O'Mara, 27 April 1940, Gallagher Papers, NLI MD MS 18,361/3. Permission granted courtesy of the National Library of Ireland.

Good, Anne: Letter to Mrs Charles Clarke, 31 March 1923, quoted by Hubert Butler, *Escape from the Anthill* (Lilliput Press, 1985, pp. 100–101). By kind permission of the Lilliput Press, Dublin.

Gregory, Lady Augusta: Diary, 12 April 1923, in Daniel J. Murphy (ed.), *Lady Gregory's Journals: Vol. 1* (Oxford University Press, 1978, pp. 445–6). Permission granted by Oxford University Press.

Gwynn, E. J.: Letter to J. H. Bernard, 6 September 1921, Bernard Papers, British Library, MS 52783, ff. 137–140. Permission granted © British Library Board.

Hackett, Francis: *Ireland: A Study in Nationalism* (B. W. Heubisch, 1918, pp. 309–12).

Harris, Emily K.: Letter to King George V, 10 November 1926, NAI D/T 5215. Permission granted courtesy of the National Archives of Ireland.

Haughey, Charles: Dáil Debates, 11 February 1992, Vol. 451, No. 6, cols. 1509–16. Republished under Oireachtas Adapted PSI Licence.

Hayes, Michael: Seanad Éireann debate, 19 December 1962, Vol. 55, No. 19, cols. 1685–9.

Heaney, Seamus: Dennis O'Driscoll, *Stepping Stones: Interviews with Seamus Heaney* (Faber and Faber, 2008, pp. 224–6). Permission granted by Faber and Faber.

Hewitt, John: Letter to R. P. Maybin, 14 May 1945, Hewitt Papers, PRONI,

D3838/3/12. Permission granted by the Deputy Keeper of Records, Public Record Office of Northern Ireland.

Hogan, Caelainn: *Dublin Review*, No. 52, Autumn 2013. Permission granted by the author.

Holland, Kitty: *Irish Times*, 12 December 2013, pp. 5–20. Permission granted by the author and © *Irish Times*.

Holland, Mary (1988): *Irish Times*, 21 March 1988. Permission granted by the estate of Mary Holland and © *Irish Times*.

Holland, Mary (1998): *Observer*, 12 April 1998. Permission granted by the estate of Mary Holland and *Guardian* News and Media, 2016.

Holloway, Joseph: 'Impressions of a Dublin Playgoer', NLI MD, Holloway Papers, 2 MS 1900, 7–19 February 1926. Permission granted courtesy of the National Library of Ireland.

Hourihane, Ann Marie: *She Moves Through the Boom* (Sitric Press, 2001, pp. 105–11). Permission granted by the author and the Lilliput Press, Dublin.

Hussey, Gemma: Hussey Papers, 16 March 1985. By kind permission of the author.

Inglis, Brian: *Spectator*, 5 July 1963. Permission granted courtesy of the *Spectator*.

Irish Independent **report (1926)**: *Irish Independent*, 9 December 1926.

Irish Messenger: Extracts from 'The Question Box', 1948. Permission granted by Donal Neary on behalf of the publication.

Irish Times **correspondent [possibly Renagh Holohan]**: *Irish Times*, 11 November 1971. Permission granted © *Irish Times*.

Irish Times **report (1928)**: *Irish Times*, 12 March 1928.

Jacob, Rosamond: Diary, 7 December 1931, Jacob Papers, NLI MD 32,582 (68). Permission granted courtesy of the National Library of Ireland.

Kavanagh, John: 'Emigration: A Letter', Bell, Vol. XIX, No. 10, November 1954, pp. 54–8.

Keating, Mary Frances: John O'Brien (ed.), *The Vanishing Irish* (Ebury Press, 1954, pp. 166–7 and 175–6). Permission granted by Catherine Keating on behalf of the Keating family.

Kelleher, J. V.: *Foreign Affairs*, Vol. 35, No. 3, 1957, pp. 485–95. Republished with permission of *Foreign Affairs* via Copyright Clearance Center, Inc.

Kelly, John: Dáil Debates, 9 February 1922, Vol. 377, No. 6, cols. 1583–7. Republished under Oireachtas Adapted PSI Licence.

Kelly, Morgan: *Irish Times*, 28 December 2006. Permission granted by the author.

Kelly, Reverend William: Letter to Dr Michael Browne, 12 November 1922, Galway Diocesan Archives. Permission granted by Dr Martin Drennan, Bishop of Galway.

Kenny, Enda: Dáil Debates, 19 February 2013, online text, pp. 34–5. Republished under Oireachtas Adapted PSI Licence.

Kington, Miles: *Moreover, too …* (Penguin, 1985, pp. 160–62). Copyright © Miles

Kington. Reproduced by permission of the estate of Miles Kington, c/o Rogers, Coleridge and White Ltd, 20 Powis Mews, London w 11 1jn.

Kinsella, Joseph: Joseph Kinsella, Military Archives, Ireland, BMH WS 476, pp. 4–5. Permission granted by the Military Archives.

Lee, J. J.: *Ireland: 1912–1985* (Cambridge University Press, 1989, pp. 645–8). Permission granted by the author and © Cambridge University Press.

Lemass, Seán: D/TSCH 3 / S 16920A, 19 August 1960. Permission granted courtesy of the National Archives of Ireland.

Lenihan, Brian: Letter to John Charles McQuaid, 10 December 1964, McQuaid Papers, Dublin Diocesan Archives, DDA/8/B/XVIII/9/44. Permission granted by Dr Diarmuid Martin, Archbishop of Dublin.

Leonard, Mae: Cliodhna Ní Anluain (ed.), *Sunday Miscellany: A Selection from 2006 to 2008* (New Island, 2008, pp. 273–4). Permission granted by the author.

Levine, June: *Sisters: The Personal Story of an Irish Feminist* (Ward River Press, 1982, pp. 174–82). Permission granted by Cork University Press and Ivor Browne on behalf of the estate of June Levine.

'Lia Fáil': *Leitrim Observer*, 20 January 1934, p. 3.

Lillis, Michael: Letter to the *Irish Times*, 11 May 2011. Permission granted by the author.

Lynn, Kathleen, and Richard Hayes: Sinn Féin public health circular on dangers of syphilis, NLI, ILB 300 p5/45. Permission granted courtesy of the National Library of Ireland.

Lyons, F. S. L.: *Ireland Since the Famine* (Fontana Press, 1985, pp. 550–51). Permission granted by HarperCollins Publishers Ltd © 1985, F. S. L. Lyons.

Mac Amhlaigh, Dónall: *An Irish Navvy* (Collins Press, 2003, pp. 3–6). Permission granted courtesy of the Collins Press.

McCafferty, Nell (1972): Profile, Martin McGuinness, *Irish Times*, April 1972. Permission granted by the author and © *Irish Times*.

McCafferty, Nell (1999): *Hot Press*, March 1999. Permission granted by the author.

McCausland, Nelson: *Scotch Town: Ulster Scots Language and Literature in Belfast* (Ulster Scots Agency, 2015, pp. 54–66). Permission granted by the author.

McCusker, Harold: Hansard, House of Commons Debate, 27 November 1985, Vol. 87, cols. 912–18. Permission contains public sector information licensed under the Open Government Licence v2.0. Permission granted courtesy of the National Archives (UK).

McElligott, J. J.: Memos to Maurice Moynihan, 22 March and 17 April 1937, D/TSCH 3 / S 10159. Permission granted courtesy of the National Archives of Ireland.

McElroy, Fr Edward: Report to Hierarchy, 17 June 1957, D'Alton Papers, Armagh Diocesan Archives. Permission granted by Dr Eamon Martin, Archbishop of Armagh.

Macfarlane, Deputy Governor G.: Borstal report on Brendan Behan, 1 June

1941, National Archives (UK), PCOM 9/1907. Permission contains public sector information licensed under the Open Government Licence v2.0. Permission granted courtesy of the National Archives (UK).

McGahern, John: *Memoir* (Faber and Faber, 2006, pp. 249–52). Permission granted by Faber and Faber and by Alfred A. Knopf, an imprint of the Knopf Doubleday Publishing Group, a division of Penguin Random House LLC.

McKay, Susan: *Northern Protestants: An Unsettled People* (Blackstaff Press, new and updated edition, 2005, pp. 38–42). Permission granted by Blackstaff Press.

McKee, Malcolm: *Belfast Telegraph*, 30 June 1966.

McRedmond, Louis: *Tablet*, 6 October 1979. Reproduced by permission of the publisher of the *Tablet* (www.thetablet.co.uk).

MacSwiney, Mary: Dáil Debate on the Treaty, 21 December 1921, pp. 116–17. Republished under Oireachtas Adapted PSI Licence.

Magdalen Laundries inquiry: 'Report of the Inter-Departmental Committee to Establish the Facts of State Involvement with the Magdalen Laundries', 5 February 2013.

Markievicz, Constance: *Prison Letters of Constance Markievicz* (Longmans, Green and Co., 1934).

Martyn, Edward: Letter to John Sweetman, 1 August 1922, NLI 47,591/1, Sweetman Family Papers. Permission granted courtesy of the National Library of Ireland.

Montgomery, James: Letter to Department of Justice, 23 September 1930, NAI, D/Jus/H/231/41. Permission granted courtesy of the National Archives of Ireland.

Moran, D. P.: *Leader*, 12 August 1916.

Moylan, T. K.: Diary, 26 April 1916, unpublished typescript, NLI MD MS 9620. Permission granted courtesy of the National Library of Ireland.

Murphy, Colin: *Dublin Review*, No. 38, Spring 2010, pp. 29–58. Permission granted by the author.

Murphy, Dervla: *Wheels Within Wheels* (Eland, 2002, pp. 85–90). Permission granted by Eland Books.

Murphy, John A.: *Irish Times,* 30 March 2016. Permission granted by the author.

O'Brien, Art: Chronicle of Terence MacSwiney's hunger-strike and death, 22–5 October 1920, Art O'Brien Papers, NLI MD MS 8446/3. Permission granted courtesy of the National Library of Ireland.

O'Brien, Conor Cruise: *Irish Independent*, 29 February 1992. Permission granted by Michael Williams on behalf of the estate of Conor Cruise O'Brien.

O'Brien, Edna: *Country Girl* (Faber and Faber, 2013), pp. 53–6. Permission granted by the author and Faber and Faber.

O'Brien, Kate: *Presentation Parlour* (Heinemann, 1963, pp. 135–8). Reprinted by permission of David Higham Associates on behalf of the estate of Kate O'Brien.

O'Connell, Maurice: Letter to T. Desmond Williams, 19 September 1975,

O'Connell Papers, NLI MS 47404. Permission granted courtesy of the National Library of Ireland.

Ó Donnchadha, Micheál: GAA Archives, 1955, Central Council Minute Book, GAA/CC/01/18, pp. 52–9. Permission granted by the GAA Library and Archives.

O'Donoghue, Florence: Letter to Liam Lynch, 3 July 1922, O'Donoghue Papers, NLI MD MS 31,187. Permission granted courtesy of the National Library of Ireland.

O'Faolain, Nuala: *Irish Times*, 1 February 1988. Permission granted © *Irish Times*.

O'Faolain, Sean (1934): Letter to Hanna Sheehy Skeffington [n.d. but 1934], Hanna Sheehy Skeffington Papers, NLI 33, 607 (1). Permission granted courtesy of the National Library of Ireland.

O'Faolain, Sean (1951): 'Mother and Child Scheme', *Bell*, June 1951, pp. 5–13. Permission granted by courtesy of the RCW Literary Agency on behalf of the estate of Sean O'Faolain.

O'Friel, H.: Letter to E. M. Coulson, 19 February 1930, D/TSCH 3 / S 6002. Permission granted courtesy of the National Archives of Ireland.

Ó hEithir, Breandán: *Over the Bar* (Ward River Press, 1984, pp. 215–16). Permission granted by Christine Green on behalf of the estate of Breandán Ó hEithir.

O'Malley, Desmond: Dáil Debates, 20 February 1985, Vol. 356, cols. 272–85, Republished under Oireachtas Adapted PSI Licence.

O'Meara, F. J. Q.: Letter to Cardinal John D'Alton, 19 January 1960, D'Alton Papers, Armagh Diocesan Archives. Permission granted by Dr Eamon Martin, Archbishop of Armagh.

O'Toole, Fintan: *Irish Times*, 23 May 2015. Permission granted by the author and © *Irish Times*.

Ó Tuathaigh, Gearóid: J. J. Lee (ed.), *Ireland: 1945–1970* (Gill & Macmillan, 1979, pp. 111–23). Permission granted by M. H. Gill & Co.

Oranmore and Brown, Lord: Letter to Walter Long, 28 June 1920, CAB 24/108/50, National Archives (UK). Permission contains public sector information licensed under the Open Government Licence v2.0. Permission granted courtesy of the National Archives (UK).

Palmer, Caitríona: *An Affair with My Mother* (Penguin Ireland, 2016, pp. 167–73). Permission granted by Penguin Books Ltd.

Pearse, Patrick: Letter to his mother, 1 May 1916, WO71/45, National Archives (UK). Permission contains public sector information licensed under the Open Government Licence v2.0. Permission granted courtesy of the National Archives (UK).

Power, Brenda: *Sunday Times*, 24 August 2014. Permission granted by News Syndication.

Price, Lesley: Lesley Price Barry, Military Archives, Ireland, BMH WS 1754, pp. 10–14. Permission granted by the Military Archives.

Pro-Quidnunc: 'The Country Shop closes', *Irish Times*, 19 October 1978.

Rice, David: *Sunday Times*, 10 May 1992. Permission granted by News Syndication.

Rice, Ellie: Letter to Bishop Charles O'Sullivan, 21 August 1922, O'Sullivan Papers, Kerry Diocesan Archives. Permission granted by Dr Raymond Browne, Bishop of Kerry.

Robinson, C. H.: Letter to the Under Secretary, 1 March 1922, NAI CSORP/R10. Permission granted courtesy of the National Archives of Ireland.

Robinson, Mary: Speech given at Dublin Castle on inauguration as President of Ireland, 3 December 1990. Transcript issued as press release.

Rodgers, W. R.: *New Statesman*, 8 April 1966. Permission granted by the *New Statesman*.

Ryan, John: *Studies*, Vol. VIII, No. 25, March 1918, pp. 112–26. Permission granted by Bruce Bradley, SJ, on behalf of the publication.

Scott, Michael, and Dorothy Walker: Dorothy Walker, *Michael Scott, Architect: In (casual) conversation with Dorothy Walker* (Gandon Editions, 1996, pp. 224–7). Permission granted by Gandon Editions, Kinsale.

Shaw, Fr Francis: *Studies*, Vol. LXI, No. 242, Summer 1972, pp. 113–53. Permission granted by Bruce Bradley, SJ, on behalf of the publication.

Shaw, George Bernard (1928): *Irish Statesman*, Vol. 11, No. 11, 17 November 1928. Permission granted by the Society of Authors on behalf of the estate of George Bernard Shaw.

Shaw, George Bernard (1940): Mary Hyde (ed.), *Bernard Shaw and Alfred Douglas: A Correspondence* (Oxford University Press, 1982, pp. 135–6). Permission granted by the Society of Authors on behalf of the estate of George Bernard Shaw.

Sheehy Skeffington, Hanna (1916): Official records of the Royal Commission of Enquiry set up by the command of the King in August 1916, at the Four Courts, Dublin. Permission granted by Micheline Sheehy Skeffington on behalf of the family.

Sheehy Skeffington, Hanna (1943): *Bell*, Vol. VII, No. 2, pp. 143–8, February 1943. Permission granted by Micheline Sheehy Skeffington on behalf of the family.

Singleton, Major H. (from 'Ulstermen at the Somme', 1916): Patrick Buckland, *Irish Unionism 1885–1923: A Documentary History* (The Historical Association, 1973, pp. 397–9). Permission granted by the Deputy Keeper of Records, Public Record Office of Northern Ireland, D1327/3/21.

Sinn Féin Standing Committee: Appeal to Pope, D/TSCH 3 / S 5864A. Permission granted courtesy of the National Archives of Ireland.

Stopford Green, Alice: Letter to J. C. Smuts, 19 April 1919, Stopford Green Papers, NLI MD MS 43,263/1. Permission granted courtesy of the National Library of Ireland.

Sweetman, John: Letter to Salvatore Luzio, 21 April 1923, Sweetman Family

Papers, NLI MD MS 47591/3. Permission granted courtesy of the National Library of Ireland.

Tóibín, Colm (1969): Diarmaid Ferriter, *What If? Alternative Views of Twentieth-Century Ireland* (Gill & Macmillan, 2006, pp. 1–14). Permission granted by the author.

Tóibín, Colm (1980): *In Dublin*, November 1980. Permission granted by the author.

Toksvig, Signe: Liz Pihl (ed.), *Irish Diaries 1927–1936* (Lilliput Press, 1994, pp. 382–3). By kind permission of the Lilliput Press, Dublin.

Tummon, Francis: Francis Tummon, Military Archives, Ireland, BMH WS 820, pp. 19–21. Permission granted by the Military Archives.

Tyrrell, Peter: Typescript of memoir, in Owen Sheehy Skeffington Papers, NLI MS 40544/10. Permission granted courtesy of the National Library of Ireland.

Unnamed veteran ('Two Ulstermen at the Somme', 1916): Testimony recorded by R. H. Stewart and quoted in Philip Orr, *The Road to the Somme* (Blackstaff Press, new and updated edition, 2008, pp. 193–4, 200). Permission granted by Blackstaff Press.

Walsh, J.J.: Letter to Hanna Sheehy Skeffington, 5 May 1919, Hanna Sheehy Skeffington Papers, NLI MD MS 22,689. Permission granted courtesy of the National Library of Ireland.

Walsh, Louis J.: Letter to Eamon de Valera, 5 June 1937, in Gerard Hogan, *The Origins of the Irish Constitution 1928–1941* (Royal Irish Academy, 2012, pp. 586–7). Permission granted by the Royal Irish Academy, Dublin.

Walshe, Joseph P.: Memo to Eamon de Valera, 22 April 1937, de Valera Papers, UCDA P150/2419. Permission granted courtesy of University College Dublin Archives.

Waters, John: *Irish Times*, 20 December 2013. Permission granted by the author.

Whitaker, T. K. (1969): Draft note of advice to Jack Lynch, 15 August 1969, Whitaker Papers, copy with editor. Permission granted by the author.

Whitaker T. K. (1958): 'Economic Development' (Government Publications, 1958). Permission granted by the author.

Wilson, Henry: Letter to Lord Rawlinson, 18 May 1921, Wilson Papers, IWM, HHW 2/13D/14. Permission granted courtesy of the Imperial War Museum, London.